Ocean of Eloquence

SUNY Series in Buddhist Studies
Matthew Kapstein, Editor

Ocean of Eloquence

Tsong kha pa's Commentary on the Yogācāra Doctrine of Mind

Introduced and Translated by
Gareth Sparham

In Collaboration with
Shotaro Iida

State University of New York Press

Published by
State University of New York Press, Albany

Printed in the United States of America

For information, address State University of New York Press, State University Plaza, Albany, N.Y. 12246

Production by M. R. Mulholland
Marketing by Bernadette LaManna

Library of Congress Cataloging-in-Publication Data

Tsoṅ-kha-pa Blo-bzaṅ-grags-pa, 1357-1419.
[Yid daṅ kun gźi'i dka' ba'i gnas rgya cher 'grel pa legs par bśad pa'i legs par bśad pa'i rgya mdzo. English & Tibetan]
Yid daṅ kun gźi'i dka' ba'i gnas rgya cher 'grel pa legs par bśad pa'i legs par bśad pa'i rgya mdzo: Ocean of eloquence: Tsong kha pa's commentary on the yogācāra doctrine of mind / translated by Gareth Sparham; in collaboration with Shotaro Iida.
p. cm. – (SUNY series in Buddhist studies)
Includes bibliographical references and index.
ISBN 0-7914-1479-5 (alk. paper). – ISBN 0-7914-1480-9 (pbk. : alk. paper)
1. Yogācāra (Buddhism)–Early works to 1800. 2. Dge-lugs-pa (Sect)–Doctrines–Early works to 1800. I. Sparham, Gareth. II. Iida, Shotaro. III. Title. IV. Title: Legs par bśad pa'i rgya mdzo. V. Series.
BQ7950.T754Y5 1993
294.3' 85–dc20 92-24974
CIP

10 9 8 7 6 5 4 3 2

Contents

ABBREVIATIONS

AS	*Abhidharma-samuccaya*
ASBh	*Abhidharma-samuccaya-bhāṣya*
AK	*Abhidharma-kośa-kārikā*
AAV	*Abhisamayālaṁkāra-vṛtti*
AA	*Abhisamayālaṁkāra-nāma-prajñā-pāramitopadeśa-śāstra-kārikā*
AAA	*Abhisamayālaṁkārālokā Prajñā-pāramitā-vyākhyā*
BC	*Bodhi-caryāvatāra*
D	*Yid dang kun gzhi dka' ba'i gnas rgya cher 'grel pa legs par bshad pa'i rgya mtsho*, Tsong kha pa chen po'i gsung 'bum edition, vol. Tsha:356-474. Ngag dbang dge legs de mo (New Delhi, 1977)
Guhyārtha-vyākhyā	*Don gsang ba rnam par phye ba bsdus te bshad pa* (*Vivṛta-guhyārtha/gūḍhārtha-piṇḍa-vyākhyā*)
Ke'u tshang	*Rnal 'byor spyod pa pa'i lugs kyi yid dang kun gzhi'i rtsa 'grel gyi dka' gnas gsal byed nyi zla zung 'jug*
M	*Yid dang kun gzhi dka' ba'i gnas rgya cher 'grel pa legs par bshad pa'i rgya mtsho.* Mtsho sngon mi rigs dpe skrun khang edition (1986):1113-1208
MAV	*Madhyānta-vibhāga*
MSA	*Mahāyāna-sūtrālaṁkāra*
MSam	*Theg pa chen po bsdus pa* (*Mahāyāna-saṁgraha*)
MSB	*Theg pa chen po bsdus pa'i 'grel pa* (*Mahāyāna-saṁgraha-bhāṣya*)
MSU	*Theg pa chen po bsdus bshad sbyor* (*Mahāyāna-saṁgrahopanibandhana*)
N	*Yid dang kun gzhi dka' ba'i gnas rgya cher 'grel pa legs par bshad pa'i rgya mtsho.* International Academy of Indian Culture edition. Raghu Vira (New Delhi, 1961)
O	*Yid dang kun gzhi dka' ba'i gnas rgya cher 'grel pa legs par bshad pa'i rgya mtsho.* As reproduced in Odani and Kalsang (1986)

P	*Yid dang kun gzhi dka' ba'i gnas rgya cher 'grel pa legs par bshad pa'i rgya mtsho.* In Peking edition of the Bstan 'gyur. Also Peking edition of the Bstan 'gyur when followed by a number as in P4456.
RGB	*Ratna-gotra-vibhāga-mahāyānottara-tantra-śāstra*
TK	*Triṁśikā Vijñapti-mātratā-siddhi*
SNṬ	*Ārya-gambhīra-saṁdhi-nirmocana-sūtra-ṭīkā*
VS	*Viniścaya-saṁgrahaṇī*

PREFACE

Our interest in the *Ocean of Eloquence* began in 1979 while Gareth Sparham was still a student at the Buddhist Dialectic Institute in McLeod Ganj, India. The 'Bras phung Blo gsal gling monk and scholar Dam chos rgyal mtshan gave a traditional explanation of it, according to a time-honoured rule, as a discursus during the study of the fourth chapter of the *Abhisamayālaṁkāra*. Gareth Sparham attended and debated the topics in formal session each day after classes with fellow students and jotted down a rough translation of the text for his own records. The appearance of this book owes to Dam chos rgyal mtshan and to the others at the Buddhist Dialectic Institute a debt of gratitude. They treated the *Ocean of Eloquence* as a sacred book and considered sharing its insights a religious act. Gareth Sparham remains cognizant of the generosity they showed in allowing him to participate fully.

At the University of British Columbia in 1985 work began on the text anew. Shotaro Iida suggested to Sparham, his student in the doctoral program at UBC, that he resume work on the text and collaborate on a project to make it available to the scholarly community. Iida, cognizant of the importance of Gadjin Nagao's recent work on the *Mahāyāna-saṁgraha* (the book on which the *Ocean of Eloquence* is based), felt such a collaboration would be timely. He would like to acknowledge his debt to the pioneering scholarship of Nagao. He also acknowledges the contribution made by Nobuchiyo Odani and Tsultrim Kalsang's publication of the Japanese translation. Iida translated the parts of the text not covered by Dam chos rgyal mtshan and supplied material from Japanese sources.

Sparham would like to acknowledge the support of the Indo-Canadian Shastri Institute which made work on this book possible during 1990-91 by granting a postdoctoral fellowship for research in India.

The Tibetan fonts were designed by Pierre Robillard, whom we thank for allowing us to make use of his work.

TECHNICAL NOTE

The use of Tibetan words presents difficulty since their spelling and pronunciation differ so markedly. Tibetan words are spelled out in full following Turrel Wylie's system of transliteration ("A Standard System of Tibetan Transcription," *Harvard Journal of Asian Studies* 22 [1959]:261-7), except where noted. The first letter of a Tibetan proper name is capitalized even if it is not the main letter (Tib. *ming gzhi*) of the word. Where both the Sanskrit and Tibetan equivalent of an English word are given in parenthesis the Sanskrit term comes first separated from the Tibetan word by a comma. Where just the Tibetan word is given it is preceded by the abbreviation 'Tib.' in order to avoid confusion. The symbol * intimates the Sanskrit word is a retranslation from Tibetan not actually attested in any Indian original.

The critically edited Tibetan text is based on the Mtsho sngon mi rigs dpe skrun khang edition (1986:1113-1208) of *Yid dang kun gzhi dka' ba'i gnas rgya cher 'grel pa legs par bshad pa'i rgya mtsho* (=M). It was checked against the editions of Raghu Vira (New Delhi, 1961) (=N), Odani and Kalsang (1986) (=O), Ngag dbang dge legs de mo (1977) (=D) and the edition in the Peking Bstan 'gyur(=P). To facilitate cross-referencing between the translation and Tibetan text, folio numbers to the Tibetan text reproduced in Odani and Kalsang (1986) have been inserted. Approximate cross-references are given in the translation, e.g., *Ocean of Eloquence* 8b3 for the convenience of the reader. Page numbers of the Mtsho sngon mi rigs dpe skrun khang edition have also been inserted into the Tibetan text. Roman numerals preceded by 'Mv' identify lines from Tsong kha pa's *Kun gzhi rtsa ba* (*Ocean of Eloquence* mnemonic verses). The numbering of these follows the order in Wilson (1984:766-778).

For the modern reader's convenience, chapter breaks–not found in the Tibetan text–have been inserted and in the Introduction a full citation is given in a footnote when a text or secondary source is mentioned for the first time.

It was deemed desirable to present the text in Tibetan script, rather than transliteration, to facilitate the reading of the text as a coherent entity in the original.

INTRODUCTION

The text edited and translated here is the *Yid dang kun gzhi dka' ba'i gnas rgya cher 'grel pa legs par bshad pa'i rgya mtsho* (literally, *Ocean of Eloquence: An Extensive Commentary on the Difficult Points of* Ālaya-vijñāna *and* Kliṣṭa-manas, referred to hereafter as *Ocean of Eloquence*) by the Tibetan Buddhist writer Tsong kha pa (1357-1419). It is a detailed investigation of the last two of an internally coherent system of eight consciousnesses (*vijñāna*) asserted by Yogācāra, an Indian school of thought associated with the names of Maitreya[-nātha], Asaṅga, and Vasubandhu. These two consciousnesses, which are a unique and distinquishing feature of the school, are the *ālaya-vijñāna*, an hypostasized ever-present subconscious, and the *kliṣṭa-manas*, an hypostasized, ever-present egocentered thought. As will become clear, both Sanskrit terms cover a wide range of meanings which it is difficult to capture in single English equivalents. English hybrid translation words like 'basis-of-all consciousness' and 'afflicted thinking-mind,' though more exact, will be too cumbersome for felicitous usage in ordinary English prose so the original terms are retained throughout.[1]

This Introduction is in two sections. First the *ālaya-vijñāna* doctrine is dealt with in isolation, freed from later interpretation. From the point of view of the later exegete Tsong kha pa this doctrine is a sacred truth, a 'revelation' (*buddha-vacana*) to be explained. Then the later exegesis is dealt with. This exegesis presents itself as a nonoriginal restatement of the 'revelation.' It is Tsong kha pa's *Ocean of Eloquence* itself. It is advantageous if the reader first becomes familiar with the *ālaya-vijñāna* doctrine freed from later interpretation and then, armed with a prior understanding of that revelation, approaches what Tsong kha pa has to say.

The *ālaya-vijñāna* doctrine arose on the Indian subcontinent about one thousand years before Tsong kha pa. It gained its place in a distinctly Yogācāra system over a period of some three hundred years stretching from 100 to 400 C.E., culminating in the *Mahāyāna-saṁgraha*, a short text by Asaṅga (circa 350), setting out a systematic presentation of the *ālaya-vijñāna* doctrine developed over the previous centuries. It is the doctrine found in this text in particular that Tsong kha pa, in his *Ocean of Eloquence*, treats as having been revealed in toto by the Buddha and transmitted to suffering humanity through the Yogācāra founding saints (Tib. *shing rta srol byed*): Maitreya[-nātha], Asaṅga, and Vasubandhu.

The different streams of thought which culminated finally, in the *Mahāyāna-saṁgraha*, in the complex ideas which comprise the mature classical *ālaya-vijñāna* doctrine are, in the *Ocean of Eloquence*, inextricably linked. It will be the first task of this Introduction to separate the complex notions of *ālaya-vijñāna* and *kliṣṭa-manas* set forth in the *Mahāyāna-saṁgraha* and to a lesser extent in the *Abhidharma-samuccaya* into their different parts in order to grasp what Tsong kha pa conceived as the starting point of his inquiry.

The way in which I reconstruct the 'uninterpreted *ālaya-vijñāna* doctrine' or, as Tsong kha pa would term it, 'revelation', is open to a possible misunderstanding. Recent scholarship[2] has dissected out, isolated, and traced the literary origins of the different important components in the meaning-complex that is associated with the term *ālaya-vijñāna* in its classical usage in texts like the *Mahāyāna-saṁgraha.* These different components have been identified as belonging to earlier and later historical periods. Tsong kha pa on the other hand understood them as the single revelation of the Enlightened Being set forth in the founders' texts. Nevertheless, I treat Tsong kha pa's lack of self-conscious historical awareness as unimportant and take each component separately, and as having its own history, and then simply state that all of these together should be seen as different aspects of the doctrine Tsong kha pa had in mind as a single unified revelation. I do this to utilize what seems to me the best method of conveying to a modern reader as quickly and as painlessly as possible the many different aspects of the *ālaya-vijñāna* doctrine systematized in the *Mahāyāna-saṁgraha* which, taken together, provide the necessary point of departure for Tsong kha pa's text.[3]

As will become clear, the intellectual concerns of fourteenth century Tibet differed from the immediate concerns of early Indian Yogācāra, and Tsong kha pa's presentation of the *ālaya-vijñāna* doctrine in his *Ocean of Eloquence* reflects those concerns. As Tsong kha pa's first major work (an important consideration which will be discussed below), the *Ocean of Eloquence* is important both for what it reveals of the Tibetan intellectual mileu into which Tsong kha pa was born and as a document showing the earliest stages in the development of Tsong kha pa's thought. The second section of the Introduction deals with these matters.

Before proceding, a brief word about the methodology of first explaining the *ālaya-vijñāna* doctrine in isolation, freed from later interpretation (this is what I am loosely equating with a traditional person's revelation) and then dealing later with its traditional exegesis. The approach, implicit in this Introduction, that first deals with the origins and history of an earlier 'revelation' in isolation and then with the way that 'revelation' is interpreted is entirely heuristic. It is based on the perception that I, and most western people I know, access information best when it is presented historically. But entering into the idea that the *ālaya-vijñāna* doctrine was revealed by an Enlightened Being and that Tsong kha pa, as the center of a cultic belief, did make a nonoriginal presentation would not be uninstructive for some. Persons who already have a sense of history would certainly learn from such an exercise, just as much as the believer would learn from historical analysis. This is not an attack on the value and validity (even authority) of historical truth. In a slightly different context, Daniel L. Overmyer says: "My primary methodological consideration is to avoid reductionism as much as possible, that is, to meet the subject in question at every level on which it presents itself, without distortion. It is necessary to keep faith with the human beings who are the makers of history by seeking to understand their own purposes in relationship to the total context. This principle means to understand the relationship of historical situation to sectarian belief as a dialectical one, without seeking to give undue precedence to either."[4] It is something like this that I intend.

The intellectual concerns which provide the general context for the arising of the Yogācāra *ālaya-vijñāna* doctrine

What are the wider intellectual concerns which emerge in preclassical Indian literature and which provide the broader context, in the history of Indian religious thought, for the emergence of the particular Buddhist school that first asserted an hypostasized subconscious during the early centuries of the common era? Most important is the general notion of karma,[5] a word which, as is well known, means 'action' but which comes to refer to the entire net of complex causes and effects wherein a particular action (or set of actions) is held to result in a particular sequence of results. Whatever the full story of its origins in India, a story which would entail a detailed discussion of the notion of sacrificial efficiency as well as the rich Indian tradition of grammatical speculation—both of which would carry the discussion far afield—the notion of karma became particularly important as an explanation of, and justification for, social status, particularly the notion of social status enshrined in the Vedic notion of four *varṇas* (social classes). There are two dimensions to this: first the very natural human wonder about where one came from, and second the question of why one has the position in society that one does. In the Indian context perhaps more than in other societies[6] the question of why one has the position in society that one does appears to have had a particular importance. The question of where one came from became almost inextricably mixed up with the question of one's status or social class. Karma became a far more important notion than the concept of any single creator to explain one's origins, even in distinctively theistic texts.[7] So for Brahmanical writers, Buddhist preachers of the *daśa-kuśala-patha* ('way of ten virtues'), and Jain sages seeking to avoid any action whatsoever in an attempt to rid themselves of karmic residues, some notion of karma was central to explaining how one came to be here and one's position in life.

Besides explaining, rationalising if you will, the different social classes and different good or bad fortune in life, karma had an equally important role to play as an element woven into developing Indian soteriologies. Either in pre-Upaniṣadic times as proper sacrificial action which ensured rebirth in the heavens of the fathers, or later, in ever more detailed and systematized religious philosophies as proper adherence to a code of virtuous conduct or to a course of yogic praxis which would remove the results of earlier wrongdoing, action, in the sense of the force left by previous action, was a pivot of the system. It was an idea challenged only by the very fringe of Indian society (the Carvākas and Lokāyatas) and was perhaps the most influential of all culturally received ideas defining the functioning of the Yogācāra *ālaya-vijñāna.*

Yet if there were to be one notion that, even more than karma, characterized early Indian religious thought and deeply influenced the way later thinkers conceived of the *ālaya-vijñāna* 'subconscious,' it would undoubtedly have to be that of a unifying ultimate. There is no need to dwell long on its content, well known in its general characteristics from the Upaniṣadic *brahman* and *ātman* doctrine. It is useful, however, to recall the importance of *cit* ('consciousness') in the definition of this unifying ultimate and note three aspects: a) that it is in some sense ontologically more fundamental than other things, b) that it is the origin of them, and c) that an understanding of it is liberating. Amongst the Buddhist schools, the influence of this notion is most apparent in Yogācāra. It appears to have entered into Yogācāra thinkers in what might be termed the transformational (*pāriṇāmika*) current of Indian thought. According to this transformationalist view the whole of waking reality is like waves on an ocean, not other than the one underlying reality. Diversity is only apparent, not lasting and true. We will come back to this current of thought later, in the context of a possible common heritage influencing both classical Sāmkhya and Yogācāra.

If karma and the unifying ultimate are the culturally received notions most dominant in the formulation of the *ālaya-vijñāna*, localization of the obscuring principle (one hesitates to use a word like evil in the Indian context) around the ego informs the idea of *kliṣṭa-manas.* Ego, both as the first cause of action and as the obscurer of the ultimate, is the creator of all that is imperfect. In Yogācāra most of the functions of ego attach to the *ālaya-vijñāna* itself and it overshadows, as a guiding principle, the definition of the *kliṣṭa-manas* which becomes relegated to a necessary but minor role. Because of this, because less is known about the development of the *kliṣṭa-manas* in India and because the *kliṣṭa-manas* is largely irrelevant to developments of the Tibetan *kun gzhi* (*ālaya*) doctrine, I will have much less to say about it in this Introduction than about the *ālaya-vijñāna.*

Origins of the Yogācāra *ālaya-vijñāna* doctrine

It is customary, following north Indian Buddhist traditions carried on in Tibet, to describe Yogācāra as one of two important philosophical schools of Indian Mahāyāna Buddhist thought, the other being Madhyamaka. Following the same tradition it has become customary to categorize it as an idealist philosophy on account of its doctrine of *vijñapti-mātratā* ('state of mere awareness'), i.e., the doctrine that objects have no reality beyond the awareness that knows them. The origins of the Yogācāra school are traditionally traced back to Maitreya[-nātha] (here loosely equated with the putative author of the three so-called Maitreya[-nātha] texts, the *Mahāyāna-sūtrālaṁkāra*, etc.), to Asaṅga (by whom I mean specifically the author of the *Mahāyāna-saṁgraha* and *Abhidharma-samuccaya*) and to Asaṅga's brother Vasubandhu (by whom I mean the author of the *Triṁśikā* and *Viṁśatikā*). All lived in about the fourth century.[8]

The school may conveniently be divided (still following a tradition carried on in Tibetan scholastic works) into two streams: one based primarily on the works of Asaṅga, and the other on the works of Dignāga, traditionally said to be a student of Vasubandhu, or at least *a* Vasubandhu. The difference between them is said to be one of emphasis. Whereas the former, sometimes called the 'scriptural stream' (Tib. *lung gi rjes 'brang*) stresses the *ālaya-vijñāna* doctrine and seeks to establish *vijñapti-mātratā* by way of demonstrating the logical impossibility of atomic existence, the latter, the so-called 'stream of reasoning' (Tib. *rigs pa'i rje 'brang*) seeks to do so by way of demonstrating the necessary bases for perceptual (*pratyakṣa*) and inferential (*anumāna*) authoritative cognition (*pramāṇa*).[9]

Since it is axiomatic that ideas do not just spring up from the void in the mind of even the most brilliant thinker but are rooted in an intellectual history and in the social mileu from which the writer drew his or her inspiration, an important line of recent scholarship has been to unpack the traditional explanation that the *ālaya-vijñāna* doctrine, in its final form as an integral and necessary part of an internally coherent system of eight consciousnesses (*vijñāna*), originated in the systematic treatises inspired by the compassionate insight of these founders. This research has culminated in the exhaustive study of the *ālaya-vijñāna* by the German scholar Lambert Schmithausen (1987).

Among the different meanings of the *ālaya-vijñāna* that Schmithausen identifies, the first is revealed in an early section of the *Yogācāra-bhūmi* describing a yogin's consciousness during *nirodha-samāpatti* (a state of suspended animation or deep trance).[10] Since the person enters into a quasi-insentient state during such periods and there is, therefore, a break in the person's continuum of awareness far more radical even than the apparent break in the continuum of awareness during the deepest, dreamless sleep, some early Yogācāras seem to have hypothesized that the person's consciousness entered a latent seed-form, as it were, and got stuck or laid back into (*ālaya*) the physical sense-faculties.[11] It remained there until the state of suspended animation finished. Then this *ālaya-vijñāna* (hibernating *vijñāna,* we might say) was understood to have served as the cause of the re-emerging awareness of the newly animated yogin, a necessary middle link between the person's awareness prior to, and following the deep meditative absorption, preventing what would otherwise have been a radical hiatus in the stream of consciousness and hence death.

In the first major expansion in the meaning of the term, considered narrowly within the stream of development which led to its becoming the Yogācāra eighth consciousness, the *ālaya-vijñāna* became associated with the vivifying principle (*upādātṛ*). This occured as the notion of its being the consciousness present in the otherwise unconscious states of deep trance became extended to the moment of death and then the moment of birth. The presence or absence of the *ālaya-vijñāna* explained the 'appropriation' (*upa ā √dā*) without which death ensued and the living organism lost all feeling and began to putrefy. It caused the *ālaya-vijñāna* to become associated with the feeling which imparts warmth and sensation even to the very extremities of the physical organism and the gradual withdrawal of which, at death, accounted for the gradual inward spread of coldness from the outer limbs.

Once the *ālaya-vijñāna* had become associated with the subtle consciousness present at the moment of conception it was but a short step to the notion that the *ālaya-vijñāna* was the basic constituent of personality, that it was "the ultimate or deepest objective basis to which the notion of Ego or Self (*ahaṁkāra,* etc.), the feeling of identity (*asmimāna*) and self-love (*ātma-sneha,* etc.) refers" (Schmithausen 1987:51). The compound *ālaya-vijñāna* is so suited to this particularly Buddhist interpretation (it would then be understood to mean not "mind which lays down on or sticks in [physical sense-faculties]" but "mind which is stuck to or laid down upon [as a self]") that even in its earliest usage it possibly carried something of this meaning.[12]

For Buddhist speculative thinkers it is axiomatic that if there is some sort of soul it will not partake of any ultimate reality as does the Brahmanical *ātman.* That is to say the person (*pudgala*) is necessarily contingent on (*upādāya*) the five aggregates (*skandha*) and hence somehow thought up (*prajñapti-sat*) and not materially real (*dravya-sat*). This axiom, which Buddhist speculative thinkers treat as inviolable, denies to them the onion-skin model of transmigration—that very convenient model in which life after life, an ongoing soul is said to put on, and then again take off, sheaths of coarser mental and physical material. Buddhists have always been hard pressed in the absence of such a soul to come up with a viable explanation of what forms the basis or location of personal identity and to explain just what it is that transmigrates.

The *ālaya-vijñāna* presented itself as a perfect solution to this perennial problem. As perhaps the deepest subconscious element, the one which was first on the scene and last off, so to speak, during a lifetime, it was to all intents and purposes a constant within the everchanging flux of the psychophysical constituents and eminently suited to function as a soul without actually being one. Indeed, it was so similar to the Brahmanical soul that even the *Mahāyāna-saṁgraha* says that only special Bodhisattvas would understand the doctrine without going wrong, and that if one were to teach it to certain "unskillful persons of the Śrāvaka family" they would leap to the incorrect belief that "It's me." Other Buddhists opposed to Yogācāra gleefully seized on the *ālaya-vijñāna* as being the Brahmanical *ātman* masquerading under another name.[13]

I have already referred to the fact that there were attempts to explain the mechanics of karma long preceding the distinctive Yogācāra *ālaya-vijñāna* doctrine. Foremost amongst the karmic results which these different models sought to explain was why one was born a human rather than as an animal or some other lower or higher form of life. In early Buddhist texts such a karmic result was given the specific name of a *vipāka* ('maturation') and the *ālaya-vijñāna* at an early stage in its development became synonymous with such a result, particularly when it became associated with the mind at the moment of conception.

Now, amongst the Buddhist models to explain karma one of the very earliest and most important was the so-called 'twelve-linked chain of dependent origination' (*dva-daśāṅga pratītya-samutpāda*) formula. In this model, *avidyā* (in essence, self-centeredness) produces unskillful actions which leave *saṁskāras* ('impressions, formations') on the third of the twelve links, *vijñāna* ('consciousness'). This 'consciousness,' which was conceived of as somehow carrying the *saṁskāras*, was called *sarva-bījaka* '[mind] containing all seeds.' Dependent on it arose the fourth of the twelve links, *nāma-rūpa* ('name and form,' in essence the mental and physical constituents of a new life). Just as the *ālaya-vijñāna* came to incorporate the meaning associated with the mind at the moment of conception (that is, the *nāma* of *nāma-rūpa*) similarly it soon became equated with this *sarva-bījaka-vijñāna* and it began to acquire what was to become one of its most important meanings, the consciousness in which seeds stick, or on which they are laid down.

A large conceptual leap is required to move from conceiving of the *ālaya* as a *vijñāna* that carries the seed for the maturation which is a new life to a *vijñāna* which carries the seeds of all things, physical and mental.[14] The factor most crucially involved in effecting this leap is its becoming associated with the notion of *dauṣṭhulya* (Tib. *gnas ngan len* literally, 'a state getting bad' explained more fully in the following two paragraphs). The association of the two, largely completed the process of the *ālaya-vijñāna* becoming a central Yogācāra term and being declared an eighth consciousness quite dissimilar to the sixth, *mano-vijñāna* ('thinking-mind consciousness, mental consciousness').

On reflection it is not very surprising that the newly emerging concept of *ālaya-vijñāna* as vivifying element, repository of *saṁskāras* and basis of the sense of self, should have been adapted to the notion that all motivated things are miserable (*sarva-saṁskārā duḥkhāḥ*), a sentiment so central in Buddhist canonical literature that it is traditionally held to be the first doctrine Śākyamuni uttered after his enlightenment, and indeed so pervasive an idea in Indian writing in general that it appears, in terms only slightly less absolute, in epic and classical Brahmanical writings. This doctrine enshrines the insight, or negative attitude if you will, that human existence (*saṁsāra*) is, in and of itself, a state of misery; that just being is ground for the arising of a set of manifestly painful experiences (*duḥkha-duḥkhatā*), of experiences of fleeting pleasure which necessarily end, at some point or other, in pain (*vipariṇāma-duḥkhatā*), and for a human existence that is, as the location of the experiences of old age and death, a natural magnet, a veritable black hole, for unbroken misery (*saṁskāra-duḥkhatā=dauṣtulya*).

When connected with the doctrine that all motivated things are miserable, the concept of the *ālaya-vijñāna*, as basic substratum of the living being and repository of the seeds of future experience, puts across with great force and simplicity the notion of a creature whose destiny is controlled by the force of previous unwholesome actions and buffeted by the arising, first of the maturation (*vipāka*) which is a new life, and then of the experiences which such a maturation brings on. Endowed with the emotive dimension such considerations bring, the notion of *ālaya-vijñāna* developed from being merely a neutral concept in a speculative philosophy to a position of central importance in the Yogācāra scheme of things. The *ālaya-vijñāna*, out of its nature as the sum total of all seeds of experience became, in a causal sense at least, *saṁsāra* itself. And by extension liberation (*nirvāṇa*) came to be described in terms of the removal of the *ālaya-vijñāna*, or, more exactly, by a fundamental transformation (*āśraya-parivṛtti/parāvṛtti*) of it. At the end of the long course of yogic endeavor, so painstakingly plotted out in all its detail in the Yogācāra texts, the *ālaya-vijñāna* would change from being an opaque store of residual impressions into an enlightened Buddha mind in which all things were manifestly reflected (*ādarśana-jñāna*).

This point in the development of the *ālaya-vijñāna* doctrine, when the term carries all the above connotations or facets of meaning, is roughly the stage in its development that is found in the *Mahāyāna-saṁgraha*. It is what I have been calling 'the revelation,' and it is roughly this complex notion that Tsong kha pa had in mind when, in Tibet towards the end of the fourteenth century, he undertook to explain the term in his *Ocean of Eloquence*.

Sāṁkhya and Yogācāra

The synthesis of ideas set forth in such a polished fashion in the *Mahāyāna-saṁgraha*—a synthesis wherein the *ālaya-vijñāna* functions as the eighth of a set of eight consciousnesses, receives and gives rise to experience as the store of impressions, and appears as the (mistaken) ultimate basis of the sense of self—raises a question: Why did the different streams of thought, the different ideas in the classical *ālaya-vijñāna* doctrine found in the *Mahāyāna-saṁgraha*, present themselves to Asaṅga as suggesting, or at least being capable of being brought together in, a single complex synthesis? The intellectual and literary histories of the different ideas have shown that they were separate in their origins. A model or template to explain the synthesis of ideas in the classical formulation of the doctrine would, therefore, be expected. The model would not be so obviously similar that it would detract from the *ālaya-vijñāna* doctrine's originality, but would be close enough in conception to remove the necessity to posit its miraculous revelatory production.

Such a model may be found in early *sāṁkhya*, using the word to refer not to the later classical Sāṁkhya *darśana* best known through Īśvara-kṛṣṇa's (circa 350) formulation[15] but in its original sense as a partially systematic tradition of enumeration or categorization. Such a tradition, already in a state of considerable development in the *Mokṣa-dharma* and *Bhagavad-gītā*, may have provided later Indian classical thinkers, Yogācāra as much as Sāṁkhya, with the prototype for the idea of an underlying reality (*pradhāna* or *prakṛti*) that manifests in a diversity of quasi realities (*vikṛti*).

In Īśvara-kṛṣṇa's Sāṁkhya there are a finite number of principles which explain the known universe. Amongst these there are only two which partake of any lasting ultimate reality: one, called *pradhāna* or *prakṛti* representing matter, and the other *puruṣa* representing consciousness or soul. In Īśvara-kṛṣṇa's Sāṁkhya these two partake of no other unifying principle and remain absolutely and eternally separate, imparting a strikingly dualistic character to the system.[16] The remaining principles besides *puruṣa* and *prakṛti* are present in, and emerge from, *prakṛti*: first *buddhi* (in essence a primary mediating principle for diversity), then *ahaṁkāra* ('ego'), and then, in an internally coherent fashion, the other sense- and motor- faculties and the primary and secondary elements which build up the known world. All of the evolutes are material and nonsentient and, as evolutes (*pariṇāma*), entirely contingent on and hence in some fashion less real than *prakṛti* itself.

At first sight this material universe and the mind-only universe of the classical Yogācāra school appear to be very different. Closer analysis however reveals that this difference is not as extreme as it first appears. Both classical Sāmkhya and Yogācāra are similar in conceiving of the transitory universe as illusory: the one because all results (the evolutes of *prakṛti*) do not go beyond the nature of the fundamental cause *prakṛti*, and the other because apparently external objects are in fact only internal experiences not substantially different from the awareness that knows them—awareness that arises from residual-impression seeds placed on the *ālaya-vijñāna.* Further, in that the first Sāṁkhya evolute *buddhi* is the first of the secondary twenty-three principles to emerge from *prakṛti*, it, like *prakṛti*, contains within itself as cause all the evolutes which come after it (cp. its other name *mahat*—'great one'). This is strikingly similar to the Yogācāra conception of the *ālaya-vijñāna.* The *ālaya* too has no final lasting reality. It, like *buddhi,* is not present when *mokṣa* is attained and all ignorance about reality is removed. Yet it, like *buddhi*, contains within itself and mediates all the elements explaining the known world, starting with the sense of self-identity and importance (*ahaṁkāra*) and finishing with even the gross external objects and the gross experience of them.

It is also noteworthy that in Īśvara-kṛṣṇa's Sāṁkhya, results are asserted to be present in their causes. This apparently contradictory doctrine mirrors the insight that something existent cannot come out of a nonexistent nothing. Thus Īśvara-kṛṣṇa asserts that all results (the twenty-three evolutes of *prakṛti*) are present in *prakṛti* and merely become manifest. By extension, such results would also be present in *buddhi.* Now, although Yogācāra would deny vehemently the Sāṁkhya doctrine of pre-existent results and insist that the causal impression-seed on the *ālaya-vijñāna* precedes its result, still the Yogācāra doctrine of seeds dormant in the subconscious clearly parallels much of Sāṁkhya thinking. Indeed, if one brackets the ontological status of *buddhi* for the moment, the difference between the two doctrines becomes merely words: both function similarly.[17]

There are further parallels with *kliṣṭa-manas.* Īśvara-kṛṣṇa says the first evolutes to arise from *buddhi* are *ahaṁkāra* (which like the *kliṣṭa-manas* is an ever-present egocentricism) and *manas* (which like the *mano-vijñāna* is a knowlege instrument which serves to transmit or mediate sense inputs). In the *Mahāyāna-saṁgraha* the first consciousness to arise from *ālaya-vijñāna* is *kliṣṭa-manas,* which then defines a *mano-vijñāna* with at least some of the functions of Īśvara-kṛṣṇa's *manas.*

This is not the place to enter into this in greater detail. But were these apparent parallels to be shown conclusively to owe their similarities to a common earlier model, it would hardly be surprising. I think it likely that they in fact do so. Both classical systems arose at much the same time and in the same general region and they are both equally products of the same religio-intellectual heritage.

The *ālaya-vijñāna* within the eight-consciousness model

In the *Mahāyāna-saṁgraha* we already find in completed form the Yogācāra doctrine that each ordinary being is endowed with a set of eight consciousnesses. These eight consciousnesses may be conveniently broken down into three subgroups: a) There are six consciousnesses based on the sense-faculties. These are the five sense-consciousnesses such as the eye sense-consciousness (*cakṣur-vijñāna*), ear sense-consciousness (*śrotra-vijñāna*), etc., and the sixth, thinking-mind consciousness (*mano-vijñāna*). (b) There is a seventh consciousness, called *kliṣṭa-manas* ('afflicted thinking-mind'); and c) an eighth consciousness, called *ālaya-vijñāna*.

Now Yogācāra, like most classical Indian philosophies, was essentially religious. It was concerned with an ultimate (*paramārtha*) understanding which would give liberation, and the important terms in its philosophy present themselves as prominent and requiring description or inclusion in a set of elements or basic principles to advance the writer's primary concern: namely, leading the reader first to understand and then to embrace in yogic praxis a vision of liberation. For the author of the *Mahāyāna-saṁgraha*, the completed eight-consciousness model necessarily functioned within the wider Yogācāra religious philosophy to explain first why we are enmeshed in the cyclic world (*saṁsāra*), second how we should extricate ourselves from it, and lastly the state of liberation when we are free from it.

This religious intention of Yogācāra writers leads them to give a moral dimension to their eight-consciousness model (which could equally well merely explain the basic mechanics of knowledge acquisition and development). Here one can discern an inward and outward movement.

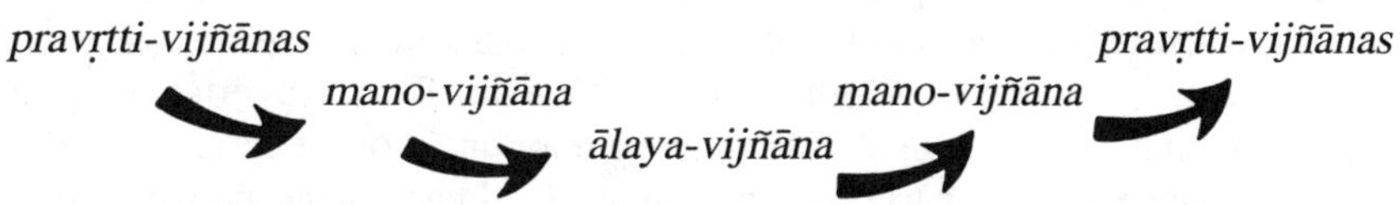

In the inward movement, the *pravṛtti-vijñānas* (sense-consciousnesses) apprehend distracting objects of desire: shapes, sounds, tastes, etc. These translate into the understandings of the sixth consciousness, *mano-vijñāna*, an immediate nonqualified inner awareness of what the object is. Always functioning alongside this inner thinking-mind is the seventh *kliṣṭa-manas* ('afflicted thinking-mind') with its ever-present sense of individual importance. It colors the impression the object makes on the sixth, thinking-mind, and gives rise to attitudes (*manaskara*) of liking, disliking, or indifference. The experience is in turn deposited as residual impressions on the eighth, the ever-present subconscious *ālaya-vijñāna.* In this, the eighth consciousness serves primarily as the receptacle or storehouse of the residual impression left by the functioning of the sixth consciousness.

In the outward movement, one's attitude towards (and implicitly general level of knowledge about) an object is explained by the maturing of the residual impression left by previous experience. This impression is stored on the eighth consciousness (*ālaya-vijñāna*). As this impression, now called a seed (*bīja*), ripens it gives rise to a frame of mind, the sixth thinking-mind consciousness (*mano-vijñāna*), endowed with a certain attitude and level of knowledge about the object appearing to one of the five sense-consciousnesses (*pravṛtti-vijñānas*).[18] The inner process occurs with the bare experience of the sense-consciousness again being filtered through the sixth, thinking-mind, and that experience is again stored in the *ālaya-vijñāna.* In this fashion, a record of painful or pleasant experiences—and similarly ignorance or knowledge—is built up, develops and evolves, and attitudes are formed and hardened.

Tsong kha pa's exegesis

As I have already mentioned, this complex *ālaya-vijñāna* doctrine systematized in the *Mahāyāna-saṁgraha* was viewed by Tsong kha pa as the single, unified revelation of an Enlightened Being and as such stands as the point of departure for his exegesis of it in his *Ocean of Eloquence.* According to Tsong kha pa's own conception of his work, it will not tell us any more about that 'revelation' than the 'revelation' itself, and in a limited sense this is true. It investigates the doctrine's difficult or knotty points (Tib. *dka' ba'i gnas* as in the concluding verse [56a5-6], not *dka' gnad* as might be expected). Largely by way of a question and answer format, it consists of, in the main, an uncovering of the different aspects of the doctrine that we have seen. There is a certain value in the text on that account alone. Of greater importance for the modern reader, however, is the value this early work retains as a landmark on the map of Tibetan intellectual history, providing a vantage point from which to view developments in the use of the Tibetan term *kun gzhi* ('basis of all'). Before turning to this, however, some information about the life of Tsong kha pa and some consideration of when the *Ocean of Eloquence* was written are in order.

Life of Tsong kha pa

The main sources for the life of Tsong kha pa have been set out in a short article by Obermiller[19] and reviewed and supplemented by Kaschewsky.[20] Both agree that the main source is Mkhas grub dpal bzang po's (1385-1438) Life (*rnam thar*) of Tsong kha pa called *Dam pa'i 'jug ngog.*[21] This forms the basis of a short Life of Tsong kha pa by Ngawang Dhargyey[22] and Thurman[23] and, indeed, for Obermiller's earlier remarks as well. Some additional bibliographical remarks are contained in van der Kuijp's review article[24] and in Wilson's[25] in-depth study of a later commentary on the *Ocean of Eloquence* by the A mdo writer Gung thang dkon mchog bstan pa'i sgron me (1762-1823).[26] There are a number of later expanded Tibetan versions of the life of Tsong kha pa, foremost amongst them the so-called *Rnam thar chen mo* by 'Brug rgyal.[27] They are based on Mkhas grub but supplement him with a combination of oral tradition and inferences drawn from Tsong kha pa's works. A partial chronology of the works of Tsong kha pa is also to be found in the *Bod rgya tshig mdzod chen mo* and *Bstan rtsis kun las btus pa.*[28]

Tsong kha pa was born in 1357 during the transitional period in Tibetan history when Phag mo gru under the leadership of the first Ta'i si tu Byang chub rgyal mtshan (1302-1371) finally wrested control over many of the important forts and monasteries of Dbus (central) and Gtsang (west-central) Tibet from the Sa skya sect. It was a period marked by ongoing competition between rival centers of religious and secular power in Dbus and Gtsang, the most important of which were at 'Bri gung, Rtse thang (the seat of Phag mo gru power), Tshal, Mtshur phu (the central Tibetan seat of the Karma bka' brgyud sect) and Sa skya. Although the rivalry was dominated from the time of Tsong kha pa by the Phag mo gru and their successors, the different factions would continue fighting one another until the middle of the seventeenth century when the by-then victorious followers of Tsong kha pa attained undisputed power.

The period of Tsong kha pa's birth also marks the end of the long translation period that stretches back to the early eighth century. Bu ston rin chen grub (1290-1364), the great encyclopaedist of Zhwa lu, had died when Tsong kha pa was seven years old, leaving behind in his editing and arranging of the Snar thang collections, what was to become the definitive redaction of the Tibetan canon (the Bka' 'gyur and Bstan 'gyur). Tsong kha pa was thus born when it was possible for the first time to read all important Buddhist texts in Tibetan translation and his primary access to Buddhist ideas was through texts in a standardized, religious Tibetan (*chos skad*), grouped in particular categories according to the traditions and insights of his Tibetan predecessors. Slightly more removed from the Indian Buddhist scene than earlier Tibetan translators, the developments in his thought owe much to this new social and intellectual reality.

Until his death in 1419, at the age of 63, Tsong kha pa wrote extensively on many aspects of Buddhist religious philosophy and practice. Van der Kuijp (1985:47) has summed up the effect of this work as follows: "... [His] output... set into motion a series of momentous controversies. . . . These contributed greatly to the further fragmentation of the Sa-skya-pa school and ultimately resulted in the establishment of the more or less autonomous Dga' ldan pa doctrinal entity." This 'doctrinal entity,' soon an important new cult, took advantage of the vacuum created by the continued fighting between the earlier Tibetan sects and families and quickly grew. Tsong kha pa's works, together with the works of his two principal disciples, Rgyal tshab dar ma rin chen (1364-1432) and Mkhas grub dpal bzang po, became the source of inspiration for the members of a new Tibetan Buddhist sect often called the Dga' ldan pa ('those associated with the Dga' ldan monastery'),[29] after the name of the first monastery he founded. Their own preferred name, somewhat tendentious, is Dge lugs pa ('those who are virtuous'). Followers of the sect are also popularly known, (especially to the English-speaking world) as 'yellow-hats', to distinguish them from members of the older Tibetan sects, the Rnying ma pa, Sa skya pa, and Bka' bgyud pa, who on ceremonial occasions wear red hats.[30] Helped in no small part by support from powerful Mongolian factions, by the early seventeenth century the sect, associated with the line of Dalai Lamas[31] and based in very large monasteries located around the central Tibetan city of Lha sa, assumed almost complete power over large sections of Tibet until the Chinese communist takeover in 1959, effectively ruling the country and defining the views of the orthodox church.

Problems of interpretation in Tsong kha pa's earlier and later works

In his later years Tsong kha pa formulated a distinctive view[32] that was the outcome, in part at least, of a mystical communion with Mañjuśrī, with whom he first communicated through a charismatic medium, the enigmatic Bka' gdams pa mystic, lama Dbu ma pa.[33] It caused Tsong kha pa to modify his earlier opinions and, in particular, caused a crystallization of his views concerning the *ālaya-vijñāna* and *kliṣṭa-manas.* Thus one finds that his treatment of the *ālaya-vijñāna* in the *Ocean of Eloquence* and in *Legs bshad gser phreng* (finished in 1392) differs from his treatment of the *ālaya-vijñāna* in his later works such as *Legs bshad snying po* (written between 1407 and 1408) and, particularly, in *Dgongs pa rab gsal* and his commentary on the *Guhya-samāja-vyākhyā-tantra Vajra-jñāna-samuccaya* (discussed in more detail below), definitive texts on sūtra and tantra written within two years of his death. Whereas in the *Ocean of Eloquence* Tsong kha pa accepts, or, at the very least considers it possible, that the hypostasized seventh and eighth consciousnesses exist in some way, in his later books he is unequivocal in his assertion that both notions are completely fictitious and are merely heuristic devices.

Recently some important later works of Tsong kha pa have appeared in English translation.[34] It is timely, therefore, in introducing this earlier work of Tsong kha pa, perhaps even his very earliest work, to bring up some of the problems of interpretation arising from the elaborate historiography of Tsong kha pa built up in the various Lives.

Mkhas grub's Life (*rnam thar*) of Tsong kha pa and all of the later Lives belong to the same literary genre as the Life of Bu ston[35] translated by Ruegg some twenty-five years ago. Although all contain some historical information, they have an innate tendency to distort historical reality because of the presuppositions that are the genre's defining feature. The origins of the genre are yet to be fully investigated but by the mid-fourteenth century, at least, two unquestioned premises inform its perspective. First, the important religious figure who is the subject of the "biography" is presented embedded within a complex tantric buddhology, a sort of modified docetism wherein, in essence, the religious figure is accepted to have been enlightened (or to at least function as if enlightened) even before birth. The different events in the Life reveal different aspects (Tib. *rnam pa*) of enlightenment for the benefit of disciples and are in that sense not historical but rather appearances manifested for the sake of living beings. The second premise of the genre, connected to the first, is that the views of the subject of the "biography" and the explanations of the sūtra and tantra path (*mārga*) which it spawned are not original in any respect but are rather the unmistaken presentation of what the Enlightened Being Śākyamuni, and Nāgārjuna, his foremost exegete, held to be truth (Tib. *dgongs pa mthar thug*).

What this means, in practical terms, is a tendency in the Lives to attribute to the religious figure supernatural abilities at an early age. Thus we find equally in the Lives of Bu ston and Tsong kha pa that both are said by their biographers to have been able to comprehend difficult Buddhist texts at age six or even three. While one should not think that educated Tibetan or Mongolian readers were unaware of the a-historical dimensions introduced by the literary form (both the Bu ston and the Tsong kha pa Lives set out, in pretty much historical fashion, their subject's actual course of study in later chapters; and there can be no doubt that there always has been, and there remains, a sophisticated ability in the traditional reader to discount the a-historical on one level while "believing" in the supernatural on another), it is also undeniable that the complexity of the literary genre itself tended to lead writers into dating events earlier than they in fact happened. It also leads the biographer to gloss over, or to conceal within a complex hermeneutical gymnastics, developments and changes that occured in the thought of the religious figure over the course of his life.

In arriving at decisions about the dates of events in Tsong kha pa's life and about the development in his thought, therefore, one has to keep these factors in mind and be aware that the presentation of historical reality will be affected by them.[36] The same considerations apply to the works of Tsong kha pa himself. Equally with his later followers, he believed that his insights were free from originality and that his vision was the exact vision of the Buddha and the Mādhyamika saints described in their various sūtras and śāstras (this is in part why I have called the understanding of the classical *ālaya-vijñāna* that served as the point of departure for his *Ocean of Eloquence* a 'revelation'). And equally Tsong kha pa's world was populated by enlightened figures. Though he did not refer to himself as an enlightened being, it remained only for his followers to add a name, a more familiar modern icon, to make him a part of the pantheon. Thus not only traditional books about Tsong kha pa but, paradoxically, even books written by Tsong kha pa himself can obfuscate the historical development of his thought.

Early teachers and date of the text

It is probably not without significance that both the teachers to whom Tsong kha pa offers reverent praise at the end of his *Ocean of Eloquence* are from the Sa skya sect. The first is his tutor and abbot Don grub rin chen. Like Tsong kha pa, Don grub rin chen was from Mdo khams smad (north-eastern Tibet—popularly known as A mdo). He had travelled earlier in his youth to the seats of learning in Dbus and Gtsang where, if he did not distinguish himself, one can imagine that he had at least been blessed by the spirit of great learning. Far to the north-east in A mdo, many months journey by foot from Lha sa over a series of mountain passes, it would have been ennobling for a monk simply to have spent time in central Tibet, to have gone on pilgrimage to the sacred spots, and to have sat in the presence of luminaries such as the great Bu ston. Tsong kha pa, a fourth child of ordinary nomadic herders, was given away to this relatively ordinary but sanctified monk while still young and,[37] according to Mkhas grub, Don grub rin chen set out Tsong kha pa's early course of study. Don grub rin chen held that a student should first focus on the *Abhisamayālaṁkāra* (a book closely associated with the *Pañca-viṁśati-sāhasrikā*, a Yogācāra version of the *Prajñā-pāramitā-sūtra*) and study in detail two fundamental Yogācāra texts: the *Mahāyāna-sūtrālaṁkāra* and *Abhidharma-samuccaya*. Tsong kha pa's interest in Yogācāra in general, and in the *ālaya-vijñāna* doctrine in particular during his early years can thus be traced to the guidelines set down for him, while still a young student in A mdo, by Don grub rin chen.

When Tsong kha pa came of age he too left north-eastern Tibet, as had his teacher before him, to study in the monasteries of Dbus and Gtsang. He is said to have travelled in ordinary style with little in the way of belongings or companions. We are told that after studying medicine for a short period he went first to 'Bri gung and then visited other important centers, eventually arriving in Sa skya where he met the second of the two persons reverently mentioned in his *Ocean of Eloquence* colophon, the Sa skya lama Red mda' ba gzhon nu blo gros (1349-1412), the most influential of all Tsong kha pa's early teachers.[38] Red mda' ba was a scholar who had already at a quite early age inherited the mantle of the Sa skya scholar-saints. He was to be Tsong kha pa's main guide through the great edifice of scholastic Buddhism, providing him with the foundations on which Tsong kha pa would erect his exposition of the Prajñā-pāramitā literature *Legs bshad gser phreng*.

As far as I have been able to determine, this work *Legs bshad gser phreng* is the first text of Tsong kha pa that can be positively dated. Other works stated in the later Lives to be earlier than *Legs bshad gser phreng* contain no information in the surviving editions of the texts themselves about when they were written.[39] The detailed colophon to *Legs bshad gser phreng*, which is similar to the *Ocean of Eloquence* in that Don grub rin chen and Red mda' ba are the only two teachers mentioned, explicitly tells us that the work was started in Tshal between 1390 and 1391 when Tsong kha pa was thirty-two and that more work was done on it there a year later. As corroborated by Mkhas grub, *Legs bshad gser phreng* was finished in 1392 in Bde ba can monastery, probably in May or June.

The colophon of the *Ocean of Eloquence* mentions, besides the two teachers Don grub rin chen and Red mda' ba gzhon nu blo gros, that it was written in Sa skya. It does not, unfortunately, say in which year. Still, even if the exact date is uncertain, that it was written in the first part of Tsong kha pa's intellectual life during what Mkhas grub calls his 'Prajñā-pāramitā study period' (a period that ends approximately with the writing of *Legs bshad gser phreng*) is suggested by the way Tsong kha pa interprets a verse from Sa skya Paṇḍita's *Tshad ma rigs gter*.[40] Dreyfus[41] suggests that the interpretation of this verse in the *Ocean of Eloquence*, which agrees with Sa skya Paṇḍita's authentically Dharmakīrtian approach to universals (*sāmānya, spyi*), is absent from Tsong kha pa's mature work. It is an interpretation later rejected by Tsong kha pa[42] in favour of a more phenomenological or experiential interpretation associated with a tradition of Dharmottara and Śāntarakṣita introduced into Tibet by Ngog legs pa'i shes rab and found in particular in the Gsang phu ne'u thog monastery. That the *Ocean of Eloquence* was written at an early period in Tsong kha pa's life is also suggested by its subject matter. As I shall show in more detail shortly, one of the most striking characteristics of Tsong kha pa's later work is the absence of any detailed reference to the *ālaya-vijñāna*, particularly in descriptions of meditative praxis.

Although there is no specific mention of the *Ocean of Eloquence* in Mkhas grub's Life of Tsong kha pa, in the Life published by Kaschewsky it says explicitly that the *Ocean of Eloquence* was written when Tsong kha pa was twenty-one. It is noteworthy, however, that the assertion is put forward tentatively. I think it is most probably too early a date.[43]

Following Mkhas grub we can reconstruct a rough outline of the travels and study of Tsong kha pa in the four or five years leading up to the writing of *Legs bshad gser phreng* between 1390 and 1392. We are told that he spent eleven months in Sa skya with Red mda' ba, probably from late spring of 1386 to early spring of 1387. The next spring and early summer Tsong kha pa and Red mda' ba went through Stod and Byang, staying a short time in a number of different places as was the custom with lamas on tour. During this period, while teaching Tsong kha pa the *Abhidharma-samuccaya*, Red mda' ba wrote his *Abhidharma-samuccaya* commentary at Ngam ring chos sde. In the autumn (apparently of the same year) Tsong kha pa set off for north-eastern Tibet on a trip home from the Gtsang region via Lha sa. He seems to have changed his mind half way and instead stopped in Mal gro lha lung where he studied the *Pramāṇa-vārttika*. He wintered that year (1387-88) in Chos bde ba can and next spring went back to Gtsang and Snar thang, spending the summer in Snar thang studying *pramāṇa*. That autumn he studied with Bo dong phyogs las rnam rgyal in Er and apparently in a feverish period of study with many teachers went back to Sa skya with Red mda' ba where he spent at least the last part of the winter of 1388-89. During the next spring and summer he travelled in the Dbus region studying with a variety of teachers and began *Legs bshad gser phreng*.

What is striking in later Lives of Tsong kha pa, Kaschewsky's amongst them, which set out a coherent chronological sequence of events beginning with Tsong kha pa's arrival in Central Tibet in 1373, is that some of these same events mentioned by Mkhas grub, which can be dated back from the writing of *Legs bshad gser phreng*, are placed about ten years earlier. Even allowing for the fact that Tsong kha pa was a brilliant student who quickly made a name for himself, particularly when he acquitted himself with distinction in the debating courtyard (Tib. *chos grwa*) of the major monasteries, since he was an ordinary nomad from A mdo he would not have had special access, in his early years at least, to the libraries or funds which would have allowed him to progress as quickly in his learning as the later accounts would have us believe. Even allowing that there is some truth in statements that he memorized sixteen pages of scripture a day it is unlikely that Tsong kha pa would have had either the knowledge or the confidence to write the *Ocean of Eloquence* just four or five years after his arrival in central Tibet. More likely the early date assigned to the text in the later Lives (*rnam thar*) is the result of moving up events that happened some five to ten years later to an earlier period in Tsong kha pa's life in order to set out a coherent narrative. Given the premises of the genre it would have been natural to do so.

Before leaving the question of the exact date of the *Ocean of Eloquence*, it is instructive to consider the relationship between it and *Legs bshad gser phreng*. While a detailed analysis of the contents of this latter book must await further research, it is notable that in one of its later chapters (Tib. *skabs bzhi pa*) there is an acceptance, or at least agnosticism, concerning the status of the *kliṣṭa-manas* and *ālaya-vijñāna* similar to that found in the *Ocean of Eloquence* and in contrast to the unequivocal rejection found in Tsong kha pa's later works.[44] Since Tsong kha pa makes no cross-reference to either *Legs bshad gser phreng* or the *Ocean of Eloquence* in either book, the presence of such a similar perspective might possibly warrant the view that Tsong kha pa had it in mind, when he was writing

Legs bshad gser phreng, to write a separate treatise on the *ālaya-vijñāna* at a later time. I consider this unlikely, if only because the *Ocean of Eloquence* reads in part like an attempt to work through and understand a difficult subject and lacks *Legs bshad gser phreng*'s sheer size and sophistication. Moreover, in an earlier section of *Legs bshad gser phreng* (Tib. *skabs dang po*) there is a detailed consideration of *gotra* ('buddha nature') from the point of view of different Buddhist schools.[45] Here Tsong kha pa seems to have already moved to a position that certain Yogācāras do not assert the *ālaya-vijñāna*[46] and to be already using a language devoid of any reference to mind and mind nature (on this language see below) when describing Madhyamaka opinions about the ultimate, this suggesting a stage in Tsong kha pa's thinking slightly more advanced than that found in the *Ocean of Eloquence.* It may also be significant that *Legs bshad gser phreng* itself lacks a detailed explanation of the *ālaya-vijñāna.* Although in most respects an extremely detailed commentary, it mentions the *ālaya-vijñāna* only in passing, and even after taking into account the fact that the *Abhisamayālaṁkāra* (the root text that *Legs bshad gser phreng* is explaining) does not explicitly mention the *ālaya-vijñāna* or *kliṣṭa-manas*, and that Tsong kha pa may perhaps, even at this stage in his life, have had some notion of a different *Mdo sde spyod pa'i dbu ma rang rgyud pa* (the equivalent Sanskrit would be *Sautrāntika-svātantrika-madhyamaka*) point of view,[47] such an absence is striking in this systematic and detailed work.

Taking into consideration all these factors, my opinion is that the *Ocean of Eloquence* was probably written before Tsong kha pa began to write *Legs bshad gser phreng*, either when he stayed in Sa skya in the winter of 1389-90, or, perhaps, even earlier in the summer or fall of 1386.

Kun gzhi in Tsong kha pa's later works

It is not of great consequence, in the context of the investigation I am engaged in, whether or not the formulation of the ideas of so-called Indian Mādhyamika and Yogācāra thinkers by Tsong kha pa accorded with what those earlier Indian writers actually intended. Indeed, it would be of no consequence even if, in his interpretation of Candrakīrti, or of later Mādhyamikas like Kamalaśīla, he were to have mistakenly understood those writers to be saying what was in fact set forth in a Yogācāra text of Asaṅga. What is of importance is that Tsong kha pa, over the course of his intellectual life, came to conceive of two different systems of thought, one he called Madhyamaka and the other Yogācāra, and that he believed that of these two only one embodied the final, definitive statement about reality.

That Tsong kha pa held such an opinion throughout his intellectual life is clear from even a cursory reading of his works. Even allowing for the necessary development in his thought over the forty or more years of his intellectual life, there is no evidence to show that, having held the *vijñapti-mātratā* doctrine earlier as his own final opinion on reality he then, later in his life, changed and embraced the doctrine of *śūnyatā* as set forth by Nāgārjuna. He always held, first no doubt as an act of faith and then as a personal belief, that Nāgārjuna as interpreted by Candrakīrti was correct. This is not surprising since all of his teachers such as Red mda' ba, etc., are located squarely in traditions which held that point of view.

Nevertheless it is equally apparent that his opinion about the final ontological status of *kun gzhi* ('basis of all') changed during the course of his intellectual life. *Kun gzhi* is the standard Tibetan translation of *ālaya* and may or may not be a short form of *kun gzhi rnam par shes pa* ('basis-of-all consciousness'), the standard Tibetan translation of *ālaya-vijñāna.* I will retain it untranslated in my following remarks. Not only is Tsong kha pa's presentation of *kun gzhi* in the *Ocean of Eloquence* extremely convincing, but, as I have already shown (note 44), he is explicit in *Legs bshad gser phreng* that only Hīnayānists (Tib. *nyan thos sde pa*) as distinct from Mahāyānists deny a set of eight consciousnesses.

That is not to say Tsong kha pa was unequivocal in his acceptance of *ālaya-vijñāna* in his early years. Nowhere in his early works does he make as clear a statement to the effect that the *ālaya-vijñāna* exists as he does in his later works that it does not. He seems, rather, to be unsure about the matter. At the end of the *Ocean of Eloquence*, for example, he says[48]

> Would those who are learned in the Vijñapti-[mātrin] texts which are as vast as a great ocean please make a just and fair appraisal of this consciousness, satisfactory or otherwise. If you think something is satisfactory please accept it. Since it is certainly not impossible that somebody with my sort of knowledge could make mistakes on subtle [topics], if [something] is not [satisfactory] please do otherwise.

Such exhortations are also common in *Legs bshad gser phreng* and suggest a formative stage in the original thoughts which would later distinguish Tsong kha pa's views from those of his earlier teachers and contemporaries.

If he is, at best, ambivalent about the status of *kun gzhi* in his early life (an ambivalence that remains even in early passages of the *Lam rim chen mo*)[49] why, in his later formulation of Buddhist truth based on his visionary experiences, did Tsong kha pa feel it was necessary to explicitly reject *kun gzhi*? We are fortunate that he spells out the reasons clearly in a short explanation of the *Guhya-samāja-vyākhyā-tantra Vajra-jñāna-samuccaya* written shortly before his death.[50] This text, written after his definitive *Madhyamakāvatāra* commentary *Dgongs pa rab sel,* must be considered one of his last works and as containing a final definitive statement on the *kun gzhi* question.

The larger context for Tsong kha pa's clear and unequivocal rejection of the *kun gzhi* in his *Vajra-jñāna-samuccaya* commentary is a detailed explanation of the origin, divisions into, emergence of, and dissolution of three transcendental wisdoms (the *vajra*-jñānas mentioned in the title of the short text). Having discussed the emanation of the *anāntara-bhāva-dehin* (an embodied spirit that lives between lifetimes) from luminosity (*prabhāsvara*) at death, and the coming into being of a fetus at conception, Tsong kha pa takes up what is a parallel question in Buddhist tantra, i.e., the macrocosmic evolution/emanation of the known universe (470.5ff). He discusses both its arising and final dissolution. The luminosity (*prabhāsvara*, i.e., starting point of all that exists) is ultimate reality (*paramārtha*), but, in accord with Tsong kha pa's final statement, not the ultimate reality that is realized, because were it to be so there would be no need for religious praxis since all would then be in a natural state of enlightenment. Using the metaphor of child and mother (the same person but at different periods), Tsong kha pa says that 'child luminosity' (Tib. *bu 'od gsal*) is the content of the visionary experience before death that is the outcome of a long cultivation of the ultimate truth realized in a properly graduated course of study. Through meditation it becomes an integrated experience. When integrated, it is 'mother luminosity' (Tib. *ma'i 'od gsal*), the actual death experience, and becomes, through the process of recognition, part of a natural process such that one realizes the Dharma-kāya ('Truth Body') and remains in an enlightened state. It is at this point in his discussion that the discursus on *kun gzhi* arises (472.5), at the end of which (478.1) he sets forth the reason why it must be rejected.

> [Question:] Even though a *kun gzhi* which is *svabhava-siddha* ('inherently real') is rejected, still one may accept one which, substantially different (Tib. *ngo bo tha dad*) to the set of six, is the illusion-like *sarva-bījaka* of all good and bad.
>
> [Response:] Should one accept such a *kun gzhi* one would have to accept shapes and sounds, etc., which ripening from *kun gzhi* residual impressions, are mere appearances without objective content (Tib. *don med*). But in this [definitive] text [on Buddhist truth, i.e., the *Guhya-samāja* commentary] it says, "One gets the knowable through knowing; without a knowable there is no knowing. So why not assert the nonexistence of understanding and understood?"
>
> Here, then, the ontological status of a knowable and knowing are equated. If one were not to exist the other would not either. This is no different to what we find in the *Madhyamakāvatāra* where it says the object-known (Tib. *don*) and knowing are not to be differentiated when it comes to their ontological status: both are equally ultimately nonexistent and equally conventionally existent. The Ācārya does not accept there is a

> knowledge of something nonexternal. So he does not assert a *kun gzhi* which is substantially different to [the sixth consciousness] *mano-vijñāna.*

In essence, then, Tsong kha pa totally rejects a place for the *ālaya-vijñāna* because it gives awareness itself—what Tsong kha pa terms 'knowing' (Tib. *shes byed*)—undue weight relative to ordinary external appearances.

The term *kun gzhi* in Tibet before Tsong kha pa

Before the period of the new translations (see below), the most important context in which *ālaya-vijñāna/kun gzhi* appeared as a central term was in descriptions of an ultimate meditative praxis.[51] Probably the oldest description of such meditative praxis was Rdzogs chen (more fully *rdzogs pa chen po*—'great perfection').[52] In texts dating to the early part of the ninth century[53] *sems* (Tibetan for 'mind') is said to create the illusory, which creation then obscures its own real nature (Tib. *sems nyid*), a nature that is an unimpeded illumination pure from the beginning. This real nature of mind is called *kun gzhi* (also *gdod ma'i gzhi, ji bzhin pa'i gzhi,* etc.), an ever pure and dormant awareness (Tib. *rig pa*). In its bare outlines, the Rdzogs chen meditative praxis (and this is equally true of the Mahā-mudrā practices associated with the Bka' brgyud and Sa skya sects) consists in calming discursive thought and contacting or manifesting the nature of mind by utilizing mind's innate self-reflexive ability to know itself.[54]

The literary environment within which the term *kun gzhi* originated and functioned as a term used primarily to describe ultimate meditative praxis persisted into the period of the new translations (its beginnings traditionally dated from the work of Lo tsa ba Rin chen bzang po [958-1055] and from the time of the arrival of Atiśa in Tibet in 1042). As the numbers of Buddhist texts increased and the quality of their translation into Tibetan improved, the increasingly sophisticated Tibetan Buddhists began to scrutinize the fusion of Yogācāra and Madhyamaka doctrines more carefully. This scutiny was sharpened, after the eleventh century, by the increasing popularity of the *Prāsaṅgika-Madhyamaka of Candrakīrti (whose works were carefully translated by Pa tshab nyi ma grags [born 1055] and his disciples) which was far less accomodating of Yogācāra terminology and views than the Yogācāra-Madhyamaka first introduced into Tibet by Śāntarakṣita and his students at the end of the eighth century.

This influence of *Prāsaṅgika can be traced in the 'tenet system' (Tib. *grub mtha'*) type taxonomies set forth by Mimaki based on his work on the Bka' gdams pa Dbu pa blo gsal's *Grub pa'i mtha' rnam par bshad pa'i mdzod.*[55] What one observes is that, as *Prāsaṅgika emerges more clearly as a distinct and unique form of Madhyamaka, there is a corresponding devaluation of the syncretistic Yogācāra-Madhyamaka. There is first a sharpening of the awareness of the difference between the schools of thought, then an association of the views of the Yogācāra school with the surface (*saṁvṛti*) level of truth, then a distinction drawn between those Madhyamaka schools associated or not associated with Yogācāra, and finally a clear and definitive differentiation between *Yogācāra-Svātantrika and *Prāsaṅgika, where the former is squarely placed in the non-Prāsaṅgika (and hence wrong) category.[56]

The problem of interpreting the meaning of *kun gzhi* during the new translation period lies in the different ways Tibetan thinkers understood the two—ultimate (*paramārtha*) and surface (*saṁvṛti*)—levels of truth. Are the seventh and eighth consciousnesses of Yogācāra, a) completely nonexistent (Tib. *shes bya la mi srid*), like the hair of a turtle, or is it b) that they do not exist ultimately (Tib. *don dam du med*), when the transcendent state beyond the four extremes is actualized? If the latter, the seventh and eighth consciousnesses might still exist on a surface level of reality (Tib. *kun rdzob tu yod*). As already mentioned, Tsong kha pa in his later works is unequivocal in his rejection of any truth status whatsoever for the seventh and eighth consciousnesses, considering them merely heuristic devices (Tib. *sems tsam pa'i lugs gzhi gzhag na yod*) completely devoid of reality. Tibetan writers previous to Tsong kha pa, however, do not reject *kun gzhi* in such a clear and unequivocal fashion. Rather, as a strategy for dealing with the challenge of *Prāsaṅgika's rejection of Yogācāra, they include it in, or even equate it with, the lower truth (*saṁvṛti-satya*), which is the category of ordinary appearance.[57]

The best known Tibetan to systematically associate Yogācāra with ordinary appearance and Madhyamaka with the ultimate level of truth was Sa skya Paṇḍita Kun dga' rgyal mtshan (1182-1251).[58] According to Sa skya Paṇḍita[59] the sphere of truth (*dharma-dhātu*) that transcends the four extremes of being (*bhava, dngos*), etc. is the Madhyamaka ('the middle way') and ordinary appearance (Tib. *snang ba*) or representation (Tib. *[rnam par] rig pa*) systematized as eight consciousnesses is Yogācāra or Cittamātra ('mind only'). The relative existence of a composite (*saṁskṛta*) *kun gzhi* within this implicitly hierarchical presentation of the two truths was not an issue for Sa skya Paṇḍita, who accepted the Yogācāra eight consciousness model, including the *ālaya-vijñāna/kun gzhi*, without comment or distortion.[60] Scriptural authority was given to this accomodation of Yogācāra with *Prāsaṅgika-Madhyamaka through a skillful reworking of the hermeneutics of the *Saṁdhi-nirmocana-sūtra.*[61] Different surface level realities explained in the doctrine of the four truths (i.e., the doctrine of what is to be given up and embraced taught in the *Saṁdhi-nirmocana-sūtra*'s first turning of the wheel of the dharma) were said to be underlayed by the intrinsically pure mind-nature (Tib. *sems nyid*) which is ultimate truth. The Prajñā-pāramitā sūtras (the second turning) were said to teach the refutation (sometimes explicitly by analytic meditation [Tib. *dpyad sgom*]) of all mind and mental factors, thus teaching the path whereby the underlying essential is revealed in its original brilliance and vacuity. In the final revelation (Tib. *bka' tha ma nges pa don gyi chos kyi rnam grangs*) transcendental wisdom was taught. It required a fundamental transformation of the *kun gzhi* in ordinary beings for it to be realized. Since it was the essence of the earlier minds and mental factors it was of a sort with them, but completely beyond dualistic appearance.[62]

Kun gzhi at the time of Tsong kha pa

What is particularly remarkable in light of the complex history of *kun gzhi* in Tibetan literature is that Tsong kha pa, at such an early age, wrote his *Ocean of Eloquence* dealing with *kun gzhi* from the Yogācāra point of view, restricting the sources for his discussion almost exclusively to Yogācāra sources. In this he may have been directly influenced by Bu ston rin chen grub. Although he is not a direct teacher of Tsong kha pa, his influence on Tsong kha pa is well attested and he is one of the few Tibetans living at approximately the same time as Tsong kha pa to have dealt with *kun gzhi* strictly in terms of an Indian Yogācāra source. In his commentary on the *Abhidharma-samuccaya*,[63] the explanation of consciousness (*vijñāna-skandha*) (201.1-257.7) is in terms of the *ālaya, kliṣṭa-manas*, and *pravṛtti-vijñānas*. The major part of Bu ston's discussion (202-244), which covers most of the Indian sources which Tsong kha pa later drew on for his *Ocean of Eloquence*, concerns the *ālaya* and is the most detailed treatment of the subject based on Yogācāra sources, prior to Tsong kha pa, that I have, to date, been able to locate. Bu ston bases his explanation of the operation and cessasion of the *ālaya-vijñāna* on five rubrics found in a verse from the *Viniścaya-saṁgrahaṇī.* These have been summarized by Wilson (1984:365-6) as a) operation of the *ālaya-vijñāna* in the context of its objective supports, b) operation in the context of the accompaniers with which it is in similar association, c) operation in the context of the engaging (*pravṛtti*) consciousnesses and their acting as causes of each other, d) the number of sets of consciousness in conjunction with which *kun gzhi* operates, and e) its own actual operation. Tsong kha pa, however, makes no reference to this verse in his *Ocean of Eloquence* or to Bu ston's explanation of it.

One of the early teachers of Tsong kha pa whose views on *kun gzhi* are relatively well known is Sa bzang Ma ti Paṇ chen, with whom the young Tsong kha pa studied Sanskrit prior to meeting Red mda' ba. Ma ti Paṇ chen was a student of the influential Jo nang pa teacher, Shes rab rgyal mtshan (1292-1361). In his commentary on the *Abhidharma-samuccaya*,[64] Ma ti Paṇ chen mentions two *kun gzhis:* one a *saṁvṛti* consciousness and the other, ultimate wisdom. The former is coterminous with the surface and the latter with ultimate truth.

> . . . one must know the distinction between the two truths concerning mind (Tib. *sems*) and *kun gzhi* . . . . With regards to *kun gzhi*, there are two factors: (1) the nature which is conventional, a substratum of [final] nature, and consciousness; and (2) the factor which is ultimate, [final] nature, and wisdom. [This latter is] the Buddha essence.[65]

Ma ti Paṇ chen says that, depending on the angle one is looking from, one can interpret this 'Buddha essence' (i.e., *tathāgata-garbha*) as surface or ultimate level *kun gzhi*.[66] The surface level *kun gzhi* is not real because (this is the Jo nang pa 'emptiness of other' [Tib. *gzhan stong*] view)[67] *saṁvṛti-satya* lacks reality in its entirety. The ultimate *kun gzhi* on the other hand is nondual wisdom. This interpretation harks back to the Jo nang pa view that one reveals the ultimate by the removal of the surface (*samsāra*) *saṁvṛti* level. As Shes rab rgyal mtshan says in his *Nges don rgya mtsho*,[68] "The pure wisdom *kun gzhi* is an emptiness of other (Tib. *gzhan stong*), it is empty of all phenomena of cyclic existence."

Although there is little evidence of any direct influence of Jo nang pa views on Tsong kha pa's presentation of *kun gzhi* in his *Ocean of Eloquence* it is likely that even at this early point in his life he was beginning to view the Jo nang pa in a negative light. In his important mature work *Legs bshad snying po* many of Tsong kha pa's arguments are directed against the Jo nang pa views of Shes rab rgyal mtshan and it is known that Red mda' ba, Tsong kha pa' s most influential early teacher, disagreed strongly with the Jo nang pa position.

Red mda' ba's opinions about *kun gzhi* are not known in detail since his commentary on the *Abhidharma-samuccaya*, written at about the same time as the *Ocean of Eloquence* is not available.[69] It is interesting, however, in the context of an investigation of Tsong kha pa's earlier and later presentations of *kun gzhi*, to note that even Red mda' ba in his commentary on *Madhyamakāvatāra* (verse 39)[70]—in the context of explaining Candrakīrti's refutation of the Yogācāra school[71]—formulates his refutation of *kun gzhi* in a way that does not clearly eliminate it as existing, as an eighth consciousness, on the *saṁvṛti* level. Red mda' ba's presentation is easily reconcilable with the views of the Sa skya Paṇḍita set out above and indeed, in the Sa skya school, Red mda' ba's works are treated as authoritative.

In the *Ocean of Eloquence* itself, Tsong kha pa's presentation is distinguished by a novel division into basis (Tib. *brten du byur pa*) *kun gzhi* and based-on (Tib. *brten pa*) *kun gzhi*. Although both are equally given the name *ālaya-vijñāna*, Tsong kha pa says they are different. The former is the basis of the residual impressions and the latter is the residual impressions themselves. They are, he says, not materially the same nor are they materially different. Understanding the relation between them is to understand the profound dependent origination (*pratītya-samutpāda*), the heart of the Buddha's doctrine. This differentiation between basis and based-on *kun gzhi* was an innovative interpretive strategy devised by Tsong kha pa himself. It had the advantage of making more intelligible at least some of the diverse ideas fused together in the classical Yogācāra *ālaya-vijñāna* doctrine

Tsong kha pa also grapples at some length in the *Ocean of Eloquence* with the question of how the *tathāgata-garbha* exists for a person caught in the distortion of an imperfect world, or—to phrase the problem differently—how the seed of transcendental wisdom can be placed on the *ālaya-vijñāna*.[72] Tsong kha pa's proposed solution is a reframing of the question in terms of the gradual versus spontaneous (or all-at-once) enlightenment dispute.[73] In this his conclusions anticipate his position in his famous *Lam rim chen mo*, where great emphasis is placed on the role of gradual learning in the liberation process, and spontaneous enlightenment is explicitly and unequivocally rejected.

Concluding remarks

The general effect of Tsong kha pa's treatment of *kun gzhi* on later Tibetan writers who carried on traditions originating before Tsong kha pa's time was a heightened awareness of the "error" in the Yogācāra eight-consciousness system. Stag tshang shes rab rin chen (see note 46) attacked Tsong kha pa's mature opinion about *kun gzhi* and reaffirmed what he believed to be the earlier position set forth by Sa skya Paṇḍita. Besides any merit they may have intrinsically, Stag tshang's comments are interesting for identifying what was perceived as unorthodox in Tsong kha pa's work. Other writers simply show in their presentation of Yogācāra that they are aware of Tsong kha pa's views, and perhaps they slightly modify earlier explanations to avoid criticism.[74]

In time, Tsong kha pa's *Ocean of Eloquence* gave rise to its own commentarial tradition. The large Dge lugs pa monasteries each had their own favored interpretation and considerable scholastic heat was generated about abstruse points of Yogācāra doctrine. The 'Bras phung Go mang writer, Gung thang dkon mchog bstan pa'i sgron me, in his *Mkhas pa'i 'jug ngog*,—the basis of Wilson, 1984—is of particular interest because of Gung thang's attempt to track down the opinions of Tsong kha pa's early teachers. Ke'u tshang Blo bzang 'jam dbyangs smon lam's commentary, *Nyi zla zung 'jug*, was consulted by Odani and Kalsang for their Japanese translation of the *Ocean of Eloquence*.[75] Another commentary enjoying relatively wide currency is the early twentieth century *Kun gzhi'i thal phreng* by the 'Bras phung Blo gsal gling writer Blo bzang chos dbying.[76] What is of particular interest in this commentarial tradition is that it has developed even though it is accepted that the object of study, the Yogācāra *ālaya-vijñāna*, does not exist at all and to that extent is "wrong." The comments of Wilson (1984:36-7) in respect to the Dge lugs pa sacred environment in which this occurs are illuminating.

> The study of Buddhist doctrine . . . is not a case of philosophizing . . . rather, an instance of the interpretation of texts . . . with a set goal in mind . . . to train the students mind in critical analysis and . . . to cause the student to become conversant with artificial or constructed images of reality and to be able to apply rational criteria in determining their validity. In this way he can see at first hand the transformative power that rationality has in religious life and, having become convinced of its efficacy, transfer its use from external doctrinal formulations to an analysis of the thought patterns innate in his own mind. Thereby, he can eliminate misconceptions and false modes of thinking and achieve a truly transformative vision of reality as it is. It is said among Tibetan students of doctrine that even the study of what is known to be untrue in the final event can be a liberative internalization of the Buddhist doctrine.

Notes

1. The reader should also be aware that the word *ālaya-vijñāna* in phrases like '*ālaya-vijñāna* doctrine' is used throughout this Introduction to refer loosely to both the *ālaya-vijñāna* and *kliṣṭa-manas* in order to avoid cumbersome repetition.

2. In particular the recent work of Lambert Schmithausen contained in his *Ālaya-vijñāna. On the Origin and the Early Development of a Central Concept of Yogācāra Philosophy*, Studia Philologica Buddhica Monograph Series IVb (Tokyo: The International Institute for Buddhist Studies, 1987). His meticulously annotated work is the main source for the discussion of the different meaning-components of the classical *ālaya-vijñāna* doctrine that follows and readers are directed to that work for a full and detailed presentation of the many sources, analysis, and reasoned conclusion.

3. Another possible approach to the problem of dealing coherently with the number of different meanings included under the classsical term *ālaya-vijñāna* is suggested by Ronald Mark Davidson's notion of 'environment specific systems' ("Buddhist Systems of Transformation: *Asraya-parivrtti/paravrtti* Among the Yogācāra," Ph.D. dissertation, University of California at Berkeley, 1985). Although Davidson is concerned with an explanation of fundamental transformation (*āśraya-parāvṛtti*), i.e., the change from the ordinary suffering state that is the *ālaya-vijñāna* to the state of enlightenment, his remarks on environment suggest an alternative approach to the different facets of meaning of *ālaya-vijñāna*, wherein one would view them as different ways of framing a question or different responses to a problem when viewed from different perspectives.

4. Daniel L. Overmyer, *Folk Buddhist Religion: Dissenting Sects in Late Traditional China* (Cambridge: Harvard University Press, 1976), p. 13.

5. Sanskrit *karman* is treated as an English loanword and spelled karma.

6. There is a vast literature devoted to explaining social class or caste in India. The work of Louis Dumont merits particular mention.

7. At the very beginning of the *Bhagavad-gītā*, for example, Arjuna tells Kṛṣṇa, who is later to appear as the creator and destroyer of the universe, that misguided action not only results in a personal downfall, but effects the very tenor of the time and disturbs the balance (*ṛta*) of society. "The eternal religious rites of one's caste (*jāti*) and family (*kula*) are destroyed by these evil deeds of the family destroyers who mingle the social classes." The *Gītā* goes on to develop a complex theory of karma around the notion of disinterested purposeful action.

8. The most recent attempt to sort out the historical problems associated with these writers is Davidson (1985) who provides the bibliographical references.

9. This rationale for the division was suggested by Christian Lindtner during a series of conversations in 1988. As I will point out later (note 46), Tsong kha pa's mature view that some Yogācāras (the *rigs pa'i rje 'brang*) do not assert an *ālaya-vijñāna* is offensive to some Tibetan thinkers.

10. Unpublished manuscript of the *Yogācāra-bhūmi* p. 78b5, quoted by Schmithausen 1987:note 146.

11. Schmithausen's association of the radically idealistic, even spiritualist Indian concept of *ālaya-vijñāna* with a fundamentally materialistic origin is absent from later development of the idea in India and Tibet, although the bridging function of the *ālaya-vijñāna* is certainly present. It raises many questions, particularly in light of Paul J. Griffiths' (*On Being Mindless: Buddhist Meditation and the Mind-Body Problem,* La Salle Illinois: Open Court Publishing Co., 1986) choice of this doctrine as a point of departure for a consideration of the body-mind problem in Buddhism. As noted by Stcherbatsky and Frauwallner, the nature of the *indriyas*, physical yet translucent in nature and closely connected with a transmigrating spark, raises many questions about the way early Indians thought about, and differentiated, the conscious and unconscious elements in their systems. Although the scope of this Introduction does not allow me to pursue the matter further here one possible direction for future research is an investigation of the origins of Indian objectivism; that is, the process which led to *indriya*-based *pramāṇa* becoming a primary source of authoritative knowledge.

12. In some early passages of the *Yogācāra-bhūmi* (for references see Schmithausen 1987:51ff) *ālaya-vijñāna*, as the ultimate basis of personal identity, is even understood in the sense of an appropriating or vivifying (*upādāna*) consciousness (cp. the ubiquitous *upādāna-skandha*), and appears as a quasi person. In such contexts the term *ālaya-vijñāna* means 'the sticking or grasping mind.'

13. Bhavya was said to be a particularly strong critic of the *ālaya-vijñāna* doctrine.

14. The former was a notion already current, as the older *pratītya-samutpāda*

doctrine shows, long before the rise of the Yogācāra school. The notion of carrying all seeds, seeds of not only the basic consciousness of the person in the next life but even of the person's sense-faculties and finally of every experience the person would undergo, would transform the *ālaya-vijñāna* to something eminently suited to play a central role in explaining *vijñapti-mātratā*, the doctrine that objects do not partake of an external atomic reality but, caused by seed-impressions left in the mind, are like dream-objects substantially the same as the awareness of them.

15. *Sāṅkhya Kārikās*, ed. by Pandit Sri Harirām Shukla (Banaras: Chowkhamba Sanskrit Series, 1932).

16. In post-Sāṁkhya systems, particularly Vedānta, there is the tendency, anticipated in the Upaniṣads, to merge the attributes of both into a single ultimate principle that lies behind phenomenal reality. This is not unlike the Yogācāra notion of inexpressible emptiness and mere awareness. This appears to have influenced the Tibetan understanding of *kun gzhi*, particularly as it appears in the writing of Tsong kha pa's teacher Ma ti Paṇ chen, who was a student of the famous Jo nang pa Dol pu pa/ba Shes rab rgyal mtshan.

17. The Sāṁkhya universe that evolves from *prakṛti* is illusory and, in the words of Īśvara-kṛṣṇa, recedes back when liberation (*kaivalya*) is attained into the one mother nature that then, like an embarrassed bride, draws back from *puruṣa* when its true illusory nature is seen for what it is. The description of the actual process of attaining *mokṣa* is metaphorical: an unclear element in the otherwise coherent classical Sāṁkhya model. Perhaps the Yogācāra explanation of the fundamental transformation of the *ālaya-vijñāna* containing residual impressions into a mirror-like wisdom allows us better to discern how liberation was conceived as taking place–a process which necessarily became obscured in the classical formulation which retained (stressed?) the dualistic character of *prakṛti* and *puruṣa*.

18. This process of experience/knowledge formation exposes the similarities, mentioned earlier, between the functioning of Sāṁkhya *ahaṁkāra* and *manas* on the one hand and Yogācāra *kliṣṭa-manas* and *mano-vijñāna* on the other.

19. E. Obermiller, "Tsong-kha-pa le Pandit." MCB 3 (1934-5):319-338.

20. Rudolph Kaschewsky, *Das Leben des Lamaistischen Heiligen Tsongkhapa Blo-bzaṅ-grags-pa* (Wiesbaden: Otto Harrassowitz, 1971).

21. The full title is *Rje bstun bla ma tsong kha pa chen po'i ngo mtshar ma du byung ba'i rnam par thar pa dam pa'i 'jug ngog*, Lhasa gsung 'bum, vol. Ka:2-144 (New Delhi: Ngawang Gelek Demo, 1977).

22. Geshe Ngawang Dhargyey, *A Short Biography and Letter of Je Tzong-k'a-pa* (Dharamsala: LTWA, 1975).

23. Robert A.F. Thurman, ed. *Life and Teachings of Tsong Khapa* (Dharamsala: LTWA, 1981).

24. Leonard W.J. van der Kuijp, "Apropos of a Recent Contribution to the History of Central Way Philosophy in Tibet: *Tsong Khapa's Speech of Gold*" (review of Robert A.F. Thurman, *The Speech of Gold. Reason and Enlightenment in Tibetan Buddhism,* Princeton University Press, 1984; reprint ed. Delhi: Motilal Banarsidass, 1989) (Berliner Indologische Studien Band 1,1985).

25. Joe Bransford Wilson, Jr., "The Meaning of Mind in the Mahāyāna Buddhist Philosophy of Mind Only (*Cittamātra*): A Study of a Presentation by the Tibetan Scholar Gung tang jam bay yang (Gung thang 'jam pa'i dbyangs) of Asanga's Theory of Mind-Basis-of-All (*Ālaya-vijñāna*) and Related Topics in Buddhist Theories of Personal Continuity, Epistemology and Hermeneutics," Ph. D. Dissertation (University of Virginia, 1984).

26. *Yid dang kun gzhi'i dka' gnas rnam par bshad pa mkhas pa'i 'jug ngog,* in Collected Works of Gung thang dkon mchog bstan pa'i sgron me, vol. 2:275-402 (New Delhi: Ngawang Gelek Demo, 1972).

27. 'Brug rgyal dbang blo bzang 'phrin las rnam rgyal's *'Jam mgon chos kyi rgyal po tsong kha pa chen po'i rnam thar,* ed. by Tshe-tan Zhabs-drung (Xi-ning: Quinghai People's Publishing House, 1984). Another important early source is a Life of Tsong kha pa by Gnas rnying pa kun dga' bde legs (1446-1496) mentioned by van der Kuijp (1985:52).

28. *Bod rgya tshig mdzod chen mo* (Beijing: Mi rigs dpe skrun khang, 1984); Tshe-tan Zhabs-drung, *Bstan rtsis kun las btus pa* (Xining: Quinghai People's Publishing House, 1982).

29. The early 'doctrinal entity' is also sometimes called Bka' gdams gsar pa reflecting Tsong kha pa's links with Rwa sgreng monastery where he composed his most famous work, the *Lam rim chen mo.*

30. Mention should also be made of the Bon sect, which shares many characteristics in common with the Rnying ma.

31. Tib. *bla ma* is treated as an English loanword and spelled lama.

32. In essence what Gser mdog paṇ chen Śākya mchog ldan (1428-1507) calls *kun rdzob tshad sgrub:* the doctrine of a fully comprehensible and describable ultimate reality (i.e., *śūnyatā*) co-emergent with, and not exclusive of, an authoritative surface level of operational truth (*tha snyed pa'i tshad ma, *vyavahāra-pramāṇa*).

33. See Thurman (1984:78ff) who stresses the importance of this mystical experience in the development of Tsong kha pa's thought. One might add that Tsong kha pa was described by some (according to van der Kuijp 1985:48) as being "inspired by an evil demon."

34. There are partial translations of the *Ngags rim chen mo* and *Dgongs pa rab gsal* by P.J. Hopkins in *Tantra in Tibet* (London: Allen and Unwin, 1977) pp. 81-169 (being a translation of the opening section of the *Rgyal ba khyab bdag rdo rje chang*

chen po'i lam gyi rim pa gsang ba kun gyi gnad rnam par bye ba) and *Compassion in Tibetan Buddhism* (Valois, N.Y.: Gabriel/Snow Lion, 1980) pp. 93-230 (being a translation of chapters 1-5 of *Dbu ma la 'jug pa'i rgya cher bshad pa dgongs pa rab gsal*); a complete translation of the *Legs bshad snying po* by Thurman(1984) (being a translation of *Gsung rab kyi drang ba dang nges pa'i don rnam par phye ba gsal bar byed pa legs par bshad pa'i snying po*); and two partial translations of the *Lam rim chen mo* by Alex Wayman and Elizabeth Napper in Alex Wayman, *Calming the Mind and Discerning the Real* (New York: Columbia, 1978; reprint ed. Delhi: Motilal Banarsidass, 1979) (being a translation of the *Lhag stong chen mo*); and in Elizabeth Napper *Dependent Arising and Emptiness* (Boston: Wisdom, 1989), (being a translation of the *dgag bya dngos 'dzin* section of *Lhag stong chen mo*). See also Mark Tatz, *Asanga's Chapter on Ethics With the Commentary of Tsong-Kha-Pa.* (Lewiston/ Queenston: Edwin Mellen Press, 1986) and Alex Wayman, *Ethics of Tibet* (Albany: State University of New York, 1991).

35. D. Seyfort Ruegg, *Life of Bu ston Rin po che*, Serie Orientale Roma XXXIV (Roma: IsMEO, 1968). Pages 47-56 are a translation of *Chos rje tham cad mkhyen pa bu lo tsa ba'i rnam par thar pa snying po'i me thog* by Sgra bshad pa, who succeeded Bu ston as abbot of Zhva lu.

36. Again, this does not necessitate the rejection of the premises that underpin the various religious beliefs and rituals which make up the widespread cult of Tsong kha pa and are the vitalizing elements, as it were, of the elaborate traditional literature which serves to increase the Dga' ldan pa believer's faith, first, in the doctrines of Tsong kha pa, and second, in the transcendent status of the center of the cult, Tsong kha pa himself. The final form of the cult, focusing on the worship of a triumvirate comprised of Tsong kha pa and his two main disciples, Mkhas grub and Rgyal tshab (Tib. *rje yab sras gsum*), emerged soon after. It is today the single most important defining characteristic joining together the many diverse branches of the Dge lugs pa sect.

37. This would not have been an unusual action by Tsong kha pa's parents, who hailed from the same region as Don grub rin chen, especially because when Don grub rin chen returned to his native region he founded two monasteries which, though not very successful in attracting bright monks, would have given him a reputation as an educator and abbot. The giving of young children to monks fits a pattern seen even today amongst Tibetans and in no way requires, or even suggests, a theory of incarnate lamas, though Don grub rin chen no doubt recognized quite early on the precociousness of his young charge.

38. It is said that Tsong kha pa was sent to this teacher when the famous Jo nang pa scholar Nya dpon kun dga' dpal, whom Tsong kha pa had approached with a request to learn the *Abhidharmakośa*, pleaded old age and suggested Red mda' ba as a worthy substitute. This is not without some irony. The followers of Tsong kha pa were to wipe out most of the Jo nang pa sect in the mid seventeenth century under the pretext of preserving Tsong kha pa's doctrine from a terrible heresy.

39. Kaschewsky (1971 vol. 2 III,6r.5-6; III,12r and III,12v5-III,13r.1) lists the

following as pre-dating *Legs bshad gser phreng*: *Dge bdun nyi shu bsdus pa, zhugs dang gnas pa'i skyes bu chen po rnams kyi dka' gnas* (alternative name *Dge bdun nyi shu bsdus pa rjes gnang dang zhugs gnas*?) P6147 (168.1.1-170.2.2); *Bsam gzugs zin bris* P6148 (170.2.2-173.4.1); *Zhugs pa dang gnas pa'i skyes bu chen po rnams kyi rnam par bzhag pa blo gsal bgrod pa'i them skas* P6146 (173.4.1-196.5.6) and the *Ocean of Eloquence*. All have recently been published in a single volume under the title *Legs bshad gser gyi phreng ba* (Mtsho sngon mi rigs dpe skrun khang, 1986).

40. *Tshad ma rigs pa'i gter*, in *Complete Works of the Great Masters of the Sa skya sect of Tibetan Buddhism*, vol. 5:158.2.5-6 (Tokyo: The Toyo Bunko, 1968).

41. George Dreyfus does not refer to this verse directly in his Ph. D. dissertation ("Ontology, Philosophy of Language, and Epistemology in Buddhist Tradition," University of Virginia, 1991) but in a series of personal communications has expressed this opinion. His dissertation, which advances earlier work by van der Kuijp (1983), is particularly valuable because of its detailed analysis of another aspect of Tsong kha pa's oeuvre, his presentation of *pramāṇa* (Tib. *tshad ma'i rnam gzhag*). It shows that though original in the sense that it differs from the presentation of Sa skya Paṇḍita, Tsong kha pa's presentation of *pramāṇa* is on that account by no means closer to an older Indian tradition. Rather Tsong kha pa's view represents the re-emergence of a pre-Sa skya Paṇḍita interpretation that, if not distinctly Tibetan, is nevertheless perhaps less what Dharmakīrti himself intended than the one it replaces. Whether Tsong kha pa's mature presentation of *kun gzhi* is original or anticipated in Bka' gdams pa works is yet to be ascertained.

42. Besides the small text *Sde bdun la 'jug pa'i sgo don gnyer yid kyi mun gsel* Tsong kha pa wrote little under his own name on *pramāṇa*. Nevertheless it is thought that the work of his disciple Rgyal tshab records his opinions and my remarks are based on a tentative acceptance of that point of view.

43. Kaschewsky III,12v5-III,13r1 *yang sa skyar bzhugs pa'i skabs shig sems tsam pa'i lugs kyi nyon yid kun gzhi'i dka' gnas bstan pa'i rtsa tshig dang / de'i rgya cher 'grel pa legs bshad rgya mtsho zhes bya ba brtsams // gsung 'di ni sems tsam pa'i lugs shes 'dod dag la shin tu phen pa'i legs bshad yin no // bstan bcos 'di dus phyis shig brtsams pa yin nam brtag* (indecipherable) *lar (→par) bya'o*. Immediately following this begins another year "When he was 22 . . . ."

44. This is in a later part of *Legs bshad gser phreng*, (Tsho sngon ed. p. 717ff) perhaps suggesting that (parts at least of) the first chapter were written later than the fourth chapter. The passage contains a seven-part discussion of *samāpatti*. First, discussing the type of religious individual capable of *samāpatti*, Tsong kha pa says "ordinary people and *srota-āpannas* do not enter [*samāpatti*] by wisdom through the *vimukti[-mārga]s*. This is because removal of the *kliṣṭa-manas* and attainment of the *bhavāgra* mind are needed to enter it and the first does not have the first and the others do not have the latter." He then quotes from the *Daśabhūmika-sūtra* to the effect that a seventh level Bodhisattva enters *samāpatti* and says the statement in the *Daśabhūmika* does not contradict what he is saying because *samāpatti* in that sūtra is referring to the

ultimate sphere. From this statement, which is based on the understanding that the Bodhisattva does not remove *kliṣṭa-manas* until the eighth level, it appears Tsong kha pa is treating the *kliṣṭa-manas* as real. An even clearer statement of its and the *ālaya-vijñāna's* reality is found just following this when (p. 718) Tsong kha pa describes what is stopped in *samāpatti.* Without any statement that he is talking specifically from the point of view of the Yogācāra school (though referring directly to the *Viniścaya-saṁgrahaṇī*) Tsong kha pa says pointedly that though the Śrāvaka texts say only six consciousnesses are stopped, in reality seven are, only the *ālaya-vijñāna* remaining (*gnas skabs de yang kun gzhi yod pas sems ldan yin te*). The difference between the view set forth in *Legs bshad gser phreng* and Tsong kha pa's later texts was also noted by Tibetan writers. Elizabeth Napper (1989:417) says: "The Golden Rosary . . . as Sha mar den dzin puts it [Zha dmar bstan 'dzin, *Lhag mthong chen mo'i dka' gnad rnam brjed byang du bkod pa dgongs zab snang ba'i sgron me* (Delhi: Mongolian Lama Guru Deva, 1972), p. 25.5], was written 'prior to [Dzong ka ba's] showing the mode of having completed the analysis of the view.'" Such circumlocutions are the convention, in Dga' ldan pa sacred literature, for referring to the developments in Tsong kha pa's ideas over the course of his life.

45. Tsong kha pa (*Legs bshad gser phreng*, Tsho sngon ed. pp. 332-340) first sets out the Yogācāra view of lineage (*gotra*) based on a passage from the *Guhyārtha-vyākhyā:* "The *pariniṣpanna* ('final outcome') is of two sorts: one permanent and the other impermanent. The impermanent is of two sorts: the nature (Tib. *bdag nyid*) and the seed of pure transcendental wisdom. As to the latter, its *bdag nyid* is of two sorts: the naturally abiding (*prakṛtistha*) lineage (henceforth n.a.l.) and the lineage which has come about fully [from conditions] (*samudānīta*);" and "The pure (Tib. *rnam par byang ba*) n.a.l. is also contingently (Tib. *ltos nas*?) given the name *ālaya-vijñāna* because, as the *Śrī-mālā-siṁha-nāda-sūtra* says, 'Relative to the seed of the pure all living creatures are in possession of the *tathāgata-garbha.*'" Hence the n.a.l. is the potential for the arising of the stainless on the *ālaya* (*kun gzhi*). It is not the nature (Tib. *ngo bo*) of the *ālaya-vijñāna* since it is its antidote. A transformation like the separation of milk and water takes place. The MSam n.a.l. is therefore made (*saṁskṛta*). The MSA n.a.l is also *saṁskṛta.* It is not thusness (*tathatā*) "since apart from a mere conceptual separability (Tib. *chos can tha dad*) there is no divisions in its [*tathatā's*] actual stream of being (Tib. *rang rgyud pa'i dbye ba med pas*)." Also (334) since in the MSA the Hīnayāna lineage finishes with nirvāṇa it cannot be *tathatā* since this latter always endures. The three sorts of lineage relative to three sorts of interest, etc. set forth in the MSA (and in the *Viniścaya-saṁgrahaṇī*) "intend different sorts of seeds on the *kun gzhi.*" Where the *kun gzhi* is not posited, as in the Bbh and the *Śrāvaka-bhūmi*, (note that Tsong kha pa already seems to identify Yogācāras that do not assert the *ālaya-vijñāna*) the two sorts of n.a.l. and lineage which has come about fully [from conditions] are still set forth as 'the specialness of the six sense-bases' (*ṣaḍāyatana-viśeṣa*). The inner *āyatanas* are what the essential materiality of a person consists in (Tib. *sems can kyi rdzas kyi rtsa bar gyur pa*). They are the specialness (Tib. *khyad par*) making a person a person. The inner *āyatanas* are thus the special basis (Tib. *khyad gzhi*) of the lineage. This means that in the MSA the unbroken stream of the mind is the location of the n.a.l and the n.a.l. is the potential for creating enlightenment

situated on it. They are materially indivisible but you cannot say the six sense-bases (i.e., the stream of the mind) is itself the actual n.a.l. Tsong kha pa ends his explanation of Yogācāra lineage by saying one should understand that apparently contradictory explanations of lineage in Yogācāra texts as *saṁskṛta* and *asaṁskṛta* are in terms of the lineage being a material cause of enlightenment (Tib. *rgyu rkyen*) or a meditational content which, when contemplated, brings enlightenment (Tib. *dmigs rkyen*). If the former it is referred to as *saṁskṛta* and if the later as *dharmatā* ('fundamental reality') (337).

The Madhyamaka position is that the n.a.l. is the *dharmatā* (338-9). There is a fundamental difference in how the Yogācāra and Madhyamaka construe the adventitious nature (*āveṇika*, *glo bur ba*) of what is to be removed. The Yogācāra understand the different states of mind and mental factors as obscuring the clear nature of mind. These minds are materially real but based on a misconception and hence removable. In Madhyamaka they are removable because they do not partake of final reality (340). For the Madhyamaka (340) getting rid of what is to be removed is like two illusory bulls locking horns, and trying to articulate or pin down just what the final reality is only leads to exhaustion and no result.

46. Stag tshang shes rab rin chen in his *Grub mtha' kun shes nas mtha' brel grub pa* (Thim phu: Kun bzang stobs rgyal 1976:126a.1-126b.2; quoted Wilson 1984:89-90 and 100ff) says all Yogācāras assert the *ālaya-vijñāna*, a position still implicit perhaps in some (earlier?) parts of *Legs bshad gser phreng* but already being questioned in other later parts (see notes 44 and 45).

47. See van der Kuijp (1985:53-4) for some of the complications associated with such statements and Donald S. Lopez (*A Study of Svātantrika*, Ithaca: Snow Lion, 1987:325-42) for a later Dge lugs pa text written after such taxonomy had become accepted.

48. *Ocean of Eloquence* 56b2: *rgya chen rgya mtsho lta bu yi / rnam rig gzhung la sbyangs gyur pa // de dag gis ni rnam shes 'di / gzu blos rigs dang mi rigs dpyad / gal te rigs pa lta na blang.* The Dge lugs pa scholar Doboom Tulku, director of Tibet House, New Delhi, in a personal communication said that one should understand *rnam shes 'di* to refer to *kun gzhi* itself and interpret the verse as a definitive statement that Tsong kha pa did not accept the eight-consciousness model even at this stage of his intellectual development.

49. For example at *Lam rim chen mo* 161a.1-2 where there is still a faint ambiguity about the status of the *ālaya-vijñāna*.

50. *Dpal gsang ba 'dus pa'i bshad pa'i rgyud ye shes rdo rje kun las 'tus pa'i rgya cher bshad pa rgyud bshad thabs kyi man ngag gsal bar bstan pa*, *Lhasa gsung 'bum*, (New Delhi: Ngawang Gelek Demo, 1977), vol. Ca:450-586. Given the statement (474.4-5) that he has already explained Candrakīrti's rejection of *kun gzhi* (*kun gzhi khas mi len pa la gnod pa bstan pa'i spang dka' ba rnams kyi skyon spong... bshad zin to*) this text must have been written after his *Madhyamakāvatāra* commentary *Dgongs pa rab sel* and be considered one of his last works. It is therefore Tsong kha

pa's final definitive statement on the *kun gzhi* question. As to why he turned away from the syncretistic language of Yogācāra-Madhyamaka when describing the ultimate meditative praxis, a full answer requires much further research. One factor does seem to be that Tsong kha pa perhaps saw the *tathāgata-garbha/ālaya-vijñāna* or *sems nyid/sems* division as somehow prone to abuse in that it relativized monks' modes of conduct which he felt must be, if not philosophically absolute, socially absolute.

51. In general the understanding and usage of the term *kun gzhi* before Tsong kha pa was influenced by a complex of earlier doctrines and opinion, amongst them a) the Yogācāra *ālaya-vijñāna* doctrine, b) the *tathāgata-garbha/gotra/dhātu* doctrines, c) the *śūnyatā/dharmatā/tathatā* and *prabhāsvara-citta* doctrines, and d) tantric *bodhicitta* and the *ṣaḍaṅga-yoga* ('sixfold practice') of the Kāla-cakra tantra. Other factors were e) the (possibly non-Buddhist) absolute *dharma-kāya* associated in later times with the Jo nang pa sect, f) distinctive Tibetan terminology (such words as Tib. *kha dag, gdod ma'i gzhi, kun tu bzang po, phyi mes chen po* and *ye phyi mo*), and g) strategies for acceptance or rejection of the terminology and ideas of the Yogācāra school by different Mādhyamikas.

52. Rdzogs chen has been compared to Ch'an, and while the issue of its relation or lack of relation with that Chinese school need not detain us, it has repeatedly been associated with a spontaneous model of enlightenment. It is pertinent that Rdzogs chen is primarily a description of, or guide to, meditative praxis (Tib. *sgom khrid*). The school's theoretical literature (Tib. *lta khrid*) is secondary.

53. *Rig pa'i khu 'jug* and *Sbas pa'i rgum chung* (Indian Office Library numbers 647 and 594) have been analyzed and translated by Samten Gyaltsen Karmay in *The Great Perfection (rDzogs chen). A Philosophical and Meditative Teaching in Tibetan Buddhism* (Leiden: E.J. Brill, 1988).

54. In the standard description of ultimate meditative praxis, the term *kun gzhi* at best only partially corresponds to the Yogācāra *ālaya-vijñāna*. It is intimately connected with tantric *bodhicitta* (for the little that is known about this doctrine see S.B. Dasgupta, *An Introduction to Tantric Buddhism* [3d ed., University of Calcutta, 1974]). The Yogācāra *ālaya-vijñāna* creates only saṁsāra, while the meditative praxis *kun gzhi* incorporates the creative potential of the *tathāgata-garbha* and partakes of a reality that extends to and in that sense creates nirvāṇa as well. The mind that looks at itself is *kun gzhi* as creator of saṁsāra. The mind that looks at itself and manifests its own nature in a self-reflexive insight is *kun gzhi/khams(dhātu)* looking at itself as "creator" of nirvāṇa. This sort of *ālaya-vijñāna/dhātu* ambiguity is already found in nonsystematic Indian texts like the *Ghana-vyūha* and *Laṅkāvatāra* (see Ruegg 1969 and 1989:17) and is evident in the opening verse from the *Mahāyānābhidharma-sūtra*. The term *sems* ('mind,' in the sense of what creates the illusory which then obscures its own real nature in the meditation) is more closely connected with the Yogācāra *citta* (translated into Tibetan as *sems*) and often specifically equated with the *ālaya-vijñāna*. The linkage is made through a creative etymology (*nirukti*) which derives *citta* from root √*ci* 'to accumulate' [seeds]. For references see *Ocean of Eloquence* 30b3 (translation chap. 4, n. 40) and 32b2 (translation chap. 5, n. 19). Finally, the description of

kun gzhi in the ultimate meditative praxis may be phrased in the positive language of Vedāntic monism. As Karmay (1988:177) puts it: "... the Primordial Basis of rDzogs chen is fundamentally positive and conceived in the sense of a cognitive being (*yul can*). It is the transcendental state of the *sems* (*sems nyid*), but at the same time it is also capable of being a creator through its phenomenal aspect (*sems*)."

55. K. Mimaki, *Blo Gsal Grub Mtha'* (Kyoto: University of Kyoto, 1982); "The *Blo Gsal Grub Mtha'* and the Mādhyamika Classification in Tibetan *grub mtha'* literature," in E. Steinkellner and H. Tauscher, eds., *Contributions on Tibetan Buddhist Religion and Philosophy* (Vienna: Universität Wien, 1983):161-67.

56. See Lopez's translation (1988:57) of Lcang skya rol pa'i rdo rje's (1717-1786) *Grub mtha'i rnam par bzhag pa* which represents the culmination of this trend.

57. The sources for the stratification of the diversity of Indian Buddhist opinion into higher and lower stages leading to a highest view (Tib. *dgongs pa/lta ba mthar thug*) in Tibetan *grub mtha'* literature have been discussed by Mimaki (1983) and Lopez (1988). Amongst them the ninth chapter of Śāntideva's BCA is particularly important for providing a model for later interpretation of Yogācāra doctrines. There, having stated that all of the Buddha's other teaching is to lead the disciple to a correct wisdom (*prajñā*), Śāntideva says (following the explanation of Prajñākara-mati, *Bodhi-caryāvatāra with the Commentary Pañjikā* [Buddhist Sanskrit Texts 12, ed. by P.L. Vaidya, Mithila Institute, Darbhanga 1960], pp. 178ff) that the content of such wisdom is twofold: ultimate reality (*paramārtha*) and a surface level of what is conventionally true (*saṁvṛti*). The former is transcendent, the latter ordinary or mundane. Śāntideva then sketches a ladderlike, ascending scale of religious insight, beginning with the insight (or lack of it) of the ordinary person (*prākṛtaka*), who is concerned with things or material reality (*vastu-tattva*), as distinct from the insight of the yogin, who is concerned with fundamental reality (*pradhāna-tattva*). Amongst the latter (yogins) there are ordinary ones still concerned with the covering level of reality which, on account of their intellectual and spiritual shortcomings, they are unable to see for what it is; and, finally, transcendent yogins. The view of each more actualized yogin refutes (*bādhyante*) the less realized yogin's insight.

58. Sa skya Paṇḍita's views are anticipated in the works of Grags pa rgyal mtshan (1147-1216).

59. *Thub pa'i dgongs pa rab tu gsal ba* and *Sdom pa gsum gyi rab tu dbye ba'i bstan bcos*, in *Complete Works of the Great Masters of the Sa skya sect of Tibetan Buddhism* (Tokyo: The Toyo Bunko, 1968), vol. 5:1-50 (loosely trans. Geshe Wangyal and Brian Cutillo in *Illuminations: A Guide to Essential Buddhist Practices* [Novato, California: Lotsawa, 1988]) and vol. 5:297-321.

60. In *Sdom gsum rab dbye* (300.3.6) Sa skya Paṇḍita equates the *su/tathāgata-garbha* with the luminous part (Tib. *gsal cha nyid*) of the *kun gzhi* while denying that it is either *kun gzhi* or any other awareness (Tib. *rig pa*) beyond *kun gzhi*. At the same time he denies that the *tathāgata-garbha* is the sphere of truth (*dharma-dhātu*) on the grounds that the latter extends to all that is inanimate while the former is found only

within animate creatures. In *Thub dgongs rab gsal* (43.5-44.4) Sa skya Paṇḍita states that since all perception is necessarily caught in the net of *prapañca*, within the bifurcation into subject and object, the transcendental wisdom of an enlightened being must be beyond the four extremes and cannot be said to be, or not be, something with an object or knowledge content. He sets forth two aspects to transcendental wisdom: a) knowledge of reality from the point of view of its diversity (*yāvad-[bhāvika]-jñāna*) and b) knowledge of reality from the point of view of its unifying ultimate (*yathāvad-[bhāvika]-jñāna*) that come from or are paralleled by the Yogācāra and Madhyamaka doctrines, respectively. Sa skya Paṇḍita interprets the second and third 'turning of the wheel of the dharma' (see below) as teaching emptiness (*śūnyatā*), which he conceives of as an ultimate luminosity (Tib. *don dam 'od gsal*) and surface luminosity (Tib. *kun rdzob 'od gsal*), respectively, where the latter is the transformed *kun gzhi*.

Sa skya Paṇḍita's new ordering of Yogācāra and Madhyamaka in accord with the two levels of truth (an ordering which responded to the increasing influence of the new translations of *Prāsaṅgika texts but retained the balance between Yogācāra and Madhyamaka) was skillfully used by the third Karma pa Rang 'byung rdo rje (1284-1339) in a short but influential work *Rnam shes ye shes 'byed pa'i bstan bcos* ("On the differentiation of ordinary and transcendental consciousness"), in *Dbu ma gzhan stong skor bstan bcos phyogs bsdus deb dang po*, pp. 49-62 (Gangtok: Karma Shri Nalanda Institute, 1990). Rang 'byung rdo rje uses Nāgārjuna's Madhyamaka to show how everything is empty and unoriginated and says that since all is unoriginated all is therefore just mind (Tib. *sems tsam*), i.e., a hollow appearance. He takes the eight sorts of consciousness, with the *kun gzhi* foremost amongst them as a taxonomy of, or at least a guide to, ordinary appearance. He goes on to explain how the eight consciousnesses transform into the five transcendental wisdoms (*jñāna, ye shes*), and sets up a further correspondence between those wisdoms and the three Buddha bodies (*kāya, sku*). The eighth mind, the *kun gzhi*, is finally transformed into the Dharma-kāya ('Truth Body'), the *kliṣṭa-manas* and *manas* into the Sambhoga-kāya ('Enjoyment Body') and the five sense-consciousnesses into the Nirmāṇa-kāya ('Transformation Body'). Underlying them all and encompassing them, neither one with nor different from them, is an inexpressible reality called Dharma-dhātu ('Sphere of Truth'), free from all conceptuality. This is the Svābhāvika-kāya ('Fundamental Nature Body'). Enlightenment is the manifestation of the Buddha bodies, the defiled states of mind are all *kun gzhi*. They are removed by the path, which is produced by the power of the undefiled *tathāgata-garbha*.

61. The grand synthesis is worked out by Klong chen rab 'byams pa dri med 'od zer (1308-1363) in *Sems dang ye she kyi dri lan. Zhal gdams dris lan skor, chos gzhi rin po che'i phreng ba*:377-393, (in *Miscellaneous Writings* [*Gsung thor bu*] vol. 1:247-393 [Delhi: Sanje Dorje, 1973]). The *Saṁdhinirmocana Sūtra* has been translated from Tibetan by Étienne Lamotte, *Saṁdhinirmocana Sūtra: L'Explication des mysteres* (Louvain 1935); for Tsong kha pa's use of the hermeneutics see also Thurman 1989; see the first volume of Snellgrove's *Indo-Tibetan Buddhism* (2 vols., Boston: Shambhala, 1987) for a presentation of Buddhism using the hermeneutics as a historical model. Klong chen pa's hermeneutics are anticipated by Ratnākara-śānti and are worked out explicitly (see note 60), if less systematically by Sa skya Paṇḍita.

On the inaccessibility of Klong chen pa's work to his contemporaries see van der Kuijp (1985:58).

62. In passing, it is interesting to note that this grand synthesis was important in later Tibetan history. The fifth Dalai Lama, advised by Paṇ chen lama Blo bzang chos kyi rgyal mtshan, employed a revised version of it as a theory that would allow followers of the Rnying ma and Sa skya sects to join him in his coalition against the Bstan skyong princes of Gtsang. This is the Dben sa brnyan brgyud (a secret oral tradition reputedly going back to Tsong kha pa himself) that became the Dge lugs bka' brgyud and was much later expounded by Gung thang dkon mchog bstan pa'i sgron me. It reflects a liberal tendency to reincorporate different views rejected by orthodox Dga' ldan pa/Dge lugs pa scholastics. It also informs the Ris med movement of the late nineteenth century and has remained an important doctrine down to the present day for those opposed to triumphant Dge lugs pa sectarianism (see the final essay by Tenzin Gyatso, Dalai Lama XIV, in *Kindness, Clarity and Insight*, eds. Jeffrey Hopkins and Elizabeth Napper [Ithaca: Snow Lion, 1984]).

63. *Chos mngon pa kun las btus kyi ṭīk rnam bshad nyi ma'i 'od zer*, in *The Collected Works of Bu-ston*, ed. Lokesh Chandra from the collection of Raghu Rai (New Delhi: International Academy of Indian Culture, 1967), vol. 20:79-748.

64. *Dam pa'i chos mngon pa kun las btus pa'i 'grel pa shes bya ba rab gsal snang ba* (Gangtok: Gon po Tseten, 1977) 85b6-86a1 and 86a6-86b2. Quoted by Gung thang (trans. in Wilson 1984:469)

65. Translation based on Wilson (1984:467). Cp. Sa skya Paṇḍita's equation of the two truths with Yogācāra and Madhyamaka. Cp. Gung thang's comments (Wilson 1984:467).

66. Wilson (1984:473) translates "The *kun gzhi* which is not beyond being conventional, consciousness, and the nature is characterized as impermanent, suffering, empty and selfless. The *kun gzhi* whose nature is ultimate, nondual wisdom is the final culmination, the perfection of purity, self, bliss and permanence."

67. For an introduction to the Jo nang pa see D. Seyfort Ruegg, "The Jo nang pas: A School of Buddhist Ontologists According to the *Grub Mtha' Śel gyi me loṅ*," JAOS 83.1 (1963):73-91. According to Wilson (1984:554) Red mda' ba was much averse to the Jo nang pa view of Shes rab rgyal mtshan (whence presumably Tsong kha pa's strong disagreement with Jo nang pa views in *Legs bshad snying po*). Shes rab rgyal mtshan held that there was a *dharma-kāya* pure from the beginning and adorned with all the Buddha marks (*lakṣaṇa*). It became emptied of another and quite adventitious saṁsāra where the former is *kun gzhi* as *ye shes* and the latter *kun gzhi* as *rnam shes*. The terminology of two such *kun gzhis* is also accepted by Śākya mchog ldan in his *Shing rta chen po'i srol gnyis kyi rnam par dbye ba bshad nas nges don gcig tu bsgrub pa'i bstan bcos kyi rgyan*, in *Collected Works*, vol. 2:471-619 (Thimpu 1978).

68. Quoted by Gung thang (Wilson 1984:486).

69. Some verses from the commentary are quoted in later literature. Of particular interest is Red mda' ba's opinion (quoted unfavorably by Gung thang, Wilson 1984:619) that "... examination of whether the residual impressions are intrinsically abiding or newly produced is an examination of what is not a place [for examination]." This same view is found in the *Ocean of Eloquence* (8a3).

70. Red mda' ba gzhon nu blos, *Dbu ma la 'jug pa'i rnam bshad de kho na nyid gsal ba'i sgron ma* (Sakyapa Students' Union: Sarnath, 1982), pp. 140ff, 149.

71. *Madhyamakāvatāra* v. 39, "Since its cessation is not through its own nature (*sva-bhāvena*), because even in the absence of *kun gzhi* there is this potential..." (Tib. *gang phyir rang bzhin gyis de mi 'gag pa/de phyir kun gzhi med kyang 'di nus phyir*); also trans. Huntington (1989:162).

72. The main sources for Tsong kha pa's presentation of the *tathāgata-garbha* within the *ālaya-vijñāna* doctrine are the following: a) *Bodhisattva-bhūmi* (Wogihara's ed. 2.3) b) *Viniścaya-saṁgrahaṇī* (VS) (Bhattacharya 1957:25.1): c) VS (P5539:235.4. The Sanskrit reconstructed from Hakamaya's fragments of the ASBh is: *sāsravānantaram anāsravam, anāsravānantaram sāsravaṁ, laukikānantaraṁ lokottaraṁ, lokottarānantaraṁ laukikam utpadyate. na ca teṣāṁ tathā bījatvaṁ yujyate.*); d) VS (P5539:237.4.4-6. The Sanskrit reconstructed by Schmithausen is: *yad ālaya-vijñānaṁ mokṣa-bhāgīya-nirvedha-bhāgīya-kuśala-mūla-bīja-parigṛhītaṁ ... na samudaya-satya-hetuḥ ... pravṛtti-vairodikatvān mokṣādi-bhāgīyānāṁ kuśala-mūlānām.*); e) VS (P5539:246.2.8-3.1. The following is from Schmithausen 1987:78 and note 570: *de ltar na 'jig rten las 'das pa'i chos rnams skye ba'i sa bon gang yin / de dag skye ba'i sa bon gyi dngos po gnas ngan len gyi rang bzhin can yin par ni mi rung ngo zhe na / smras pa / 'jig rten las 'das pa'i chos rnam ni de bzhin nyid la dmigs pa'i rkyen gyi sa bon dang ldan par skye'i bag chags bsags pa'i sa bon dang ldan pa ni ma yin no /*); f) *Mahāyānābhidharma-sūtra* 1.1 (quoted in *Ocean of Eloquence* 39b2); and g) the MSam.

Besides the Indian Yogācāra and Tibetan sources for Tsong kha pa's views already referred to, mention should be made of two streams of Yogācāra interpretation, the Nālanda tradition (associated in particular with the interpretation of Dharmapāla and set forth in Hsüan Tsang's *Vijñapti-mātratā-siddhi*) and the Valabhi tradition associated in particular with the interpretation of Sthiramati. According to Gung thang (Wilson 1984:67) Tsong kha pa's interpretation of the MSam follows the latter tradition. Be that as it may, in the period after the MSam three opinions about the seed of transcendental wisdom (i.e., the *tathāgata-garbha* in the Yogācāra *ālaya-vijñāna* doctrine) are presented in the *Guhyārtha-vyākhyā* (431a2-3) and are similar to those in Hsüan Tsang's *Vijñapti-mātratā-siddhi* (Trans. by la Vallée Poussin, *Vijñapti-mātratā-siddhi, La Siddhi de Hiuan-tsang* 1927-8:102ff): a) The assertion that residual impressions, and in particular the residual impression which ripens into a liberating vision, are there naturally (*prakṛtyā*), independent of a tainter; they are not generated out of *bhāvanā* (habituation to a truth). The residual impressions do, however, increase (*vṛdh, utkarṣ, puṣ*) by the force of *bhāvanā*. They are not produced by, yet nevertheless are increased by *bhāvanā* because they are *anādikālika*; i.e., because there is always the necessity of a previous experience to explain any residual impression; b) A second assertion that all residual impressions are created by a tainter (i.e., by a previous experience). Previous to an experience such residual impressions are not there. At the same time, the experience which leaves a residual impression nurtures the seed placed by previous experience; and c) A third assertion, that there is an increase or nuturing of a residual impression that is, of itself, there naturally, this being the seed of transcendental wisdom that is inseparable from fundamental reality. At the same time there is also a placing of what was previously not there, this needed to account for the residual impression left by ordinary experience.

73. References to the ever growing literature on this topic can be found in D. Seyfort Ruegg, *Buddha-nature, Mind and the Problem of Gradualism in a Comparative Perspective* (London: School of Oriental and African Studies, 1989) and *Sudden and Gradual Approaches to Enlightenment in Chinese Thought*, ed. by P. N. Gregory, Studies in East Asian Buddhism no. 5 (1987). Ruegg's suggestion that we view a number of important events and controversies in Tibetan religious history as reflecting an inherent polarity or tension between gradual and spontaneous enlightenment models is particularly helpful. Although Ruegg is concerned, in large part, with understanding the diverse literature documenting opposition between the quietist Dhyāna (Ch'an) Buddhism of Chinese Hva shang Mahāyāna (Ho shang Mo ho yen) and Indian Kamala-śīla's scholastic gradualism–an opposition that has been traced back in some sources to a debate that took place in Dbus in the late eighth century–the polarity he suggests offers a way of looking at Tsong kha pa's earlier and later presentations of *kun gzhi*, particularly if the gradual and spontaneous extremes are changed slightly to contrast analytic meditative praxis (Tib. *dpyad sgom*) and nondiscursive meditative praxis (Tib. *'jug sgom*), respectively.

74. See Rong ston shes rab kun rig's (1367-1449) explanation of lineage in *Shes rab kyi pha rol tu phyin pa'i man ngag gi bstan bcos mngon par rtogs pa'i rgyan ces bya ba'i rnam bshad tshig don rab tu gsal ba* (Delhi: Ngawang Tobgay, 1972), 187.5-188.6 and the discussion of *nirodha-samāpatti* from the point of view of different schools 388.3-389.4. Go rab 'byams pa bsod nams seng ge appears to be influenced by Tsong kha pa's new hermeneutics which relegates Yogācāra to a relevance that is purely heuristic. In the context of an investigation of the *tathāgata-garbha*, Go rab 'byams pa, having commented on the fact that it may have many names, e.g. *kun gzhi* in the *Laṅkāvatāra*, makes the statement (*Sdom pa gsum gyi rab tu dbye ba'i rnam bshad rgyal ba'i gsung rab kyi dgongs pa gsal ba*, in *Works of the Great Masters of the Sa skya sect of Tibetan Buddhism*, 138.3.4 [Tokyo: The Toyo Bunko, 1968]) *'on kyang sems tsam pa'i 'dod pa ltar gyi kun gzhi bde gshegs snying por smra ba ni ma yin te / de dag gis bshad pa'i kun gzhi yod par mi 'grub pa'i phyir ro.* See also the later Bka' brgyud and Rnying ma writers Mi bskyod rdo rje (the eighth Karma pa 1507-1554) and Sog zlog pa blo gros rgyal mtshan (1552-1624) quoted by Karmay (1988:181-2). Cp. however the Rnying ma writer Rong zom chos kyi bzang po, in his *Theg chen la 'jug pa'i tshul* (written ca. 1050) who, while formulating the difference in terms of tantric *bodhicitta*, already identifies a defiled *kun gzhi* spoken of in the lower vehicle (Tib. *theg pa 'og ma*), i.e., Yogācāra, and the *gdod ma'i gzhi*

('primordial basis') of the higher vehicle: *theg pa 'og ma ba'i tshul gyis / kun gzhi'i mtshan nyid ni zag pa dang bcas pa'i chos thams cad kyi rgyu dang 'bras bu'i ngo bor gnas shing smin pa yin pas / shing thog dang 'dra la / zag pa med pa rnams kyi rten dang gnas tsam yin te / dug gi bum pa'i nang na sman gnas pa lta bu'o / zhes bshad / theg pa gong ma'i tshul las ni / kun gzhi'i mtshan nyid gdod ma nas byang chub kyi sems zhes bya la / nyon mongs pa dang gnas ngan len gyi bag chags ni glo bur gyi dri ma ste gser g.yas g.yogs pa'am / nor bu rin po che 'dam du bsubs pa bzhin yon tan cung zad mi snang bar zad de / rang bzhin nyams par byas pa med do /* (quoted by Karmay 1988:179).

75. *Rnal 'byor spyod pa'i lugs kyi yid dang kun gzhi'i rtsa 'grel gyi dka' gnas gsal byed nyi zla zung 'jug. Ke'u tshang gsungs 'bum*, vol. 1:181-254 (Dharamsala: LTWA, 1984).

76. Published in Buxa, Arunachal Pradesh: Shes rig 'dzin skyong slob gnyer khang, 1964. Mention should also be made of the Bla brang Bkra shis 'khyil writer Blo bzang 'jigs med's *Yid and kun gzhi'i rtsa ba'i mchan 'grel* in *Rare Texts of the Bla-brang Bkra-sis-'khyil Tradition* (New Delhi: Kalsang Thabkay, 1974), and Blo bzang dam chos rgya mtsho's *Rnam rig pa'i lugs kyi yid and kun gzhi'i don cung zad bshad pa ngo mtshar gzugs brgya 'char ba'i me long* in *Collected Works of Blo bzang dam chos rgya mtsho*, vol. 1 (New Delhi: Ngawang Sopa, 1975).

TRANSLATION

OCEAN OF ELOQUENCE: AN EXTENSIVE COMMENTARY ON THE DIFFICULT POINTS OF *ĀLAYA-VIJÑĀNA* AND *KLIṢṬA-MANAS*

One

Introduction: Origins of the Mind Only Doctrine

Homage to Bhagavan [Mañjuśrī], the Sovereign of Words.

> I bow my head to those learned even amongst the learned,[1] who have admirably expounded, without errors or complications, out of their faithful understanding, the beautifully preached, the excellent paths, the road traversed by the Buddhas and Bodhisattvas.
>
> I compose this treatise according to the Lama's instructions on the *[kliṣṭa-]manas* and the *ālaya-vijñāna*, the difficult points in the Vijñapti-[mātratā] texts, in order to clarify them, as well as to refresh my own memory of them. [Mv I]

Upon commencing a discourse on *manas* and *ālaya-vijñāna* one might ask, "When did the Mind Only (*citta-mātra*) school originate?"

> Ārya Nāgārjuna was prophesied as holder of the Mahāyāna by the highest teacher [i.e., the Buddha]. Following the spread of the Mahāyāna [by Nāgārjuna] Asaṅga, who was prophesied, established [the Mind Only] school. [Mv II]

After the Buddha had passed into the calm equipoise in the sphere of existence, Mahāyāna doctrine disappeared from this world (*jambū-dvīpa*). At this time just the Hīnayāna doctrine remained and the proponents of the Buddhist teaching were only the Vaibhāṣikas, etc. Since there were none who venerated and practiced the Mahāyāna sūtras, Abhidharmas like the *Śata-sāhasrikā-prajñā-pāramitā-sūtra* ('The Perfection of Wisdom in One Hundred Thousand Lines') were lost. It is said that all profound and extensive *Prajñā-pāramitā-sūtras* then remained in the palace of the Dragon-kings. *Śiṣya-lekha* says:[2] [4b]

> The teaching, like the best jewel, is excellent and is beneficial. In its purity, venerated by the dragons with hooded heads as though a crown

> jewel (*cuḍa*),[3] it illuminates the darkness that exists at the bottom of the earth.

And also in the *Lankāvatāra-sūtra* it says:[4]

> Please say who will hold [this teaching] when you pass into nirvāṇa.
> Mahāmati, you should know the following: When the Tathāgata has passed into nirvāṇa the teachings will be held, after much time has elapsed, by a monk with dignity and fame. He will hail from the country of Vedalī in the south. He will have the name Nāga ('Dragon'). Destroying those extremes of existence and nonexistence he will show the world that my vehicle [i.e., teaching] is the peerless Mahāyāna, then realize the first and joyous stage (*pramuditā-bhūmi*) and will go to the Heaven of Great Bliss.

Thus it was prophesied that Nāgārjuna, the great being, would be born in the southern country of Vedalī, take Buddhist ordination, and then bring back from the land of the dragons all the *Prajñā-pāramitā-sūtras*. Then, in order to make clear to this world the Mahāyāna doctrine of the absence of inherently existing phenomena, he composed the Six Treatises of Reasoning,[5] etc., which remove all the faults in Buddhist and non-Buddhist tenets.

Following him, as it says in the *Manjuśrī-mūla-tantra*,[6] came the Buddhist scholar Asaṅga.

> Then a bhikṣu called 'Asaṅga' will understand the meaning of the treatises. He will delineate the definitive and the interpretative meaning of sūtras in many ways. He is the one whose true nature is to teach insight in the world and he will become the one who is adept at the analysis of the treatises. The one who [5a] realizes this analysis will be called Śāladūti. By the power of the retention (*dhāraṇī*) of [Śāladūti] superior insight will be born. Thus, in order that the teaching will remain long, he [Asaṅga] will gather the true meaning of the sūtras. After a life span of one hundred and fifty years he will proceed to a heavenly abode. Then, having experienced much happiness during cyclic existence, the great one will ultimately achieve enlightenment.

Having achieved his practice of realization of Ārya Maitreya [by the samādhi based on *śamatha-vipaśyanā*], as prophesied, Asaṅga beheld [Maitreya] face to face and went to the Tuṣita heaven.[7] There he heard the teaching of the 'Five Books [of Maitreya]'[8] and then returned with them to this world. He himself also composed the *Mahāyāna-saṃgraha* etc., thereby opening wide the trail of the Mind Only system. As it says:[9]

> In order to help all worlds, the man called 'Asaṅga' drank [as it were] a scoop of water by hearing [the flow of nectar] poured forth from the vase of Ārya Maitreya. [That nectar] is the flow of the nectar of samādhi which results from the [samādhi] called 'Flow of Dharma.' I bow to this [Asaṅga].

Question: What, then, was the Mahāyāna view that existed before Asaṅga blazed the trail of the Mind Only system?

> Previously there was only Madhyamaka. [Mv III]

Prior to Asaṅga, there was no explanation other than that of the Mādhyamikas who interpreted the deep purport of the Tathāgata's words as "the avoidance of the two extremes of eternalism and nihilism which is precisely interdependent existence (*pratītya-samutpada*)." For there was no one, apart from Nāgārjuna, [5b] who elucidated the Mahāyāna. Hence, the *Mahāyāna-sūtrālaṃkāra*,[10] the *Bodhi-caryāvatāra* and the *Madhyamaka-hṛdaya*, etc. would prove the Mahāyāna to be the Buddha's word, because, when Nāgārjuna was propagating Mahāyāna doctrine in this world, those scholars who held lower tenets said, blasphemously, that the Mahāyāna was not Buddha's word by reason of the fact that a) they had never heard of Mahāyāna, and b) because it was incompatible with those certain parts of the scriptures that they held to be authoritative (*pramāṇa*).

Ācārya Nāgārjuna himself also established that the Mahāyāna was Buddha's word. Nāgārjuna demonstrated that 'being empty in its own nature' (*svabhāva-śūnya*) is the deep purport of the Buddha's words with a) reasoning (*yukti*) and b) scripture (*āgama*): He logically refuted [in his *Mūla-madhayama-kārikā's*] any elaborations (*prapañca*) such as the eight extremes [of cessation (*nirodha*), production (*utpāda*), etc.] in interdependent existence and b) quoted as scripture the Hīnayāna sūtra[11]

> Śākyamuni Buddha, understanding both functioning and nonfunctioning things, refuted [the reality of] existence and nonexistence in his teaching to Kātyāyana.

He then said that, "Whoever has intelligence could not criticize that," [5b.4] thereby establishing the Mahāyāna to be Buddha's word.

Thus, after Nāgārjuna, Asaṅga blazed wide the path of the Mind Only system and then Bhāvaviveka and others, the direct disciples of the master [Nāgārjuna], set out the Mind Only tenets at length and rejected them. Thus the state of affairs which came about is as follows: After the Buddha passed into nirvāṇa, Vaibhāṣika scholars, etc., having composed the 'Seven Treatises of the

Abhidharma,' etc., propagated their own system widely and, [6a] by interpreting the sūtras other [than in the correct manner], tainted the precious dharma. As it is said [in the *Abhidharma-kośa*]:[12]

> When the Teacher's worldly eye is closed and nearly all who were witness [to him] have died, those evil philosophers, who did not see him and are unrestrained, disturb the doctrine.

And also[13]

> And they [mistakenly] say this [Abhidharma] is said by the Teacher.

Such quotations show that after Buddha had entered nirvāṇa deluded action was very forceful and most people followed their own scriptural sources and were attached to naive realism. For this reason, the Bodhisattva Nāgārjuna, who had achieved the first stage, i.e., the Joyful, wrote treatises such as the *Madhyamaka-kārikā*, etc., based on the Mahāyāna revelation [in the *Prajñā-pāramitā-sūtras*] of an emptiness which is the nonexistence of a differentiating mark.

Thus for a long time [after the Buddha passed into nirvāṇa] Hināyāna tenets became very widespread and not even the name 'Mahāyāna' was heard. Then Nāgārjuna blazed the path of the Mahāyāna and spread it wide. Then the master Asaṅga blazed wide the path of the Mind Only system. Therefore, although prior to Nāgārjuna and Asaṅga the mere designation Madhyamaka and Cittamātra did exist, it was these two, as already stated, who wrote the commentaries of the two [distinctive schools] on the basis of the deep purport of the sūtras. If it were otherwise one would have to show a scholar and his works which establishes the Mahāyāna by explaining the deep meaning of the Buddha's words prior to Nāgārjuna and Asaṅga. These are not to be found.

During which periods of time did these two masters, prophesied by the Tathāgata, live? [6b]

[Answer]: First, in regard to Nāgārjuna, as it is said in the *[Mañjuśrī-] mūla-tantra*:[14] "Four hundred years after I have passed into nirvāṇa. . . ." And as it says in the seventy-fifth folio of [Won ch'uk's] *Chieh sh'en mi ching shu* ('Extensive Commentary on the *Saṁdhi-nirmocana-sūtra*'):[15]

> Two hundred some years after the nirvāṇa, Bodhisattva Nāgārjuna, on the basis of the *Prajñā-pāramitā-sūtras*, composed several treatises such as the *Mahā-prajñā-pāramitopadeśa* and the *Madhyamaka-kārikā*, etc. In these works, by refuting the imagined nature of dharmas, he has shown the guiding principle (*naya*) of the marklessness [of all dharmas]. Then Āryadeva and others took this up as perfect and by transmitting it from one to

the other propagated it. Then, nine hundred some years after the nirvāṇa, Bodhisattva Maitreya, on the basis of the *Saṁdhi-nirmocana-sūtra*, composed the treatises such as the *Yogācāra-bhūmi* and the *Madhyānta-vibhāga*. Ācāryas Asaṅga and Vasubandhu took these texts up as perfect and propagated them. Since at that time the doctrine was of one taste, there was no controversy between those asserting emptiness and those asserting existence (*bhava*). This is the reason why Ācārya Nye ba'i 'od (=Bandhu-prabhā/ Prabhā-mitra)[16] said: "A thousand years ago the taste of Buddha's teaching was one. Thereafter, mindfulness (*smrti*) and wisdom (*prajñā*) gradually deteriorated and those asserting emptiness and those asserting existence (*bhava*) spread widely in the world."

Notes

1. For Tsong kha pa's early teachers see Introduction pp. 13-14.

2. This *Śiṣya-lekha* is attributed in the Bstan 'gyur to Candragomin (ca. 650 according to Tatz 1985:8).

3. Certain cobras are said to carry in their hood a jewel which they treasure and guard with great care.

4. *Laṅkāvatāra-sūtra* (Nanjio 1956:286); translated by Suzuki (1968:239-240).

5. The *rigs tshogs dgug* "Six Treatises of Reasoning". They are: a) *Mūla-madhyamaka-kārikā*, b) *Śūnyatā-saptati*, c) *Vigraha-vyāvartanī*, d) *Yukti-ṣaṣtikā*, e) *Vaidalya-sūtra*, and f) *Ratnāvalī*. Cp. Lindtner (1982).

6. The translation is based on the Sanskrit quoted in Odani and Kalsang (1985:114, n. 6). *Mañjuśrī-mūla-tantra*, Buddhist Sanskrit Texts 18:482.15-23. The emendations of v. 453c-d are from Obermiller's "Bu ston's *History of Buddhism* and the *Mañjuśrī-mūla-tantra*," JRAS (1935:305). Cp. Wilson 1984:208, n. 2.

7. The person of Maitreya-nātha is still debated. For references see Ruegg (1969:39-70), Nagao (1982:5-13), and Davidson (1985). In passing it is interesting to note Tsong Kha pa's view.

8. These are a) *Mahāyāna-sūtrālaṁkāra*, b) *Madhyānta-vibhāga*, c) *Dharma-dharmatā-vibhāga*, d) *Ratna-gotra-vibhāga-mahāyānottara-tantra-śāstra*, and e) *Abhisamayālaṁkāra*. Davidson (1985:39) speculates that the five treatise tradition began with Rngog lo tsa ba.

9. See Bu ston's *History of Buddhism* (Obermiller 1986:141).

10. Cp. MSA (Levi 1907:1-8).

11. *Madhyamaka-kārikā:* 15.7. The Sanskrit is *kātyāyanāvavāde cāstīti nāstīti*

cobhayam / pratiṣiddhaṁ bhagavatā bhāvābhāva-vibhāvinā // (deJong 1977:19).

12. AK8.41 (Shastri 1981:1187) *nimīlite śāstari loka-cakṣuṣi kṣayaṁ gate sākṣijane ca bhūyasā / adṛṣṭa-tathair niravagrahaiḥ kṛtam kutārkikaiḥ śāsanam etad ākulam.* This is quoted in the *Abhidharmakośa-bhāṣya* 3.41.

13. AK1.3d (Shastri 1981:14) *uditaḥ kilaiṣa śāstrā.*

14. For the Sanskrit see *Mañjuśrī-mūla-tantra*, Buddhist Sanskrit Texts 18:482.8

15. The Sanskrit given along with its Tibetan name *'phags pa dgong pa zab mo nges par 'grel pa'i mdo'i rgya cher 'grel pa* (trans. by Chos grub ca. 755-849) is *Ārya-gambhīra-saṁdhi-nirmocana-sūtra-ṭīkā.* On the proper name of Won ch'uk (613-696) (variously Wen tshegs, Wen tsek; Yüan ts'ê according to Nagao) see Wilson (1984:965 n. 12 and 867 n. 24). The passage is found at P5517:16.2.3-3.1. This passage has been translated previously by Iida (1977:355-356).

16. This master is thought to be the author of the *Butsujikyōron/Fo-ti-ching-lun*, to have hailed from Magadha, and to have been a disciple of Dharmapāla.

Two

Ālaya-vijñāna as Basis

What, then, are the *ālaya-vijñāna* [7a] and the *kliṣṭa-manas* that are found in the system of tenets held by these [Vijñapti-mātrins]?

> The *ālaya-vijñāna* and the *kliṣṭa-manas* should be understood under the following four subsections: a) their definitions, b) their proofs, c) the refutation of nine [*vijñānas*], and d) the refutation of one [*vijñāna*]. [Mv IV]

The *ālaya-vijñāna* and the *kliṣṭa-manas* should be understood under four rubrics: a) ascertainment of their definitions, b) their proofs, c) the refutation of the assertion of a set of nine [*vijñānas*], and d) the refutation of the assertion of a set of one [*vijñāna*]. This is a summary. The more detailed explanation now follows.

The definitions are two: a) the definition of the *ālaya-vijñāna* and b) of the *kliṣṭa-manas.* In regard to the former there are again two parts: a) definition of the *vipāka* ('fruition') *ālaya-vijñāna* which is *āsraya* ('basis') and b) definition of the *bīja* ('seed') *ālaya-vijñāna* which is *āśrita* ('dependent').

> Of the two definitions, *ālaya-vijñāna* we accept to be defined in two aspects in accord with the division of basis and dependent. [Mv V]

> Question: What is the definition of the *ālaya-vijñāna* as basis?

> Of these, the *ālaya-vijñāna* as a basis cognizes objects (*artha*), sentient being (*sattva*), and residual impressions (*vāsanā*); is without any particular individuation [i.e., is not a cognition of the sort that knows this is X and that is Y]; is not a subject of moralizing (Tib. *lung ma bstan=avyākṛta*) and is endowed with five [mental factors] such as contact, etc. [Mv VI]

Thus the *ālaya-vijñāna* as a basis should be understood by these four: a) objective support (*ālambana*), b) form (*ākāra*), c) nature (*svabhāva*), and d) [the mental faculties] that accompany (*saṃprayukta*) it.

First, there are the following three components to its objective support: 1) five objects, i.e., forms, sounds, smells, tastes, and feelings; 2) a 'sentient being,' which is five sense-faculties, i.e., eye, ear, nose, tongue, and body; and 3) the residual impression (*vāsanā*) [left] by settling on the thoroughly imagined nature (*parikalpita-svabhāva*) of persons and dharmas.

Second, the form of the cognition is such that though the world and what is in the world appear, it is neither able to determine what is appearing, nor to give rise to certainty later [about what appeared].

Third, the nature of the *ālaya-vijñāna* as a basis is unobscured and not a subject of moralizing (*anivṛtāvyākṛta*). [7b]

Fourth, it is always endowed with feeling (*vedanā*), cognition (*samjñā*), volition (*cetanā*), contact (*sparśa*), and attention (*manaskāra*). Therefore it is said [in the *Madhyānta-vibhāga*][1] that

> [*ālaya-vijñāna*] arises as the consciousness of the appearance of objects [of the senses] and of living beings.

And also it is said in the *Triṃśikā-kārikā*:[2]

> It [*ālaya-vijñāna*] has [within itself] the representations of consciousness of not-clearly-recognizable objects and places. It has associated contact, mental attention, feeling, cognition, and volition. Its feeling is equanimous. It is unobstructed and not a subject of moralizing. The same for its contact, etc..

Residual impressions as objective support

Question: How do the the residual impressions, which are not describable as being substantially one with, or [substantially] other than, the maturation (*vipāka*), become the objective support of the maturation [i.e., *ālaya-vijñāna*]?

> [Answer]: Because, by the power of the seeds, the place, objects, and body appear they are considered to be an objective support. [Mv VII]

Thus, although the seeds do not appear and become an object (*viṣaya*), nevertheless, they are posited as objective support since it is through the power of these [seeds] that the places, i.e., the bases of the sense-faculties; the body, i.e., the sense-faculties; and the objects, i.e. the five [sense]-objects making up the world and what is in the world appear to the maturation *ālaya-vijñāna*. For example, since, by the power of an object [i.e., the actual thing out there], a consciousness arises endowed with the form of that object, it [the thing out there] is accepted to be the objective support [of that consciousness], even though it does not appear [to it].

Question: Do the world and what is in the world also appear to the *ālaya-vijñāna* of the formless [realm]?

> The grasped portions (Tib. *gzung cha*) of the *ālaya-vijñāna* are beheld by the five consciousnesses and are, in turn, labeled by the sixth [thinking mind (*manas*), i.e., are bifurcated into senses and external objects]. Hence, they [the senses and external objects] are exclusive to the two [lower] realms [of desire and form]. Were this not the case, the formless [realm] would not proceed beyond the thought processes (*samjñā*) of the form [realm] and would be in a level of consciousness that has forms. This is because there is nothing external, only physical appearances in consciousness. [Mv VIII]

[8a] Since objects directly appearing to the *ālaya-vijñāna* are beheld by the five sense-consciousnesses, and since the thinking-mind (*manas*) labels both sense-faculties and objects, therefore the world, and what is in the world, do not appear to the formless *ālaya-vijñāna.* This follows because no thinking-mind that labels forms exists in the formless [world]. For this reason, the five objects that appear directly to the *ālaya-vijñāna* of a single basis [i.e., person] are not hidden from the five sense-consciousnesses of that basis.

Question: In that case would not a single object become something that two consciousnesses grasp? If one agrees, how does one meet the objection that no object can be grasped in common, since, if it was, two consciousnesses would become substantially the same on account of the fact that whatever appears to a consciousness has the essence of that [consciousness]?

[Answer:] There is no flaw here. The statement that whatever appears to consciousness has its essence, or is neither the same nor different from that consciousness, is pertinent at the time of [vigorous scholarly] investigation [of the nature of consciousness and its object]. At that time we deny a common object [to two consciousnesses]. We accept a common object in the situation where there is no [vigorous] examination and investigation and, [in such a context] deny that it has the essence of that consciousness. Otherwise, it leads to destruction of the concept of the five aggregates;[3] to imaginary hairs, to yellow conchs [where there is a white conch], etc., and to dream objects being substantially real; and to the unwelcome conclusion that forms, [i.e., the object of eye-consciousness] and sounds, [i.e., the object of ear-consciousness] etc., have an emotional dimension (Tib. *myong ba*).

If the world and what is in the world appear to the formless *ālaya-vijñāna*, living beings of the formless [realm] would not proceed beyond the thought processes of the form [realm]. This is because the world, and what is in it, which have forms, appear directly to the consciousness of those [in the form realm]. It is not possible to agree with this because it is said:

> Also, [in the formless world], the discrimination of impediment ceases, and discrimination of multiplicity (*nānātva*) as well. [8b]

Furthermore, something formless would come to be endowed with form. This follows because an actual physical world, and what is physically in the world, would appear directly to the former [formless realm] *ālaya-vijñāna*. There is no lack of certainty about this because even in the two upper realms there is no externally established form, only physical appearances in consciousness.

Thus, it is the force of the meditation on formless absorption (*samāpatti*) that incapacitates the seeds that produce appearances of form in the *ālaya-vijñāna*. For as long as the person remains in the formless realm, nothing which has form can appear. It is like the force of the meditation on the absorption of the thought processes which incapacitates the seeds of the six consciousnesses in the *ālaya-vijñāna*. For as long as that absorption does not wane the six consciousnesses cannot arise.

Question: Would it not follow, however, that the formless *ālaya-vijñāna* becomes without any objective support? For the world and what is in it, which have forms, do not appear, and it is meaningless to posit residual impressions as its objective support. If one agrees with this one is led to accept a consciousness devoid of objective support [an absurd proposition].

Answer: There is no flaw in this. For as it is said in the MSam:[4]

> When [conscious of] the past, etc., dreams, and the two kinds of images [i.e., those which appear in certain samādhis and in a mirror] there is no actual objective support [but still one is conscious of them]. Therefore, since one can be conscious (*ā-lamb*) of these, [consciousness does not need an actual objective support].

All consciousnesses, therefore, are not necessarily contingent on an existing objective support. In particular, the *ālaya-vijñāna* is present through a propulsive force [which throws the living being into saṁsāra] and is not contingent on the appearance of an *ālambana*. For the previous virtuous or nonvirtuous action brings forth this basis of a happy or bad migration that is not removed, even for one instant, until the time of death.

Thus, in the formless [realm] (because there are neither objects nor sense-faculties), of the three objective supports [possible for the *ālaya*] there is only residual impression. And although there is no residual impression that is a directly appearing object, [9a] since it is by its power that the appearances of place, object, and body are facilitated, it becomes the objective support. For example, since a seed in storage can turn into a sprout when it meets with appropriate conditions, one says it is the condition for a sprout. Thus it is untenable to say that the physical world, and what is in it, appear to the formless realm *ālaya-vijñāna.*

Question: Granted it is like this in the formless realm. But how about the two lower realms? Do the world and what is in it appear to a single *ālaya-vijñāna*?

> Also in the [two] lower [realms], if all the world and what is in it appeared to a single person's *ālaya-vijñāna*, the flaming molten-iron hell, etc. would begin to appear to the form [realm] gods, and the celestial world and what is in it would begin to appear in hell. Not only this but then the various objects of knowledge of those with special talents would appear to common ordinary beings. [Mv IX]

Also in the two lower realms, if all the material of the world and what is in it appeared to a single *ālaya-vijñāna*, all of the appearances of the flaming molten-iron hell, etc., would arise for the gods of the form realm. If we accept this, the pains of that suffering also exist for them, because an *ālaya-vijñāna* seed which [produces] the appearance of a real sight of hell has been activated. [The reason] is not unproven because this sight of hell appears directly in the *ālaya-vijñāna* and is contingent on the activation of a residual impression. There is no lack of certainty because, when the direct appearance of these is by the force of a seed, it affects one positively or detrimentally. It is similar to, for example, the time one is dreaming. Then pleasant or unpleasant appearances affect one positively or detrimentally. [9b]

[Attempted defense of the discredited thesis:] "Since the world of similar types of person is created from both a) action that gives rise to appearance (Tib. *snang 'gyur gyi las*) and b) action that gives rise to engaging in something (Tib. *spyod 'gyur gyi las*) it can help them or harm them. The worlds of dissimilar types of person, on the other hand, are created from action that gives rise to appearance but not from action that gives rise to engaging in something. Hence they do not help or harm."

[Answer:] One cannot say this because certain objects—forms, sounds, etc.—affect certain similar types of person in differing ways: some see them as a help and others as harmful. Furthermore, since we do not accept any world except that appearance of form to inner consciousness, help and harm comes about merely from the appearance of something that seems to be really (Tib. *rang mtshan pa*) pleasant or unpleasant. [Help and harm] are not contingent on engaging in something. For example, an apparitional Yama (King of Death) appearing as a real Yama produces terror. Just an apparitional damsel appearing as a real damsel produces lust. [One does not need to engage with anything more real to experience the pain and the pleasure.]

There is another way to consider this. Is that appearance of hell to the human *ālaya-vijñāna* appearing just as it does to a hell-being or not? In the first case [i.e., if hell appears to a human just as hell appears to a hell-being], the appearance of hell is not caused by the power of the karma of a hell-being. If one accepts this there is conflict with the following passage [from the *Bodhicaryāvatāra*][5]

> Who made the ground of molten iron? From where did the coven of women come? The Buddha said they all have come from the mind that is bad.

Furthermore, one has to accept that the world that appears to the human *ālaya-vijñāna* appears in just the same way to the hell-being's *ālaya-vijñāna*. In that case one has the [unwelcome] necessity of throwing out all the quotations (like this following one [from the MSam])[6] which disprove externally existing objects:

> Since there are different perceptions of one thing [10a] according to the type of being—hungry ghost, human, animal, god—it is asserted that an [external] object is not established.

If one says that such appearances [of hell to humans] are visible to the sense-consciousness of those sentient beings, but that they are not the same as appearances visible to their *ālaya-vijñāna*, we answer that both of those appearances of the five objects to the sense-consciousness [i.e., the appearance of hell to humans and of the human realm to hell-beings] are also beheld by the *ālaya-vijñāna*. The two quotations, "Consciousness arises as the appearance of objects [of the senses] . . ." [7b1] and "[The grasped portions of *ālaya-vijñāna*] are beheld by the five sense-consiousnesses . . ." [7b4] have already demonstrated this.

In the second case, [if one accepts] the appearances to be, at once, not the same appearance visible to a hell-being yet an appearance of a real sight of hell, it is absurd. The pleasure of happy lives would also appear to everyone. What this means for the remaining four beings [hungry ghosts, animals, *asuras*, and *devas*] can be inferred by this reasoning.

Thus, certain Ābhidharmikas maintain that "[everything] from the eight hot hells to the fourth concentration (*dhyāna*) appears on one *ālaya-vijñāna*." Others maintain that except for the fourth concentration, which comes about through a unique karma, [everything] appears [to a single *ālaya*]. And others assert, having considered the statement in [Vasubandhu's] *Pratītya-samutpādādi-vibhaṅga-nirdeśa*:[7]

> . . . since there is no way to distinguish between the objects perceived [by *ālaya-vijñāna*] and the manner of its perception . . .

that the material of the entire world, and what is in it, which are not capable of being delimited (Tib. *tshad kyis bcad*), appear to [a single] *ālaya-vijñāna*.

[The quotation] does not establish [that position]: it damages it. [If one says] "Not so, this very quotation damages [the assertion that everything does not appear to a single *ālaya*]." We respond: the quotation is not teaching that all the world and what is in it—since it cannot be delimited—appears. The meaning is that an *ālaya-vijñāna* does not have the capacity to distinguish clearly, and then give rise to a subsequent certainty about things. It cannot be said [of *ālaya-vijñāna*] that "when there was such and such an objective support it beheld it in such and such a form." [10b] Were it to do so, the above unwelcome consequences (Tib. *gnod byed*) would ensue.

Question: What kind of world, and what is in it, appears [to the *ālaya*] in the two lower realms?

> The following are also posited as objects of the *ālaya-vijñāna*: a) one's sense-faculties and their objects [which the *ālaya* perceives] directly, and b) whatever is capable of appearing as the object of the sixth of the set [of consciousnesses,[8] which the *ālaya* perceives] indirectly. [Mv X]

The objects [which the *ālaya*] perceives directly are the objects which appear to the person's own sense-faculties. Whatever is capable of appearing as the object of that person's sixth of the set [of consciousnesses] is also posited as being, indirectly, the object of that person's *ālaya-vijñāna*.

Question: Is this not damaged by the passage from the *[Madhyānta-vibhāga]-bhāṣya* [explaining] 'living beings'[9] which says:

> 'Living beings' refers to an appearance as five sense-faculties in one's own or another's continuum.

[Answer: No, because] this passage is saying that the sense-faculties which appear to the *ālaya-vijñāna* are the five sense-faculties in one's own or another's continuum. It is not saying that the five sense-faculties of oneself, and of others, appear directly to one *ālaya-vijñāna*. Were this not the case, and were the sense-faculties in another's continuum, directly appearing to one's *ālaya-vijñāna*, to be someone else's actual-sense faculties, then all beings would have a single continuum [an absurd proposition]. And also we find [it stated in the MSam][10] that all body and physical *vijñaptis* [i.e., transformations of consciousness] arise from the designation residual impression (*abhilāpa-vāsanā*). That residual impression is one that is not capable of harming one's own *ālaya-vijñāna* by what someone else is conscious of.[11]

Question: Given that all objects of the sixth consciousness are objects of *ālaya-vijñāna*, do mental objects like the twelve divisions of Buddha's teaching and abstractions such as 'the past,' etc., also become objects of *ālaya-vijñāna*?

> The things, other than sense-faculties and objects, which are the objects of the sixth [i.e., *mano-vijñāna*] [11a] are not the objects of the *ālaya-vijñāna*, because the sixth has abstract objects while the *ālaya-vijñāna* is free of grasping at constructs (*citrīkāra*). [Mv XI]

Objects of thinking-mind—other than sense-faculties, objects, and residual impressions—such as the twelve divisions of Buddha's word and abstractions like 'the past,' etc., do not become objects of *ālaya-vijñāna*. This is a) because they simply function as objects after having been fabricated by the thinking-mind, and b) because the naming process which grasps constructs is absent from *ālaya-vijñāna*.

Nature of the *ālaya-vijñāna*

Why is it that the *ālaya-vijñāna* is not posited as being virtuous or nonvirtuous and is definitely unobstructing and not a subject of moralizing?[12]

> [The *ālaya-vijñāna*] is ascertained to be unobstructing and not a subject of moralizing a) because it is the basis of perfuming residual impressions, and b) because virtue and nonvirtue become manifest and present in a single continuum. [Mv XII]

The *ālaya-vijñāna* is established to be nonobstructing and not a subject of moralizing because it is a) the basis of the perfumes, i.e. residual impressions (*vāsanā*) left by virtuous and nonvirtuous [states of mind], and b) because manifest virtuous and nonvirtuous states of mind occur in a single continuum within a given period. [It follows] because something afflicted [i.e., nonvirtuous] or virtuous cannot be the basis of residual impressions.

Five mental factors

Question: Why is it said to be "endowed with just five" [7b1] associated mental factors (*caitta*) "such as contact, etc.?"

> Since it [*ālaya-vijñāna*] is not a subject of moralizing and [its objective support] is not clear, its [mental factors] are limited to the five such as contact, etc. [Mv XIII]

Since it is nonobstructed and morally neutral, the eleven virtuous mental factors and the [six] root and [twenty] closer afflictions are not present. And since it is not capable of clear particularization, the five ascertainers of objects are not present either. The four changeable mental factors are not found [11b] with it because the bases on which they are imputed are not present.[13]

Always present with [*ālaya-vijñāna*] are five omnipresent mental factors: These are:

a) contact (*sparśa*), because it is the cause of all mental factors,
b) [*vedanā*], because all minds are concerned with one or another of the three sorts of [pleasant, unpleasant, or neutral] experience,
c) a basic (Tib. *tsam*) delimitation of the object [*saṁjñā*],
d) a basic stirring [in the mind] relative to the object [*cetanā*], and
e) a basic turning of the mind towards its objective support [*manaskāra*].

These are found with all minds.

Question: Which of the above three experiences is the feeling associated with *ālaya-vijñāna*?

> The feeling here is the one in between. [Mv XIV]

The feeling is, in essence, neither happiness nor suffering. It is an equanimous (*upekṣā*) experience of what is between. This is because, when [the *ālaya*] perceives, it has no feeling of happiness or suffering. Why is this so? Because if there was a feeling of associated happiness, those states above the fourth concentration (*dhyāna*) [which are defined as devoid of all happy and suffering feelings] would become levels with happiness. Also, fruitional happiness would [absurdly] be found in hell. And if *duḥkha* ('suffering') were to be associated [with the *ālaya*] there would be extensive [inconsistencies]: virtuous and inexorable action would propel fruitional suffering, [an absurd proposition], and the formless states, for example, would become levels where suffering is found.

Etymology of *ālaya-vijñāna*

Question: Why is the matured consciousness (*vipāka-vijñāna*) which has become the basis called *ālaya-[vijñāna]*?

> It is called *ālaya-[vijñāna]* because it is adhered to as self.[14] [Mv XV]

It is called *ālaya* [derived from prefix *ā* 'from all sides' + √*lī* 'to sink down on'] because the afflicted minds (*kliṣṭa-manas*) of the five sorts of [i.e., all] creatures [sink down on], i.e., adhere to, this as a self. The object which is viewed by the afflicted mind as self is the maturation portion of the *ālaya-vijñāna*.

Question: Until which point is this maturation portion of the *ālaya-vijñāna* present? At what point is it removed?

> It is continually present until nonresidual [nirvāṇa] and the [12a] diamondlike [samādhi]. [Mv XVI]

It is removed after Hīnayāna *nirupadhiśeṣa-nirvāṇa* ('nonresidual nirvāṇa') and Mahāyāna *vajropama-samādhi* ('diamondlike meditative stablization'), respectively. Previous to that it is present unceasingly. Thus it is said [in the *Triṃśikā-kārikā*]:[15]

> The residual impression left by action, along with the residual impression left by a 'dual' [i.e., subject/object] apprehension, cause another maturation [of seeds] to occur where the former maturation has been exhausted.

Thus the maturation *ālaya-vijñāna*, impelled by a virtuous or nonvirtuous action in an earlier life, operates until the death of this life. There is no breaking of the continuum because, even though it [the earlier *ālaya-vijñāna*] stops when the potency of that action finishes, a dream [-like maturation] produced by a later action comes into being.

Question: Why is only the basis consciousness called the maturation? Surely the eye sense-faculty and so forth are also maturations?

Answer: There is no flaw here. A maturation must have three attributes: a) it must be unobstructed by [defilement] and not a subject of moralizing, b) it must be present without break for as long as there is life, and c) it must be a result impelled by previous virtue or nonvirtue. There is nothing except the *ālaya-vijñāna* and [the five mental factors] associated with it that satisfies the above three attributes of a maturation. It is not contradictory for a nonobstructed phenomenon which is not a subject of moralizing to be the maturation of virtue or nonvirtue. It is contradictory, however, for a virtue or a nonvirtue to be the maturation of a nonvirtue or virtue, respectively. This is because they are both dissimilar and each other's antidote.

Question: Given that something nonvirtuous is itself the maturation of nonvirtue and something virtuous itself the maturation of virtue there is no contradiction. It is not necessary, therefore, for maturations to be exclusively not a subject of moralizing.

Answer: Then [12b] there is the flaw that complete affliction (*saṁkleśa*) would never be stopped. For such maturations would operate without a break until death in every life. If there was a virtuous maturation there would not be even one instant when a virtuous mind was not present. In such cases there would be no occasion for complete affliction to arise, and if its arising did not exist, the cessation of its earlier presence would not exist either [and hence there could be no nirvāṇa]. If the maturation was nonvirtuous there would be no break in nonvirtuous minds and therefore its antidote would have no occasion to arise. Without it complete affliction could not be stopped. Also a person whose root of virtue (*kuśala-mūla*) was cut, for example, would still be manifestly virtuous. And there are untold other flaws as well. Thus the *ālaya-vijñāna* is necessarily unobscured and not a subject of moralizing. As [the MSam][16] says:

> Why are dharmas which are the maturation (*vipāka*) of virtue and nonvirtue (*kuśalākuśala*) all called nonobscured maturations which are not subjects of moralizing? By being nonobscured and not subjects of moralizing they do not contradict with virtue and nonvirtue, while virtue and nonvirtue are mutually incompatible. Furthermore, if a maturation were to be virtuous or nonvirtuous complete affliction could never go away. For this reason the matured consciousness (*vipāka-vijñāna*) is not obscured and is neutral.

Also the MSam[17] says:

> Since the interruption of the stream of the matured consciousness (*vipāka-vijñāna*) does not take place except at the linking up (*pratisaṃdhi*) [i.e., passing from the intermediate stage to a new life] . . . .

Therefore, since maturation must be present for the entire life it must remain until death. Since it can be seen that eyes and so forth are removeable before death, they are [13a] not real maturations.

Also it says in the *Abhidharma-samuccaya*:[18]

> What is a maturation? It is the *ālaya-vijñāna* and its associated [mental factors].

Thus only the basis *ālaya-vijñāna* is a maturation.

With this, the explanation of the basis [*ālaya-vijñāna*] is complete.

Notes

1. The Sanskrit of MAV 1.3 as found in the MAVBh (Nagao 1964) quoted by Anacker (1984:425) is *artha-sattvātma-vijñapti-pratibhāsaṁ prajāyate / [vijñānaṁ].* Cp. Schmithausen 1987:100-103, esp. n. 724). The English translation is based on the Tibetan version which takes *°sattvātma* not as a dvandva but as a bahuvrīhi and appears to read **pratibhāsa-vijñānaṁ* in place of *vijñapti-pratibhāsaṁ.*

2. The Sanskrit of TK3-4ab (Anacker 1984:422) is *asaṁviditakopādisthāna-*

vijñaptikaṁ ca tat / sadā sparśa-manaskāra-vit-saṁjñā-cetanānvitam // upekṣā vedanā tatrā nivṛtāvyākṛtaṁ ca tat /. Anacker (1984:186) translates "Its appropriations, states and perceptions are not fully conscious yet it is always endowed with contact. . . ."

3. If *rūpa-skandha* were substantially the same as the perception of it, then it would no longer be *rūpa* (form) and one could no longer speak of an aggregate of forms. Cp. Gung thang (Wilson1984:545-48).

4. MSam (Lamotte 1938:31; Nagao 1-72). The translation is based on the probable Sanskrit original. That all the editions read *gnyis po* in place of *gnyis la* in pada b is best explained by the difficultly inherent in consistently translating *ālambana* and the various forms of *ā √lamb* into Tibetan with *dmigs (pa)*. The similar change in pada d, *de la dmigs → de ni dmigs* in some editions, is probably again because of the same tendency, of Tibetan writers, when more removed from Sanskrit syntax, to construe *dmigs pa* as an object. For references to later commentary and a translation of this passage see Wilson (1984:499 and 930 nn. 16 and 17). The Sanskrit is retranslated by Nagao (1982) as **atītādau tathā svapne pratibimba-dvaye' pi ca / asannālambanatvāc ca tadālambana-yogataḥ.*

5. The Sanskrit of BCA 5.7ab-5.8ab (Bhattacharya1960:54) is *taptāyaḥ-kuṭṭiṁ kena kuto jātāś ca tāḥ striyaḥ // pāpa-citta-samudbhūtaṁ tat tat sarvaṁ jagau muniḥ //.* Translated from the Tibetan by Batchelor (1979: 45).

6. MSam (Lamotte 1935:31; Nagao I-72). The Tibetan has been reconstructed into Sanskrit by Nagao (see also Lamotte 1938:104-5) as **preta-tiryaṅ-manuṣyāṇāṁ devānāṁ ca yathārhataḥ / tulya-vastu-manobhedād arthāniṣpattir iṣyate//1//.*

7. *Pratītya-samutpādādi-vibhaṅga-nirdeśa*, rendered extremely literally, in the Bstan 'gyur, as *Rten cing 'grel bar 'byung ba dang po dang rnam par dbye ba bshad pa.* The alternative correct title (cp. Tucci:1930:612, n.1) is *Pratītya-samutpāda-vyākhyā.* A line similar to that quoted here is found at P5496:288.1.6 which reads *'o na de'i dmigs pa dang rnam pa gang zhe na // dmigs pa dang rnam pa yongs su ma chad pa'o.* The same reading is found in the *Pratītya-samutpādādi-vibhaṅga-nirdeśa-ṭīkā* (alternatively *Pratītya-samutpāda-vyākhyā-ṭīkā*) by Guṇamati at P5496:339.3.3-4. Cp. Frauwallner (1956:43-49); Matsuda (1982:63-66). Wilson (1984:533) mentions ". . . those such as the Nepali Jahu . . ." as possibly making such a statement.

8. Cp. this translation of Tibetan *tshogs* with Wilson's explanation of the term (1984:223) as a 'collection'.

9. This is referring to the *Bhāṣya* ('Commentary') on the the MAV (quoted above 7b4) "[the *ālaya-vijñāna*] arises as the awareness of the appearance . . . of <u>living beings.</u>" The Sanskrit of the MAVBh (Nagao 1964) quoted by Anacker (1984:425 line 23) is *sattva-pratibhāsaṁ yat pañcendriyatvena sva-para-santānayor.* Wilson (1984:584) points out that "the phrasing of the textual source . . . is closest to that found in the Tibetan translation of Won ch'uk's *Saṁdhi-nirmocana* Commentary."

10. MSam (Lamotte 1938:25; Nagao 1982:59).

11. The reasoning here is hard to follow. If person X is going to harm person Y, the harm to Y comes about because of the ripening of a residual impression left on Y's *ālaya*. The *abhilāpa* residual impression, which merely produces the body and the sense-faculties, is not a type which produces such harm. Now, if X's sense-faculty of hearing were to be damaged it would not cause Y's hearing to be impaired. This is because the *abhilāpa* residual impression, which produces the sense-faculty, does not cause similar damage in another continuum. Hence each person's sense-faculties appear in a unique manner to each person's *ālaya*.

12. The scheme may be represented as follows:

1. *kuśala* (virtuous)
2. *akuśala* (nonvirtuous)
3. *avyākṛta* (neutral)

a) *nivṛtāvyākṛta* (obstructed and neutral); b) *anivṛtāvākṛta* (nonobstructed and neutral)

Tsong kha pa's approach to the moral status of the *ālaya-vijñāna* is directed primarily by the requirements of systematic consistency.

13. For an explanation of different mental factors (*caitta*) and their functions see AS (Pradhan 1950:5-7; Rahula 1971:7-14).

14. Cp. MSam (Lamotte 1938:4; Nagao I-3) *sattvās tadālīnā ātmatvenety ālaya-vijñānam* discussed by Schmithausen (1987:n. 137).

15. The Sanskrit of TK19 (Anacker 1984:423) is *karmaṇo vāsanā grāha-dvaya-vāsanayā saha / kṣīṇe pūrva-vipāke'nyad vipākaṁ janayanti tad //.* The translation follows Anacker (1984:188).

16. MSam (Lamotte 1938:24; Nagao I-62); discussed by Schmithausen (1987:154 n. 974).

17. MSam (Lamotte 1938:24; Nagao I-52).

18. AS translated by Rahula (1971:50). Cp. the Sanskrit retranslation by Pradhan (1950:30) *vipākaḥ punar ālaya-vijñānaṁ sasaṁ prayogaṁ draṣṭavyam.*

THREE

ĀLAYA-VIJÑĀNA AS SEED

Question: What is the definition of the dependent seed *ālaya-vijñāna*?

> The seed *ālaya-vijñāna*, which is something dependent (*āśrita*) [as distinct from something which is a basis (*āśraya*)], is the potential placed on the location of perfumes by the perfumer when it [the perfumer] is ceasing. [Mv XVII]

[The seed *ālaya-vijñāna*] is that potential—the seeds of virtue, nonvirtue and of what is not the subject of moralizing—placed on the location of perfumes by the perfumer. [The so-called perfumer] is the set of seven consciousnesses, at the time it is ceasing. The set of six consciousnesses [i.e., excluding *kliṣṭa-manas* and *ālaya-vijñāna*] places the seeds of both virtue and nonvirtue and also what is not a subject of moralizing. This is because in this group [of six] is found all three [types of minds], such as a virtuous [mind], etc. The *kliṣṭa-manas* and its associated [mental factors] only leave neutral perfumes since they always remain, in essence, what is not a subject of moralizing.

Question: How is it ascertained that the perfumer is the group of seven [consciousnesses] and their associated [mental factors]?

[Answer:] Entering (*pravṛtti*) consciousnesses and the *ālaya-vijñāna* continually adhere to each other, each functioning as cause and result of the other. For, all such entering consciousnesses, by nurturing the older seed, function as the empowering condition (*adhipati-pratyaya*) of the seed part of the *ālaya-vijñāna* and, by placing a new seed, as its causal condition (*hetu-pratyaya*). Thus [the MSam][1] says:

> These two consciousnesses become a condition for each other (*anyonya-pratyaya*). For the *Mahāyānābhidharma-sūtra* says:
>
> > All dharmas adhere to *[ālaya]-vijñāna* and likewise this [*ālaya-vijñāna*] adheres to them, in the sense of being the result and [13b] the cause of each other.

This explanation is from the point of view of simultaneous cause and effect. From the nonsimultaneous point of view, [the set of six consciousnesses] also place the seeds which give rise to the maturation part of a future life's *ālaya-vijñāna.*

Moreover, the perfuming occurs as the basis is ceasing and the perfumer arising. This is simultaneous. It is like, for example, sesame (*tila*) and the sesame flower which are there together, one arising as the other is perishing, so that later on the flower does not exist, but its fragrance is left, placed in the sesame seed.[2] Thus it is also said:[3]

> Here, the entering consciousness functions in two ways as a condition of the *ālaya-vijñāna.* It is posited [as a condition of *ālaya*] from the point of view of nurturing seeds fully in this life and, since in a future life it [the *ālaya*] is caused to become manifest, from the point of view of directing (Tib. *yongs su 'dzin pa*) the seed. For this reason, just as, with the full expanding of the seeds in this life, virtuous, nonvirtuous [minds], and those not the subject of moralizing arise contingent on the *ālaya-vijñāna,* to a similar extent, by way of a simultaneous coming into being and ceasing, they perfume that upon which they depend.

Mechanics of seed formation

Question: What are the prerequisites for something to be the location of perfumes?

> The location of perfumes has five particulars: it is a) stable, b) not a subject of moralizing [i.e., neither virtue nor nonvirtue], c) perfumed, d) related to the perfumer, and e) a basis in its own right.[4] [Mv XVIII]

The location of perfumes is posited as having five qualities.[5] What are these five?

a) It is stable. This means that it must be something like a sesame seed, etc., the continuum of which is ongoing. It cannot be like sound or lightning which is unstable and not suitable to be a location of perfumes. Such things are not accepted to be imbued with any residual impression. They are phenomena which lose whatever they are imbued with. This [word 'stable'] teaches [14a] that the set of seven consciousnesses and forms cannot be the location of perfumes. For [the *Triṁśikā-kārikā*][6] says of these:

> The arising of a mental consciousness takes place continually, unless in a state without thought processes, in one of the two absorptions, in a torpor, a faint or a state devoid of mind.

and[7]

> But it [*kliṣṭa-manas*] does not exist on the transcendental paths or in the cessation absorption.

Thus, because [forms] are not in the form or formless realms, and because [the set of seven consciousnesses] sometimes cease, they cannot be the location of perfumes.

Question: In this case the *ālaya-vijñāna* also cannot be the location of perfumes because it also sometimes ceases, because, as it is said [in the *Triṁśikā-kārikā*]:[8]

> After the state of the Arhant it turns back.

[Answer:] There is no flaw here. It is enough that [the *ālaya*] remains without break for as long as there are perfumers.

b) It is not a subject of moralizing. Strong (Tib. *mi mnyam pa*) smells like garlic and sandlewood cannot imbue all seeds while bland smells like sesame can do so.[9] Thus, something not the subject of moralizing, with a bland type of smell, is not incompatible with extremely clear virtuous and nonvirtuous minds. This [not being a subject of moralizing] teaches that virtuous and afflicted minds cannot be the location of perfumes.

c) It is perfumed. This means it must have the capacity to be perfumed. This is saying, then, that impermanent, as distinct from permanent, phenomena can be imbued, and hence that noncomposite phenomena (*asaṁskṛta*) cannot be the location of perfumes.

d) It is related to the perfumer. This means there must be a relation such that the perfumer is arising and the location of perfumes is perishing at the same time. This teaches a) that different streams of consciousness and b) phenomena which exist at different times cannot be perfumer and location of perfumes, respectively.

e) It is a basis in its own right. This means it is a basis in its own right, [14b] not just one through a process of synonymity. This eliminates [the five omnipresent mental factors] such as contact, etc., associated with a main mind (*mūla-citta*), from being the location of perfumes. For these [mental factors] depend on a main mind, the *ālaya-vijñāna*, and are not, therefore, a basis in their own right.

Question: In that case, then, do these [the five omnipresent mental factors] such as contact, etc., perfume their constituent *ālaya-vijñāna* or not? If the former, then there will be a perfumer other than the group of seven consciousnesses. If the latter, these [five mental factors] will then have no cause.

[Answer:] There have been two opinions,[10] one saying: "They must perfume, for otherwise they would have no cause," and the other saying, "The [associated mental factors] are extremely indistinct and are not a subject of moralizing. Therefore they do not perfume. However, since they are a maturation of past action they are propelled [into existence] and remain until death." The latter [explanation] is better, otherwise the *ālaya-vijñāna* also will itself have to perfume and there will be the flaw of not finding the location of perfumes.

Divisions of *vāsanā*

Question: How many divisions of propensities are there?

Answer: There are four: a sixfold division, a threefold division, and two fourfold divisions. First the sixfold division.

Sixfold division of *vāsanā*

> Outer, inner and the indistinct two, then the conventional and the absolute: these are accepted as the six types of seeds.[11] [Mv XIX]

a) Outer seeds are such things as barley and the lotus-root.

b) Inner seeds are the seed portion of *ālaya-vijñāna.*

c-d) The two indistinct [seeds] are explained as follows: [First the word] 'indistinct.' Because [such seeds] are not the subject of moralizing, neither affliction (*samkleśa*) nor purity is distinct within them. Alternatively, neither virtue nor nonvirtue is distinct. [The word] 'two' refers to outer and inner seeds. According to one explanation (Tib. *ṭīg byed*) of the MSam[12] [15a] which reads 'indistinct as two' [instead of 'the indistinct two'], something which is not the subject of moralizing, when analysed, is not distinct as afflicted and pure nor as a virtue and nonvirtue.

The following interpretation is also given for 'two.' In that *ālaya-vijñāna* itself has the seeds of harmful phenomena, on account of which fact harmful phenomena originate [from it], it has a cause and effect relation with them. And in that it functions as the basis or place of all the seeds of pure phenomena it has a cause and effect relation with them too. Thus it says in the *Guhyārtha-vyākhyā:*[13]

> In regard to 'the two indistinct [seeds],' the derivation is as follows: Not distinct as either the two, virtue and nonvirtue; or the two, complete affliction and purity, [hence] completely indistinct, i.e., something that is neutral (*avyākṛta*). Some read '[seeds indistinct] as two,' and get the following meaning: Not distinct, when analysed, as either afflicted and pure; nor distinct, when analysed, as virtue and nonvirtue, i.e., neutral. Of these,

an outer seed is neutral and because of its neutrality is indistinct. And an inner seed is indistinct in that it is not discernable as being virtuous, etc.

And also in the *Upanibandhana*:[14]

By 'indistinct' is meant not a subject of moralizing. By 'two' the outer and inner [seeds] or, [in another interpretation], effects and causes. There are two aspects of the *ālaya-vijñāna* that has these [latter] two dimensions. Thoroughly afflicted and pure phenomena arise because of the cause [15b] and basis functioning that takes place.

e) Conventional seeds are outer seeds because they are simply the object of ordinary wisdom (*vyavahārika-prajñā*).

f) Ultimate seeds are inner seeds because, even under analysis [by transcendental wisdom], one must assert that they exist.

In the earlier explanations set forth in the above passages from the *Guhyārtha-vyākhyā* and *Upanibandhana* the first, third, and fifth types of seeds [i.e., the ordinary external seed] are merely incidental. In the latter explanation set forth in the *Upanibandhana* [which explains the 'two' in terms of a cause and effect relation] they [ordinary seeds] are incidental. And thus the MSam says:[15]

Outer, inner, the indistinct two, then the relative and the absolute: these six types of seeds are accepted. Being stable, not a subject of moralizing, perfumed, and related to the perfumer, and not other than the perfumer: these characterize a residual impression.

Threefold division of *vāsanā*

Or there are three residual impressions: of designation, view of self, and *bhavāṅga* ('the branch [i.e., cause] of [cyclic] existence'). [Mv XX]

Thus it is said in the MSam:[16]

What are the divisions of this *ālaya-vijñāna*? In short one should discern three and four sorts. Relative to the three particular types of residual impression there are three: a) the designation residual impression (*abhilāpa-vāsanā*), b) the view of self (*ātma-dṛṣṭi*), and c) the *bhavāṅga* ('the branch [i.e., cause] of [cyclic] existence').

As this says, then, there are three types. The first residual impression [i.e., *abhilāpa-vāsanā*] leaves on the *ālaya-vijñāna* the seeds of all the names and signs of every phenomena, from form to omniscience. It is, in short, the causal condition for the thinking-mind that gives linguistic expression to various things. [16a] It is called the residual impression [left] by elaboration (*prapañca*) because it is the seed of the thinking-consciousness's elaboration of a variety of objects. It is also called the designation residual impression because it is the seed of the form of thinking-consciousness that says [to itself] "an eye is an eye" and "a form is a form."

Question: In that case, how does one interpret the MSam where it says:[17]

> The *vijñaptis* ('representation of consciousness')[18] of body, possessor of body and experiencer; the *vijñapti* of the object experienced [by the first three], the *vijñapti* of the subjective experience [of that]; the *vijñaptis* of [past, present and future] time, of number, of place and of linguistic expression all originate from the designation residual impression-seed.

Answer: I believe there is no flaw here. The 'seed of the thinking-consciousness' mentioned above [at 16a.2, where it says, "It is called the residual impression [left] by elaboration because it is the seed of the thinking-consciousness's elaboration of a variety of objects"] is from the point of view of what [the designation residual impression] mainly is. The teaching here [in the MSam] is, I think, that the dependent phenomena (*paratantra*) seeded on the *ālaya-vijñāna*, are the imagination of the unreal (*abhūta-parikalpa*) systematized as representations of consciousness. And it is all these representations of consciousness from 'body' to 'linguistic expression' that originate from, of the three sorts of *vāsanā*, the designation propensity. This is because they do not arise from the other two [propensities, i.e., *ātma-dṛṣṭi-* and *bhavāṅga-vāsanā*] and are all [i.e., all nine representations of consciousness are] objects which thinking-consciousness designates [as being this or that]. Hence, from the point of view of being designated, it is only the thinking-consciousness and associated [mental factors] which cause the residual impression (*vāsanā*) to be placed, and it is only the thinking, labeling consciousness that is produced [from those residual impressions].[19]

Second, the view of self residual impression. This is the seed placed by *kleśas* ('affliction emotions') [16b] and their associated [mental factors]. It gives rise to the diffentiation-into-self-and-other (*sva-para-viśeṣa*) representation of consciousness. As [the MSam] says:[20]

> For the diffentiation-into-self-and-other representation of consciousness arises from the view of self residual impression-seed (*ātma-dṛṣṭi-vāsanā-bīja*).

It is also called *sat-kāya-dṛṣṭi-vāsanā* [residual impression left by mistakenly viewing the five aggregates, which are perishable and a collection, as a permanent and single soul]. This is because it is the seed of that [mistaken] view of the perishable [aggregates].

Third, the *bhavāṅga* residual impression. This is the seed, placed by virtuous or nonvirtuous entering (*pravṛtti*) consciousnesses, of the dawning of existence, [i.e.], happy or bad lives, of death and rebirth. As [the MSam] says:[21]

> The happy-and-bad-lives-death-and-rebirth (*sugati-durgati-cyutyupapatti*) representation of consciousness arises from the residual impression-seed which is the branch [i.e., cause] of [cyclic] existence.

This is also called the maturation (*vipāka*) residual impression because it gets its nature from the fully ripened maturation.[22]

Question: The sense-faculties and [sense-] objects referred to here [in the MSam] are termed representations of consciousness (*vijñapti*). Are they so called because they are, in fact, awareness?

[Answer:] No.

Question: What, then, are they?

[Answer:] When one examines those things appearing as five sense-faculties and as five sense-objects such as form, sound, etc., they seem to be external and cut off from [mind]. At that time these are not accepted to be, in fact, consciousness. We make a presentation of them just as is generally accepted in the world and as it appears to impure perception. When they are examined carefully, however, such appearances are not describable as identical with, or other than, consciousness. They are completely imaginary (*parikalpita*).

Looking at what is appearing, then, an ultimate soul or fundamental principle such as non-Buddhist schools imagine, or the atoms [17a] imagined by the lower Buddhist schools are not established. This is because they are not viable as appearances. They are further refuted by the arguments disproving subject-object bifurcation (*grāhya-grāhaka*). Since experience is graspable as being material (*dravya*), they are, in fact, appearances of the inner consciousness itself. They are superimposed on that by thought. Thus it says in the MSam:[23]

> By these representations of consciousness are demonstrated the characteristic marks which are dependent phenomena, the imagination of the unreal (*abhūta-parikalpa*), systematized as all [*kāma, rūpa* and *ārūpya*] realms, states of birth (*gati*), places of birth (*yoni*), and afflictions. A *vijñapti's vijñapti-mātratā* ("a representation of consciousness's state of being merely a representation of consciousness"), which is the basis of the appearance of the nonexistent spurious object contained in the imagination of the unreal is the characteristic mark of a dependent phenomenon (*paratantra-lakṣaṇa*).

> Question: What is the characteristic mark of a completely imaginary phenomenon (*parikalpita-lakṣaṇa*)?
>
> [Answer:] It is whatever has no reality, but appears just as the objective content of a representation of consciousness.
>
> Question: What is the characteristic mark of a thoroughly established phenomenon (*pariniṣpanna-lakṣaṇa*)?
>
> [Answer:] It is the complete nullification (*atyantābhāvatā*) of the object's characteristic mark (*artha-lakṣaṇa*) [=completely imaginary phenomenon] in the locus of that characteristic mark that is a dependent phenomenon.

Also:[24]

> Question: What is an example (*dṛṣṭānta*) for these representations of consciousness of which it is said, "They are mere representations of consciousness (*vijñapti-mātra*), for they are without any objective content (*arthābhāva*)?"
>
> [Answer:] One should look at the example of a dream, etc. In a dream, although there is no objective content, mere consciousness (*vijñāna-mātra*) appears in a variety of aspects: as form, sound, smell, taste, feelings, a home, forests, earth, and mountains, etc. These lack all objective content whatsoever. From this example one should become convinced of all things being just representations of consciousness. One should understand from the word 'etc.' other [suitable] examples such as an illusion (*māyā*), a mirage (*marīci*), [17b] and imaginary falling hair (*timira*).

Fourfold division of *vāsanā*

Third, the first [of the two] fourfold division[s].

> The four types of seeds are a) common, b) uncommon, c) having feeling, and d) without feeling. [Mv XXI]

Common (*sādhāraṇa*) seeds are seeds on the *ālaya-vijñāna* which give rise to the vessel-like outer world of inanimate things. Uncommon (*asādhāraṇa*) seeds are those which give rise to [the sap of] what is in the world [i.e., the person]. These two seeds are also termed 'the seed from which things lacking feeling originate' and 'the seed from which things having feeling originate,' respectively. This is because the vessel, not being delimited by a mind,[25] does not appear as the basis of pleasure and pain while the sap [i.e., person] is the opposite of that. Thus [the MSam] says:[26]

Question: What are the divisions of these [seeds] by way of characteristic marks?

Answer: There are a) the one of which the characteristic mark is being common, b) of which the characteristic mark is being uncommon, c) of which the characteristic mark is being the seed from which things lacking feeling originate, and d) of which the characteristic mark is being the seed from which things having feelings originate. The common one is the seed of the vessel-like world. The uncommon one is the seed of each person's *āyatanas*.[27] The common one is the seed from which everything lacking feeling arises. The uncommon one is the seed from which arises all that has feeling.

Fourth, the second fourfold division [of residual impressions].

> Also four [other residual impressions] are mentioned: a) the state that invites pain, b) pliability, c) those already used, and d) those not yet used. [Mv XXII]

The seeds of a state that invites pain (*dauṣṭhulya*) are the seeds of all root afflictions like attachment and anger, and of all close-by afflictions such as wrath and spite. The seeds of pliability (*praśrabdhi*) are the seeds of [18a] all ordinary virtue. Already-used seeds are the seeds of virtue and nonvirtue which reach maturation in a happy or bad state of rebirth, and terminate in that maturation. For they are like food that has been cooked and cannot again be brought to maturation. Seeds not yet used are the designation residual impressions (*abhilāpa-vāsanā*).[28] For they have been issuing forth from a time without beginning, bringing about, in the continuum of all living beings right from their birth without any prompting the multitude of mental constructions [based on] the subject-object [bifurcation]. Thus [the MSam] says:[29]

> Also there is [a residual impression], the characteristic mark of which is being a state that invites pain, and [a residual impression], the characteristic mark of which is pliability. The ones marked by being a state that invites pain are the seeds of afflictions and close-by afflictions. The ones marked by pliability are the seed of all contaminated virtuous phenomena.

and[30]

> Also there are [residual impressions], the characteristic marks of which are being already used and not yet used. The ones marked by being already used are the seeds of virtue and non-virtue which reach maturation and

> terminate in that maturation. The ones marked by being not yet used are the designation residual impression-seeds, for they are seeds of the mental construction which has come about from time without beginning.

Hence, they [are wrong] who say[31] that the two [seeds] 'already used and not yet used' spoken of in the MSam [should be understood] in the following order: Just as the essence of the seed is destroyed when the shoot has arisen, similarly, when the residual impressions [left by] maturation as a happy or bad state of rebirth have already matured into fruitions [as new *vipāka/ālaya-vijñānas*], since they are non-existent, they are not things which can be nurtured [and hence are called 'already used']. Since the residual impressions for results which have not yet originated are new residual impressions, therefore these second [sort] can be nurtured [and are called 'not yet used']. It [18b] is not the intention of the MSam.

Relation of the seeds and basis

Question: Are such residual impressions as these substantially the same as, or separate from, the consciousness which is their basis?

> Furthermore those residual impressions are neither substantially the same as nor different from the basis. [Mv XXIII]

Question: Why are they not the same?

> They are not the same because a) seeds would then have an objective support (*ālambana*) and aspect (*ākāra*) [as does a consciousness], b) the seeds of the five states of rebirth would get muddled up, and c) the realms would get muddled up as well. [Mv XXIV]

The *ālaya-vijñāna* and the seeds are not substantially the same. Otherwise the seed part of the *ālaya-vijñāna* would have to have an objective support and aspect. If one agrees that it does have these, one will contradict [the scriptural] explanation that, "seeds have neither objective support nor aspect."

Furthermore, the seeds of the five states of rebirth will become muddled up because one must admit they are all substantially the same. How so? Because when seeds of all five states of rebirth are on one basis they must be there at one and the same time, and one must then admit that all those will be substantially the same as the single instant of the *ālaya-vijñāna* that is their basis. Now, since that instant is without parts, those five seeds become a single substance without parts. [19a] This is so because they have the nature [as seeds on the *ālaya-vijñāna*] of a [single instant of] consciousness which is a partless singularity. If one agrees that this is indeed so, the [absurd] consequence would be that a nonvirtue could set down a seed that matures as a happy state of rebirth. This is because [the hypothetical single instant of the basis *ālaya-vijñāna* which is substantially the same as the composite of the seeds of the five states of rebirth] would be a seed that could mature as a bad state of rebirth. Also there would be the [absurd] consequence that a virtue could set down the seed that matures as a bad state of rebirth. This is because [the hypothetical single instant] would be a seed that could mature as a happy state of rebirth.

A person who does not strive for the unconfined intelligence of the wise, and to whom only a surface understanding of the words (Tib. *sgra spyi*) has occurred, may think: "The seeds of the five states of rebirth do not have to be each apart from the other [1143] because the thing (*bhāva*) and [its] form (*rūpa*) are different [but not separable from each other]."[32] Let us examine this.

Is this thing which is held to be substantially the same as the form, [made up of] the substance of the form or not? If the former, your assertion [that the relation between the five seeds is like the relation between a thing and its form] is not established. For you accept that [the] thing, which is substantially the same as a form, to also be substantially the same as [its] sound, smell, taste, and feeling. But being [made up of] the substance of form [the thing] would have nothing to do with them. And saying "It is not [made up of] the substance of form. It is substantially the same as it, but [made up of] the substance of something different" is the raving of a lunatic! We are not going to debate with someone who is insane!

In this vein the Lord of Scriptures [Sa skya Paṇḍita] says [in his *Tshad ma rigs gter*]:[33]

> If the thing which is *vyāvṛtta* ('reversed') from 'not-tree' were to be an agaru tree[34] then other [trees] would not be trees. If the other [tree] were to be a tree then an agaru tree would not be. This is because, [when a generality, e.g., 'tree' is substantially the same as a particular, e.g., an agaru tree, then the generality] would be its [the particular's] nature, not any other [particular's nature].

This is saying that the thing which is *vyāvṛtta* ('reversed') from 'not-tree' is either identical with an agaru tree or not identical as far as its substance is concerned. If the former [i.e., if the substance of 'tree' is identical to the substance of an agaru tree] all particular trees, other than the agaru tree, will become not-tree. In the latter case [i.e., if the substance of 'tree' is not identical to the substance of an agaru tree] the agaru tree will become not-tree for it will not be *vyāvṛtta* ('reversed') from what is not-tree. If one accepts that those [trees] different to the agaru tree are also substantially the same as 'tree' then the agaru will not be a tree. [19b] The reason for this is like that found in the statement:

"Because all the substances would exist all mixed up with each other." Thus, for as long as one accepts a substantially established generality beyond all the particulars, one is not able to eliminate the faults that crop up[35] from being substantially the same or different.

Furthermore, given that there is no contradiction in admitting something to be substantially the same, but at the same time accepting two parts [to it], then even the Buddha himself cannot refute the fact that a constituent part (*avayava*), and that which has constituent parts (*avayavin*), are substantially the same.

Also, [the three] realms would become muddled up. In this case, [where residual impressions and the basis *ālaya-vijñāna* are asserted to be substantially the same], by the force of meditation on a form-realm god's absorption (*samāpatti*), there is a seed that will give rise to the state of being a form-realm god that would have to be on a desire-realm *ālaya-vijñāna*. This is because one has to assert that the *ālaya-vijñāna* is substantially the same as that [residual impression left by meditation which is the seed for rebirth as a form-realm god]. Also that seed would only be categorized [1144] as being on a desire-realm level because that newly placed seed would be an *ālaya-vijñāna* of the desire realm. Hence, there are unlimited types of logical analysis, like this, that one can use if [the *vāsanās* and the basis *ālaya-vijñāna*] are [asserted to be] substantially the same.

Question: Why are they not substantially different?

> They are not different because two *ālaya-vijñānas* would then occur on one basis [i.e., person]. [Mv XXV]

If they were to be substantially different, [still, the seed *ālaya*] would not be a form, a nonassociated phenomenon (Tib. *ldan min*) or seven of the set [of eight consciousnesses]. This is so because [the seed *ālaya*] is a) substantial [and is, therefore, not a nonassociated phenomenon], b) exists in the formless [realm and is, therefore, not a form], and c) is present when the set of seven [consciousnesses] are absent, respectively [and is, therefore, not one of those seven consciousnesses]. Thus it would have to be a second *ālaya-vijñāna*. If one were to accept this, then there would have to exist two *ālaya-vijñānas* on one basis and hence a multitude of mental continuums would come about.

[Objection:] This is not necessary because even though many associated mental factors (*caitta*) occur together with a single mind (*citta*), and even though the set of seven [consciousnesses] exists together [20a] with the *ālaya-vijñāna* still a multitude of mental continuums do not come into being.

[Response:] This is not the same. [The mental factors] are present contingent on the single mind and the set of seven [consciousnesses] are present in dependence on a single *ālaya-vijñāna*. If, on the other hand, there were to be two *ālaya-vijñānas* one would not be contingent on the other because both would be stable consciousnessess having an independent status. So the fault [in asserting the two *ālayas* to be substantially different] remains.

Question: In which way, then, do these residual impressions abide?

> Therefore they are inexpressible as one with or other than the basis since they are mere imputations. [Mv XXVI]

Since they are, then, neither a substantial singularity or plurality they are not established as being either the same as or different from the basis consciousness. They are, therefore, just like imputations. They are essentially that *[ālaya-]vijñāna's* potential which is lying dormant. For as [the MSam] says:[36]

> Question: How do the *ālaya-vijñāna* and the seeds of completely afflicted dharmas abide? Are they substantially different, or not different, from each other?
>
> Answer: Those [residual impressions] which are on [the *ālaya-vijñāna*] are neither substantially different nor substantially not different. So the *ālaya-vijñāna* which has the capacity to produce those, in that it does so, is [called] 'the [consciousness] with all the seeds.'

Commenting on this the *Guhyārtha-vyākhyā* says:[37]

> Since on either side these two flaws appear, it says "... those which are on it are neither substantially different, etc." The statement, "They are those which are not describable as being one with, or other than, the *ālaya-vijñāna*" conveys the intended meaning.

Also commenting on this the *Upanibandhana* says,[38]

> The statement, "... those on it are neither substantially different, nor [20b] substantially not different" says residual impressions are on the *ālaya-vijñāna* in a manner completely beyond difference and nondifference in that they are in the form of special capacities (*śakti-viśeṣa*). These capacities are, moreover, not describable as being either one with, or other than, what has capacity. This question, "Are they different or not different from each other?" does not lead to something else because they [residual impressions] are imputed when what has capacity [the basis *ālaya*] is viewed in a different light.

Since, by this exegesis, this Ācārya [Asvabhāva] believes potentials to exist as imputations (*prajñapti-sat*), and what has potentials to be substantially existent (*dravya-sat*) it comments to the effect that the residual impressions and *ālaya-*

vijñāna are a) not substantially different and b) not the same isolate.[39] The assertion that the two are, therefore, substantially the same, within being different isolates, is the mistaken dharma statement of other schools and hence is not a statement uttered by us.[40]

Furthermore, since in [Yaśomitra's] *Vyākhyā* to the second chapter of the *Abhidharmakośa*, which explains Ācārya Vasubandhu's own system it says[41] that a seed, potential (*śakti*) and residual impression all have the same meaning; that a seed exists as an imputation and is not substantially existent, Asaṅga's and Vasubandhu's opinions [on this matter] are the same. Hence this tainting seed, a section of the *saṁskāra-skandha* ('aggregate of composites'), is an attainment (*prāpti*) that is a nonassociate composite. This is so because it is a) a composite, b) is not a form, and c) is not a mind or mental factor. Also because as the *Abhidharma-samuccaya* says:[42]

> Question: What are the associated ones (*samanvāgama*)? They are like the [related ones (*saṁprayoga*)] defined earlier and are threefold in division: associated with seeds, associated with the controller [21a], and associated with activity.

Question: In that case how does one interpret the above [MSam. quoted 15b5]?

> Relative to the three particular types of residual impression there are three . . .[43]

and the *Guhyārtha-vyākhyā* where it says that there is a twofold division of *ālaya-vijñāna* into seed and maturation.[44]

[Answer:] There is no flaw here. Generally, the use of the word 'consciousness,' even for the seed *ālaya*, is in rough expositions where seeds and maturation are not separately identified. For, if they are separately identified, and if one inquires whether they are substantially the same or different, it is taught that they are neither. And, in the case of this specific quotation from the *Guhyārtha-vyākhyā*, it is an expansion following naturally out of the earlier condensed explanation.[45] And both commentaries [*Guhyārtha-vyākhyā* and *Upanibandhana* quoted 20a5-20b3] are in accord in their explanation of the passage "Are they different, [or not different], from each other?" quoted [from the MSam at 20a4]. And it says in the *Guhyārtha-vyākhyā*:[46]

> The presence of the continuum of the earlier seed is the causal condition only for the seed of a separate later time. It is not an empowering condition because it is a cause establishing something similar (Tib. *skal bar*

> *mnyam*). It is not an immediately preceding corresponding condition because it is, in essence, neither [mind nor] mental factor. And it is not an objective support condition because there is no taking of a seed as an objective support.

And, [finally, there is no flaw] because in the *Upanibandhana*[47] it says that "the mere residual impressions are not the *ālaya* consciousness." So it is not correct to find a flaw [and argue that seeds substantially exist] just because of seeing the mere word ['consciousness' applied to the seed part of the *ālaya*].

Question: Saying that the seeds are functioning things but not accepting them to be substantial is surely a completely original point of view [without scriptural basis]?

There is no flaw here either. This Ācārya [Vasubandhu], [21b] his brother [Asanga] having separated functioning things (*vastu*) into substantial (*dravya*) and imputed (*prajñapti*), held that nonassociated phenomena were composite [functioning things] but also held that they were not substantial. So this nonmixing and delineation of each of the two Ācāryas' systems is wise and scholarly and something one can feel confidence in.

Characteristics of *vāsanā*

Question: Are these residual impressions virtuous, nonvirtuous, or not the subject of moralizing?

> The placer [of the residual impression] is virtuous, etc.; the residual impression which is placed is not a subject of moralizing. [Mv XXVII]

The word 'unobscured' has been left out [i.e., this is saying that a residual impression is both unobscured and not a subject of moralizing (*anivṛtāvyākṛta*)].

[Objection:] This is not correct because it is contradicted by both scripture and reasoning. [The scripture] is the *Abhidharma-samuccaya* where it says, talking of virtuous and nonvirtuous residual impressions:[48]

> What are virtuous in terms of what follows on (*anubandhataḥ*)?
> [Answer:] Just the residual impressions of those [virtuous states of mind].

and[49]

> What are nonvirtuous in terms of what follows on?
> [Answer:] Just the residual impressions of those [nonvirtuous states of mind].

[The reasoning is as follows]: If one accepts all perfuming residual impressions to be *avyākṛta* ('not a subject of moralizing') it would lead to the unwelcome consequences that a) they would not act as the cause of matured [consciousnesses, *vipāka-vijñāna*], b) that the seed giving rise to virtuous, nonvirtuous and neutral entering consciousnesses would not give rise to a result similar to the cause, and c) that after receiving ordination there would not be the arising of a continuum of virtue that remained until death. This is so because a) matured [consciousness] is always propelled forth by a virtue or nonvirtue, b) because a result similar to the cause must be like the cause, and c) because at the time when all the set of six [consciousnesses] are eliminated and there is no manifest thinking-mind, only the seed, you say that this seed is not a subject of moralizing [and cannot, therefore, be virtue. Hence the continuum of virtuous ordination would be broken].

[Response:] What you say is not correct. And why? Because . . .

> There is no proof for the assertion that there are real virtuous and nonvirtuous [residual impressions]. [Mv XXVIII]

Objection: But the above quotations and reasons are the proof.

[Response:] These are not valid proofs that real virtuous or nonvirtuous residual impressions exist. And why? There are two parts to the answer: Why the quotations do not stand as textual proof and why the reasoning does not stand as logical proof.

First, if the quotation beginning "What are virtuous in terms of what follows on (*anubandhataḥ*)?" were to establish residual impressions to be really virtuous or nonvirtuous, then [absurdly] a real form would come about in the formless realm. This follows because the so-called 'forms in terms of what follows on' would be real [forms]. This is because [such forms in terms of following on, viz. the physical sense-faculties in dormant] seed [form which give rise] to the physical [sense-faculties in a future life] exist in this [formless realm]. Furthermore there would [absurdly] come to exist real nonvirtues in the two upper realms [since nonvirtues in terms of what follows on, i.e., seeds giving rise to subsequent nonvirtuous states of mind, exist there].

Second [why the reasoning does not stand as a proof]. This has three parts.

First, in regard to the reason that "they would not act as the cause of matured [consciousnesses]." If by this you mean that they would not act as the propelling cause of matured [consciousnesses] we agree, because those residual impressions have themselves been propelled by the virtuous and nonvirtuous perfumers, and it is, therefore, those perfumers themselves which are the propelling causes. If, on the other hand, you mean that they do not produce a matured [consciousness] there is no pervasion. Otherwise, the previous instants of the *ālaya-vijñāna* [which you accept to be] not a subject of moralizing (*avyākrta*) will not be so.

Second, in regard to the reason that "... [an *avyākṛta* residual impression] would not give rise to a result similar to the cause." This also does not harm us because [the results] are similar to the placers [of the residual impressions], and that alone is enough to fulfill the requirement that the result be similar to the cause.

Third, in regard to the reason that ". . . the continuum of an ordination would not come into being." Again there is no harm, because, for so long as, having generated a sense of embarrassment, shame, and mindfulness, one has the power to restrain oneself from misguided conduct in any situation which could be an occasion for doing something contrary to the moral code, from just that the earlier [22b] ordination can be posited as existing and, at that time, furthermore, ongoing. Moreover, both commentators [authors of the *Guhyārtha-vyākhyā* and *Upanibandhana* quoted above 15a3-5, 15a5-b1] explain the above 'indistinct' [seed mentioned in the MSam] to refer to something that is not a subject of moralizing. It is, therefore, established that [the residual impressions] are not a subject of moralizing.

Question: Does this not contradict, though, the *Guhyārtha-vyākhyā* where it says:[50]

> It is also a little indistinct in regard to the inner [seed]. Anything produced by inner virtuous and nonvirtuous dharmas will be virtuous and nonvirtuous.

and

> Since all residual impressions are nonobscured and not a subject of moralizing, from them come only those dharmas which are nonobscured and not the subject of moralizing. It is not possible that virtuous and nonvirtuous dharmas arise from what is nonobscured and not the subject of moralizing.

Answer: The latter quote is just the presentation of an opposing idea and is not definitive. Otherwise, a neutral mind would not function as the immediate condition for a virtuous or nonvirtuous mind [which is patently absurd].

In regard to the former quotation: It just forms a sufficient explanation (Tib. *na yams*) for the discussion of the so-called 'indistinct' [residual impressions].[51] The position asserted [by the *Guhyārtha-vyākhyā*] takes as sufficient explanation the earlier of the passages quoted above ["Not distinct as either the two, virtue and nonvirtue" 15a3ff] because it says in the *Guhyārtha-vyākhyā* apropos the example [given in the MSam, quoted below] of a dye-mix [made from] various kernels:[52]

> In that [the residual impressions] operate through the consciousness which is the basis [*ālaya-vijñāna*] of the residual impressions functioning as cause they are not different. In that [the residual impressions] are not graspable as virtuous or nonvirtuous there is no range to them.

When residual impressions, then, they [the seed portions of the *ālaya-vijñāna*] are not different nor is there a range to them. [23a] Both the opponents' positions and the position that is asserted as correct explain in this manner.

Objection: If the residual impressions are not different from the *ālaya-vijñāna* and if the range of virtues and nonvirtues do not appear, results with different natures and the range of virtues and nonvirtues, etc., would not be able to come about from it. This is so because it is illogical to posit a range of results where there is no range of causes.

[Response:] There is no fault here as one can understand from the following passage in the MSam:[53]

> Question: How can it be that the residual impressions, which are not different and diverse, function as the cause of different dharmas?
>
> [Answer:] For example, a cloth treated with a dye-mix [made from] various kernels does not appear with a range of colors, but yet, when it is dipped in the vats of dye, all the various sorts of different colors show up on the cloth [one after the other]. Similarly, though a range of residual impressions taint the *ālaya-vijñāna*, while they are still residual impressions they do not appear in diversity. But when directly dealing with the different pots of dye which make the results manifest, dharmas are revealed in an unlimited diversity. This is the most profound and subtle Mahāyāna dependent arising (*pratītya-samutpāda*).

Notes

1. MSam (Lamotte 1938:13; Nagao I 27). The Sanskrit of the verse from the sūtra found in MAVṬ 34.1, quoted by Nagao (1964:31), is *sarva-dharmā hi ālīnā vijñāne teṣu tat tathā / anyonyaṁ phala-bhāvena hetu-bhāvena sarvadā//.* The English translation is aided by Schmithausen (1987: n. 136). Also translated by Friedmann (1984:43).

2. The same example is found in the MSam (Lamotte 1938:9; Nagao I 14).

3. Tsong kha pa perhaps intends this as a summarizing paraphrase of MSam (Lamotte 1938:9-10; Nagao I 14-17).

4. Cp. MSam (Lamotte 1938:12; Nagao I 23) quoted below.

5. According to Nagao (1982:29) the MSam maintains the *ālaya-vijñāna* has four qualities (*dhruve 'vyākṛta-bhāve ca bhāvaka-saṃnibandhake / bhāvanā na tad-anyeṣu vāsanā-lakṣaṇaṃ hi tad*). The *Vijñapti-mātratā-siddhi* is similar.

6. The Sanskrit of TK16 (Anacker 1984:423) is *mano-vijñāna-saṁbhūtiḥ sarvadā saṁjñikād ṛte / samāpatti-dvayān middhān mūrchanād apy acittakāt.* The translation is aided by Anacker (1982:187).

7. The Sanskrit of TK7cd (Anacker 1984:422) is *na nirodha-samāpattau mārge lokottare na ca.* Also quoted below 35b1.

8. The Sanskrit of TK5a (Anacker 1984:422) is *tasya vyāvṛttir arhatve.*

9. The idea seems to be that the smell of the flower is passed along into the seed and a bland smell would not preclude the presence of another stronger smell (cp. Gung thang in Wilson 1984:346, 350). Alternatively, Gung thang in his first interpretation (Wilson 343) construes *la* not as a conjunction but as denoting the object. Griffiths (1986:85) refers to the "... extremely common image of the sesame seed ... [that is] itself 'perfumed' by the plant which bore it with the 'tendency' to produce plants which are similarly perfumed,[and] produces the 'tendency' in the flowering plant which grows from it to have a certain perfume, even though the seed itself no longer exists."

10. The former is held by Bu ston (*Nyi ma'i 'od zer* 208:6-7) who rejects the latter view without mentioning who held it. Gung thang (Wilson 1984:349) says the source of Tsong kha pa's explanation is the *Guhyārtha-vyākhyā.* Gung thang (Wilson 598ff) also quotes from Ma ti Paṇ chen(89a4-5) to show he also held the former view which Gung thang says Tsong kha pa learned from Red mda' ba. Cp. Wilson's translation pp. 601-2.

11. This verse is identical to the version of the verse quoted from the MSam (Lamotte 1938:12; Nagao I 22) discussed below. Explained by Gung thang (Wilson 1984:383-6).

12. MSBh P5551:155a7ff. The Chinese translation by Hsüan Tsang is translated in part by Lamotte (1938:vol 2, 39).

13. *Guhyārtha-vyākhyā* P5553:69.1.1-4.

14. MSU P5552:251b7; cp. Lamotte (1938:vol. 2, 39-40).

15. MSam (Lamotte 1938:12, Nagao I 22). An additional śloka separates the two verses in the original: *skad cig pa dang lhan cig 'byung // de ni rgyun chags 'byung bar 'dod // nges dang rkyen la ltos pa dang // rang gi 'bras bus bsgrubs pa'o //*. Cp. Lamotte's translation of the first of these three verses: "Le germe externe (*bāhya*) et le germe interne (*ādhyātmika*) sont indifférenciés (*avyākta*). De ces deux germes, [le premier] est purement conventionnel (*saṁvṛta*), [le second] est absolu (*pāramārthika*). On admet qu'ils sont des germes à six caractéres (*ṣaḍākāra-bīja*)."

16. MSam (Lamotte 1938:22; Nagao I 58).

17. MSam (Lamotte 1938:25; Nagao II 2).

18. The Sanskrit equivalents for these *vijñaptis* are *deha, dehin, bhoktṛ* (1-3), *upabhogya* (4), *upabhoga* (5), *adhvan* (6), *saṃkhyā* (7), *deśa* (8), and *vyavahāra* (9). In total eleven *vijñaptis* are mentioned. Besides the above nine there are *sva-para-viśeṣa* 'differentiation into self and other' (10), and *sugati-durgati-cyutyupapatti* 'death and rebirth in good or bad destinations' (11).

19. The issues just touched on here are dealt with at length by Tsong kha pa in his *Legs bshad snying po* (translated by Thurman 1989). Particularly helpful is Thurman's long note on p. 234 in which there is a translation of the function of the *abhilāpa-vāsanā* given by Tsong kha pa's disciple Mkhas grub.

20. MSam (Lamotte 1938:25; Nagao II 2).

21. Ibid.

22. The *vipāka-vijñāna* is the basis *ālaya-vijñāna* which is the continuum giving continuity to the events of a single lifetime.

23. MSam (Lamotte 1938:25-6; Nagao II 2-4).

24. MSam (Lamotte 1938:26; Nagao II 6).

25. The point of this discussion is to say that while the external world is unconscious, not delimited by a single awareness but accessible to the minds of others, the internal world of the individual is the opposite of that: delimited by a single awareness and not immediately accessible to the minds of others.

26. MSam (Lamotte 1938:22-3; Nagao I 59-60).

27. The twelve *āyatanas* (i.e., six senses and their respective objects) are to be understood as the elements by which an individual knows and is known.

28. See 15b5.

29. MSam (Lamotte 1938:23; Nagao I 61).

30. Ibid.

31. Cp. MSBh P5551:169b7-170a6.

32. The view is informed by Dharmakīrti's statement that all *bhāvas* ('things') are real insofar as they perform the function which defines them (*artha-kriyā*); and by his theory of *apoha* ('exclusion [theory of knowledge]').

33. *Tshad ma rigs pa'i gter.* 158.2.5-6.

34. The *amyris agallocha.*

35. Apparently a passive sense of *brtags* 'present itself for examination.'

36. MSam (Lamotte 1938:10; Nagao I 16).

37. *Guhyārtha-vyākhyā* P5553:66.4.8-5.1

38. MSU P5552:248b5-249a5.

39. The term *ldog pa gcig* literally 'the same reverse' is difficult to translate. It conveys a particularly Tibetan development of the idea of *vyāvṛtta* and refers to the bare datum stripped of any shared attribute.

40. The passage is obscure. Wilson (1984:673) translates "... is a misappropriation of the doctrinal vocabulary of other major texts and hence does not appear as the vocabulary of (Indian Cittamātrins following Asaṅga)." Gung thang, in his comments, associates the mistakes with Ma ti Paṇ chen.

41. This is a paraphrase of AKVy (Shastri 1981:218-9), especially *śakti-viśeṣa eva bījam / na bījaṁ nāma kiṁcid asti prajñaptivat* (p. 219).

42. AS (Pradhan 1950:35): *samanvāgamaḥ katamaḥ / lakṣaṇataḥ purvavat // tat-prabhedaḥ punaḥ tri-vidhaḥ / bīja-samanvāgamo vaśiṣṭā-samanvāgamaḥ samudācāra-samanvāgamaḥ*. Translated by Rahula (1971:57).

43. The threefold division is *abhilāpa-vāsanā*, *ātma-dṛṣṭi* and *bhavāṅga*.

44. A paraphrase of *Guhyārtha-vyākhyā* P5553:67.1.6-7.

45. The translation is conjectural.

46. *Guhyārtha-vyākhyā* P5553:67.4.2-4.

47. MSU P5552:239b4. Taishō 1, 383b.

48. AS (Pradhan 1950:22). The Sanskrit is *anubandhataḥ kuśalaṁ katamat / teṣām eva yā vāsanā*; translated by Rahula (1971:35).

49. Ibid. The Sanskrit is *anubandhato 'kuśalaṁ katamat / teṣām eva yā vāsanā*.

50. *Guhyārtha-vyākhyā* P5553:69.1.4-5.

51. See above 15a1ff where the seeds are described as such because "neither affliction nor purity is distinct within them."

52. *Guhyārtha-vyākhyā* P5553:68.3.5-6

53. MSam (Lamotte 1938:10; Nagao I 18-19). Wilson (1984:633), following Gung thang, translates "... this is like cotton which when treated with the juice of fruit pits does not appear variegated, but when put into a vessel of dye displays many different varieties of color."

FOUR

SEEDS OF DELIVERANCE

Question: Are the residual impressions such that they have been on the *ālaya-vijñāna* forever, or is it that they are perfumed anew?

> There are three ways in which residual impressions are placed: they are asserted a) to be there naturally, b) produced and not previously there, and c) both. [Mv XXIX]

Among Yogācāra scholars there are three schools of thought as to the way in which the residual impressions are placed. What are they? They are:

a) the assertion that [the residual impressions] are there naturally, independent of a perfumer,
b) the assertion that a perfumer places [residual impressions] previously not there, and that a perfumer nurtures what was placed previously, and
c) the assertion that there is [both] the nurturing of [residual impressions] that are there naturally and the placement of what was previously not there. [23b]

These schools of thought are set out in the *Guhyārtha-vyākhyā* where the faults they find with each other, and the way the faults are handled, are dealt with at length.[1] In that book the first school of thought is accepted as correct but here it is the third that has been accepted.

I shall examine them from the point of view of a) seeds of uncontaminated transcendent wisdom, b) outflow (*niṣyanda*) seeds, and c) maturation (*vipāka*) seeds.

Of these the first, being the naturally abiding lineage (*prakṛti-stha-gotra*), is there naturally. As it says in the *Bodhisattva-bhūmi*:[2]

> Of these, the naturally abiding lineage is the specialness of the six-sense bases of all Bodhisattvas. For it is obtained naturally and comes down, one from the other, from time without beginning in an unbroken succession.

The two seeds: a) outflow (*niṣyanda*) and b) maturation (*vipāka*), are newly placed seeds. This is because: a) virtuous, nonvirtuous, and neutral engaging consciousnesses which are simultaneous with the *ālaya-vijñāna*—one coming into being as the other is going out of existence—leave a seed that will, in future, give rise to an engaging consciousness of a similar type; and b) because one must posit the seed of a maturation as [the residual impressions], produced by manifest virtuous and nonvirtuous states, which propel a [good or bad] maturation. This is one way, then, [to delineate the way seeds are placed on the *ālaya*] based on whether they are contingent on a certain placer, or not, and whether they are naturally there or are newly placed.

If one considers [residual impressions] from the point of view of whether they are beginningless or have a beginning, one finds that lineage (*gotra, rigs*) has no beginning and is not dependent on a placer, while the latter two have both [i.e., both have a beginning and in particular instances do not have a beginning]. [The outflow (*niṣyanda*) seed, in general, has no beginning because] the perfumer [which places] anew the outflow seed itself arises from a previous seed that is an outflow [24a], and that seed one must, again in turn, posit to have had a placer which was an outflow.

If, however, in specific instances of outflow seeds as well there were to be no beginning [it would be absurd]. Then virtuous or nonvirtuous minds occuring at the present time would not set down seeds which give rise to a similar class [of virtuous or nonvirtuous states of mind] in future [because such seeds would have been there for ever and there would, therefore, be no need to engage in virtuous behaviour and no use in refraining from nonvirtue]. Were the maturation seed, [in general], to have a beginning, [it would be absurd] because then cyclic existence would also have to have a beginning. If, however, also in specific instances there were to be no beginning [to seeds of maturations it would be absurd] because then a current meritorious, or nonmeritorious, course of action would not set down a seed of a maturation.

One must examine the following statement:[3]

> When a newly placed, weak residual impression [left by] listening [to the doctrine] is nurtured later on by [further] understanding, a) the nurturing of the outflow seed and b) the nurturing of the uncontaminated seed is newly established. Were the residual impression [left by] listening [to the doctrine] to be there naturally, then all persons would [absurdly have to] awaken into the lineage of liberation. [This is not, in fact, the case] because such a residual impression [left by] listening is the lineage which has been established.

In line with this, the residual impression left by listening is not placed anew by a placer and the three—listening, thinking, and contemplating—simply foster [an earlier understanding]. Were this not the case [then the residual impression left by understanding, which is simply the naturally abiding lineage by a different name] would not be naturally there. Thus the residual impression left by listening [i.e., naturally abiding lineage] is not placed anew by listening, and the mere residual impression that is naturally there is not the lineage which has been established. Since this is the case, just the presence [of the residual impression left by listening] does not entail awakening into the lineage [of liberation].

Question: What are naturally abiding lineage and developed lineage?

[Answer:] The naturally abiding lineage is not contingent on any placer, and is that seed of all uncontaminated dharmas [24b] which exists innately (Tib. *ngo bo nyid kyis gnas*). Having met with another's voice [explaining the doctrine] and a proper [religious] attitude [on the part of the listener], it becomes the ground for the increase of listening, thinking, and contemplation.

Why is it called the naturally abiding lineage? Because it is not placed anew by a placer and exists, on account of its nature, from beginningless time.

Why is it called the residual impression [left by] listening? Because, when the Buddha and Bodhisattvas are met with (Tib. *sphrad*) it, the dharma-element, the extremely pristine outflow, becomes the ground for the understanding of, for example, the twelve divisions of the Buddha's [profound] dharma.[4]

Why is it called the specialness of the six sense-bases? Because, in whoever's continuum it is found as a possession, it makes the six sense-bases of that being more special than others.

The developing lineage is posited as that same naturally abiding lineage when, having met with another's voice [explaining the doctrine] and a proper [religious] attitude [on the part of the listener], and fostered by listening, thinking, and contemplating, it has moved into a state of heightened potential. This is so because a) both of these [lineages] are seeds on the matured consciousness, b) because it is said the seed of uncontaminated [transcendental wisdom] is not something merely fostered by listening, thinking, and contemplating and is not placed anew, and c) because it is not accepted that the established lineage exists naturally, nor that it is a lineage placed anew. Thus the *Guhyārtha-vyākhyā* says:[5]

> That essential seed has two forms: the naturally abiding [25a] and that which comes about fully (*samudānīta*) from conditions.

Why is this [lineage] called fully established, developed, or that which comes about fully from conditions? It is because the very seed that exists by virtue of ultimate reality (Tib. *chos nyid kyis gnas*) is, contingent on listening, thinking, and contemplating, either established in, or else caused to be developed into, a state of heightened potential, or else because, [contingent on listening, etc.] it comes about fully, [passing] from a weak [potency] to middling and from middling to great.

Thus, this very seed is posited as the naturally abiding lineage from the point of view of its being there naturally, and as the developed lineage from the point of view of what has come about fully from conditions.

When interpreted in this manner, the earlier quotation from the *Guhyārtha-vyākhyā* [quoted at 25a1] and Ārya Vimuktisena's explanation of the Mind Only view [in his *Abhisamayālaṁkāra-vṛtti*][6]

> Others say the lineage is the special quality of the six *āyatanas*. There are two—that which comes about fully from conditions and the naturally abiding one.

are both correct.

Therefore the actual lineages accepted by Ācārya Asaṅga are as explained above. The statement that appears in certain of this Ācārya's work [*Ratna-gotra-vibhāga*][7] that ultimate reality (*dharmatā*) is the basis, ultimate reality is the lineage . . . is to be interpreted as follows. Just as one gives the name 'lineage' to [ultimate reality] simply by virtue of its being the basis of the four: the *dhātu*, enlightenment, qualities and, [enlightened] activity; and of the resultant Triple Gem [i.e., the seven subjects discussed in the seven chapters of the *Ratna-gotra-vibhāga*], similarly one gives the name 'basis-lineage' [to ultimate reality] just because, when one strives on the path with ultimate reality as objective support, the special qualities of the three vehicles come about. Were it to be otherwise [25b] many flaws would arise: a) there would not be three functionally different lineages, b) one could not say the Śrāvaka lineage stops when remainderless [nirvāṇa is attained], and c) the teaching of the MSam[8] that if there were no *ālaya-vijñāna*, transcendental purity would not be possible because there is no place, other than *ālaya-vijñāna*, for the seed of transcendental mind would not be our [Yogācāra] unique position.

[Mādhyamika objection:] If this were the case, then a) when one attains the developed lineage the naturally abiding lineage would not exist, and b) the cause of the Svābhāvika-kāya ('Fundamental Nature Body') would be a composite phenomenon. This is because the developed lineage is simply that very seed of stainless [wisdom] when conditions foster it, because it is explained that both [naturally abiding and developed lineage] are causes and not results, and because the naturally abiding lineage is spoken of as being the cause of the Nature Body. Hence your [Yogācāra] system is not best.

Let me answer these objections.

The first fault does not damage [our position]. When the seed of stainless [wisdom] is fostered by conditions it simply increases—to weak by a great deal of listening, to middling by a great deal of thinking, and to great by a great deal of contemplation. The seed does not produce the actual phenomenon anew. By force of the simultaneous condition of fostering, and the causal condition of the previous seed of a similar type, there is a positive increase. At such a time both [the seed] which is naturally abiding and [the seed] which has come about fully from conditions are there. The statement that they exist as causes and not as effects was made with the unstated proviso that certain conditions had not been encountered.[26a]

The second fault also does not damage [our position].[9] This is because a) where it says in the MSam that[10] the seed of stainless [wisdom] is the seed of the Dharma-kāya ('Truth Body'), both commentaries[11] [*Guhyārtha-vyākhyā* and *Upanibandhana*] explain Dharma-kāya [in that context] to [refer to] the suchness of the abandonment of the two obscurations [*kleśa-jñānāvarana*], along with the residual impressions [left by them], which [suchness] is the basis of all [Buddha-]quality dharmas such as the [ten] powers, etc.;[12] b) because it also says, in regard to the statement that the first lineage is the cause of the Svābhāvika-kāya, that nonconceptual transcendental wisdom in a state of equipoise is the cause of the Dharma-kāya and the postmeditative state (*pṛṣṭha-labdha*) is the cause of the Rūpa-kāya ('Form Body');[13] and c) because it also says in other places [i.e., Nāgārjuna's *Ratnāvalī*][14] that the two—[the wisdom] collection (*jñāna-saṁbhara*) and [the merit] collection (*puṇya-saṁbhara*)—are the causes of these two [Dharma- and Rūpa-]kāyas respectively.

Furthermore, were one to require two lineages to correspond to the noncomposite and composite bodies then, since the composite has two quite different bodies—of Saṁbhoga ('Enjoyments') and Nirmāṇa ('Emanations')—one would also require two quite different lineages for them. Thus there would not be definitely two lineages; instead there would [absurdly] be three. And one is not able to [validly] argue that "This [fault] does not come about [to holders of the Madhyamaka position] because both [the lineage which leads into the attainment of Saṁbhoga-kāya and the lineage which leads into the attainment of Nirmāṇa-kāya] are the developed lineage."[15] This [Madhyamaka assertion] does not go beyond the above [Yogācāra assertion] which simply is that, given the different characteristic marks of the Svābhāvika-kāya and Rūpa-kāya, one has to assert both a noncomposite lineage and composite lineage for them.

And [Mādhyamikas] also cannot [validly] argue [as in the *Abhisamayālaṁkāra*][16] that, "Though we assert lineage to be ultimate reality (*dharmatā*) still the flaw of there not being three different functional lineages does not ensue because we delineate the different [lineages] in terms of the attributes qualifying the basis." That [argument] would be acceptable were [the doctrine of] three vehicles (*yāna*) to be an interpretative teaching (*neyārtha*) [as in Madhyamaka]. But it is not acceptable given the [Yogācāra] assertion that there [definitely] are three vehicles which reach [three different] final destinations. [26b] For in their treatise [*Mahāyāna-sūtrālaṁkāra*, Asaṅga][17] says, "In that one observes [amongst Śrāvakas, Pratyeka-buddhas, and Bodhisattvas] different personalities (*dhātu*), different interests, definitely practicing or not practicing, and differing results from the seeds, there are three different lineages." Hence [Yogācāras], taking into consideration the results, infer that there are different causes. They do not teach that there are different lineages because the bases are different. And in their commentary on " . . . thus is attained . . . "[18] they explain, as does the *Bodhisattva-bhūmi* [quoted above 23b3], that [the naturally abiding lineage] "is the specialness of the six sense-bases."

In this [Yogācāra] way [of thinking], then, the seed of uncontaminated [wisdom] that is on the matured [*ālaya*] consciousness is not *ālaya-vijñāna*, since it is an antidote to *ālaya-vijñāna.* When, through a great deal of fostering by the conditions of listening, thinking, and contemplation, the pure seed increases and the seed of the afflictions is impeded, then, just as the swan, without grasping milk and water separately, coagulates the milk and causes clear water to come about, similarly, though the seed [of transcendental wisdom] and the *ālaya* function within not being grasped as separate, when the seed of complete affliction is impeded and purity expands, a fundamental change takes place and the three kāyas manifest themselves. Thus we read in the MSam:[19]

> Unlike that, transcendental purity would not be possible in the absence of consciousness with all the seeds (*sarva-bījaka-vijñāna*) because the residual impression left on that [*sarva-bījaka-vijñāna*] by listening would not be able to fully grasp [i.e., ripen] its seed.
>
> [Question:] How, though, if matured consciousness with all the seeds is cause of afflictions (*saṃkleśa-hetu*), could it still be the seed of the transcendental mind which is their antidote? The transcendental mind is not mixed [with ordinary experiences], so there is no residual impression left by it. In the absence of a residual impression [27a] left by it one has to explain from what seed [transcendental wisdom] would arise.
>
> [Response:] [Transcendental wisdom] comes from the residual impression left by listening, an outflow seed of the extremely pure dharma element.
>
> [Question:] Well then, is the essence (Tib. *ngo bo*) of the residual impression left by understanding *ālaya-vijñāna* or not? If the essence is *ālaya-vijñāna* how can it be a seed of the antidote to the [*ālaya-vijñāna*]? If it is not, show how [*ālaya-vijñāna*] can be the place (*āśraya*) where the seed of the residual impression left by listening abides?
>
> [Response:] That which, contingent on the Buddhas' enlightenment, becomes a residual impression left by listening enters the place it abides.[20] It enters that matured consciousness in the sense of being 'combined' with it like milk and water. It [the residual impression left by listening] is not *ālaya-vijñāna* because it is the seed of its antidote. Based on a weak

residual impression, a middling residual impression comes about. Based on a middling residual impression, a great residual impression comes about. This is accompanied by a great deal of work listening, thinking, and contemplating. One should consider the weak, middling, and great residual impressions left by listening as seed of the Dharma-kāya. Since they are the antidote to *ālaya-vijñāna* they are included amongst what is not, essentially, *ālaya-vijñāna.* Hence, though they are ordinary, since they are an outflow of the transcendental extremely pure, dharma element,[21] they become the seed of transcendental mind. [27b] One should consider that, even though transcendental mind is yet to come about, still they are the antidote to the complete entanglement of afflictions, the antidote to going to a bad rebirth and the direct antidote to getting involved in all wrongdoing. They are conducive to meeting with Buddhas and Bodhisattvas. Though ordinary in respect of new Bodhisattvas they are included in the Dharma-kāya and they are included in the Śrāvakas' and Pratyeka-buddhas' Vimukti-kāya ('Liberation Body'). They are not *ālaya-vijñāna,* they are included in the Dharma-kāya and in the Vimukti-kāya. To the extent that they gradually increase through weak, middling, and great, the matured consciousness declines and there is a fundamental transformation (*āśraya-parāvṛtta*). When the fundamental transformation has occurred the matured consciousness with all the seeds becomes seedless and is completely abandoned.

How does the abiding of *ālaya-vijñāna* and what is not *ālaya-vijñāna,* an abiding together like water and milk, come to decline from that [state of togetherness]?

It is just like the fundamental transformation that occurs when milk in water is drunk by a swan or when, freed from ordinary attachment, the residual impressions of nonequipoise levels (*asamāhita-bhūmika-vāsanā*) decrease and the residual impressions of equipoise levels increase.

Tell us about [28a] a) "a seed which is an outflow of the extremely pure dharma-element" [27a1], b) " . . . [being] contingent on the Buddhas' enlightenment . . . " [27a3], c) the difference between the Dharma-kāya and Vimukti-kāya ('Liberation Body'), and d) the two examples for fundamental transformation.

[Response:] First, it says in the *Upanibandhana*:[22]

> The cause similar to the Buddhas' extremely pure dharma-element, free of adventitious obscuration, is the doctrine which is taught. Insofar as it [the doctrine] has issued from that cause [the pure dharma-element], it is similar to it. To give ear to that [doctrine] is to understand [literally,

'listen']. The residual impression [left] by that is the seed of the uncontaminated, transcendental mind [not of the *ālaya*], because the *ālaya-vijñāna* is not similar to it [and does not necessarily issue forth from it].

Second, again from the same [commentary]:[23]

The meaning of the statement "... contingent on the Buddhas' enlightenment ..."[24] is as follows. The transcendental wisdom, scentless and unhindered, [an enlightened mind] is the ground[25] of the residual impression of understanding doctrines which are taught, i.e., the sūtras, etc. The *ālaya-vijñāna* is not the ground. It proceeds simultaneously with that [residual impression].

Understanding doctrine, for example, is the ground of increase; the *ālaya-vijñāna* is the ground of the basis.[26]

Third, again from the same [commentary]:[27]

The difference between the Dharma-kāya and Vimukti-kāya is as follows: The Vimukti-kāya is simply being without afflictive obscurations (*kleśāvaraṇa*). It is like, for example, when a villager is released from shackles, etc. Suffering is removed. That is the entire result, there is no greater special thing like attaining majesty, etc.

The Dharma-kāya is the liberation from afflictive obscurations and from obscurations to knowing (*jñeyāvarana*) [28b] along with their residual impressions, ornamented by many amazing qualities such as the [ten] powers and the [four] fearlessnesses.[28] It is the ground of all endowments and, since one enjoys as one wishes, it is the attainment of the most excellent freedom. It is like, for example, when a prince is freed from shackles. At once he is anointed and invested with complete and most excellent majesty.

Fourth, the swan example [for fundamental transformation] is from the point of view of something well-known to ordinary people, while the freedom from attachment example is from the point of view of what is well-known in the scriptures.

Thus those scholars who assert that the seed of uncontaminated [transcendental wisdom] is an *ālaya-vijñāna* are seen to have an unrefined opinion because they hold a view contrary to this [MSam] quotation.

Now, setting aside this discursus, let us return to our general explanation.

Derivation of the word *ālaya*

Question: Why is this seed part of the *ālaya* called *ālaya*?

> It is called *ālaya* because thoroughly afflicted dharmas meet back to it, either as result or as cause entities. [Mv XXX]

I will explain in accord with [the MSam], which says:[29]

> Why are these [seeds] called *ālaya-vijñānas*?
> They are called *ālaya-vijñāna* because all thoroughly afflicted dharmas which arise adhere (*ālīna*) to it as results (*phala-bhāva*) or because it adheres to them as [their] cause. It is also called *ālaya-vijñāna* since all living beings adhere to it as a self.

These three word derivations, given as though the derivation of the word for a single thing, are from the point of view of the seed and matured parts [of the *ālaya*] not having been separately delineated. They are explained separately as follows.

Generally, the meaning of the term *ālaya* is [29a] 'that to which all dharmas meet back.' In particular, the seed part of the *ālaya* is termed *ālaya* because the set of seven consciousnesses are included [as transformations of it] or because, since [the *ālaya*] functions as causal condition for all thoroughly afflicted dharmas—*kleśa*, action, and birth—they meet back to it as its results. Alternatively, in that these dharmas function as cause entities of that same [seed] *ālaya* they meet back to it. Hence it is called *ālaya*.

The matured part of *ālaya-vijñāna* is termed *ālaya-viijñāna* because all five types of migrators, on account of *kliṣṭa-manas*, adhere to it as themselves.[30]

Cessation of *ālaya-vijñāna*

Question: At what point does that sort of seed part [of *ālaya-vijñāna*] stop?

> Hence the Empowered One and Arhant do not have *ālaya-vijñāna* since the two placers are not present. [Mv XXXI]

'Hence' [means]: Because of the fact that thoroughly afflicted dharmas meet back to the seed *ālaya* either as its result entities or else as its cause entities, and because of the fact that this [*ālaya*] is adhered to as a self by *kliṣṭa-manas*. Because of that, therefore empowered Bodhisattvas—those of the eighth level and above—and Śrāvaka and Pratyeka-buddha Arhants are, specifically, free of the seed part of *ālaya-vijñāna*, and, in general, free of *ālaya-vijñāna*. This is because, having eliminated all afflictive emotion (*kleśa*), neither of the two placers are there at all. This [reason] is not unproven (*asiddha*) for it says [in the MSam]:[31]

> Śrāvakas and trainee (*śaikṣa*) Bodhisattvas are characterized by revealing [the elimination of] a portion [of *kleśa-* and *jñeyāvaraṇa*]. Applicable to Arhants and Pratyeka-buddhas is the characteristic of revealing [the elimination of] afflictive obscuration in its entirety [29b] and, to Tathāgatas, the characteristic of revealing [the elimination of] obscuration to understanding in its entirety as well.

Specifically, the *Guhyārtha-vyākhyā* explains when the three residual impressions[32] are removed:[33]

> The residual impression-seeds that are branches of existence are there until the resultant maturation comes about. The seeds of *sat-kāya-dṛṣṭi*[34] and the residual impression-seeds [left] by harmful elaboration (*prapañca*) are there until their antidote is achieved. The residual impression-seeds [left] by virtuous and neutral elaboration (*prapañca*) are there until Śrāvakas and Pratyeka-buddhas pass completely into nirvāṇa. In the case of Tathāgatas, the continuum of [those elaboration seeds], in the sense of their merely having a presence, remains until the diamondlike [*samādhi*].

[Objection:] If the *ālaya-vijñāna* is not present in Empowered Ones and Arhants, does one have to assert that eight consciousnesses are present in their continuum or not? If one does have to [assert eight consciousnesses], then an *ālaya-vijñāna* must be present, otherwise it would be a consciousness not included in the group of eight. If one does not have to [hold that eight consciousnesses are present] it damages one's assertion that the maturation [*ālaya*] remains until diamondlike [*samādhi*] and nonresidual [nirvāṇa].

[Response:] There is no flaw here. Though the *ālaya-vijñāna* is always a maturation consciousness, maturation consciousness is not always an *ālaya-vijñāna*. An Empowered One and Arhant have maturation consciousnesses but [to talk of] their having the *ālaya-vijñāna* would be meaningless. The second fault is thus avoided.[35] And when, in teaching the set of eight [consciousnesses], the *ālaya-vijñāna* is formulated as the eighth, [a consciousness] of that type is intended, not the material reality (Tib. *rdzas*) itself. [30a] Otherwise, [if an actual *ālaya-vijñāna* was meant, in the context of defining the relationship between entering and *ālaya* consciousnesses], it would have been improper [for Asaṅga, in the *Viniścaya-saṁgrahaṇī* of the *Yogācāra-bhūmi*, as quoted below 30a4] to have mentioned the *nirodha-samāpatti* ('absorption into cessation') of the Arhants, and Bodhisattvas on the eighth level and above, as the side[36] where there is [both] no entering consciousness and no *ālaya-vijñāna*.

It is also not proper to say that [Asaṅga means Arhants and empowered Bodhisattvas] have no seed part of the *ālaya-vijñāna* [but do have basis *ālaya-vijñāna*], because he says maturation part is *ālaya-vijñāna* to the extent that the *kliṣṭa-manas* adheres to it as a self [and *kliṣṭa-manas* has been removed from their minds]. Thus it says in the *Guhyārtha-vyākhyā*:[37]

> In regard to the statement, "It applies to maturation consciousness." It does not necessarily follow that this refers to the *ālaya-vijñāna*, because, though that [*ālaya*] does not exist in the continuum of Bodhisattvas who are on the eighth level, etc., nor in the continuum of Arhants and Pratyeka-buddhas, the maturation consciousness does.

And it also says in the *Viniścaya-saṁgrahaṇī* that there are four sides to the relation [between *ālaya-vijñāna* and *pravṛtti-vijñāna*].[38] It says the [first] side of the relation, where there is *ālaya-vijñāna* but not entering consciousness, is the five states of unconsciousness. The opposite to this [i.e., where there is entering consciousness but no *ālaya-vijñāna*] is the conscious state of nontrainees [Arhants] and irreversible Bodhisattvas. The [third] side, where there are both, is when there is any other conscious state. [The side where] there is neither is the state of *nirodha-samāpatti* ('absorption into cessation') and nonresidual nirvāṇa of nontrainees and irreversible Bodhisattvas.

Also the *Trimiśikā-kārikā* says:[39] [30b]

> After the state of the Arhant it turns back.

One should, therefore, take what we have explained above about the limits of the *ālaya-vijñāna* to be the last word on the matter.

Thus, the eighth consciousness found in the continuums of empowered Bodhisattvas and Arhants is called maturation consciousness or "the consciousness taken after deaths beyond number." It is not called *ālaya-vijñāna*.[40]

Question: If you say this in respect of Empowered Ones and Arhants then they would have no minds, for it is said [in the MSam]:[41]

> And why is it called *citta* ('mind')?
>
> . . . because it is the external accumulation [*ācitatva* from √*ci*, to accumulate] on account of the residual impression-seeds left by different dharmas.

[Response:] This quotation's meaning is not applicable. A mind (*citta, sems*), thinking- mind (*manas, yid*), and consciousness (*vijñāna, rnam shes*) are spoken of in the sūtra.[42] A third category that is mind, different again to thinking-mind and consciousness, is mentioned [here]. Apart from *ālaya-vijñāna* such a mind is not to be found. In this context the mind (*citta*) has to be explained as an accumulation, and while the *ālaya-vijñāna* is an accumulation (*ācita*) of all the residual impressions, thinking-mind and consciousness do not fulfill such a meaning. This is what is intended here. Nevertheless, even though there is nothing different from thinking-mind and consciousness that has accumulated residual impressions other than these [*ālaya-vijñāna*], there still is [another, more general understanding of] mind that fulfills the concept set forth in the statement that "consciousness is what beholds an object."[43] This is so a) because 'mind' does not definitely mean only what has accumulated residual impressions, and b) because no other manner of positing the *ālaya* beyond the three or two ways[44] has been mentioned.

The MSam also says in the same vein:[45] [31a]

> There is no third category that is mind, outside of *ālaya-vijñāna*, to be found. For this reason *ālaya-vijñāna* is established to be the category mind (*citta*).

Let us now examine this. Some scholars say that it is Hīnayānists who assert that the maturation part [of the *ālaya-vijñāna*] is removed after Hīnayāna nonresidual [nirvāṇa] is attained. Well then, let us see if this assertion [that the maturation part is removed after attainment of Hīnayāna nonresidual nirvāṇa] is made by deficient (*hīna*) Vaibhāṣika and Sautrāntika philosophers, or if it is asserted by those who are stationed on deficient Śrāvaka and Pratyeka-buddha paths. It cannot be the former because neither of those propounders of tenets accept the existence of any consciousness other than the group of six. And it is not the latter either. One would have to show the system whereby they ascertain the coming about and removal of the *ālaya-vijñāna* and that is not to be found.

So, then, whose assertion is it? [Answer:] This extensive presentation of the coming about, and removal of, the *ālaya-vijñāna* occurs in Yogācāra texts.

[Objection:] In that case, from the point of view of a Mahāyāna school, there could be a Hīnayāna [yogin] who finishes and eliminates obscurations to knowledge (*jñeyāvaraṇa*) because, when nonresidual nirvāṇa [is attained], the maturation part [of the *ālaya-vijñāna*] is removed.

[Response:] There is no flaw here. At the time of such nonresidual nirvāṇa there is no elimination of all obscurations to knowledge through the Hīnayāna path gradually making their potential weaker and weaker. Nevertheless, obscurations to knowledge are removed in the sense that their continuum is cut, because the continuum of the five aggregates is stopped [at that time].

This reason is not unproven. At the time of nonresidual [nirvāṇa] the Arhant casts off the composite life. It is a given that, if, after death, awareness were to occur then birth [31b] would have to be taken. Because he has eliminated all action and afflictive emotion (*kleśa*), and because the matured aggregates produced by those have been removed, he does not take rebirth through the force of action and afflictive emotions. Furthermore no form of action and afflictive emotions has the potential to produce a body because this is a state of utter peace and because the locus [for a person] (Tib. *rten*) has stopped. Hence, this [state of nirvāṇa] is simply the calming of all elaborations (*prapañca*), the sphere without signs that is the severance of the continuum of the ongoing composites.

[Objection:] This then would be no different to the sphere without signs of the Mahāyāna.

[Response:] Not so. This is just the calming [i.e., nonexistence] of the ongoing composites. From that peaceful sphere the body that does the work of others does not shine out, because on the path there was no meditation for the sake of others. And in the *Viniścaya-saṁgrahaṇī*, as referred to above, it says that nonresidual nirvāṇa is the side where there is neither *ālaya-vijñāna* nor entering consciousness [so that nirvāṇa differs from the Bodhisattva's enlightenment where the consciousnesses transform into wisdoms]. Also, one cannot say "this is comparable to the Hearers" because this is a time when one is ascertaining if *ālaya-vijñāna* exists.

Hence, the Vaibhāṣikas accept that, at the time of nonresidual [nirvāṇa], the cutting of the continuum of the composite [skandhas], which is an analytic cessation, is a substantially established noncomposite phenomenon. The Sautrāntikas, on the other hand, accept it [nirvāṇa] to be a void, nonaffirming, utter negation of the composite and accept that there are no aggregates at all. They thus accept a nonsubstantially established noncomposite phenomenon. Both of these schools think that this [nonresidual nirvāṇa] is the meaning of the sūtra:

> When the body is at ease, feeling is cooled, discrimination is negated, volition is at peace, and when consciousness has subsided: the end of suffering is like this. [32a]

Specifically, Sautrāntikas, since it says that the Arhant's mental liberation is like the extinguishing of a flame:

> Their minds become liberated like a flame that has gone out.

model their philosophy in accord with that.

Cittamātrins assert [nirvāṇa] to be the final reality (*tathatā*) where material and mental activity is stilled, where there is no sensory happiness but where there is the stable happiness of the freedom from pain; not a void, nonaffirming, utter negation; not something substantially established but yet permanently unchanging. Therefore, [according to the Cittamātrins], entrance into the Mahāyāna is possible right up to residual [nirvāṇa]. Following that it is not. As it says in the *Viniścaya-saṁgrahaṇī*:[46]

> Does the Śrāvaka who will get to become fully enlightened establish incomparable, completely perfect enlightenment stationed in the sphere of nirvāṇa with the residue of the aggregates, or does he do so stationed in the sphere of the nirvāṇa without the residue of the aggregates?
>
> He does so while in the sphere of the nirvāṇa with the residue of the aggregates. For when one is in the sphere of the nirvāṇa without the residue of the aggregates there is no work on any undertaking at all and the continuum of all striving is cut.

Some, who do not differentiate between such assertions, and take Madhyamaka and Cittamātra as a single unit, [mistakenly] assert that the maturation consciousness is removed at the stage of Hīnayāna nonresidual nirvāṇa, while others [32b] [mistakenly] assert that it is not removed [at that stage], since there has to be entry into the Mahāyāna even from the nonresidual stage. Such persons have confidence in a position that is agonizingly difficult [to defend].

A more extensive teaching along these lines can be found in the commentary on the *Viniścaya-saṁgrahaṇī's* outline for [the nirvāṇas] with aggregates and without aggregates[47] and also in the *Abhisamayālaṁkārālokā's* explanation[48] of [*Abhisamayālaṁkāra* 2.2]:[49] " . . . [Mahāyāna lineage] has a definite place and is pervasive . . . ."

At this stage it goes without saying that one could tie in what is found in the great texts and deal with Niḥsvabhāva-vādin and Cittamātrin views about the sūtras which mention three vehicles or one vehicle along with their proofs as to whether [these sūtras] are interpretive (*neyārtha*) or definitive (*nītārtha*). But those of dull intelligence can go insane if there is too much said so I shall leave it there.

This completes the explanation of all the difficult points concerning the maturation and seed *ālayas*.

Notes

1. *Guhyārtha-vyākhyā* P5553:80.2.6ff. See the *Vijñapti-mātratā siddhi* (La Vallée Poussin 1928-9:102ff) where such views are associated with Candra-pāla, Nanda and Śrīsena, and Dharma-pāla, respectively. Gung thang (Wilson 1984:607-

12) says Bu ston says that Sthiramati asserts the first position, Paramārtha the second, and Paramasena and Nandasena the third. Gung thang, quoting 'Jam dbyangs bshad pa says Ma ti Paṇ chen also associated the views with these writers. Also see Introduction note 72.

2. Bbh (Dutt 1966:2) *tatra prakṛti-sthaṁ gotraṁ yad bodhisattvānāṁ ṣaḍ-āyatana-viśeṣaḥ sa tādṛśaḥ paraṁparāgato' nādikāliko dharmatā-pratilabdhaḥ.*

3. Tsong kha pa is perhaps paraphrasing the *Guhyārtha-vyākhyā.*

4. An analogy for this might be when a child goes to school and learns the first letters of the alphabet. The initial understanding leaves an impression on the mind, i.e., a seed on the *ālaya.* On subsequent days the child returns to learn the alphabet. The seeds laid down by the earlier correct understanding are awakened and the increasing understanding again lays down a yet stronger residual impression. As the child continues studying, and learns the entire alphabet, corrects all mistakes and becomes habituated to the letters, a deeper ability of the human child, the ability (*vāsanā*) to learn to read sentences, paragraphs and finally complex connected passages in a language has been awakened. This deeper ability is innate and unlearned.

5. Cp. *Guhyārtha-vyākhyā* P5553:51.4.2. Obermiller (1931:100) paraphrases: "Absolute reality (*yongs grub*) manifests itself in two forms: the active and the immutable (*nitya*). The first of these has again two varieties—the pure transcendental wisdom of the Buddha and the germ of this transcendental wisdom [see Introduction note 45]. It is . . . of two kinds, viz. the primordial and that which becomes developed."

6. The full title is *[Ārya]-pañcaviṁśati-sāhasrikā-prajñāpāramitopadeśa-śāstrābhisamayālaṁkāra-vṛtti.* The Skt. (Pensa 1967:76) is *ṣaḍ-āyatana-viśeṣo gotraṁ tad dvi-vidhaṁ: prayaya-samudānītaṁ, prakṛtyavasthitaṁ cetyapare.*

7. Although Tsong kha pa possibly is quoting directly from the *Ratna-gotra-vibhāga-mahāyānottara-tantra-śāstra* (Johnston 1950:73.14-16) *sarvatra dharmataiva pratiśaraṇam / dharmataiva yuktiś citta-nidhyāpanāya citta-saṁjñāpanāya,* translated by Obermiller (1931:231) "In every case, for the accurate investigation of the spiritual element and correct knowledge about it, the Absolute Essence must be resorted to, and represents a logical foundation" it is more likely he is simply summarizing the RGV, particularly I 149 (Johnson 1950:73ff=Obermiller 1931:229ff). Cp. the statement in *Legs bshad snying po* (translated by Thurman 1989:259).

8. A paraphrase of MSam (Lamotte 1938:18; Nagao I 44).

9. Tsong kha pa's argument defending the Yogācāra doctrine of two lineages against the Mādhyamika's second charge, namely, that the cause of the Svābhāvika-kāya would be a composite phenomenon, is difficult to follow. It presupposes the Yogācāra doctrines: a) that ultimate reality consists of an emptiness inexpressible as being one with, or different from, the wisdom which knows it; b) that emptiness is noncomposite and wisdom is composite; c) that buddhahood is described under the rubric of Dharma-kāya and Rūpa-kāya, the former the outcome of the wisdom

collection (*jñāna-saṁbhara*) and the latter the outcome of the merit collection (*puṇya-saṁbhara*); d) that Dharma-kāya is subdivided into Svābhāvika-kāya and Jñāna-dharma-kāya; e) the Svābhāvika-kāya is again subdivided (this is probably a uniquely Tibetan contribution to Yogācāra) into 'Body of naturally pure own-being' (*Svabhāva-śuddha-svabhāva-kāya) and 'Body of own-being purified of temporary defilement' (*Āgantuka-mala-śuddha-svabhāva-kāya); f) that the Rūpa-kāya is subdivided into Saṁbhoga-kāya and Nirmāṇa-kāya; and g) that all kāyas, apart from the Svābhāvika-kāya and its subdivisions, are composite and require a cause or lineage which is composite.

10. Cp. MSam quoted below "... the residual impression left by listening, an outflow seed of the extremely pure dharma element" (Nagao I 45) and "One should consider the ... residual impression left by listening as seed of the Dharma-kāya" (Nagao I 48).

11. MSU P5552:263a2-3 trans. by Lamotte (1938:vol. 2, 69).

12. This is a literal translation. It is saying that "The Dharma-kāya is a fundamental reality revealed by the removal of all hindrances to full enlightenment. This fundamental reality is itself the basis of all the qualities which define full enlightenment." In Asaṅga's statement that "The seed of stainless [wisdom] is the seed of the Dharma-kāya," Dharma-kāya refers only to *Svabhāva-śuddha-svabhāva-kāya and *Āgantuka-mala-śuddha-svabhāva-kāya, both of which are noncomposite and require a noncomposite cause.

13. The point is that 'Dharma-kāya' in this context refers to the composite Jñāna-dharma-kāya, the lineage or cause of which is the composite developed lineage.

14. Cp. *Ratnāvalī* (Hahn 1982:3 and 12).

15. Cp. RGV I 149-50 (Johnson 1950:71-2) *gotraṁ tad-dvi-vidham jñeyaṁ nidhāna-phala-vṛkṣavat / anādi-prakṛtisthaṁ ca samudānītam uttaram // buddha-kāya-trayāvāptir asmād-gotra-dvayātmatā / prathamāt prathamaḥ kāyo dvitīyād dvau tu paścimau.*

16. Cp. AA 1.39 which reads (Wogihara 1973:76) *dharma-dhātor asambhedād gotra-bhedo na yujyate/ ādeya-dharma-bhedāt tu tad-bhedaḥ parigīyate.*

17. The Sanskrit of MSA 3.2 (Levi 1907-11:10-11) is *dhātūnām adhimukteś ca pratipatteś ca bhedataḥ / phala-bhedopalabdheś ca gotrāstitvaṁ nirūpyate // ... asti yāna-traye gotra-bhedaḥ.*

18. The exact passage to which Tsong kha pa is referring has not been identified.

19. MSam (Lamotte 1938:18-20; Nagao I 44-49). For more suggestions as to the probable Sanskrit see also Schmithausen (1987:nn. 574, 580, and 582). Cp. also the discussion by Schmithausen (pp. 79-81 especially n. 572). Translated by Davidson (1985:215-17). It is difficult to agree with Davidson's comment that "the seed of the auditory traces ... as is obvious from the section is foreign to the *ālaya-vijñāna.*"

20. Cp. Lamotte's translation of Hsüan Tsang's version of this passage (1938:vol. 2, 67) "Jusqu'à ce qu'on obtienne l'illumination des Buddha, cette imprégnation d'audition, selon qu'elle réside dans n'importe quel lieu de fonctionnement qui lui sert de support (*āśraya-pravṛtti-sthāna*), réside provisoirement dan la connaissance-rétribution...."

21. The Sanskrit is *suviśuddha-dharmadhātu-niśyanda* ('a necessary outflow of the pure dharma element.') Schmithausen (1987:81 and n. 582) translates "outflow of true reality completely freed from [accidental impurities]." Tib °*rgyu mthun* could be a literal rendering, if the Tibetan translators understood a bahuvrīhi "of which the necessary outflow is the pure dharma element," and added the word *rgyu* ('cause') as the understood noun being qualified. If this is the case one should translate °*rgyu mthun* as "the concordant [result] when the pure dharma element is cause." Although this may be the case, a less contrived reading of the Tibetan is "a cause similar to, or concordant with, the dharma element." Because of the peculiar manner in which Buddhist thinkers understood *nisyanda* both translations come to mean the same thing.

22. MSU P5552:261b6-8.

23. MSU P5552:262a1-2.

24. If one reads *kyis*, the passage is rendered "All the Buddhas, contingent on [their] enlightenment..."

25. Nagao gives the Sanskrit of *gnas* 'ground' as *āśraya*. It means 'cause.'

26. That is, understanding doctrine leaves residual impressions which cause the seed of transcendental wisdom to develop to maturity. Other residual impressions function as a basis for further contaminated ordinary experiences. Also see n. 4.

27. MSU P5552:263a1-2. Cp. Lamotte's translation of Hsüan Tsang's version of this passage (1938:vol. 2, 69).

28. The ten powers attributed to Bodhisattvas are: 1) devotion to the Buddha's teaching, without attachment, 2) increase in devotion, 3) expedient ability to instruct people and alter their conduct, 4) ability to understand others' thoughts, 5) ability to satisfy others' desires, 6) continuous exertion, 7) the inclusion of all vehicles without abandoning the Mahāyāna, 8) ability to show the appearance of the Buddhas in all worlds in each pore of the body, 9) ability to cause people to turn toward the Buddha's teachings and to lead them to perfection, and 10) ability to satisfy all types of people with only a single phrase. The four fearlessnesses attributed to Bodhisattvas are: Their discourses are fearless since they 1) do not forget, 2) are in tune with the listeners' abilities, 3) solve difficult points, and 4) answer every question. Thus, whereas the Śrāvakas and Pratyeka-buddhas achieve merely the Vimukti-kāya, a liberation from worldly turmoil, Bodhisattvas come to command a fearless freedom within the world on the basis of their attainment of a Dharma-kāya.

29. MSam (Lamotte 1938:4; Nagao I 3). The translation is aided by Schmithausen (1987: n. 137).

30. As above *Ocean of Eloquence* 11b5-6.

31. MSam (Lamotte 1938:24; Nagao I 61).

32. These are listed above *Ocean of Eloquence* 15b4: a) the designation residual impression (*abhilāpa-vāsanā*), b) the view of self (*ātma-dṛṣṭi*), and c) the branches of existence (*bhavāṅga*).

33. *Guhyārtha-vyākhyā* P5553:69.2.3-4.

34. Tibetan *'jig tshogs la lta ba* translates Sanskrit *sat-kāya-dṛṣṭi* (literally "holding to the dogma of the reality of the physical body"). The Tibetan is explained, as above, as mistakenly viewing (Tib. *lta ba*) the five aggregates, which are perishable (Tib. *'jig*) and a collection (Tib. *tshogs*), as a permanent and single soul.

35. Wilson (1984:375-6) translates "the two faults."

36. There are three- or four-sided (Tib. *mu=koṭi*) relationships. The former (Tib. *mu gsum*) obtains between, for example, Socrates and man. A four-sided relationship (Tib. *mu bzhi*) obtains (as in the quotation from the VS below) between, for example, Socrates and a youth. The youth Socrates is the first side, the old man Socrates the second side, a youth other than Socrates the third side, and a rabbit the fourth.

37. *Guhyārtha-vyākhyā* P5553:80.5.5-6; discussed by Schmithausen (1987: n. 580).

38. An expansion of VS P5539:10a8. Discussed by Schmithausen (1987:81 nn. 586 and 588).

39. TK5a quoted above *Ocean of Eloquence* 14a2.

40. Cp. Schmithausen (1987:79 especially n. 580).

41. MSam (Lamotte 1938:6; Nagao I 9). Cp. also AS (Pradhan 1950:12) quoted below, *Ocean of Eloquence* 35b2.

42. Dīgha-nikāya I 21 according to Lamotte (1938:vol. 2, 15).

43. This is the meaning conveyed in the statement in, for example, AK2.34 (Pradhan 1967:61) *cittaṁ mano' tha vijñānam ekārtham* "mind, thinking-mind and consciousness have the same meaning."

44. Apparently referring to the two causes of the *ālaya* set forth in TK19 (quoted above *Ocean of Eloquence* 12a1-2) and the three prerequisites of an *ālaya* set forth at 12a4-5.

45. MSam (Lamotte 1938:6; Nagao I 8. The translation has been aided by Lamotte (1938:vol. 2, 22-3).

46. VS P5539:140b2. Cp. Schmithausen (1969:58).

47. VS P5539:136b8. Cp. Schmithausen (1969:40).

48. AAA (Wogihara 1973:129-137).

49. AA2.2 (Wogihara 1973:137) *viṣayo niyato vyāptiḥ*.

Five

Definition of *Kliṣṭa-manas*

How is the *kliṣṭa-manas* ('afflicted thinking-mind') defined?

> The *kliṣṭa-manas* is defined as that obscured (*nivṛta*) [mind], not the subject of moralizing, which views the maturation part of *ālaya-vijñāna* as self and has only nine [mental factors like contact, attachment, etc.]. [Mv XXXII]

Of the seed and maturation parts of *ālaya-vijñāna* it is the latter which is its objective support (*ālambana*). This is because its objective support must be something similar to an I. It is in the form (*ākāra*) of a belief that its objective support is I. As it says in the *Guhyārtha-vyākhyā*:[1]

> It is from the point of view of the idea (*ākāra*) of I arising, not from the point of view of its [the *ālaya's*] presenting its actuality.

Hence, even though the substance of the maturation does not actually appear, and thereby become the object [33a] of *kliṣṭa-manas*, it is, nevertheless, posited as the object [of *kliṣṭa-manas*] insofar as the force of that maturation consciousness causes it, itself [*vipāka-vijñāna*], to be simply mistaken for I.

[The *kliṣṭa-manas*] is *nivṛta* ('obscured') and not a subject of moralizing (*avyākṛta*).

What, though, do *nivṛta* and *anivṛta* ('unobscured') mean?

[Response]: By *nivṛta* is meant repeatedly polluted by afflictive emotions (*kleśa*) because this *[kliṣṭa-]manas* has been repeatedly polluted by the four root afflictive emotions (*kleśa*). By *anivrta* is meant not stained by afflictive emotions as, for example, the five sense-faculties or the eleven [virtuous mental factors] like faith.

Some persons hold the following opinion on this. Thinking that during the Ārya's meditative equipoise (*samāpatti*) there is no *kliṣṭa-manas*, but there is *ālaya-vijñāna*, they assert a) [that something is *nivṛta* if] it hinders (*nivṛta*) equipoise and [*anivṛta* if] it does not hinder meditative equipoise; and, thinking that liberation is not gained until all afflictive obscurations (*kleśāvaraṇa*) are eliminated they assert b) [that something is *nivṛta* if] it hinders liberation and [*anivṛta* if] it does not hinder liberation. Such persons do not know what *nivṛta* or *anivṛta* actually entails. Their idea is too restrictive because it defines both [*nivṛta* and *anivṛta*] only in relation to *kliṣṭa-manas* and *ālaya-vijñāna*.

Thus, the meaning of these two [i.e., whether a dharma is, or is not, *nivṛta* is to be decided] from examining whether or not a phenomenon is itself obscured (*nivṛta*) or unobscured, not whether it does or does not obscure something else. Otherwise, a) [in response to the first part of the above assertion], the portion of the Arya's virtuous or neutral thoughts which is a distraction [to being absorbed in contemplation of the ultimate] will [absurdly] be *nivṛta* because it is a hindrance to meditative equipoise. And b) [in response to the second part of the above assertion] since none of the three [Śrāvaka, Pratyeka-buddha, and Bodhisattva] liberations[2] is possible unless all the causes which definitely impel another rebirth are eliminated, the meritorious and unmoveable (*aniñjya*) karmas which definitely impel another rebirth [33b] would [absurdly] also be *nivṛta*.

And one cannot say of these [karmas which definitely impel another rebirth] that they are *nivṛta* because they are karmas which are thoroughly afflicted (*saṁkliṣṭa*). This is a) because an obscuration (*āvaraṇa*) is said to be either an afflictive emotion (*kleśa*) or else a physical, verbal or mental nonvirtue motivated by that, and b) because *anivṛta* virtues and thoroughly afflicted (*saṁkliṣṭa*) life would [absurdly] become *nivṛta*. Thus the *Abhidharma-samuccaya* says:[3]

> a) Nonvirtues and b) the *nivṛtas* which are not a subject of moralizing are afflicted (*kliṣṭam*). The *nivṛtas* which are not a subject of moralizing are a) *kleśa* associated with the mind that wanders [from rebirth to rebirth] (*sarvatraga-manas*), b) view that the perishable aggregate [is a single, permanent soul] (*sat-kāya-dṛṣṭi*), and c) extremism (*antagrāha-dṛṣṭi*) which arises simultaneously in association with the thinking-mind consciousness (*manovijñāna*), and d) which is associated with the [thinking-minds] of the form and formless realms as well.

and[4]

> Virtues and the *anivṛtas* which are not a subject of moralizing are not afflicted.

And the MSam says:[5]

> Being afflicted (*kliṣṭam*), the *[kliṣṭa]-manas* is a *nivṛta* ('something obscured') which is not a subject of moralizing. Always the four *nivṛta*

> *kleśas* ('obscured afflictive emotions') are in association with it. Like the afflictive emotions operating in the form and formless realms, this is a *nivṛta* which is not the subject of moralizing. This is because the afflictive emotions operating in the form and formless [realms] are embraced by calm-abiding [and are therefore obscured, and not the subject of moralizing], while the *[kliṣṭa-]manas*, which is always present, [will be the same].

[Question:] This, then, is what being *nivṛta* entails. Now, how is it ascertained that [*kliṣṭa-manas*] is never the subject of moralizing (*avyākṛta*)?

[Response:] Since it is afflicted (*kliṣṭam*) it is not virtuous, and since virtuous thoughts become manifest at the same time as it, in one continuum, it is not a nonvirtue either. Otherwise, [if *kliṣṭa-manas* were not *avyākṛta*], manifest virtuous and nonvirtuous thoughts could not arise in ordinary people. This is because this *[kliṣṭa-]manas* operates in a permanently manifest state until the Ārya path is produced.

[34a] Its associated [mental factors] are contact (*sparśa*) and the other four [omnipresent factors, mentioned above, 7b2-3] along with attachment, ignorance, pride, and opinion about self: in total nine. It says in the *Guhyārtha-vyākhyā*:[6]

> It has only nine mental factors associated with it—the four afflictive emotions and the five omnipresent ones taught earlier.

And the *Triṃśikā-kārikā* says:[7]

> Situated and fully derived from this [*ālaya-vijñāna*], and with that place as its objective support, is [*kliṣṭa-*]*manas*. It is a mind in the form of the thought "this is me." It is a *nivṛta* ('obscured') which is not the subject of moralizing and it is always assisted by four afflictive emotions: opinion about I (*ātma-dṛṣṭi*), stupidity about I (*ātma-moha*), pride in I (*ātma-māna*), and self-love (*ātma-sneha*). It is of that [level] on which it was born and there are also the other [five mental factors associated with it] such as contact, etc.

What feeling (*vedanā*) is associated with it?

[Response:] The feeling is always neutral (*upekṣā*). If [the feeling] were happiness (*sukha*) it would have to be mental happiness, in which case, since that would entail continually manifest mental happiness, ordinary people would then [absurdly] not experience pain at all. Also [the four formless meditative states (*āyatana*)] above the fourth concentration (*dhyāna*) would [absurdly] become levels where there was a feeling of happiness.[8] Also, there would [absurdly] be constant mental happiness even in the deepest region of hell.[9] This is not uncertain (*anaikāntika*) [i.e., it is not the case that at certain times there is one feeling and at certain times another], because, no matter which of the three realms [*kāma-*, *rūpa-* and *arūpya-dhātu*], there are not more or less [mental factors] associated [with *kliṣṭa-manas*. Hence one cannot posit a time when *vedanā* is absent]. And, since [*kliṣṭa-manas*] is a constant consciousness, it is a primary mind (*maula-citta*) and its mental factors (*caitta*) come into, and go out of, being at the same time as it does. [Hence the *vedanā* associated with it must always be the same.] One can infer from this reasoning why the feeling [associated with the *kliṣṭa-manas*] is not suffering.

Therefore, the pleasurable aspect of the *kliṣṭa-manas* is not in the form of a feeling of pleasure, [34b] it is in the form of pleasurable attachment, for the *Triṁśikā-kārikā* explains,[10] without specifying any feeling in particular, that the same five [mental factors] such as contact, etc., associated with *ālaya-vijñāna* are associated with the *[kliṣṭa-]manas* as well. Also the *Guhyārtha-vyākhyā* says:[11]

> Although there is a pleasurable aspect to it, there is no mental feeling. This is because, when [*Trimśikā-kārikā* 7a, quoted 34a3] says: "It is of that [level] on which it was born . . . ," it enumerates, as in the context [of the *ālaya*], just those such as contact, etc. Were the feeling to have been different it would have been specified.

And,

> If [the feeling] is neutral (*upekṣā*) how could there be a pleasurable aspect to [*kliṣṭa-manas*]?
>
> [Response:] Because of the association of self-love.

How could its surrounding [mental factors] be only nine? Are there not also the following six: a) distraction (*vikṣepa*) implicit[12] in [the opinion] "I am here," b) carelessness (*pramāda*) implicit in attachment and stupidity, c) fixation implicit in attachment; and d) absence of faith (*aśraddhā*), e) laziness (*kausīdya*), and f) dullness (*styāna*) implicit in the stupidity part? Are there not, therefore, fifteen [mental factors] surrounding [*kliṣṭa-manas*]?

[Response:] Although those [six mental factors] are said to be there, still the number [of mental factors associated with *kliṣṭa-manas*] is exactly nine. This is because the bases for imputing these six are the material realities (Tib. *rdzas*) of the four afflictive emotions [opinion about I, stupidity about I, pride in I, and self-love]. [The six] do not exist apart from those four. That there is no mental factor beyond the material realities of these nine can be understood in detail from the *Vivṛta-guhyārtha-piṇḍa-vyākhyā*.[13] Fearing prolixity and because it is not really a difficult idea, I will not pursue it here.

Fifth,[14] investigation of the levels.[15]

Question: Is the *kliṣṭa-manas* [on the same level as] the level on which the person,[16] in whose [mind-]stream it exists, was born or not? If the former [i.e., if the *kliṣṭa-manas* is always the same level as its *ālaya-vijñāna*], when an ordinary desire-[realm] person [35a] becomes freed from attachment to objects of the desire-[realm] he would, [absurdly], still not have removed [desire-realm] *kliṣṭa-manas* [because the desire-realm *ālaya-vijñāna* remains and, in this first case, the *kliṣṭa-manas* and its *ālaya-vijñāna* are said to be the same level]. Hence desire[-realm] afflictive emotion [such as the four afflictive emotions associated with the *kliṣṭa-manas*] would, [absurdly], still be manifestly operating in the [mind-] stream [even when they have been removed]. If the latter, [i.e., if the *kliṣṭa-manas* is not always the same level as its *ālaya-vijñāna*], given that the *kliṣṭa-manas* and its surrounding [mental factors] cling to the person's *ālaya-vijñāna* as I, since there would be impartiality, desire[-realm] afflictive emotions would not increase.[17]

[Response:] We do not accept the latter view because [*Trimśikā-kārikā* 7a, quoted at 34a3] says

> It is of that [level] on which it was born

and because there are the faults just described.

[Objection:] There are also faults in the first view outlined above.

[Response:] There is no fault here. The meaning of an ordinary person being without attachment to objects of the desire[-realm] is as follows. Principally, it is being without attachment to sexual intercourse (*maithuna*). And, if there is none of the unpleasantness of the mental unhappiness (*daurmanasya*) [encountered] prior to achieving calm abiding, and, if manifest longing for the five objects of desire (*kāma-guṇa*) does not make the [mind-]stream feel unpleasant, then, just a certain amount of greed and anger [but not all] will be eliminated by directing one's attention to outer [shortcomings]. The *kliṣṭa-manas* is associated with the ingrained view of I, however, and until the power of its antidote—uncontaminated wisdom—is produced it cannot be removed.

When does the *kliṣṭa-manas* cease to operate?

> [It] temporally [ceases] during cessation, absorption, and, finally, at the time of the Empowered One and Arhant. [Mv XXXIII]

There are two times when it is removed: first a time of temporary removal and second a final removal. The first is up to the eighth [Bodhisattva] level, on occasions when someone who has not attained the path of no-more-learning (*aśaikṣa-mārga*) enters cessation or during an Ārya's meditative equipoise. The second is [35b] [at the stage of] empowered Bodhisattvas—those of the eighth level and above—and Śrāvaka and Pratyeka-buddha Arhants. Thus the *Triṁśikā-kārikā* says:[18]

> It does not exist [at the stage of] Arhant; it does not exist when absorbed in cessation; it does not exist on the transcendental path. This change [of *kliṣṭa-manas* to a transcendental wisdom] is the second one. [The first is the fundamental change of the *ālaya-vijñāna*].

Also the *Abhidharma-samuccaya* says:[19]

> What is *manas*?
>
> It is the continual selfishness (*manyanā*) that has the *ālaya-vijñāna* as its objective support and has associated with it four afflictive emotions: opinion about I, attachment to I, and pride and ignorance in the thought "I am." Except when the path [i.e., direct vision of the ultimate] is manifest, when absorbed in cessation or on the level of no-more-learning it goes with every virtuous, nonvirtuous and neutral [state of mind]. It is also the consciousness that ceases just prior to the six consciousnesses.[20]

Therefore *manas* is two[fold]: the egotistical *manas*, and the just-prior *manas*. These are also called 'ultimate *manas*' and 'conventional *manas*,' because [the ultimate *manas*][21] is not contingent on another consciousness and exists self-sufficiently as a material reality and [conventional *manas*] is not posited apart from the group of six's [consciousnesses]. The first, then, [i.e., egotistical *manas*] produces all that is contaminated and thoroughly afflicted by functioning as that basis on which the six [kinds of consciousness'] enthralment with marks comes about. The second [i.e., the just-prior *manas*] functions as the immediate condition of the six, giving the next consciousness the occasion to arise by force of its removal. Thus it is said [MSam]:[22]

> There are two aspects to *manas*. [First] is the ground for the production of consciousness (*vijñāna*), [called] [36a] "the *manas* that ceases just prior to consciousness."[23] It is basis in that it functions as immediately preceding condition (*samanantara-pratyaya*). The second is the *manas* that is afflicted (*kliṣṭaṃ*). With it are always associated four afflictive emotions: view that the perishable aggregate [is a single, permanent soul] (*sat-kāya-dṛṣṭi*), pride in the thought "I am" (*asmimāna*), self-love, and ignorance. It is basis for the thorough affliction of consciousness. A consciousness is, then, produced by the basis supplied by the first and caused to be afflicted by the second. It is consciousness (*vijñāna*) since it perceives an object

(*viṣaya-prati-vijñapti*). Thus, since there is one just-previous (*samanantara*) and an egotistical thought (*manana*) *manas* is twofold.

[Objection]: If empowered Bodhisattvas, Arhants, and Āryas in meditative equipoise have no *kliṣṭa-manas*, then they would [absurdly] have no thinking-mind consciousness (*mano-vijñāna*) [i.e., the sixth of the set of eight consciousnesses] either. This is because the *kliṣṭa-manas* which is the governing condition (*adhipati-pratyaya*) of thinking-mind consciousness would, [absurdly], not exist. Empowered Bodhisattvas and Arhants would also [absurdly] obtain the transcendental wisdom of the sameness [of all] (*samatā-jñāna*). This is because it is said that[24]

> when *kliṣṭa-manas* fundamentally transforms it is to be called the transcendental wisdom of the sameness [of all]

and their *kliṣṭa-manas* has stopped in that way.

[Response:]

> Person-grasping (*pudgala-[ātma]-graha*), the thing that makes the afflicted one [*kliṣṭa-manas*] what it is, has stopped. Nevertheless, a) because its mere continuum (*rigs*) exists[25] and b) because the potential to produce dharma-grasping (*dharma-[ātma]-graha*) has not been stopped, both the flaw a) of there being no *mano-vijñāna* and b) of getting sameness [wisdom] are avoided. [Mv XXXIV]

In answering this I shall examine a) whether *manas* exists during meditative equipoise or not, and b) whether that *manas* has been contaminated (*āsrava*) or not.

First, [36b] even during meditative equipoise the stopping of *manas* is not because of its continuum of material reality being cut. This is because as we find in the *Saṁdhi-nirmocana-sūtra* a) even when *ālaya-vijñāna* is very much alone, one consciousness *manas* operates along with it, b) during meditative equipoise its objective support, the *ālaya*, is at hand, c) the *ālaya* furnishes [its] causal condition (*hetu-pratyaya*), and d) unlike the set of six [consciousnesses], which do not come about in the absence of different sorts of experiences like "This is the look of a shape," "This is the sound of a noise," [*kliṣṭa-manas*] operates as the same sort of thing until the end of cyclic existence. Thus the *Guhyārtha-vyākhyā* says:[26]

> The *mano-vijñāna* is not nonascertainable during the trainee's transcendental meditative equipoise because, even at that time, a

manas-evolute (Tib. *yid gyur pa*) remains. For the *Saṁdhi-nirmocana-sūtra* says:[27]

> Sometimes . . . as when there is *manas* . . . there is one [*vijñāna*],

and

> Sometimes . . . as when there is *mano-vijñāna* . . . there are two [*vijñānas*].

And, if [one points out that] what comes about at that time [of meditative equipoise] is something that is not *[kliṣṭa]-manas*, in regard to this, [when] what is not *[kliṣṭa]-manas* occurs it also explains that

> Sometimes . . . as when there is *mano-vijñāna* . . . there is one.

Furthermore, in regard to [the statement]

> Since, at the time of fainting, etc., the set of entering consciousnesses (*pravṛtti-vijñāna*) that are produced contingent on objects are not present, their continuums are cut.

How, given that a) *manas* is the same sort of thing until the end of cyclic existence, b) its objective support is at hand, [and] c) it comes about from the *ālaya-vijñāna* can its continuum be cut?

Second, the investigation of whether that *manas* is contaminated or not. There are systems of the two Cittamātrin Ācāryas [Asaṅga and Vasubandhu].

[37a] The first system holds that the *manas* during meditative equipoise is uncontaminated. This is because an afflicted and an uncontaminated consciousness do not exist in an ongoing manner at the same time in a single continuum, and the continuum of *manas* has not been cut. The four [afflictive emotions] such as the view [that] the perishable [aggregate is a single, permanent soul] remain, at that time, in mere seed-form. Furthermore, during meditative equipoise the *mano-vijñāna* with a direct vision of selflessness becomes uncontaminated. Just as the *ālaya* changes because of the presence of its seed of uncontaminated [wisdom], at that time the *manas* also, because of the nature (*dharmatā*) of the seed of uncontaminated [wisdom], changes and operates in an uncontaminated [fashion] together with the *ālaya*. When one arises [from meditative equipoise] and a contaminated virtuous thought, for example, becomes manifest, then the four root afflictive emotions also become manifest from the seeds of the four afflictive emotions [such as self-love, etc.] and make the *manas* afflicted (*kliṣṭa*). Thus the *Guhyārtha-vyākhyā* says:[28]

> Some say that *manas* is uncontaminated at that point. According to them, all the afflicted, the continuum of which does not come about because of

> the Ārya's meditative equipoise, enter a temporary seed-period. Uncontaminated in its own lineage from a time without beginning, and similar to the Ārya path which makes selflessness (*nairātmya*) manifest, an [uncontaminated] *ālaya-vijñāna* comes about.

In this system, then, since the four afflictive emotions are not manifest during meditative equipoise, there is also no *kliṣṭa-manas* polluted with their stains. Nevertheless, since a now uncontaminated *manas* devoid of those four [afflictive emotions] is asserted, they hold that there is still an empowering condition (*adhipati-pratyaya*).

In the second system[29] *manas* is asserted to be present during meditative equipoise and is also asserted [37b] to be contaminated, but, should one ask if it is contaminated by afflictive emotions the answer is no. How, otherwise, is it contaminated? [In response we say]: This *manas* which is the seventh [of the set of eight consciousnesses] has two potentials (Tib. *nus pa*): a) the potential to produce afflictive emotions when it again views the *ālaya* as self and b) the potential that comes from it functioning as the simultaneously arising basis of the *mano-vijñāna* that designates [things] with various expressions (*vyavahāra*). [This latter potential] produces dharma-grasping, the obscurations to knowing (*jñeyāvaraṇa*).

The first [potential] is what defines *manas* as afflicted. It is ongoing until such time as all afflictive emotions are removed, and stops when ignorance and wrong view are eliminated. Hence [Bodhisattvas] on and above the eighth level, and Arhants, remove the potential which produces person-grasping by their having eliminated every root and secondary afflictive emotion. Since, with removal of these [afflictive emotions], there is no longer the positing of anything as afflicted on their account, therefore the *kliṣṭa-manas* ('afflicted thinking-mind') is removed as well. The potential that produces dharma-grasping is not, however, removed [from] that *manas* and, since the continuum of the bare material reality of the clarity and knowing of that *manas* has not been cut, there is not the flaw of there being no *mano-vijñāna* on account of *mano-vijñāna* having no empowering condition. And, since the transcendental wisdom of the sameness [of all] is attained [only] when one is free from absolutely every stain, that transcendental wisdom does not come about because dharma-grasping is yet to be overcome.

Just this is correct. For it is accepted that consciousness arises when there is the completeness of each necessary condition. This *manas* which is the seventh [of the set of eight consciousnesses] gets to be afflicted by the force of the other four [afflictive emotions], not through its own actual identity. Thus it is correct to say that if its surrounding afflictive emotions—those afflictive obscurations (*kleśāvarana*)—are eliminated it is removed. [38a] It is not correct to hold that *manas* is removed even to the last part of its identity. For we assert that the meaning of fundamental change (*āśraya-parāvṛtti*) is one's nature becoming clear when, through the force of the path, all the adventitious flaws are brought to an end. Hence the *Guhyārtha-vyākhyā* says:[30]

> Some say it is defiled because, according to them, it possesses two potentials.

A detailed investigation of the latter system would also be as follows. Before the transcendental path arises grasping at persons and dharmas exist at the same time. If someone is an Ārya Śrāvaka, during meditative equipoise that *manas* does not superimpose a self of persons (*pudgalātman*) and understands clearly the meaning of the selflessness of persons (*pudgala-nairātmya*). In regard to dharmas [i.e., the superimposition of a self of dharmas (*dharmātman*)], the superimposition has not been removed so [*manas*] does not understand [*dharma-nairātmya*] clearly. [Four mental factors]: an ignorance, view, pride, and attachment that are not afflictive emotions are associated with [*manas* during an Ārya Śrāvaka's meditative equipoise]. Since they are not afflictive emotions they do not block the attainment of the Śrāvakas' result [the nirvāṇa where all *kleśāvarana* have been removed]. Still, they are not virtuous [mental factors].

If someone is an Ārya Bodhisattva, during meditative equipoise there is a direct vision of both selflessnesses. Therefore, since neither grasping at persons nor grasping at dharmas, which block the vision of the two selflessnesses, come into being [the *manas*] is uncontaminated. Thus the *Guhyārtha-vyākhyā* says:[31]

> Contingent on that ignorance which hinders[32] the simultaneous vision of the two selflessnesses, like imagining a snake where a wrong conception of the shape of a length of rope has gone before, the two views associated with *kliṣṭa-manas*: [38b] a) imagining persons and b) imagining dharmas arise together. Since, when the transcendental path arises, an Ārya Śrāvaka has a vision of the selflessness of persons, there is no superimposition of a self of persons. That *manas* is not [however] clear about dharmas and it comes about with the dullness (*moha*) and opinion (*dṛṣṭi*) of superimposition associated with it. Since these [mental factors such as dullness], which are not afflictive emotions, do not block the Śrāvakas' result, since they cause the desired result and since they cause nirvāṇa to be attained they are not virtuous [mental factors].

and[33]

> In regard to the dharma which is not afflicted, it has associated attachment and pride as well.

and[34]

> If someone is a Bodhisattva who has dedicated themself to enlightenment or who is naturally inclined that way,[35] during the period [of meditative equipoise] there is a totally uncontaminated [state] wherein both selflessnesses become manifest.

Question: How, then, is there an empowering condition (*adhipati-pratyaya*) for mental consciousness (Tib. *yid shes*) at the Buddha level?

[In response] it asks in the *Guhyārtha-vyākhyā*[36] if mirrorlike transcendental wisdom (*ādarśana-jñāna*) is perfumed with residual impressions or not? If it is perfumed then earlier Buddhas would [absurdly] be more powerful because the perfuming of the residual impressions would have been there for a longer time, while later Buddhas would [absurdly] be less powerful because theirs would have been there for less time. Also, it would no longer be a hard and fast rule that the location of perfumes [i.e., the consciousness carrying the seeds] is not a subject of moralizing [because transcendental wisdom, unlike the neutral *ālaya-vijñāna*, is always virtuous]. If [on the other hand, transcendental wisdom] is not perfumed then there will be no cause for the infinite good qualities such as [the Buddha's ten] powers (*bala*) and [four] fearlessnesses (*vaiśāradya*), etc.

The answer to this [again paraphrasing the *Guhyārtha-vyākhyā*][37] is along the following lines:

> At the time of diamondlike concentration (*vajropama-samādhi*)[38] all of the seeds of uncontaminated [wisdom] are together at the stage of their ultimate potential so that, independent of new residual impressions, the continuum [of transcendental wisdoms] comes into existence.

One should understand, then, either that the consequence is that just the uncontaminated mental consciousness (Tib. *yid shes*), produced [39a] immediately after the penultimate moment [in the Bodhisattva's career], is the operation of the stream [of transcendental wisdoms] that has come into existence from the potential having reached its maximum; or[30] that the transcendental wisdoms into which the consciousnesses (*vijñāna*) have completely changed are, mutually, condition and conditioned relative to each other.

If one explains in the above manner, the statement that, even at the ninth [Bodhisattva level] mental consciousness (Tib. *yid shes*) undergoes a fundamental change (*āśraya-parāvṛtti*) has been made having only coarse [transformation] in mind. This is because mastery of transcendental wisdoms comes with attainment of the four analytic knowledges (*pratisaṁvid*) [i.e., only at the time of enlightenment] and because [at the ninth Bodhisattva level] the smallest of the small abandonments (*heya*) of the path of meditation still remains. If, though, the change of the mental consciousness was entire, then, since residual impressions [left] by elaboration (*prapañca*) would, in that case, have been eradicated in their entirety there would [absurdly] be no consciousness arising in the form of a name or mark and hence obscurations to knowing, in their entirety, would [absurdly] have to have been eliminated [at the ninth Bodhisattva level].

Hence, in regard to the statements that from the eighth level on a) nonconceptual, transcendental wisdom comes about in an unbroken continuum, and b) endeavor is at peace, and effortless (*anābhoga*) activity comes about, the intention in these [statements] is to say that the endeavor [entailed] in the ego-centered conceptualization (Tib. *gang zag du zhen pa'i rtog pa*) that "I am in equipoise," and "I am doing this for the benefit of others" is at peace, not that the obscuration to knowing (*jñeyāvarana*)—the fluidity of the *manas* that designates [things] with various expressions—[is at peace]. Hence it is said that although the Empowered One and the Arhant have the material reality of the clarity and knowing of *manas* it is not called *kliṣṭa-manas*, and that, although they have maturation consciousness (*vipāka-vijñāna*) it is not called *ālaya-vijñāna*. This is because the content of those two is not complete in them.

There is much to be said about this, it is true, but that is enough for now.

This completes the definition of the *kliṣṭa-manas* and ends the first *le'u* ('chapter'),[40] "Ascertainment of Definitions," from my *Ocean of Eloquence: An Extensive Commentary* [39b] *on the Difficult Points of Ālaya-vijñāna and Kliṣṭa-manas.*

Notes

1. The source of this quotation has not been identified.

2. Since Tibetan has *thar* and not *rnam thar* it is unlikely that the three well-known *vimuktis–śūnyatā, animitta, and apraṇihita*—are intended.

3. AS Sanskrit version (Pradhan 1950:21) reads *akuśalaṁ nivṛtāvyākṛtaṁ ca kliṣṭam / nivṛtāvyākṛtaṁ punaḥ sarvatraga-manaḥ saṁprayuktaḥ kleśo rūpārūpya-pratisamyuktaś ca*; translated by Rahula (1971:33) "... l'indéterminé recouvert [est divise en] l'organe mental présent partout (*sarvatraga*) les associés [aux passions] (*saṁprayukta*), et les souillures associés aux états de la Forme et du Sans-Forme." The Sanskrit of the additional Tibetan (cp. Pradhan 1950:21, n. 8) is **mano-vijñāna-saṁprayukta-sahajāta-sat-kāya-[dṛṣṭy]-anta-graha-dṛṣṭi.*

4. AS Sanskrit (Pradhan 1950:21) is *kuśalam anivṛtāvyākṛtaṁ vākliṣṭam.*

5. MSam (Lamotte 1938:6; Nagao I 7c); cp. P5553:379b3. Lamotte emends *yid* to *nyon mongs pa* on the basis of Paramārtha's commentary and translates (1938:

vol. 2, 22) "Car, d'une part, les passions du domaine matériel et immatériel sont bornées (*āliṅgita*) par le quietude (*śamatha*), d'autre part, ce *manas* demeure toujours." All the Tibetan versions read *yid* for *nyon mongs pa.* The change of *°nyid do* to *°nyid de* in some editions appears to be a later attempt to construe the Tibetan *°ldan pa'i phyir* successfully.

6. This quotation has not been located.

7. The Sanskrit of TK5b-7a (Anacker 1984:422) is *tad āśritya pravartate / tad ālambanaṁ mano-nāma vijñānaṁ mananātmakam // kleśaiś caturbiḥ sahitaṁ nivṛtāvyākṛtaiḥ sadā / ātma-dṛṣṭyātma-mohātma-mananātma-sneha-saṁjñitaiḥ // yatra jas tanmayair anyaiḥ.*

8. In both the AK and AS the division of *vedanā* is, initially, into *duḥkha, sukha,* and *upekṣā* ('neutral'). The two former are again subdivided into suffering and happiness associated with sense-perception and *manas,* respectively. In the fourth *dhyāna* and above (as explained below) there is only *upekṣā.*

9. Tibetan *mnar med* is the *avīci,* the most terrible of the hot hells.

10. That is, TK7b ("there are also the other [five mental factors associated with it] such as contact, etc.") quoted above *Ocean of Eloquence* 34a3 and TK3 (". . yet it is always endowed with contacts, mental attentions, feelings, cognitions, and volitions") quoted above 7b2.

11. This quotation has not been located.

12. *'dogs pa* literally means 'to tie on,' particularly in a figurative sense as in *ming 'dogs* 'to name.'

13. Tsong kha pa perhaps uses the long title here to point out its meaning as "an extensive explanation (*vyākhyā*) having compartmentalized (*vivṛta*) the condensed (*piṇḍa*) secret meaning (*guhyārtha*)."

14. The first four, unnumbered, rubrics under which the discussion of the *kliṣṭa-manas* has been conducted are *ālambana, ākāra, sva-bhāva,* and the number of mental factors.

15. 'Level' (*bhūmi, sa*) does not refer here to the Bodhisattva levels but to the nine levels set forth in the Abhidharma. These nine levels are as follows. There are three realms: the *kāma-, rūpa-,* and *arūpya-dhātus* and the *kāma-dhātu* is the first level. The four concentrations (*dhyāna*)–which are the subdivisions of the *rūpa-dhātu*–are the second to fifth levels. The four absorptions (*samāpatti*)–which are the subdivisions of the *arūpya-dhātu*–are the sixth to ninth levels.

16. 'Person' renders *rten* (*āśraya*), literally 'basis' hence *ālaya-vijñāna.* In such contexts it means, to all intents and purposes, the person. For Tibetan speculations about the *ālaya-vijñāna* as an instance (Tib. *mtshan gzhi*) of a person see Wilson 1984.

17. Perhaps Tsong kha pa's reasoning is as follows. Selfishness, the origin of all

desires, is explained in terms of the *kliṣṭa-manas*'s attachment to the *ālaya* as self. If it were not intimately attached to its own *ālaya*, i.e., if it could rise to a higher mental level than its *ālaya*, there would be no selfishness. In that case, longings to satisfy selfish desires would not get stronger and stronger.

18. TK7-8 (Anacker 1984:422) *cārhato na tat / na nirodha-samāpattau mārge lokottareṇa ca // dvitīyaḥ pariṇāmo 'yam.* See also above *Ocean of Eloquence* 14a2.

19. The Sanskrit according to Pradhan (1950:12) is *manas katamat / yan nitya-kālaṁ manyanātmakam ālaya-vijñānam [→ālaya-vijñānālambakaṁ] caturbhiḥ kleśaiḥ saṁprayuktam ātma-dṛṣṭyātma-snehāsmimānenāvidyā ca / tac ca sarvatragaṁ kuśale 'py akuśale 'py avyākṛte 'pi sthāpayitvā mārga-saṁmukhībhāvaṁ nirodha-samāpattim aśaikṣa-bhūmiṁ ca yac ca ṣaṇṇāṁ vijñānāṁ samanantara-niruddhaṁ vijñānam.* Cp. MSam I 9 quoted at 30b2. Usually *citta*, *manas*, and *vijñāna* are treated as having the same meaning. As above (30b3), in the AS (Gokhale 19.14; Rahula 1971:17) *citta* has the specific meaning *ālaya-vijñāna* and *manas* the specific meaning *kliṣṭa-manas.* Also cp. AK1.16 (Shastri 1970:50-51).

20. This is a creative etymology which derives the word *manas* 'thinking-mind' from *samanantara* (*sam+an+antara* 'in which there is no gap at all'→) 'immediately before or after.' Rahula (1971:17) translates "..et aussi la conscience qui vient de cesser à l'instant parmi les six consciences."

21. The *kliṣṭa-manas* is conceived of as a stable, subtle consciousness which, by virtue of its being continually present, provides the basis for personal experience. Steady, deep, and a necessary prerequisite for personal experience, this hypostasized seventh mind is unlike the other *manas*, the sixth of the set of six, which continually flits in and out of existence. Venerable Blo bzang rgya' mtsho's comments were most helpful in understanding this part of the text.

22. MSam (Lamotte 1938:5; Nagao I 6).

23. Alternatively, as above, "the *manas*, just previous to which, consciousness ceases."

24. Sa skya Paṇḍita in his *Thub pa'i dgongs pa rab tu gsal ba* (47.3.4) says the statement comes from Candragomin's *Sangs rgyas kyi sa.* Demiéville (1987:25) says the *ādarśa-jñāna* is not found in India before the fourth century C.E.

25. Amongst the many different readings (in P there are differences even between the reading in the connected root text and in the root text inserted into the commentary) *de'i rig tsam yid phyir dang* (P174.1.8) means "because its mere knowing (Tib. *rig*) is *manas*."

26. *Guhyārtha-vyākhyā* P5553:61.5.2-7.

27. These statements appear to be reformulations of the passage quoted below *Ocean of Eloquence* 39b6-40a1.

28. *Guhyārtha-vyākyā* P5553:61.5.7-8.

29. This is probably the position of Tsong kha pa; cp. Ke'u tshang (235.2-4) *rang lugs slob dpon gzhan gyis bzhad pa ltar....*

30. *Guhyārtha-vyākhyā* P5553:62.1.2.

31. Ibid. 62.1.2-6.

32. If one reads *gnas su gyur* (*āśraya-parāvṛtti*) this would mean 'fundamentally transforms into.'

33. *Guhyārtha-vyākhyā* P5553:62.1.8.

34. Ibid. 5553:62.2.1.

35. For a further explanation of a *nges pa'i rigs can* literally "one whose lineage (*gotra*) is definite," see MSA:3.6 and AAA (Wogihara 1973:77).

36. Paraphrasing *Guhyārtha-vyākhyā* P5553:69.4.2-4.

37. Ibid. 69.4.4-5.

38. This is the end of the continuum (Tib. *rgyun mtha'*), i.e., the penultimate moment in the Bodhisattva's career.

39. This answer is not found in the *Guhyārtha-vyākhyā.*

40. Tsong kha pa divides his text into four *le'u* which one might ordinarily translate as 'chapter.' In that his first two *le'u* comprise nearly the entire text, however, and include topics of great diversity, I have taken the liberty of breaking them up into seven chapters. The last two *le'u* are included in Chapter 8.

SIX

PROOFS OF *ĀLAYA-VIJÑĀNA*

If one asserts an *ālaya-vijñāna* and *kliṣṭa-manas* different to the six consciousnesses how does one prove their existence?

> From believable scriptural authority (*āgama*) and through reasoning (*yukti*) one should come to understand that there are a *[kliṣṭa-]manas* and *ālaya-vijñāna* different from the six consciousnesses. [Mv XXXV]

There are two ways to establish them: by scriptural authority and by reasoning. In regard to the scriptural authority for *ālaya-vijñāna* and *kliṣṭa-manas*, first, the *ālaya-vijñāna*. The *Mahāyānābhidharma-sūtra* says:[1]

> There is an element which has no beginning in time that is the basis of dharmas. By reason of its existence there are all places of rebirth and also the attainment of nirvāṇa.

and [the *Mahāyānābhidharma-sūtra*] also says:[2]

> All dharmas adhere to the consciousness with all seeds. I therefore explain the *ālaya-vijñāna* ('consciousness which is basis of all') to the excellent ones.

The *Saṁdhi-nirmocana-sūtra* says:[3]

> The *ādāna-vijñāna* ('appropriating consciousness') is deep and subtle. It flows on with all seeds like a surging river. I do not, however, teach it to simpletons lest they suppose it to be a soul (*ātman*).

And the *Ārya-laṅkāvatāra-sūtra* says:[4]

> The mind (*citta*) is *ālaya-vijñāna*, the egotistical thought is *manas*, and the awarenesses of the objects [of the senses] are *pravṛtti-vijñānas* ('entering differentiated cognitions').

There are an infinite number of such Mahāyāna sūtra references.

Second, scriptural authority for *kliṣṭa-manas.* The *Saṁdhi-nirmocana-sūtra* says:[5]

> Sometimes there is one consciousness [40a] operating with *ālaya-vijñāna* as when there is *manas*, sometimes there are two as when there is *manas* and *mano-vijñāna*, and sometimes all seven entering consciousnesses are operating with it.

And in the tenth folio of the *Suvarna-prabhāsottama-rāja-sūtra* it says:[6]

> With the purification of the *manas* that is situated on the *ālaya-vijñāna* the *Saṁbhoga-kāya* ('Enjoyment Body') is attained.

The passages in the *Ārya-ghana-vyūha-sūtra*[7] and the *[Ārya]-lankāvatāra-sūtra*,[8] etc., which mention eight consciousnesses also serve as proof.

Eight proofs for the existence of *ālaya-vijñāna*

Second, in regard to reasoning (*yukti*), there is reasoning [which establishes the existence] of *ālaya-vijñāna* and of *kliṣṭa-manas.* First:

> Although there are an infinite number of reasonings given in the Yogācāra school's texts [to establish *ālaya-vijñāna*], I will explain eight which systematize them: the impossibility of a) taking [rebirth], b) a first [mind], c) clarity, d) seeds, e) action, f) physical experience, g) meditative absorption, and h) passing away. [Mv XXXVI]

In the MSam[9] five reasons are treated at length along with related matters. These are the impossiblity of being afflicted (*saṁkliṣṭa*) a) by afflictive emotion (*kleśa*), b) by action, and c) by birth; and the impossibility of d) ordinary and e) transcendental states of purity. In [Vasubandhu's] *Pañca-skandha-prakaraṇa* there are four reasons. In the latter part of the *[Yogācāra]-bhūmi-vyākhyā* there are seventeen scriptural proofs and also proofs based on reasoning. In [Guṇamati's] *Pratītya-samutpādādi-vibhaṅga-nirdeśa-ṭīkā* there are some of the MSam's proofs. And the way it is established as set forth in the *Abhidharma-samuccaya* is this: The *Viniścaya-saṃgrahaṇī* [of the *Yogācāra-bhūmi*] says:[10]

> There would be the impossibility of a) taking, b) the first, c) clarity (*spaṣṭatva*), d) seeds, e) action, f) physical feeling, g) mindless meditative absorption (*acitte samāpatti*), and h) passing away.

These are formulated [40b] in the *Abhidharma-samuccaya-bhāṣya* as eight reasons as follows:[11]

> One should understand the existence of the *ālaya-vijñāna* in eight ways. If there were no *ālaya-vijñāna*, a) taking a body would be impossible, b) emergence of an initial [consciousness] would be impossible, c) emergence of clarity would be impossible, d) being a seed would be impossible, e) action would be impossible, f) physical experience would be impossible, g) mindless meditative absorption would be impossible, and h) consciousness that passes away would be impossible.

Since these include nearly all [of the different proofs set forth in the above texts] I shall discuss these eight.

First proof

The first proof is as follows. Why is it impossible to take a body [at link-up (*pratisaṁdhi, nying mtsham sbyor ba*)] if there is no *ālaya-vijñāna*? [In response we say] that if one does not assert an *ālaya-vijñāna* there can be no *kliṣṭa-manas*. In that case, it would be the set of six [consciousnesses] which would have to take a body. There are five reasons [set forth in the ASam] for it being impossible for them to do so. These are as follows:

[First:] The *ālaya-vijñāna* is the maturation of a previous action and therefore operates for the length of the power of that action and is, therefore, present even at the time of link-up and can take a body. The set of six [on the other hand are different]. This is because they are said in a sūtra "... to arise by the power of the inner sense-faculty, the external object, and mental attitudes (*manaskara*) such as the desire to see, etc..." and because they arise, after the body has come into being, from conditions at hand in this life, and do not, therefore, exist at link-up.

[Second:] And even if one says, "The set of six take the body because, even at link-up, there are entering consciousnesses (*pravṛtti-vijñāna*) which are the maturation of a previous action and mental consciousnesses (Tib. *yid shes*)," still they could not do so. This is because, whereas true maturations (*vipāka*) and consciousnesses there at link-up would be maturations that link up at the initial birthplace and would be, necessarily, not a subject of moralizing, those [set of six consciousnesses] are, however, also seen to be virtuous and nonvirtuous as well.

[Third:] And even if one says, [41a] "Although those six can be virtuous and nonvirtuous there are [some of them] that can also be unobscured and not a subject of moralizing, and it is those that are the maturations so there is no fault," still they could not [take the body]. This is because, whereas the maturation part which is not a subject of moralizing operates, without a break, for the length of a life, the set of six do not operate without break for that length of time.

[Fourth:] Furthermore, given that the set of six were to take the body, the continuums of the consciousnesses taking the body would not pervade it. Any place not pervaded would not be vivified (*upātta*) by consciousness and would, therefore, become corpselike. Since the set of six are on strictly defined substrata [i.e., sight operates only in the eyes, hearing in the ears, etc.] only substrata where that consciousness occured would be vivified and all the other parts of the body would not be vivified by it. This would come about because an entering consciousness has no potential to arise pervading all the body at one and the same time.

[Objection:] Since the body [i.e., tactile] sense-faculty pervades the whole body, the substratum of the thought-area [i.e., the whole living organism] is vivified by it.

[Response:] This cannot be. For [the body sense-faculty] is itself nonconscious and does not, therefore, vivify [the thought-area].

[Fifth:] Furthermore, if those set of six take the body there would be the flaw that in one life a body would be taken many times. This is so because those [six] sometimes occur, and sometimes do not occur.

Hence, if there were to be no *ālaya-vijñāna* one would have to assert that the set of six takes the body. And since, [on the one hand] there are the five causes why this is impossible and since, [on the other hand] we see that a body is taken one must agree that it is the *ālaya-vijñāna* that takes the body. Thus it is said [in the *Abhidharma-samuccaya-bhāṣya*]:[12]

> Why would it be impossible to take the body?
>
> [Response:] It is explained fivefold: The *ālaya-vijñāna* has for its cause a previous volition (*pūrva-saṁskāra*). Eye-consciousness and the other entering consciousnesses, however, arise from the conditions at hand as expounded at length in such statements as: "Consciousnesses arise by the power of the sense-faculty, object, and mental attitudes (*manaskara*)." This is the first reason. [41b] The set of six consciousnesses are seen to be virtuous and nonvirtuous. This is the second reason. Also none of the six consciousnesses is seen to be a sort which would be categorized as being a maturation which is not a subject of moralizing. This is the third reason. Also the set of six consciousnesses operate on strictly defined substrata. That being the case, whatever the consciousness, it vivifies only that substratum by means of which it operates [as a consciousness]. It does not vivify other [substrata] and so it is impossible [for such a consciousness to take the body]. The one that does vivify [i.e., the body sense-faculty] could not possibly [really vivify] because it is nonconscious. This is the fourth reason. There is the fault that

again and again one would take a body. This is because an eye-consciousness sometimes occurs, and sometimes does not occur. The other [entering consciousnesses] are like this. This is the fifth reason.

Second proof

The second proof [for an *ālaya-vijñāna*] is as follows: Some say that if one asserts the *ālaya-vijñāna* there is a fault, because, in that case, two consciousnesses would come about simultaneously—the *ālaya-vijñāna* which operates continuously and an entering consciousness which arises from time to time. [In response we say:] You are finding a fault where no fault exists. It [two consciousnesses coming about simultaneously] is something that we assert.

Were two consciousnesses not to occur together [i.e., if there were no *ālaya-vijñāna*], then, given a situation where a person a) wishes to perceive all six objects—from seeing to being mentally aware of an object, i.e., is impartial in mental attitude, and b) [where one sense-faculty] is not closer[13] [to its particular object than another], then not even one specific consciousness would arise first. This is because the objects, sense-faculties, and mental attitudes [42a] which cause those entering consciousnesses are all present and there is no special factor [which would cause one set of causes to bring about one particular result].

Even though [the *Abhidharma-samuccaya-bhāṣya*] speaks as though the six mental attitudes towards the six objects exist at the same time, since two thoughts—that I want to see and that I want to hear—cannot exist simultaneously, one should construe [the *Abhidharma-samuccaya-bhāṣya* to mean], given impartiality and given that no [sense-faculty] is closer or farther away from its respective object, then [there could be] no [first entering consciousness] whatsoever.

[Defense of discredited thesis:] Even though one cannot say definitely, given that mental attitudes are impartial, that "where an object and sense-faculty are closer, this one of the six consciousnesses will arise first," nevertheless, once one [consciousness] has arisen another consciousness does not arise together with it. This is so because a situation does not exist wherein one mental attitude [such as "I want to see"] gives rise to two simultaneous consciousnesses of a corresponding sort.

[Response:] You are quite right that two ideas would not exist at one and the same time were the mental attitude of, for example, wanting to look at an object such as a shape a necessary cause [for eye-consciousness]. However, in that when all four conditions[14] are gathered together the consciousness which is their result arises, two do come about simultaneously. For the causal conditions (*hetu-pratyaya*) as well as the objects and sense-faculties of these six are there at the same time and the immediately preceding conditions (*samanantara-pratyaya*) which have just perished, are functioning.

[Objection:] Does this not contradict the statement that

> Occurrence of two consciousnesses simultaneously is groundless and never happens.

[Response:] It does not contradict this statement which intends [to say] that two consciousnesses of a similar type [do not come about simultaneously]. Thus it also [says in the *Abhidharma-samuccaya-bhāṣya*]:[15]

> Why is a very first entering [consciousness] impossible?
>
> If one person says "If there is an *ālaya-vijñāna* then two consciousnesses will come into being simultaneously," [in response we say] that what you think to be a fault should be explained to be no fault at all. This is because there is indeed the simultaneous operation of two consciousnesses. [42b] And why is this so? Because no first entering consciousness whatsoever would be possible for a person simultaneously wanting to see, and so forth, up to wanting to be mentally conscious of something [if there were no *ālaya-vijñāna*]. This is because in such a case the mental attitudes, sense-faculties and also the objects [which cause those entering consciousnesses] are present and there is no special factor [which would cause one set of causes to bring about one particular result].

Third proof

The third proof is as follows: If two consciousnesses were not to occur simultaneously the *mano-vijñāna* would not operate more clearly. Why is this so? One sees that the subsequent, conceptual *mano-vijñāna's* apprehension (Tib. *'jug*) of an object beheld by sense-consciousness proceeds with greater clarity. The apprehension of a mind (*manas*) recollecting an object experienced previously by sense-consciousness, on the other hand, is not so clear. Therefore, since one has to accept that the apprehension of a present, sense-consciousness object is clearer, two consciousnesses can come about at the same time and there is more clarity in the apprehension of that *manas* [which operates simultaneously with a sense-consciousness]. Were this not the case there would be no clearer, or less clear, subsequent conceptual *mano-vijñānas*.

If one says that, even though not there at the same time as the sense-consciousness, the *manas* which has an object in the present is clearer, and a *manas* with an object in, for instance, the past less clear, [in response we say] this cannot be. This is because, when either of these two *manas* understand their object it is not the object's specific characteristic marks (*sva-lakṣaṇa*) which appear. There is, moreover, no consciousness which grasps clearly an object existing, not in the past, but at the same time as it does. Thus it is said [in the *Abhidharma-samuccaya-bhāṣya*]:[16]

> Why, if two consciousnesses do not come about simultaneously, would the *mano-vijñāna* that operates together, subsequent to eye sense-consciousness, etc., not become the clearer?
>
> When there is recollection of a previously experienced object [43a] the *mano-vijñāna* comes about but it is not the clearer. That *manas* dealing with a present object does not lack clarity in this way. Therefore [two consciousnesses] do occur simultaneously and the *mano-vijñāna* can be clearer.

Fourth proof

The fourth proof is as follows: There would [absurdly] be no seeds of virtue and nonvirtue, etc., if there were no *ālaya-vijñāna*. There is no indefiniteness [in the pervasion] because only the *ālaya-vijñāna* is the place where all residual impressions are gathered.

If one says that there is no fault because the set of six are the basis of the seeds, [in response we say] this is not right. When the perfuming [i.e., laying down the taint] of a seed takes place it has to occur with the arising of the perfumer, and the cessation of the location of the perfume, happening simultaneously. [The location of the perfume must, therefore, be neutral (*avyākṛta*) because a nonvirtuous mind could not be the location of a virtuous perfume nor a virtuous mind the location of a nonvirtuous perfume.] Yet, nonvirtuous states of mind come about after virtuous states of mind and vice versa, and, similarly, transcendental states of mind come about after ordinary ones.

Furthermore, when the continuums of the set of six are cut the basis of the residual impressions would not exist and therefore the continuum of those [seeds] would also be cut. Future minds would then be bereft of a cause. Thus it is said [in the *Abhidharma-samuccaya-bhāṣya*]:[17]

> Why is it that the set of six are not a seed-state for each other?
>
> Since nonvirtues come about after virtues, virtues come about after nonvirtues and [states of mind] that are not a subject of moralizing come about after both of these, since [states of mind] in the fine realm[18] come about after those in the bad realm, [states of mind] in the fine realm come about after those in the middle realm, and so on down to [states of mind] in the bad realm come about after those in the fine realm; and since contaminated [states of mind] come about after uncontaminated ones, transcendental [states of mind] come about after worldly ones, and worldly

> [states of mind] come about [43b] after transcendental ones, it is impossible for these to be seed-states. Also, it is impossible [for the set of six consciousnesses to be the location of seeds] because a continuum that has been severed, even for an extended period, comes forth after a long period of time.

This explains the five reasons given in the MSam [quoted above 40a4].

Fifth proof

The fifth proof is as follows: If a number of consciousnesses could not occur simultaneously the [absurd] consequence would be that a) the narrow, pathlike *bhājana-vijñapti* [see below], b) the marching of feet *āśraya-vijñapti*, c) the *aham iti vijñapti*, and d) the stones and earth on the path in front of one that is the *viṣaya-vijñapti* would not occur together. If one asserts [that indeed they do not occur simultaneously] it is said that while walking along quickly, etc., one should observe and it will be clear.

The four combined *vijñaptis* ('representations of consciousness') are: a) the *bhājana-vijñapti* ('world as a representation of consciousness'). This is the appearance of the stable outer world. b) The *āśraya-vijñapti* ('substratum as a representation of consciousness'). This is the appearance of the moving world—the material reality of the living being—the six senses (*āyatanas*) and their bases. c) The *aham iti vijñapti* ('self-awareness as a representation of consciousness'). This is the introspective, continually operating thought "I am." And d) the *viṣaya-vijñapti* ('objects as a representation of consciousness'). This is the appearances of shapes, sounds, etc. Hence, since one notices that, at one and the same time, the external and internal appear, that there is self-grasping and that there is grasping at one or other of the six sense-objects, many consciousnesses do indeed occur simultaneously. It would be impossible for a single consciousness to have such essentially different actions as these.

Why are these four [*vijñaptis*] called karma ('actions')? It is evident [that they are called] karma from the point of view of agent (*kartṛ*) and action (*karman*) because the appearances [described in the *Abhidharma-samuccaya-bhāṣya*] are of an I and mine.[19]

If one asserts that there is no *ālaya,* these four are impossible. They are possible, however, if one accepts the *ālaya.* This is because a) the *vijñapti* that is the external and internal appearance, i.e., the appearance of object and sentient being,[20] is the *ālaya,* b) the *vijñapti* that is the appearance of a self is *kliṣṭa-manas,* and c) the appearances as objects are the set of six, for, as it is said [in the *Triṁśikā-kārikā*][21]

> Third are those [six entering consciousnesses] that observe the six objects.

Thus it is said [in the *Abhidharma-samuccaya-bhāṣya*] [44a]:[22]

> Why would action not exist if two consciousnesses did not come about at the same time?
>
> In short, for such an action there are aspects: the idea of a containing vessel, the idea of a location, the idea thinking 'I am here', and the idea of objects. These ideas are discerned to come about simultaneously moment by moment. For one instant of one consciousness cannot have such essentially different actions as these.

Sixth proof

The sixth proof is as follows: Were there to be no *ālaya-vijñāna*, it would be impossible to have the feeling experienced as pervading the entire body on all occasions, whatever the mental state, be it proper or improper, etc. This is because that feeling is produced in the body in the sense that it [the body] provides a substratum for it, and in the absence of a basis of operation [for that body] there would be the fault of there being no seed which is its causal condition. Thus it is said [in the *Abhidharma-samuccaya-bhāṣya*]:[23]

> Why, if there were no *ālaya-vijñāna*, would physical feeling be impossible?
>
> Because those physical feelings which are experienced in the body of someone, whether thinking properly or improperly, whether in a state of subsequent analysis or whether in meditative equipoise or not in meditative equipoise, [because those feelings] in all their variety and of many different sorts would not come about, and would not be observed, therefore the *ālaya-vijñāna* exists.

Seventh proof

The seventh proof is as follows: If there were no *ālaya-vijñāna* both meditative absorptions[24] would be impossible. This is because, if it did not exist, there would be the [absurd] consequence that [for] people practicing either meditative absorption, consciousness would cast off the body, since the set of six [consciousnesses] would have stopped and there would be no *ālaya-vijñāna*. If one asserts this, one stands opposed to the statement which explains that the difference between those [practicing mediative absorptions] and the dead is that "their consciousness has not passed away from the body." [44b]

If one says that there is no fault because, since an unclear *mano-vijñāna* is present [during meditative absorption], one is not devoid of consciousness, [in response we say] this is impossible. Where there is consciousness there is *gsum 'dus pa'i reg pa* [contact which happens when there is the coming together of the three: object, sense-faculty, and sense-consciousness]. Where that [contact] exists there is feeling (*vedanā*) and discrimination (*saṁjñā*) as well. Hence the [authoritative] statement that

> Feeling and discrimination cease with meditative absorption

would [absurdly] become incorrect.

[Objection:] In that case, even when the *ālaya-vijñāna* is present [during meditative absorption, as you assert it to be], it would also be incorrect to hold that feeling and discrimination are negated, because feeling and discrimination, as omnipresent [mental factors], are there at that time as well.

[Response:] That is true. However, in that the feeling and discrimination associated with the set of six operate in a coarse fashion, they are necessarily absent [during meditative absorption]. The feeling and discrimination associated with the *ālaya*, on the other hand, are an extremely subtle form of awareness (Tib. *dmigs rnam*) and hence do not block absorption into [a vision of ultimate] cessation. Thus, although they are present there is no fault. It is not the same. Thus it is said [in the *Abhidharma-samuccaya-bhāṣya*]:[25]

> Why, if there were no *ālaya-vijñāna*, would unconscious meditative absorption be impossible?
>
> It is because the actual consciousness of one absorbed in no-thought meditation or in the meditative absorption into cessation would pass away from the body. But it does not pass away or else there would be simply death. It is as the Buddha has said: "Their consciousness is not separated from the body."

Eighth proof

The eighth proof is as follows: If there were no *ālaya*, passing away would be impossible. This is because, in the absence of an *ālaya*, and given that one accepts that consciousness casts off the body and passes away, one would have to assert that this [casting off the body] is [done] by the mental consciousness (Tib. *yid shes*). In that case, a gradual contraction of body heat would be impossible, because, right up until the instant of passing away, a nonoccurence of mental consciousness would be impossible.

[Objection:] It is the same with the *ālaya* because its continuum is uncut right up until life stops.

[Response:] As it says in [Vasubandhu's] *Pratītya-samutpādādi-vibhaṅga-nirdeśa*:[26]

> The *ālaya-vijñāna* pervades the entire [body-]cavity. [45a]

Hence the *ālaya-vijñāna* pervades the entire body and is constant. When the force of a propelling action (*karman*) is exhausted and the *ālaya-vijñāna* can no longer remain in a region of the body it contracts from that region. When this happens the sense-faculties which depend on that also cease and the heat dissipates. Gradually all the sense-faculties are cast away and the warmth is dissipated from the whole body causing one to pass away. Mental consciousness (Tib. *yid shes*), on the other hand, is not something that pervades the entire body and it contracts, region by region, from the body. It is, therefore, not the same.

Thus death is casting off the body on account of the feeling of heat gradually contracting. Nothing besides a consciousness could do this [casting off] because, in the absence of consciousness, one does not see such a thing taking place. Even though the body is cast off by a consciousness it is not, however, by one of the five door-consciousnesses [i.e., sense- consciousnesses]. If it were, since they are in only a section of the body, it would lead to the [absurd] consequence that in the rest of the body where they are absent there would be no feeling of heat. Also one would die when one faints, etc. [because those sense-consciousnesses stop at such times].

In regard to mental consciousness (Tib. *yid shes*), even though it is not [only] in a section of the body [like a sense-consciousness, still it is not suitable to be the consciousness that casts off the body because] unlike the *ālaya-vijñāna* it does not pervade the body in its entirety. If its presence precluded casting off the body, the feeling of heat would not contract until the very final moment when life is cut. Since we see that the feeling of heat does, in fact, contract before that time, and since we see that the body is cast off when the feeling of heat has all contracted, it is the *ālaya-vijñāna*, we assert, that casts off the body. Thus it says [in the *Abhidharma-samuccaya-bhāṣya*]:[27]

> Why, if there were no *ālaya-vijñāna*, would death be impossible?
>
> The consciousness of someone who is dying cools down the upper or lower parts of the body and casts it off. There is no time when the *mano-vijñāna* is not operating. So, then, it is seen that it is in the absence of the *ālaya-vijñāna* alone, the [consciousness] which takes the body, that there is a cooling of the body and a lack of feeling [45b] in the body. This does not happen in the absence of the *mano-vijñāna* so it is not that one. It is not right [to say it casts off the body].

Thus the first, fourth, sixth, seventh, and eighth reasons explain the fault in there being no *ālaya-vijñāna* and directly prove its existence. The other three are in order to eliminate objections.

Discursus

Is this *ālaya-vijñāna* found only in Mahāyāna sūtras or is it found in Hīnayāna sacred books as well?

> Such an *ālaya-vijñāna* is also found in Hīnayāna sacred books where it is referred to as *ālaya* ('basis of all') and *mūla-vijñāna* ('root consciousness'), *bhavāṅga* ('branch [i.e., cause] of [cyclic] existence') and *ā-saṁsārika-skandha* ('one with an aggregate that lasts for the length of saṁsāra'). [Mv XXXVII]

Thus this *ālaya-vijñāna* is taught, not only in Mahāyāna sūtras under such names as *jñeyāśraya* ('substratum of the knowable') and *ādāna-vijñāna* ('appropriating consciousness'), but it is also taught in Hīnayāna sacred texts under the [above] synonyms. The MSam says:[28]

> The *Tathāgatotpāda-catur-vidhānuśaṁsā-sūtra*, in the Ekottarikāgama, says:[29]
>
> > Those persons who delight in the *ālaya*, enjoy the *ālaya*, for whom the *ālaya* is all, who have a real liking for the *ālaya*: they want to hear and they pay attention when, in order to remove the *ālaya*, the doctrine is taught to them. They approach all-knowing and practice in accord with the doctrine. When the Tathāgata is in the world this amazing, most excellent doctrine comes into the world as well.
>
> By this partial synonymity (*paryāya*),[30] the *ālaya-vijñāna* is referred to in the Śrāvaka-yāna as well. [46a] In Mahā-saṁghika scriptures, moreover, it mentions a *mūla-vijñāna* ('root consciousness'), a synonym (*paryāya*) referring to this same [*ālaya-vijñāna*]. [The idea behind the name is] that just as the tree is contingent on a root [so all states are dependent on a root consciousness]. Mahīśāsaka scriptures refer to an *ā-saṁsārika-skandha* ('one with an aggregate that lasts for the length of saṁsāra'), again a synonym referring to the same thing. [The idea is] that even though certain physical and mental continuums seem to be cut the continuum of their seeds on the *ālaya-vijñāna* never is. And in the scriptures of the Ārya Sthavira-vādins we also find reference to:[31]
>
> > *bhavāṅga* ('[the consciousness which is] the branch [i.e., cause] of [cyclic] existence'), sight, knowledge, disturbance, movement, realization, and, seventh, the initiator.
>
> That the *jñeyāśraya* ('substratum of the knowable') is thus referred to as *ālaya-vijñāna* ('foundation consciousness'), *ādāna-vijñāna* ('appropriat-

ing consciousness'), *citta* ('mind'), *ālaya* ('foundation'), *mūla-vijñāna* ('root consciousness'), *ā-saṁsārika-skandha* ('one with an aggregate that lasts for the length of saṁsāra'), and *bhavāṅga* ('[the consciousness which is] the branch of [cyclic] existence') simply extols the great *ālaya-vijñāna* path.

If the *ālaya-vijñāna* is taught in the Śrāvaka-yāna how do you interpret the passage in the MSam which says:[32]

> Since this [Mahāyāna] doctrine thus [set forth under ten topics] is not seen elsewhere, since these [ten topics] are seen to be the cause of great enlightenment, and since [the total ten] topics are taught, it is a special Mahāyāna doctrine held to have been revealed by Buddha (*buddha-vacana*).

[Response:] There is no flaw. In the Śrāvaka-yāna [the *ālaya*] is taught by means of different synonyms such as *bhavāṅga*, etc., while in the Mahāyāna it is taught in a straightforward and complete fashion with words like *ālaya-vijñāna*, *ādāna-vijñāna* ('appropriating consciousness') and *jñeyāśraya* ('substratum of the knowable'). Such teaching is not found in the Śrāvaka-yāna. [46b]

Why is such teaching not found in the Śrāvaka-yāna?

[Response:] Though there is a need to teach in the Śrāvaka-yāna as is taught in the Mahāyāna, nevertheless it is not proper to do so because it will lead to a fault. How come it is not proper to do so? It is because the subject matter of a teaching on *ālaya-vijñāna* systematizes the very subtle knowable,[33] [i.e., emptiness, which is understood when everything is seen to arise from the awakening of residual impressions, and not from external objects]. A Śrāvaka does not need to understand this very subtle knowable to achieve the desired aim. The Vimukti-kāya ('Liberation Body') which is the removal of all afflictive obscuration is actualized [by a Śrāvaka] just by practising the meaning of the four-line stanza ["All composites are impermanent; everything contaminated is suffering; all phenomena are selfless and empty; and nirvāṇa is bliss"]. The Arhant Cūla-panthaka, for example, [attained liberation in such a fashion].[34]

Why, if one does teach this, does it leads to a fault? [In response we say:] It is because, if one teaches that the consciousness which is the substratum of the seeds of all phenomena and hence is the cause of the world and what is in the world; which operates until the very end of saṁsāra without its continuum being cut and which is the underpinning of all bondage and of all liberation is the *ālaya* then, certain unskillful persons of the Śrāvaka family (*gotra*) will think "It's me!" Such ego-grasping is not proper. It is necessary, however, to teach this in the Mahāyāna because a Bodhisattva cannot attain omniscience without practicing the very subtle knowable. Also, even though the *ālaya* is taught in the above manner, it only gives rise to the understanding [in the Bodhisattva's mind] of an impermanent, contingent phenomenon so the fault [of ego-grasping] does not arise. Thus the MSam says:[35]

> Why, in the Śrāvaka-yāna, is that mind not taught as the *ālaya-vijñāna* or *ādāna-vijñāna* ('appropriating consciousness')?
>
> It is because it systematizes the subtle knowable and the Śrāvakas are not of the group that understands all knowables.[36] Hence, although this is not taught to them they achieve their knowledge.[37] So it is not taught. [47a] The Bodhisattvas are of the group that understands all knowables so it is taught to them. This is because without this understanding it is not easy for them to achieve omniscience.

In regard to the Śrāvaka-yāna teaching, "Those persons [who delight] in the *ālaya* . . . " [Aṅguttara-nikāya II 131, quoted at 45b4], how, then, do Śrāvaka thinkers (Tib. *grub mtha' smra ba*) explain the meaning of this sūtra?

> Vasumitra, Vāmana and Ghoṣaka assert that aggregates, feelings and *sat-kāya-dṛṣṭi*,[38] respectively, are intended in such references to the *ālaya*. [Mv XXXVIII]

The venerable Vasumitra[39] says that the five grasping aggregates (*pañcopādāna-skandha*) are intended in the sūtra [Aṅguttara-nikāya II 131, quoted 45b4] because they are the substratum of those persons who come to delight [in the *ālaya*].[40] Similarly, the venerable Vāmana[41] and venerable Ghoṣaka[42] assert that the feeling of happiness and *sat-kāya-dṛṣṭi*, respectively, are the intended meaning. The MSam says:[43]

> Also one person thinks that in the Buddha's long (*vistara*) discourse about "Those persons who delight in the *ālaya*" the five grasping aggregates are being called *ālaya*. Another person thinks that it is the feeling of happiness along with desire (*rāga-sahita-sukha-vedanā*) which is the *ālaya*. Yet another thinks the *sat-kāya-dṛṣṭi* is *ālaya*. They are all confused about the [actual] *ālaya-vijñāna* and think this way because of [their inappropriate] scriptures and the [limited] scope of their intellects.

[Question:] Is the way these scholastics interpret the meaning of that *[Tathāgatotpāda-catur-vidhānuśaṁsā-]sūtra* also suitable in the Mahāyāna?

> Although the instruction in the lower vehicle is not at all improper, [47b] nevertheless the Mahāyānists assertion that that sacred scripture is refer-

ring to the *ālaya-vijñāna* is far better. This is because the explanations of Vasumitra, etc., each have certain faults. [Mv XXXIX]

Lower vehicle persons are not the intended recipients of instruction about *ālaya-vijñāna*. Since they would be confused by it, it is not improper to explain [the word *ālaya* quoted at 45b4] differently. There is not even a tiny deficiency.[44] Nevertheless, far better is the assertion of Mahāyānists who do not become confused, [who say] that the '*ālaya*' spoken of [at 45b4] is referring to the *ālaya-vijñāna*, since the assertions of the three venerable ones are flawed while the assertion that it is the *ālaya-vijñāna* is perfect.

What are the flaws in the assertions of the three venerable ones?

[Response:] As it is said [in the MSam]:[45]

> Although the instruction presented in the Srāvaka-yāna setting out [the meaning of] these [words] is, indeed, not improper, the presentation of *ālaya* setting it out based on its being the *ālaya-vijñāna* is much better.
>
> And why is it much better? [In response we say:] It is because the five grasping aggregates [which Vasumitra understands by the word *ālaya*] are not at all agreeable to those who are born in the extreme suffering of a bad state of rebirth. So adherence[46] to these [aggregates], for which there is an extreme dislike, is impossible. Those [suffering beings] wish to be separated from them. The feeling of happiness along with desire does not exist above the fourth concentration (*dhyāna*). So adherence (*ālīnā*) to it, on the part of those living beings who have [attained] those [meditative concentrations], is impossible since it is not agreeable to them. [Hence Vāmana is incorrect to say the word '*ālaya*' refers to such happiness.] Also the *satkāya-dṛṣṭi* is not agreeable to those Buddhists who believe in selflessness. So adherence to it [48a] on their part is impossible. [Ghoṣaka is, therefore, incorrect to say the word '*ālaya*' refers to it.]

How is the assertion that the *ālaya* refers to the *ālaya-vijñāna* flawless?

[Response:] As it is said [in the MSam]:[47]

> As for the assertion that the *ālaya-vijñāna* is the inner self (*antarātmabhāva*). Even though those who are born in the extreme suffering of a bad state of rebirth wish to see the destruction of their painful aggregates, those who are bound by love for the *ālaya-vijñāna* as themselves never ever wish for the destruction of it. Even though those born above the fourth concentration do not find agreeable the feeling of happiness along with desire, there is still the self-love complex focussed on the *ālaya-vijñāna*. And similarly with those Buddhists who believe in selflessness.

> Even though they do not find agreeable the view of self (*ātma-dṛṣṭi*), the self-love complex focussed on the *ālaya-vijñāna* is still there. Thus it is established that [interpreting] the *ālaya* [in the sūtra quoted above at 45b4] to be the *ālaya-vijñāna* is much the better presentation.

This is what these teach. For the meaning of *ālaya* ('foundation') is *ālīna* ('that which is adhered to') and living beings adhere to this in the sense that they settle on it as a self. Those in bad states of rebirth, those above the fourth concentration without the feeling of happiness, and Buddhists who believe in selflessness, all adhere to this *ālaya-vijñāna* in the sense that they settle on it as a self. This seems to be the idea.

When handled like this, the Ācārya's [Asaṅga's] [48b] explanation that there is no *ālaya-vijñāna* after the *kliṣṭa-manas* completely changes is without any blemish.

This finishes the explanation of the proof of the *ālaya-vijñāna* together with a discursus.

Notes

1. The Sanskrit (quoted MSam, Lamotte 1938:4; Nagao I 1) is *anādi-kāliko dhātuḥ sarva-dharma-samāśrayaḥ / tasmin sati gatiḥ sarvā nirvāṇādhigamo 'pi ca //.*

2. The Sanskrit (quoted MSam, Lamotte 1938:4; Nagao I 1) as reconstructed by Nagao (1982:9) is **ālīnaṁ sarva-dharmeṣu vijñānaṁ sarva-bījakam / tasmād ālaya-vijñānaṃ sadbhyo mayaiva deśitam //.* Schmithausen (1987: n. 136) retranslates **ālayaḥ sarva-dharmānāṁ* etc., and translates "Mind containing all seeds is the *ālaya* of all dharmas; therefore it is [called] *ālaya-vijñāna*; I have taught it [only] to the excellent [disciples]."

3. The original of *Saṁdhi-nirmocana-sūtra* 5.7 according to Schmithausen (1987: n. 321) reads *ādāna-vijñāna gabhīra-sūkṣmo ogho yathā vartati sarva-bījo / bālāna eṣo mayi na prakāśit mā haiva ātmā parikalpayeyuḥ//.*

4. The Sanskrit of *Laṅkāvatāra-sūtra* verse 102 (Nanjio 1956:278; translated by Suzuki 1968:234) which is similar is *cittam ālaya-vijñānaṁ mano yan manyanātmakam / gṛhyāti viṣayānyena vijñānaṁ hi tad ucyate.*

5. *Saṁdhi-nirmocana-sūtra* 5.4. The statements in the *Guhyārtha-vyākhyā*, quoted *Ocean of Eloquence* 36b3-5, appear to be reformulations of this passage.

6. Taisho 16, 363b; 409a according to Odani and Kalsang 1986.

7. Taisho 16, 739 according to Odani and Kalsang 1986; Wilson 1984 cites P778 vol. 29.

8. See *Laṅkāvatāra-sūtra* (Nanjio 1956:1.29); Wilson (1984:424 nn. 9 and 10) quotes Vaidya's ed. (p. 20) and translates "Just so the river of the basis-of-all, / Agitated by the winds of various objects / Moves on, dancing with the waves / Of the various consciousnesses."

9. MSam (Lamotte 1938:13ff; Nagao I 29ff). The opening summary reads: *de ltar rnam par bzhag pa'i kun gzhi rnam par shes pa med par / 'di ltar kun nas nyon mongs pa dang rnam par byang ba mi rung ste / nyon mongs pa'i kun nas nyon mongs pa dang / las kyi kun nas nyon mongs pa dang / skye ba'i kun nas nyon mongs pa yang mi rung ngo // 'jig rten pa dang / 'jig rten las 'das pa'i rnam par byang ba yang mi rung ngo.*

10. The Sanskrit of this is quoted in Jinaputra or Sthiramati's ASBh (Tatia 1976:11) *tad etad ālaya-vijñānam astīti kathaṁ vijñāyate // yasmāt tena vinaupattam ādi spaṣṭatvaṁ bījaṁ karma na yujyate / kāyiko 'nubhavo 'citte samāpattī cyutis tathā.* These reasons have been considered in detail by Schmithausen (1987: Supplement II, 194-6) and discussed in detail by Griffiths (1986:96-104) in the context of his critique of Buddhist causality and nonself theory. Griffiths translates the entire section in an appendix (129-138).

11. The Sanskrit of ASBh (Tatia 1976:11.18-22) is *viniścaya-saṁgrahāṇyām aṣṭābhir ākārair ālaya-vijñānasyāstitā pratetavyā / tad-yathāntareṇālaya-vijñānam āśrayopādānāsaṁbhavataḥ, ādi-pravṛttyasaṁbhavataḥ, spaṣṭa-pravṛttyasaṁbhavato, bījatvāsaṁbhavataḥ, karmāsaṁbhavataḥ, kāyikānubhāvāsaṁbhavato 'cittaka-samāpattyasaṁbhavato, vijñāna-cyutyasaṁbhavataś ca.* Also translated by Wilson (1984:426).

12. The Sanskrit of ASBh (Tatia 1976:12.1-11) is *keṇa kāraṇenāśrayopādānaṁ na yujyate? āha / pañcabhiḥ kāraṇaiḥ / tathā hi / ālaya-vijñānaṁ pūrva-saṃskāra-hetukam / cakṣur-ādi-pravṛtti-vijñānaṁ punar vartamāna-pratyaya-hetukam / yathoktam "indriya-viṣaya-manaskāra-vaśād vijñānānāṁ pravṛttir bhavatī"ti vistareṇa / idaṁ prathamaṁ kāraṇam / api ca kuśalākuśalāḥ ṣaḍ-vijñāna-kāyā upalabhyante / idaṁ dvitīyaṁ kāraṇam / api ca ṣaṇṇāṁ vijñāna-kāyānāṁ sā jātir nopalabhyate yā 'vyākṛta-vipāka-saṁgṛhītā syāt / idaṁ tṛtīyaṁ kāraṇam // api ca pratiniyatāśrayāḥ ṣaḍ vijñāna-kāyāḥ pravartante, tatra yena yenāśrayeṇa yad vijñānaṁ pravartate tad eva tenopāttaṁ syād avaśiṣṭasyānupāttaeti na yujyate. upāttatāpi na yujyate vijñāna-virahitatayā / idaṁ caturthaṁ kāraṇam /api ca punaḥ punar āśrayasyopādāna-doṣaḥ prasajyate / tathāhi cakṣur-vijñānam ekadā pravartate ekadā ma pravartate evam avaśiṣṭāni / idaṁ pañcamaṁ kāraṇam.* Also translated by Wilson (1984:430-31).

13. The phrase *nye ring med pa* can also mean 'impartial.'

14. These are the *ālambana-*, *adhipati-*, *samanatara-*, and *hetu-pratyayas.*

15. The Sanskrit of ASBh (Tatia 1976:12.14-19) is *kena kāraṇenādi-pravṛtti-saṁbhavo na yujyate / sacet kaścid vaded "yady ālaya-vijñānam asti tena dvayoḥ*

vijñānayoḥ yugapat pavṛttir bhaviṣyati" / sa idaṁ syād vacanīyo 'doṣa eva bhavān doṣa-saṃjñī / tathā hi bhavaty eva dvayor vijñānayor yugapat pravṛttiḥ / tat kasya hetoḥ / tathā hy ekatyasya yugapad [*draḍṣṭu* →] *draṣṭu*-(Hakamaya 1978:10)*kāmasya yāvad vijñātu-kāmasyādita itaretara-vijñāna-pravṛttir na yujyate / tathāhi tatra manaskāro 'pi nirviśiṣṭa indriyam api viṣayo 'pi.*

16. The Sanskrit of ASBh (Tatia 1976:12.20-24) is *kena kāraṇenāsatyāṁ yugapad vijñāna-pravṛttyāṁ mano-vijñānasya cakṣur-ādi-vijñāna-sahānucarasya spaṣṭatvaṁ na saṁbhavati / tathā hi yasmin samaye 'tītam anubhūtaṁ viṣayaṁ samanusmarati tasmin samaye 'vispaṣṭo mano-vijñāna-pracāro bhavati na tu tathā vartamāna-viṣayo manaḥ-pracāro 'vispaṣṭo bhavati / ato 'pi yugapat pravṛttir vā yujyate 'vispaṣṭatvaṁ vā mano-vijñānasya.*

17. The Sanskrit of ASBh (Tatia 1976:12.25-13.3) is *kena kāraṇena bījatvaṁ na saṁbhavati ṣaṇṇāṁ vijñāna-kāyānām anyonyam / tathā hi kuśalānantaram akuśalam utpadyate, akuśalānantaraṁ kuśalaṁ, tad-ubhayānantaram avyākṛtaṁ, hīna-dhātukānantaraṁ madhya-dhātukaṁ, madhya-dhātukānantaraṁ praṇīta-dhātukam, evaṁ praṇīta-dhātukānantaraṁ yāvad dhīna-dhātukaṁ, sāsravānantaram anāsravam, anāsravānantaraṁ sāsravam, laukikānantaraṁ lokottaraṁ, lokottarānantaraṁ laukikam / na ca teṣāṁ tathā bījatvaṁ yujyate / dīrgha-kāla-samucchinnāpi ca saṁtatiś cireṇa kālena pravartate, tasmād api na yujyate.*

18. The bad, middle, and good realms are the *kāma-*, *rūpa-* and *arūpya-dhātus.*

19. Tsong kha pa means that they are action (Tib. *las*) in the sense that they are associated with their agent (Tib. *byed pa→byed pa po*). For example, when an eye sense-consciousness, an action (Tib. *las*), is produced, it is necessarily associated with the person seeing–the agent. The state of awareness belongs to the agent in the sense that it is 'his sight.' Similarly, the four *vijñaptis*, though understood primarily as transformations (*pariṇāma*) of the *ālaya*, are equally, as 'representations of consciousness,' actions and hence necessarily associated with the agent.

20. The terms *don* and *sems can* have been explained (*Ocean of Eloquence* 7a4-6) as part of the *ālaya*'s objective support: "... five objects (Tib. *don*), i.e., forms, sounds, smells, tastes, and feelings; a 'sentient being' which is five sense-faculties, i.e., eye, ear, nose, tongue, and body."

21. The Sanskrit ofTK8b (Anacker 1984:422) is *tṛtīyaḥ ṣaḍ-vidhasya yā.*

22. The Sanskrit of ASBh (Tatia 1976:13.4-7) is *kena kāraṇenāsatyāṁ yugapad vijñāna-pravṛttyāṁ karma na saṃbhavati / tathā hi samāsataś catur-vidhaṁ karma bhājana-vijñaptir, āśraya-vijñaptir, aham iti vijñaptir, viṣaya-vijñaptiś ceti / etā vijñaptayaḥ kṣaṇe kṣaṇe yugapat pravartamānā upalabhyante / na caikasya vijñānasyaikasmin kṣaṇe idam evaṁ-rūpaṁ vyatibhinnaṁ karma yujyate.*

23. The Sanskrit of ASBh (Tatia 1976:13.8-11) is *kena kāraṅenāsaty ālaya-vijñāne kāyiko'nubhavo na yujyate / tathā hy ekatyasya yoniśo vāyoniśo vā cintayato vānuvitarkayato vā samāhita-cetaso vāsamāhita-cetaso vā ye kāye kāyānubhavā*

utpadyante 'neka-vidhā bahu-nānā-prakārās te na bhaveyur upalabhyante ca / tasmād apy asty ālaya-vijñānam.

24. These are a) *asaṁjñisamāpatti*, a meditative absorption so deep there is no *saṁjñā* ('discrimination,' 'thought') or *vedanā* ('feeling') and b) *nirodha-samāpatti*, a meditative state in which the person becomes completely absorbed in a vision of cessation (the ultimate) such that the knower and known are merged like water poured into water.

25. The Sanskrit of ASBh (Tatia 1976:13.12-15) is *kena kāraṇenāsaty ālaya-vijñāne 'cittā samāpattir na saṃbhavati / tathā hy asaṁjñisamāpannasya vā nirodha-samāpannasya [=pa'am 'gog pa'i snyoms par zhugs pa'i] vā vijñānam eva kāyād apakrāntaṁ syat / nānapakrāntaṁ tataḥ kāla-kriyaiva bhavet / yathoktaṁ bhagavatā "vijñānaṁ cāsya kāyād anapakrāntaṁ bhavatī"ti.*

26. *Pratītya-samutpādādi-vibhaṅga-nirdeśa* P5496:25.1.6; for suggestions as to the Sanskrit see Schmithausen (1987:216 and note 1373).

27 The Sanskrit of ASBh (Tatia 1976:13.16-20) is *kena kāraṇenāsaty ālaya-vijñāne cyutir api na yujyate / tathā hi cyavamānasya vijñānam ūrdhva-dehaṁ vā śītikurvan vijahāti, adho-dehaṁ vā / na ca mano-vijñānaṁ kadācin na pravartate / ato 'py ālaya-vijñānasyaiva dehopādānakasya vigamād deha-śītatopa[la]bhyate dehāpratisaṁvedanā ca / na tu mano-vijñānasya / ato 'pi na yujyate.*

28. MSam (Lamotte 1938:7-8; Nagao I 11-12).

29. The title means "Sūtra on the Fourfold Benefit that Comes from the Tathāgata." In *Aṅguttara-nikāya* II 131, quoted Lamotte (1938:vol. 2, 26) is a similar passage: *ālayārāmā bhikkhave pajā ālayaratā ālayasamuditā* (see Schmithausen 1987:n. 71) *sā tathāgatena anālaye dhamme desiyamāne sussūyati sotam odahati aññā cittam upaṭṭhāpeti. Tathāgatassa bhikkhave arahato sammāsambuddhassa pātubhāvā ayaṃ paṭhamo acchariyo abhuto dhammo pātubhavati.*

30. For an excellent consideration of the meaning of the term *paryāya* see Davidson 1985.

31. This verse, found in the Tibetan version of the MSam (Lamotte 1938:7; Nagao I 11) is missing from the Chinese text. Lamotte (1938:28 and notes 8-10) cites, amongst others, two passages from K'ouei ki's explanation of the doctrine of the *Visuddhi-magga* and the Sthavira-vāda, but the meaning of the seven terms remains obscure. In essence, perhaps, based on a disturbance (*āvarjana*) in the *bhavāṅga* there is movement (*iṅgita*) from which arises a bare sight (*darśana*) of an object. This, on investigation, leads to knowledge (*jñāna*) and realization (*viniścaya/prekṣā?*). The initiator (*=ākṣepaka?*) of the process is *manas.*

32. MSam (Lamotte 1938:3) Prasthāvanā 4. Cp. Lamotte's translation (1938:vol. 2, 10) based on Hsüan Tsang's Chinese version.

33. The subtle knowable (*sūkṣma-jñeya*) is the *ālaya-vijñāna* itself according

to the MSUp (Lamotte 1938:vol. 2, 23-24). Bu ston in his *Rnam bshad nyi ma'i 'od zer* (203.7) says ... *shes bya phra mo rang mtshan kun gzhi dang / spyi mtshan chos la bdag med pa ma shes na / rnam mkhyen thob pa mi srid* ... it is the *ālaya-vijñāna* in particular and *dharma-nairātmya* in general.

34. Cūlapanthaka Thera was a dullard who in the course of four months was unable to learn a single stanza. The Buddha comforted him, giving him a clean piece of cloth and telling him to repeat the words *rajo-haraṇam* ('wiping away dust') while wiping his face with a cloth. As Cūlapanthaka carried out these orders he noticed that the cloth became dirty. Then, concentrating his mind on the impermanence of all things, Cūlapanthaka finally attained Arhantship (Malalasekera 1960:vol. 1, 897-98).

35. MSam (Lamotte 1938:6-7; Nagao I 10).

36. Cp. *Guhyārtha-vyākhyā* P5553:64.4.3.

37. All versions of *Ocean of Eloquence* add "and thus achieve their liberation."

38. See chapter 4 n. 34.

39. A Vasumitra is said to be the author of the *Mahā-vibhāṣā*. Schmithausen (1987:19) mentions, besides this author of the *Vibhāṣā*, another "Vasumitra [author of] a lost work called *Paripṛcchā*." This writer is considered by Griffiths (1986:66-70) as the propounder of an *aparisphuṭa-mano-vijñāna* and an opponent of Ghoṣaka.

40. By calling the aggregates a 'basis' (*gzhi=āśraya*?) of delight, Vasumitra may, perhaps, mean that they are a basis, *the elimination of which* gives rise to delight.

41. According to Chandra Das, Vāmana is the Sanskrit of Mi'u Thung.

42. Ghoṣaka, a contemporary of [a] Vasumitra, is mentioned in the *Abhidharma-kośa-bhāṣya*. It is unclear whether this is the same Ghoṣaka who is said to be the author of a proto-Vaibhāṣika text, the *Abhidharmāmṛta*, now extant only in Chinese translation (Taisho 1553).

43. MSam (Lamotte 1938:8; Nagao I 13). Lamotte directs the reader to la Vallée Poussin's *Vijñapti-matratā-siddhi*, p. 181-82. See also Bu ston's *Rnam bshad nyi ma'i 'od zer* (204, 1-6).

44. Reading *ma tshang chung med*. If one reads *ma tsang chung mod* it means "It is true that there is a tiny deficiency. Nevertheless. . . ."

45 MSam (Lamotte 1938:8; Nagao I 13).

46. For a similar use of 'adherence to' (*ālīnā*) see *Ocean of Eloquence* 13b, 28b5-6.

47. MSam (Lamotte 1938:8-9; Nagao I 13).

Seven

Proofs of *Kliṣṭa-manas*

Second, there is reasoning (*yukti*) [which establishes the existence] of *kliṣṭa-manas.*

> Were there no *kliṣṭa-manas* there would be the following faults. There would be no a) unentangled ignorance, b) similarity with the five [sense-consciousnesses], c) specific meditative absorptions, or d) word derivation. e) There would be the fault of no ego-grasping in the continuum of those born in the [realm of] no-thought (*asaṁjñyāyatana*), and f) having ego-grasping in every case would be untenable. Hence one should realize that *kliṣṭa-manas* exists. [Mv XXXX]

The *kliṣṭa-manas* is asserted to exist because there would be six difficulties if it did not.

First proof

How come there would be no unentangled ignorance (*āveṇikyavidyā*) if there were no *kliṣṭa-manas*?

[Response:] In the MSam[1] we read that,

> Unentangled ignorance is asserted to be always a block to the mind that penetrates reality (*bhūtārtha*) and to be present at all times.

Thus this ignorance always blocks direct witness to the meaning of selflessness, and is present whenever any virtuous, nonvirtuous or neutral state of mind arises. Now, since this [unentangled ignorance] is a mental factor (*caitta*) it must be associated with a single principal mind. But since it is a *kleśa* ('afflictive emotion') and lasts without a break in its continuum until the Ārya path, it could not be possessed by either the *ālaya-vijñāna* or by the set of six [consciousnesses].

Why is it called 'unentangled ignorance'?

[In response we say:] The venerable Aśvabhāva explains that it is unentangled as to location. This is because, just like unentangled (*āvenika*)

Buddha-dharmas [which are unentangled in the sense that their location is only with a Buddha], only the *kliṣṭa-manas* is its locus. The author of the *Guhyārtha-vyākhyā* [on the other hand] explains that it is unentangled either because a) it can bring forth other *kleśas* ('afflictive emotion') by its power [49a] but those others cannot bring it forth, or b) because it is independently self-powered. The *Upanibandhana* says:[2]

> Nevertheless, since *kleśas* ('afflictive emotions') other than it, such as *sat-kāya-dṛṣṭi*, etc., are associated with it, surely it is not established as being unentangled? [In response we say:] The presentation is not right. It is not asserted to be unentangled because it is not associated with other afflictive emotions. Why is it then? It is because, just like the eighteen unentangled Buddha-dharmas, others do not have it.

And the *Guhyārtha-vyākhyā* says:[3]

> It [unentangled ignorance] is unentangled because it is self-powered ignorance, not because it has no association with other root *kleśas* ('afflictive emotions').[4] For that would lead to the absurd consequence that [ignorance] associated with [a dominating *upakleśa* ('secondary afflictive emotion')] such as fury (*krodha*) and so forth would be [unentangled ignorance] as well. Also the absurd consequence that [ignorance] unassociated with any [root] afflictive emotion or secondary afflictive emotions whatsoever would be [unentangled ignorance] does not come about. This is because that would lead to the consequence that it does not exist [while it patently does]. Thus it has associated root afflictive emotions, and, since, even in a collection of mind and mental factors other than those, it is unentangled with other substantial things it is unentangled in the sense of being self-powered.[5] It is not [unentangled] on account of its being exclusive (*nāsādhāranārthatvena*). Otherwise it would lead to an [absurd] consequence since it is associated with other consciousnesses [besides the seventh alone].

When there is the assertion [that the unentangled in 'unentangled ignorance' means] unentangled with associated [mental factors] [49b] a) if one intends thereby that it is unentangled with other root afflictive emotions, the ignorance associated with [only a secondary afflictive emotion] such as fury would [absurdly] become unentangled [ignorance], and b) if one intends thereby that it does not have any other root or secondary afflictive emotion [associated with it] at all, such an ignorance would not exist [because, according to the Yogācāra doctrine, at least three other root afflictive emotions are needed]. Hence unentangled refers to being unentangled with some other substantial thing; to being a self-powered substantial thing.

Although at this point [in the *Guhyārtha-vyākhyā*] there is no further explanation of what self-powered would entail beyond the mere assertion that:[6] "Even though, since it has a) root afflictive emotions and b) minds and mental factors other than those, unassociated-unentanglement[7] is absent [from unentangled ignorance] still, since it is unentangled with other substantial things, it is unentangled," nevertheless, later on it says:[8]

> That is the *kliṣṭa-manas.* It has a self-powered ignorance because, by its force, the [self-]love, etc., associated with it are brought forth.

Although the author of the *Guhyārtha-vyākhyā,* then, explains unentangled [as unentangled] with some other substantial thing he in fact, explains [unentangled to mean] unentangled with a force [other than its own].

Hence there are two schools of thought. And although Matamati says both are valid it seems to us that the correct [explanation of the word 'unentangled'] is unentangled as to location. This is because although, to a certain extent, [self-] love, etc., do operate on account of the force of delusion (Tib. *rmongs ba*), conversely, ignorance itself operates contingent on them. And since the [mental factors] surrounding the *kliṣṭa-manas* are mutually cause and effect of each other, there is none of which it can be said "It alone brings forth [the others]."

Second proof

Why would there be the fault of dissimilarity with the five [sense-consciousnesses] if there were no *kliṣṭa-manas*?

[Response:] In the MSam it says,[9]

> What makes apparent the existence of *kliṣṭa-manas*? [In response we say:] Were it not to exist there would be the fault that ignorance would not be unentangled. There would also be the fault that there would be no similarity between [thinking-mind consciousness and] the five [sense-consciousnesses]. Just as the simultaneous supports for the group of five consciousnesses are the eyes, etc. [the thinking-mind consciousness needs a support].

This [is interpreted] in two [ways]. The position of the *Guhyārtha-vyākhyā* is as follows:[10] [50a]

> The *mano-vijñāna* ('thinking-mind consciousness') is not only something with a past support[11] because it is also an entering consciousness (*pravṛtti-vijñāna*), for example, like the eye sense-consciousness. What this means is that the five sense-consciousnesses each have an immediately preceding *manas* ('thinking-mind') which is their past support, and there are the five sense-faculties which are their simultaneous supports. In

> that the *mano-vijñāna* is indifferentiable from these in terms of being an entering consciousness it is not correct [to say] it does not have both [supports].

The *Upanibandhana*[12] takes the position that this is not an assertion in our own system. The consciousness that would be without a simultaneous support found in the sacred texts of others is refuted. How? Since for those who do not accept more than the set of six [consciousnesses] there would be no *ālaya-vijñāna* and *kliṣṭa-manas*, the absurd consequence would be that there would be no *mano-vijñāna*, because there would be no simultaneous support for it.

In both commentaries [one finds the following objection]: This is not so. [The simultaneous support of *manas*] is the one to nine holes in the heart region.

[The response in the *Upanibandhana* is that] this is not tenable. In that case the *mano-vijñāna* would lack the conceptuality that comes from conceptual certainty (*nirūpaṇa*) and conceptual remembrance (*anusmaraṇa*) because its support would be a physcial sense-faculty, just like, for example, a sense-consciousness. Also the feeling of *mano-vijñāna* would not be a mental feeling because its support would be an accumulation of tiny atoms. And [as it says in the *Guhyārtha-vyākhyā*][13] this also contradicts the sūtra which says "*manas* is not taught as an inner *āyatana* ('sense-faculty')."

Thus, although there are two views, nevertheless, relative to the [flawed] assertion in [the *Abhidharma-kośa*],[14] that

> The support of the last [consciousness] is past. The five [consciousnesses] arise from that [i.e., past] and simultaneous [conditions] as well.

one should establish [what is correct] as in the *Guhyārtha-vyākhyā*; and one should deal, as in the *Upanibandhana*, with the [flawed] assertion that the simultaneous support of the thinking-mind consciousness is the physical heart.

Third proof

Why [paraphrasing the *Guhyārtha-vyākhyā*] would there be [50b] the fault of no specific meditative absorptions if there were no *kliṣṭa-manas*?

Were there no *kliṣṭa-manas* the two meditative absorptions[15] would be indifferentiable because, in terms of the set of six [consciousnesses] having been blocked they would be the same and, in terms of whether or not there was *kliṣṭa-manas*, there would be no difference. We [i.e., Tsong kha pa] hold that [there is a difference]. When absorbed in no-thought meditation (*asaṁjñīsamāpatti*), there is a pride in I, ego-grasping, and self-love that have not been pacified. When absorbed into [a vision of ultimate] cessation (*nirodha-samāpatti*), on the other hand, one is free from them and they are pacified.

If [paraphrasing the *Upanibandhana*] one says that, since they [*asaṁjñi-* and *nirodha-samāpatti*] differ in terms of level (*bhūmi*) and mental activity (*manaskara*), they can be specified, [in response we say] that this is not so. Although there are just those [differences], the fact remains that a difference in terms of pacified or not pacified is not possible. And if [paraphrasing the *Guhyārtha-vyākhyā*] one says that they differ in terms of being in the continuum of an Ārya or ordinary being [in response we say] that difference is also impossible. Āryas consider no-thought meditative absorption an abyss to be avoided and forsake it. They do this, not because the set of six are blocked, but because ego-grasping has not been pacified. Otherwise [if they forsook no-thought meditative absorption because the set of six consciousnesses were blocked] they would [absurdly] also have to forsake meditative absorption into [a vision of ultimate] cessation. We hold that it is possible that they do, or do not, forsake [a meditative absorption] on account of a difference in terms of pacified or not pacified. Thus it says in the MSam:[16]

> There also would be the fault that the no-thought and cessation meditative absorptions would not be specifiable. No-thought meditative absorption is a sort that has *kliṣṭa-manas* while meditative absorption into cessation is not. Were this not the case, these two would not be specifiable.

Fourth proof

Why would there be the fault that those who are born in the no-thought [heaven] (*asaṁjñisattva*) would lack ego-grasping if there were no *kliṣṭa-manas*?[17] [51a]

[Response:] Although one would come to expect an afflicted state and ego-grasping, since, at the first moment when one is born in the no-thought [heaven] a mental consciousness (Tib. *yid shes*) along with ego-grasping come into being, nevertheless, there would be no ego-grasping in that continuum from after one was born right up until the onset of the mind of death. This is because there would be no *kliṣṭa-manas* and the set of six [consciousnesses] would have been blocked.

[Attempted defense of discredited thesis. This is a paraphrase of the *Upanibandhana*:] At the first moment of birth a *manas* with ego-grasping manifests itself. After that, although ego-grasping does not actually manifest itself, since its residual impression is still there ego-grasping is present.

[Response:] This is impossible. The mental consciousness that is the support of ego-grasping is not there and it is impossible for the aggregate of form (*rūpa-skandha*) to be the location of the tainting residual impression. Were a no-thought god to have no ego-grasping, he would [absurdly] be free from affliction. If [paraphrasing the *Guhyārtha-vyākhyā*] one asserts that, then the

Āryas would [absurdly] not view being in the no-thought [heaven] as constituting an *akṣaṇa* ('lack')[18] and forsake [birth there]. They do not consider it a lack and forsake it just because the set of six [consciousnesses] are stilled. Meditative absorption into [a vision of ultimate] cessation is similar [in that respect, but they do not forsake that]. [We hold that rebirth as a no-thought god] constitutes a lack a) because, since there is *kliṣṭa-manas* there is ego-grasping and so forth on every occasion; and b) because, since there is also no set of six [consciousnesses] there is the perverted notion [something grand has been attained] and so they have to stay there for five hundred eons. Thus it says in the MSam:[19]

> If a situation where a no-thought [god] were to have no ego-grasping and pride in the thought "I am" (*asmimāna*), there would be the fault that for the duration of birth in the no-thought heaven (*asaṃjñikā*) one would be free from affliction.

Fifth proof

How come there would be the fault that no creative etymology (*nirukti*) for [*manas*] would be possible if there were no *kliṣṭa-manas.*[20] [In response we say:] Were there no *kliṣṭa-manas* the etymology, "It [*manas*] is there because there is always selfishness (*manana*)"[21] would not be applicable to any consciousness, because *ālaya* and sense-consciousnesses are not egotistical and mental consciousness and its associated [mental factors] [51b] do not always think that way (*cetanā*) either. Thus it says in the MSam:[22]

> There would also be the fault that there would be no creative etymology.

Sixth proof

Why would ego-grasping on all occasions be impossible if there were no *kliṣṭa-manas*?

[Response:] One sees ego-grasping in every mental state (Tib. *sems*), be it virtuous, nonvirtuous, or not a subject of moralizing, as when [aware that] "I am being generous," "I am murdering," "I am washing." Now, this is possible if there is a *kliṣṭa-manas* but not otherwise. This is because, if there were no [*kliṣṭa-manas*], ego-grasping would be associated with a nonvirtuous mind and then virtuous and neutral minds would never come into being. Given that there is a *kliṣṭa-manas*, however, [ego-grasping] is associated with it and, since that is not a subject of moralizing, it does not preclude the simultaneous operation of virtuous and nonvirtuous minds. Thus it says in the MSam:[23]

> And also, one sees ego-grasping at all times, on every occasion in virtuous, nonvirtuous and neutral mental states. Otherwise it [ego-grasping]

would be associated only with a nonvirtuous mind. It would not be the affliction thinking "I am," which is on every occasion of a virtuous or neutral mental state.

In this context Aśvabhāva [author of the *Upanibandhana*] explains:[24]

Where there is no ignorance (*avidyā*) this ego-grasping that arises on all occasions is not found. And that ignorance is found based solely on the *kliṣṭa-manas.*

In the *Guhyārtha-vyākhyā* [we read of the following wrong views][25] in regard to the appearance of ego-grasping on the occasion of all virtuous, nonvirtuous, and neutral minds. As a subtle factor causing distortion it is held to be there at the same time as virtuous and neutral states of mind. To say "If one does not assert *kliṣṭa-manas,* [52a] ego-grasping would occur only with a nonvirtuous mind," is not correct because the assertion, as [held by] Vaibhāṣikas, is that *sat-kāya-dṛṣṭi*[26] is *nivṛta* ('obscured') and not a subject of moralizing [and is thus the mental factor associated with the sixth mind which functions to cause ego-grasping]. And also [it is not correct] because of the assertion, as in the Sautrāntikas' and our own system, that innate ego-grasping and pride in the thought "I am" occur only with a mind that is obscured and not a subject of moralizing.

Having presented these two arguments, in response to the first the *Guhyārtha-vyākhyā* says[27] that were ego-grasping not present at all times how would the virtuous and neutral states of mind of ordinary beings come to be contaminated (*sāśrava*)?[28] [If you say that contamination is] something that serves to increase contamination when observed, they would not be contaminated in that sense. When these two states of mind become manifest, contamination is blocked from arising in the continuum and when they do not occur they do not exist, and increase relative to what does not exist is impossible. They are also not [contaminated] through the observation of other [external object] contamination, because observation of externals is not asserted. Were they [contaminated] just because their governing [condition] is contaminated this would also be true of uncontaminated phenomena as well. And if they were [contaminated] because of being related with the seed of contamination the [absurd] consequence would be that the true path [would be contaminated as well]. Therefore they are properly said to be contaminated because, where there is *kliṣṭa-manas,* manifest contamination occurs simultaneously.

And in answering the second argument it says that the nonvirtue [referred to in the context of explaining ego-grasping] is not the nonvirtue that gives rise to an unwelcome fruit, but just [bare nonvirtue, defined as] what is opposite to virtue.

This completes the proofs of the *kliṣṭa-manas* and ends the second *lc'u* ('chapter'),[29] "Discussion of the Proofs," from my *Ocean of Eloquence: An Extensive Commentary on the Difficult Points of Ālaya-vijñāna and Kliṣṭa-manas.*

Notes

1. MSam (Lamotte 1938:6; Nagao I 7).

2. MSU P5552:241a4-5; trans. by Lamotte from the Chinese (1938:vol. 2, 18).

3. *Guhyārtha-vyākhyā* P5553:60.4.3-7.

4. As, e.g., at AK5.1-3 *mūlaṁ bhavasyānuśayāḥ [i.e., kleśāḥ] ṣaḍ rāgaḥ pratighas tathā / māno 'vidyā ca dṛṣṭiś ca vicikitsā ca teṣu naḥ.* These six deadly sins, which together are the root of all painful existence, are desire, enmity, pride, ignorance, doubt and view or opinion (*dṛṣṭi*).

5. This translation of this part of the *Guhyārtha-vyākhyā*, which Tsong kha pa also seems to have found obscure, is conjectural.

6. This is a paraphrase of the passage from the *Guhyārtha-vyākhyā* quoted above 49a4-5.

7. That is to say, the unentanglement defined as the absence of any associated mind or mental factors is not present.

8. *Guhyārtha-vyākhyā* P5553:61.1.4-5.

9. MSam (Lamotte 1938:5; Nagao I 7). The translation is aided by Lamotte (1938:vol. 2, 18).

10. Paraphrasing *Guhyārtha-vyākhyā* P5553:61.3.1.

11. This takes *'das pa'i rten* (**atītāśraya*) as a bahuvrīhi.

12. This is a paraphrase of P5552:241a6-b2. Translated from the Chinese by Lamotte (1938:vol. 2, 18-19). The assertion of the Sautrāntika is that all six consciousnesses are similar in having a simultaneous material basis: the five sense-faculties and the heart region.

13. At this point, in all editions of the text, notations identifying the source of Tsong kha pa's quotations make a sudden appearance. The entire quotation or paraphrase of a passage given by Tsong kha pa has been identified by a commentator's inserting the name of the text, e.g., beginning *Don* . . . and ending . . . *gsang* or *Bshad* . . . and ending . . . *sbyar* around the entire passage. The block cutters sometimes accidentally drop out the first or last word of the title. Also *gsang* is sometimes changed to *gsung*. It is very unlikely the annotations were part of the original composition. They appear at different points in the different mss. Unless otherwise noted I have followed

the editor of N who has enclosed all such annotation in square brackets and attempted to put them in some sort of coherent order.

14. AK1.44 (Gokhale 1946:78) *caramasy āśrayo 'tītaḥ pañcānāṁ sahajaś ca taiḥ*.

15. See chapter 6 n. 24.

16. MSam (Lamotte 1938:5; Nagao I 7).

17. In the verse summary this proof is fifth. Here it is dealt with fourth because the quotation from the MSam "no-thought and . . . " mentions it.

18. There are eight 'lacks' (*akṣaṇas*, *mi khom*). Freedom from the eight ('eight freedoms') defines a perfect rebirth. A perfect rebirth is thought of as a rare and fleeting moment (*kṣaṇa*) for Buddhist religious practices. Rebirth in the no-thought heaven is *akṣaṇa* insofar as rebirth there precludes Buddhist religious practices.

19. MSam (Lamotte 1938:5; Nagao I 7).

20. In the verse summary this proof is fourth.

21. Cp. AS, quoted *Ocean of Eloquence* 35b2, "What is *manas*? It is always selfish (*manyanā*) . . . [and has] the thought 'I am,'" and MSam, quoted above 36a.

22. MSam (Lamotte 1938:5; Nagao I 7).

23. MSam (Lamotte 1938:6; Nagao I 7).

24. MSU P5552:243a3-4. Translated from the Chinese by Lamotte (1938: vol. 2, 21).

25. Paraphrasing *Guhyārtha-vyākhyā* P5553:62.4.6-8.

26. That is, ego-grasping. See chapter 4 n. 34.

27. This is a conjectural translation of Tsong kha pa's explanation of *Guhyārtha-vyākhyā* (P5553:62.3.8-62.4.2).

28. Cf. *Vyākhyā* of Yaśomitra on AK1.4 (Shastri 1981:16-17).

29. See chapter 5 n. 40.

EIGHT

TWO REFUTATIONS AND FINAL REMARKS

Third, the refutation of those who assert a set of nine consciousnesses. This has two parts: First, the thesis to be refuted (*pūrva-pakṣa*).

> It is the system of Paramārtha[1] that accepts the *ādāna-vijñāna* ('appropriating consciousness') as seventh, that mentions the *ālaya* as three, and that accepts [52b] the stainless consciousness (*amala-vijñāna*) as ninth. [Mv XLI]

Here I present the assertions about the different numbers of consciousnesses by Mahāyāna masters as they are explained by the Chinese master (Tib. *rgya'i slob dpon*) Won ch'uk. In his *Chieh sh'en mi ching shu* it says:[2]

> In the Śrāvaka baskets (*piṭakas*) there are only six consciousnesses, the seventh and eighth consciousnesses are not taught. For details it is as [one finds] in their doctrines.
>
> Now, when one turns to the Mahāyāna treatises there are two explanations. The first is by the master Nāgārjuna and so forth, who explain that there are only six consciousnesses. Thus we read in the *Tattvāmṛtāvatāra* ("Penetration into the Essence of Ultimate Reality") chapter[3] in Bhavya's *Madhyamaka-hṛdaya* ("Heart of the Middle Way") that:
>
> > There is no *ālaya-vijñāna* above and beyond the six consciousnesses. Since it is not included in the six consciousnesses such as the eye sense-consciousness it is akin to a space-flower .
>
> One should thus understand that their works treat only of six consciousnesses.
>
> The second is in the treatises of Ārya Maitreya, where, based on the *Ārya-suvarṇa-prabhāsa-sūtra* ("Ārya Golden Light Sūtra"), etc., there is a full presentation of all eight consciousnesses. Based on those treatises [of Maitreya] Indian masters then explained in three ways.

First the master Bodhiruci. He makes a presentation of two minds based on the *Vijñapti-mātratā-siddhi* ("On the Proof of Mere Representation"). He explains that, of these, the first is called the *dharmatā-citta* ('mind which is ultimate reality'). This is *tattva* ('suchness'). Although this suchness is itself called mind [53a] it does not grasp anything [literally 'does not have an objective support']. The second is the mind with associated [mental factors]. Associated with it are mental factors such as faith, attachment, etc. The *Vijñapti-mātratā-siddhi* says, in defining these:

> Though they are explained as *manas* and *vijñāna* it does not contradict [what was said earlier] because [*manas*, in this context, means] the essence of *manas* as a mere representation and [by *vijñāna* is meant] the essence of mere representation itself.

Second, based on the treatise called *Viniścaya-kośa* ("Treasury of Ascertainment"), is the presentation of what is entailed by nine consciousnesses as set forth by Paramārtha in the chapter on the nine sorts of consciousness [in his **Khyāti-vijñāna-śāstra*.] There, of the nine consciousnesses referred to, the explanation of the six consciousnesses such as the eye sense-consciousness, etc., is generally the same as in other commentaries. The seventh is *ādāna-vijñāna* ('appropriating consciousness'). Since it grasps the eighth as me and mine it has afflictive obscuration (*kleśāvaraṇa*) alone and is without dharma-grasping. There is no definite achievement of Buddhahood [when it is removed].[4] The eighth is the *ālaya-vijñāna* of which there are three types:

Some [explain as follows]: The first is the the essential *ālaya.* It has the function (*artha*) of going up to [i.e., being the substantial reality which completely transforms into] Buddhahood. The second is the maturation (*vipāka*) *ālaya.* It ranges over the eighteen elements (*dhātu*). Thus the treatise called the *Madhyānta-vibhāga-kārikā* says (This is not in our [Tibetan] translations but it clearly exists in Chinese):[5]

> From consciousness, appearances as sense-faculty, object, self and representation (*vijñapti*) arise which are similar to that [consciousness].

It is therefore explained, based on this and other treatises, [53b] that the eighth [consciousness] ranges over the eighteen elements. The third is the afflicted *ālaya.* It grasps the object suchness and four sorts of pride arise. It is dharma-grasping but not person-grasping. This is how it is explained based on the treatises of Ācārya Sthiramati.

The ninth is the stainless consciousness (*amala-vijñāna*). It is *tattva* ('suchness'). The nature of *tattva* is such that, though one, it has two significations. First of all it is the object that is observed. As such it is called *tattva* and *bhūta-koṭi* ('reality-limit'), etc. Second it is what observes. As such it is called 'stainless consciousness' or 'primordial knowledge.' For more detail it is as set forth in the teaching on nine consciousnesses and in the chapter on the nine sorts of consciousness in the treatise *Viniścaya-kośa.*

Third, based on the *Lankāvatāra-sūtra* and so forth, and on the texts of Dharmapāla, etc., the master Hsüan Tsang makes a presentation of only eight consciousnesses. He does not mention a ninth because of the analysis in Bhavya's text. As it says:

> In that authoritative presentation itself their [Yogācāra's] own sacred texts are contradicted because in all the sūtras such as the *Lankāvatāra* and so forth the eighth is the *ālaya-vijñāna.*

In this case, why is it that in the great chapter (Tib. *le'u chen po*) of the *Prajñā-pāramitā-sūtra*, etc., only six consciousnesses are mentioned? [In response we say:] In the detailed breakdown explanation of the *Vijñapti-mātratā-siddhi* master Dharmapāla [is said] to give the following explanation:

> The statement in the sūtras that there are only six consciousnesses is a door to a meaning which will come about [i.e., is a skillful means to lead readers on to a more precise understanding]. Alternatively there are six types [of consciousness] relative to the six sense-faculties that are [54a] bases. In the final analysis, however, the division of consciousness is into eight types.

But did not Nāgārjuna make a presentation of just six types [of consciousness]? We shall explain. Though in the final analysis the master Nāgārjuna believed there to be a seventh and eighth consciousness . . . .[6]

Won ch'uk, having thus presented these three systems, himself follows the system of Hsüan Tsang. In regard to the presentation of Bhavya's position, there does not appear to be such a refutation of the *ālaya* in the translation of the *Madhyamaka-hṛdaya* presently in Tibet. There is not even a chapter with a name like that.

So then, the master Won ch'uk is called Rdzogs gsal in the 'Phang thang bibliography (*dkar chag*), but according to Rig pa'i ral gri[7] it is not proper to assert that he is the Rdzogs gsal who accepts the ninth stainless consciousness, because Rdzogs gsal was Chinese while the man who accepts nine consciousnesses, Paramārtha, was an Indian.

Refuting a set of nine consciousnesses

The refutation of the assertion that there are a set of nine [consciousnesses]:

> Since any primary consciousness beyond the set of eight would [absurdly] be a permanent functioning thing there is no proof of a set of nine. [Mv XLII]

Were there to be a ninth primary consciousness which was other than the set of eight it would be both permanent and a functioning thing [i.e., impermanent] as well because it would be a) not a composite (*asaṁskṛta*) [i.e., not produced and hence permanent] and b) an object-discerning consciousness [i.e., produced and hence impermanent]. If, [in attempting to defend the discredited thesis], one says that it is a composite but not systematized in the set of eight [in response we say:] this cannot be. If it were to be something physical or a nonassociated phenomenon (Tib. *ldan min*) it could not discern. It is not a mental factor. And it is also not possible for it to be a mind either [54b] because there is neither sound reasoning nor scriptural basis (*āgama*) for asserting a consciousness not systematized in the set of eight. Furthermore a seventh, *ādāna-vijñāna* is not referred to in the Tathāgata-sūtras or in any part whatsoever of the sacred books of the King Maitreya and is not asserted by the path-blazer [Asaṅga]. Sthiramati's own ideas are, therefore, not consistent with these texts which he takes to be authoritative.

This ends the third *le'u* ('chapter'),[8] "Refuting Those Who Assert a Set of Nine Consciousnesses," from my *Ocean of Eloquence: An Extensive Commentary on the Difficult Points of Ālaya-vijñāna and Kliṣṭa-manas.*

Refuting a set of one consciousness

Fourth, the refutation of those who assert a set of one consciousness. This has two parts: the statement of the thesis to be refuted and its refutation.

> When each [of the set of six consciousnesses] goes forth based on the six sense-faculties it is just the one mental consciousness (Tib. *yid shes*) that is simply being called by each of the names. Since the "Brāhmaṇa Compilation" [in the *Udāna-varga*] and the *Dva-daśāyatanopadeśa-sūtra*

> ("Sūtra Teaching the Twelve Āyatanas") also mention [consciousnesses] as being one and mention the six consciousnesses as being the *mana-āyatana* ('mind element') all consciousnesses, they say, are the mental consciousness alone. [Mv XLIII]

This explanation is from the point of view of those who assert [all consciousnesses] to be just *bodhi-citta* ('[altruistic] mind [set on] enlightenment'). In the "Brāhmaṇa Compilation" [of the *Udāna-varga*] sole reference is made to a mind which has come into being and alone travels:

> A Brāhmaṇa, I say, is one who tames the mind (*citta*) that is hard to tame which alone travels (*ekacara*) and goes far.

And in the sūtras it says that, of the twelve *āyatanas*, the set of six consciousnesses is the *mana-āyatana* ('mind element') and that:

> The *manas* experiences the objects of the six consciousnesses. They resort to *manas*.

Thus, just the one mental consciousness, based on each of the six sense-faculties which are the bases, [55a] comes to get the name of each of the consciousnesses which go forth to each object. It is similar, for example, to lighting a single lamp in a home with many windows. Thus the MSam also says:[9]

> Some say *mano-vijñāna* itself operates from one or the other of the bases and gets the name of one or the other [of the consciousnesses] in a fashion analagous to intention (*cetanā*) being called the physical or verbal deed (*karman*).[10] Arising on all the bases, in its variety of forms, it [*manas*] comes about appearing in two ways. This is simply the appearance of the bare object and the appearance of conceptualization. Since, in the realm of the physical, *mano-vijñāna* is located in the body, one feels every part of it to be alive. This is analagous to the other five physical sense-faculties located in the body.[11] Thus it says in the *Udāna-[varga]*:[12]
>
> > A Brāhmaṇa, I say, is one who tames the mind that is hard to tame, that lies within but is not body, which alone travels and goes far.
>
> And also it says,[13]
>
> > The *manas* experiences the objects which the five sense-faculties range over. They resort to *manas*.
>
> And it also says when teaching about the twelve *āyatanas* that the set of six consciousnesses is the *mana-āyatana*.

The meaning of the passage beginning "Since, in the realm of the physical . . ." up to ". . . located in the body" is as follows: The five physical sense-faculties other than mental consciousness are located in the body. Just as the experience of harm or benefit to those [five sense-faculties is also experienced by the body], since mental consciousness in the realm of the physical is located in [55b] the body, its experiences are also the body's [experiences] and there is the appearance of getting feelings of heaviness and lightness and so forth throughout the body. The meaning of "it comes about appearing in two ways" is as follows. One part of mental consciousness (Tib. *yid shes*) perceives and settles on just the appearance of the object. This is the nonconceptual. Since the other part, which settles on and conceptualizes the appearance of the object, is also mental consciousness there is not the flaw of its being only nonconceptual. The word 'resort' in the second quotation means that they are established by the *manas* sense-faculty.

Second, the refutation:

> Since the scriptures could mean something else, since sense-consciousnesses would [absurdly] behold the hidden, and also the past and the future as well, to assert a set of one is foggy and wrong. [Mv XLIV]

First, the quotations do not prove consciousnesses to be one. By "which alone travels" is intended only mental consciousness. The statements that *manas* travels over the range of the five senses-faculties, and that *manas* is the "revealer of the sense consciousnesses" intend a) that mental consciousness grasps all phenomena, b) that by the power of mental consciousness sense-consciousnesses penetrate their objects and, c) that mental consciousness has the force to prevent them [sense-consciousnesses] going out to objects and to gather [them] inside. The statement that the set of six [consciousnesses] are the *mana-āyatana* is made because there is no other amongst the twelve *āyatanas* where they can be placed.[14] It is not teaching that they are mental consciousness since *manas* and mental consciousness are not the same thing.

Logical reasoning (*yukti*) also does not establish [a set of one consciousness]. This is because, if one, it would be mental consciousness and there would then, [absurdly], be sense-consciousnesses which infer hidden phenomena from a reason (*hetu*) and which behold [objects in] the past and future. Furthermore, mental consciousness would, [absurdly], be totally nonconceptual because it and sense-consciousness would be a single material reality. [56a]

[Attempted defense of discredited thesis:] Have we not already said that, though one, there are two parts: just the appearance of the object and conceptual settling?

[Response:] This idea that it has two parts and is also a single material reality is not the understanding that gives joy to celestial beings.

Even though the MSam does not directly refute the assertion that there is a set of one [consciousness], its establishing that there is a set of eight serves to refute it. And although the *Upanibandhana*, in its commentary on this, does not do so either, still, its refutation of the idea of the physical heart being the basis of mental consciousness quoted above [50a3] serves as a refutation.

This then is the damage that logical reasons and scriptures cause to those who say there are more, or less, than a set of eight consciousnesses. [Therefore,]

> Since credible scriptures and logical reasons establish eight consciousnesses those who are wise and do not shy away from the secret import [of the teaching] should assert exactly eight. [Mv XLV]

Scholars who are not scared of the profound import of the Tathāgatas' [teaching], i.e., the *ālaya* and the *vijñapti-mātra* ('representation only') philosophy, should assert that there is a set of exactly eight.

This ends the fourth *le'u* ('chapter'),[15] "Refuting Those Who Assert a Set of One Consciousness," from my *Ocean of Eloquence: An Extensive Commentary on the Difficult Points of Ālaya-vijñāna and Kliṣṭa-manas.*

Concluding remarks

> Thanks to my lamas, I have completely explained, according to the intent of the celebrated brothers' [Asaṇga and Vasubandhu's] works and their commentaries, and without confusing the issue, the difficult topics of *mano-vijñāna* and *ālaya-vijñāna*, extremely difficult topics which have resisted repeated efforts of others to understand.
>
> How true it is that it is almost impossible to satisfy those scholarly ghosts [56b] whose understanding, after repeated study, is merely academic; whose expertise is in a litany of assertions and who are satisfied with just words.
>
> Still, a scholar who interprets the basic doctrines enshrined in the texts of Śākyamuni and the great path breakers [Nāgārjuna and Asaṅga] without plagiarizing others, and whose intellect is oblivious to pretentious utterances, will capture a scholar's heart.
>
> Would those who are learned in the Vijñapti-[mātrin] texts which are as vast as a great ocean please make a just and fair appraisal of this consciousness, satisfactory or otherwise.

If you think something is satisfactory please accept it. Since it is certainly not impossible that somebody with my sort of knowledge could make mistakes on subtle [topics], if [something] is not [satisfactory] please do otherwise.

These joyous merits that have been obtained from this [work], an inexhaustible treasure in this and future lives, like an infinite amount of good qualities [flowing from] the gigantic treasure jar, may they be bestowed on pure and impure living beings.

And may I, life after life, follow a person who excels in keeping the precepts (*śīla*), drink the ambrosia of the teachings of the Sage and, like a servant to all, avoid arrogance.

This [completes my] *Ocean of Eloquence: An Extensive Commentary on the Difficult Points of Ālaya-vijñāna and Kliṣṭa-manas.*

[The work was composed] taking the dust of [my first lama's] feet upon my head, (Chos kyi rje Don grub rin chen,[16] if I dare to state his name), a person with indefatigable wisdom and limitless compassion for showing the path of liberation to countless people. [It was completed] by relying with reverence on the lotus feet of [my main lama] Red mda' ba gshon nu blo gros,[17] a person who was [57a] born from two vast [stores of merit and wisdom] accumulated over many lives, who comprehended, just from seeing them, most all of the Tathāgata's teachings and, who, having understood profound dependent origination (*pratītya-samutpāda*), precious in the storeroom of the Buddha's revelation, became endowed with the great dharma eye which dispels doubt. [The author of the work] is Blo bzang grags pa of Eastern Tibet (*shar mdo smad*) [who is knowledgable in] the Tripiṭaka and whose mind has got into and investigated a portion of the Buddha's revelation. By having applied myself in this way at the Vajra Seat [Bodh Gayā] of the snowy mountain ranges—the glorious Sa skya Chos grva chen po ('Great religious institution at Sa skya')—may there be benefit for the [Buddha's] teaching and for infinite numbers of living beings.

Notes

1. Paramārtha lived from 499-569. Wilson points out (1984:221) that *yang dag bden pa* taken literally suggests *samyak-satya.*

2. The following is a long, unbroken quotation from Won ch'uk's commentary *Dgong 'grel gyi 'grel chen* (P5517:103.1.2-4). On Won ch'uk see chapter 1 n. 16.

3. On the term *tattvāmṛta* in Bhavya see David Eckel, unpublished mss. of

translation of *Tarka-jvālā* V, n. 3. There is no chapter with this name in the Peking edition of the Bstan 'gyur. There the third chapter is "*Tattva-jñānaiṣanā*" and the fifth chapter, "*Yogācāra-tattva-viniścaya.*"

4. Wilson (1984:220) translates '. . . it definitely does not achieve Buddhahood.'

5. An interpolation, perhaps by Tsong kha pa.

6. This ends the long quote from Won ch'uk.

7. Cp. Odani and Kalsang (1986:122 n. 173) who refer to Yamaguchi's discussion of such a person.

8. See chapter 5 n. 40.

9. MSam (Lamotte 1938:29-30; Nagao I 69). Tsong kha pa clearly takes this quotation from the MSam as presenting the opponent's point of view (*pūrvapakṣa*). He presents the refutation of it below where he says: "Even though the MSam does not directly refute the assertion that there is a set of one [consciousness] its establishing that there is a set of eight serves to refute it. And although the MSU, in its commentary on this, does not do so either, still, its refutation of the idea of the physical heart being the basis of mental consciousness quoted above [50a3] serves as a refutation."

10. For example, the intention to kill, translated out into the deed of murder, is called the physical nonvirtuous deed (*karman*) of killing.

11. Literally the passage says "Since, in the realm of the physical, *mano-vijñāna* is located in the body there is the appearance of the beholding of feeling in all locations just like the five physical sense-faculties different from that being located in the body."

12. The Sanskrit of this (Lamotte 1938:vol. 2, 102=*Dhammapada* 37) is *dūraṁgamam ekacaram aśarīraṁ guhāśayam / damayan durdamaṁ cittaṁ tam ahaṁ brūmi brāhmaṇam //*

13. Lamotte (1938:vol. 2, 103) mentions the *Majjhima-nikāya*, p. 295: *imesaṁ kho . . . pañcannam indriyānaṁ gocara-visayam . . . mano paccanubhoti mano cesaṁ patisaraṇaṁ.*

14. The twelve *āyatanas* (see AK:1.7-20; Shāstri 1981:29-63) are the five senses and their five objects along with *manas* (a sort of sixth sense-faculty that serves as a general category for all consciousnesses). The last is the *dharmāyatana*, loosely conceived of as systematizing objects of thought.

15. See chapter 5 n. 40.

16. See Introduction pp. 13-14.

17. Ibid.

Tibetan Text

ཡིད་དང་ཀུན་གཞིའི་དཀའ་བའི་གནས་རྒྱ་ཆེར་འགྲེལ་པ་
ལེགས་པར་བཤད་པའི་རྒྱ་མཚོ་ཞེས་བྱ་བ་

[Chapter One]

བཅོམ་ལྡན་འདས་གསུང་གི་དབང་ཕྱུག་ལ་ཕྱག་འཚལ་ལོ།།

རྒྱལ་དང་རྒྱལ་བའི་སྲས་རྣམས་གཤེགས་པའི་བཤུལ། །ལེགས་གསུངས་ལེགས་ལམ་ཇི་བཞིན་
ཐུགས་ཆུད་ནས། །མ་ནོར་མ་འདྲེས་རྫོགས་པར་སྟོན་[1]མཛད་པའི། །མཁས་པའི་མཁས་པ་དེ་
ལ་མགོས་ཕྱག་འཚལ།།

རྣམ་རིག་གཞུང་གི་ཤིན་ཏུ་དཀའ་བའི་གནས། །ཡིད་དང་ཀུན་གཞི་གསལ་བར་བསྟན་པ་དང་།
།བདག་ཉིད་དྲན་བ་གསོ་བར་བྱ་བའི་ཕྱིར། །བླ་མའི་གསུང་ལ་བརྟེན་ནས་འདིར་བཤད་བྱ།།

འདིར་ཡིད་དང་ཀུན་གཞི་གཏན་ལ་འབེབས་ན་དེ་དག་གང་ནས་འབྱུང་བའི་སེམས་ཙམ་གྱི་གྲུབ་པའི་མཐའ་དེ་དུས་ཅི་ཙམ་ནས་བྱུང་ཞེ་ན།

སླ་བའི་དམ་པས་[2]ཐེག་པ་མཆོག །འཛིན་པར་ལུང་བསྟན་འཕགས་པ་ཀླུས། །ཐེག་མཆོག་རྒྱས་
པར་མཛད་པའི་རྗེས། །ལུང་བསྟན་བརྙེས་པའི་ཐོགས་མེད་ཀྱིས། །སློལ་བཏོད།

ཐུབ་པ་ཆོས་ཀྱི་དབྱིངས་སུ་སྙོམས་པར་ཞུགས་པའི་རྗེས་སུ་འཛམ་བུ་གླིང་འདིར་ཐེག་པ་ཆེན་པོའི་བསྟན་པ་ནི་ནུབ་སྟེ། ཉན་ཐོས་ཀྱི་བསྟན་པ་ཙམ་ཞིག་གནས་ལ་ནང་པའི་གྲུབ་པའི་མཐའ་སྨྲ་བ་ཡང་བྱེ་བྲག་སྨྲ་བ་[3] སོགས་འབའ་ཞིག་ཏུ་གྱུར་པ། ཐེག་པ་ཆེན་པོའི་མདོ་རྣམས་ལ་ནི་གུས་པས་གཅེས་སྤྲས་སུ་བྱེད་པ་[4]དང་། མངོན་པར་སྦྱོར་བ་པོ་མེད་པས་ཆོས་མངོན་པ་འབུམ་པ་ལ་སོགས་པ་ཆུད་ཟོས་པར་གྱུར། ཤེས་རབ་ཀྱི་ཕ་རོལ་ཏུ་ཕྱིན་པ་ལ་སོགས་པ་ཟབ་ཅིང་རྒྱ་ཆེ་བའི་མདོ་རྣམས་ནི་ཀླུའི་རྒྱལ་པོ་ཆེན་པོ་རྣམས་ཀྱི་གནས་ན་བཞུགས་པར་གྲགས་ཏེ། སློབ་སྤྲིངས་ལས།[5] [4b]

བསྟན་པ་རིན་ཆེན་མཆོག་ལྷར་བཟང་ལ་ཕན་མཛད་པ། །རྣམ་པར་དག་ཚུལ་གང་ཡིན་ཀླུ་མགོའི་
གདེངས་ཀ་ཅན། །ཆེན་པོ་རྣམས་ཀྱིས་གཙུག་གི་རྒྱན་བཞིན་གུས་མནོས་ནས། །ས་ཡི་གཏིང་ན་
གནས་པའི་རབ་རིབ་སེལ་བར་མཛད།།

ཅེས་སོ། །དེ་ནས་འཕགས་པ་ལང་ཀར་གཤེགས་པ་ལས།།

མགོན་པོ་མྱ་ངན་འདས་འོག་ཏུ། །འཛིན་པར་སུ་འགྱུར་བཤད་དུ་གསོལ། །བདེ་གཤེགས་མྱ་ངན་

---

[1] *sten* O,P. [2] *pa* O. [3] Omit *yang bye brag smra ba* O,P. [4] *byed pa ba* O,P. [5] P5410:217.1.2-3. As in M, in pada a, *phen mdzad*→*'phen med*; in b, *klu*→*klu'i*.

འདས་འོག་ཏུ། །ཚུལ་རྣམས་འཛིན་པར་འགྱུར་བ་དེ། །དུས་དག་འདས་ནས་འབྱུང་བ་ནི།[1] །བློ་གྲོས་ཆེན་པོ་ཁྱོད་ཤེས་གྱིས། །ལྷོ་ཕྱོགས་བེ་དའི་[2]ཡུལ་དུ་ནི། །དགེ་སློང་དཔལ་ལྡན་ཆེར་[3]གྲགས་པ། །དེ་མིང་ཀླུ་ཞེས་བོད་པ་སྟེ། །ཡོད་དང་མེད་པའི་ཕྱོགས་འཇིག་བྱེད། །ང་ཡི་ཐེག་པ་འཇིག་རྟེན་དུ། །བླ་མེད་ཐེག་ཆེན་རབ་བཤད་ནས། །རབ་ཏུ་དགའ་བའི་ས་བསྒྲུབས་ཏེ། །བདེ་བ་ཅན་དུ་དེ་འགྲོའོ།།

ཞེས་ལུང་བསྟན་པའི་སྐྱེས་བུ་ཆེན་པོ་ཀླུ་སྒྲུབ་ཕྱོགས་བེ་དའི་ཡུལ་དུ་སྐུ་འཁྲུངས་ནས་སངས་རྒྱས་ཀྱི་བསྟན་པ་ལ་རབ་ཏུ་བྱུང་སྟེ་ཀླུའི་ཡུལ་ནས་ཤེས་རབ་ཀྱི་ཕ་རོལ་ཏུ་ཕྱིན་པ་ལ་སོགས་པའི་མདོ་རྣམས་སྤྱན་དྲངས་ནས་འཛམ་བུའི་གླིང་དུ་ཐེག་པ་ཆེན་པོ་མཚན་མ་མེད་པའི་ཚུལ་གསལ་བར་མཛད་པའི་ཕྱིར་དུ་རང་གཞན་གྱི་སྡེ་པའི་ལྟ་བ་ངན་པ་སེལ་བར་མཛད་པ་དབུ་མ་རིགས་པའི་ཚོགས་ལ་སོགས་པའི་བསྟན་བཅོས་རྣམས་མཛད་དོ།

དེའི་རྗེས་སུ་འཇམ་དཔལ་རྩ་རྒྱུད་ལས།

ཐོགས་མེད་ཅེས་བྱའི་དགེ་སློང་ནི། །བསྟན་བཅོས་དེ་ནི་དོན་ལ་མཁས། །མདོ་སྡེ་ངེས་དོན་དྲང་བའི་དོན། །རྣམ་པ་མང་པོའང་རབ་ཏུ་འབྱེད། །འཇིག་རྟེན་རིག་པ་སྟོན་བདག་ཉིད། །གཞུང་འབྱེད་དང་ཚུལ་ཅན་དུ་འགྱུར། །དེ་ཡི་རིག་པ་གྲུབ་པ་ནི། །སྣ་ལའི་ཕོ་ཉ་[5a]མོ་ཞེས་བརྗོད། །དེ་ཡི་ཐུགས་ཀྱི་མཐུ་ཡིས་ནི། །བློ་ནི་བཟང་པོ་སྐྱེ་བར་འགྱུར། །བསྟན་པ་ཡུན་རིང་གནས་བྱའི་ཕྱིར། །མདོ་ཡིས་དེ་ཉིད་དོན་སྡུད་བྱེད། །ལོ་ནི་བརྒྱ་དང་ལྔ་བཅུར་འཚོ། །དེ་ལུས་[1120]ཞིག་ནས་ལྷ་ཡུལ་འགྲོ །འཁོར་བ་རྣམས་སུ་འཁོར་བ་ན། །ཡུན་རིང་བདེ་བ་རྗེས་མྱོང་ནས། །བདག་ཉིད་ཆེན་པོ་མཐར་གྱིས་ཏེ། །བྱང་ཆུབ་ཐོབ་པར་འགྱུར་པ་ཡིན།།

ཞེས་ལུང་བསྟན་པའི་སློབ་དཔོན་ཐོགས་མེད་ཀྱིས་འཕགས་པ་བྱམས་པ་བསྒྲུབས་པས་ཞལ་གཟིགས་ཏེ། དགའ་ལྡན་དུ་བྱོན་ནས་བྱམས་པའི་ཆོས་ལྔ་སོགས་གསན་ཅིང་སླར་འཛམ་བུའི་གླིང་དུ་བྱམས་ཆོས་རྣམས་ཁྱེར་བྱོན་ཏེ་རང་ཉིད་ཀྱིས་ཀྱང་ཐེག་པ་ཆེན་པོ་བསྡུས་པ་སོགས་མཛད་ནས་སེམས་ཙམ་གྱི་ལྟ་བའི་སྲོལ་རྒྱས་པར་བཏོད་དེ། ཇི་སྐད་དུ།

འཇིག་རྟེན་ཀུན་ལ་ཕན་ཕྱིར་ཐོགས་མེད་ཅེས་བྱ་བ། །ཆོས་རྒྱུན་ཏིང་འཛིན་སྟོབས་ཀྱིས་དྲངས་པའི་བདུད་རྩིའི་རྒྱུན། །འཕགས་པ་མི་ཕམ་ཞལ་གྱིས་[4]བྱམ་པ་ནས་བླུགས་པ། །གསན་པའི་སྙིམ་པས་གསོལ་བ་དེ་ལ་ཕྱག་འཚལ་ལོ།།

ཞེས་པ་ལྟར་རོ།།

---

[1] *yin* P,O. [2] *ba'i da* M. [3] *zhes* D,P,O. [4] *gyi* O,P.

འོ་ན་ཐོགས་མེད་ཀྱིས་སྐྱོལ་བརྗོད་པའི་སྔོན་དུ་ཐེག་ཆེན་གྱི་ལྟ་བ་དེ་ཇི་འདྲ་བ་ཞིག་ཏུ་གནས་ཤེ་ན།

སྔོན་དུ་དབུ་མ་ཉིད།

ཐོགས་མེད་ཀྱི་སྔོན་དུ་རྟེན་ཅིང་འབྲེལ་བར་འབྱུང་བ་རྟག་ཆད་ཀྱི་མཐའ་དང་བྲལ་བ་ཉིད་དེ་བཞིན་གཤེགས་པའི་བཀའི་དགོངས་པར་འགྲེལ་པ་དབུ་མའི་ཚུལ་ལས་གཞན་མེད་དེ། ཐེག་ཆེན་གསལ་བར་མཛད་པ་པོ་[5b]ཀླུ་སྒྲུབ་ཁོ་ན་ཡིན་པའི་ཕྱིར་རོ། །དེས་ན་མདོ་སྡེ་རྒྱན་སྤྱོད་འཇུག་དབུ་མ་སྙིང་པོ་སོགས་སུ་ཐེག་པ་ཆེན་པོ་བཀར་བསྒྲུབ་པ་འབྱུང་བ་ཡང་འཕགས་པ་ཀླུ་སྒྲུབ་ཀྱིས་ཐེག་པ་ཆེན་པོ་འཛམ་བུའི་གླིང་དུ་དར་བར་བྱས་པའི་ཚེ་གྲུབ་མཐའ་འོག་མའི་པཎྜི་ཏ་རྣམས་ཀྱིས་རང་ཉིད་ཀྱིས་དེ་གོང་དུ་ཐེག་ཆེན་མ་ཐོས་པ་དང༌། རང་གིས་ཚད་མར་ཁས་བླངས་པའི་སྡེ་སྣོད་ཅི་རིགས་པ་དང་མི་མཐུན་པར་འདུག་པ་རྒྱུ་མཚན་དུ་བྱས་ནས་ཐེག་པ་ཆེན་པོ་བཀའ་མ་ཡིན་ནོ་ཞེས་སྐུར་པ་བྱུང་བའི་ཚེ་དེ་དག་གི་ལོག་རྟོག་བསལ་བའི་ཕྱིར་དུ་མཛད་པ་ཡིན་ནོ།།

སློབ་དཔོན་རང་ཉིད་ཀྱིས་ཀྱང་རྟེན་ཅིང་འབྲེལ་བར་འབྱུང་བ་ལ་མཐའ་བརྒྱད་ལ་སོགས་པའི་སྤྲོས་པ་མཐའ་དག་འགོག་པའི་རིགས་པ་དང༌།

བཅོམ་ལྡན་དངོས་དང་དངོས་མེད་པ། [1121]མཁྱེན་པས་ཀཱ་ཏྱཱ་ཡ་ན་ཡི། །གདམས་ངག་ལས་ནི་
ཡོད་པ་དང༌། །མེད་པ་གཉིས་ཀའང་དགག་པ་མཛད།།

ཅེས་པ་ལྟ་བུ་ཐེག་དམན་གྱི་ལུང་ལ་བརྟེན་ནས་ཀྱང་རང་བཞིན་གྱིས་སྟོང་པ་བཀའི་དགོངས་པར་བསྟན་པ་དང

སེམས་ཡོད་སུ་ཞིག་དེ་ལ་སྨོད།།

ཅེས་གསུངས་པས་ན་ཐེག་པ་ཆེན་པོ་སངས་རྒྱས་ཀྱི་བཀར་བསྒྲུབས་པ་ཡིན་ནོ།།

དེ་ལྟར་ཀླུ་སྒྲུབ་ཀྱི་རྗེས་སུ་ཐོགས་མེད་ཀྱིས་སེམས་ཙམ་གྱི་ལྟ་བའི་སྐྱོལ་རྒྱས་པར་བརྗོད་པ་ན་སློབ་དཔོན་གྱི་དངོས་སློབ་ལེགས་ལྡན་འབྱེད་ལ་སོགས་པས་རྣམ་ཤེས་སྨྲ་བའི་འདོད་པ་རྣམས་རྒྱས་པར་བཀོད་ནས་འགོག་པར་བྱེད་དོ། །དེ་ལྟར་བྱས་ན་འདིར་དེ་དག[1] གི་དོན་འདི་འབྱུང་སྟེ། ཐུབ་པ་མྱ་ངན་ལས་འདས་པའི་རྗེས་ལ་བྱེ་བྲག་ཏུ་སྨྲ་བ་སོགས་ཀྱི་པཎྜི་ཏ་རྣམས་ཀྱིས་མངོན་པ་སྡེ་བདུན་སོགས་བརྩམས་ནས་རང་རང་གི་གྲུབ་མཐའ་རྒྱས་པར་བྱས་ཏེ་མདོའི་དོན་[6a]གཞན་དུ་བཀྲལ་ནས་བསྟན་པ་རིན་པོ་ཆེ་དྲི་མ་ཅན་དུ་བྱས་ཏེ། ཇི་སྐད་དུ།

སྟོན་པ་འཇིག་རྟེན་མིག་ནི་ཟུམ་གྱུར་ཅིང༌། །དཔང་གྱུར་སྐྱེ་བོ་ཕལ་ཆེར་ཟད་པ་ན།[2] །དེ་ཉིད་མ་
མཐོང་རང་དགར་གྱུར་པ་ཡི། །ངན་རྟོག་རྣམས་ཀྱིས་བསྟན་པ་འདི་དཀྲུགས་སོ།།

ཞེས་དང༌།

འདི་ནི་སྟོན་པས་གསུངས་སོ་ལོ།།

---

[1] *'dir dag* D, *'di dag* O,P. [2] *dbang gyur skye bo phal cher zad pa dang* D,O,P.

ཞེས་འབྱུང་བ་ལྟར། སངས་རྒྱས་མྱ་ངན་ལས་འདས་པའི་འོག་ཏུ་བདུད་ཀྱི་ལས་ཆེར་གཡོས། སྡེ་པ་རྣམས་ཀྱི་འཛིན་པ་སོ་སོ་ནས་ལངས་ཏེ་ཕལ་ཆེར་ཡོད་པ་ཉིད་དུ་ལྟ་བ་ལ་མངོན་པར་ཞེན་པས། བྱང་ཆུབ་སེམས་དཔའ་ཀླུ་སྒྲུབ་ས་རབ་ཏུ་དགའ་བ་བརྙེས་པས་ཐེག་པ་ཆེན་པོ་མཚན་མ་མེད་པའི་སྟོང་པ་ཉིད་ཀྱི་གསུང་རབ་ལ་བརྟེན་ནས་བསྟན་བཅོས་དབུ་མ་ལ་སོགས་མཛད་ཅེས་གསུངས་པ་ལྟར་རོ།།

དེ་ལྟར་དུས་རིང་མོའི་བར་དུ་གྲུབ་མཐའ་འོག་མ་ཤིན་ཏུ་དར་ལ་, ཐེག་ཆེན་མིང་ཙམ་ཡང་མེད་པ་ཀླུ་སྒྲུབ་ཀྱིས་ཐེག་ཆེན་དར་བར་བྱས་ཏེ་སྲོལ་བཏོད། དེ་རྗེས་སློབ་དཔོན་ཐོགས་མེད་ཀྱིས་སེམས་ཙམ་པའི་ལྟ་བའི་སྲོལ་རྒྱས་པར་བཏོད་པ་ཡིན་པའི་ཕྱིར། ཀླུ་སྒྲུབ་དང་ཐོགས་མེད་ཀྱི་སྔོན་དུ་[1122]དབུ་མ་དང་རྣལ་འབྱོར་སྤྱོད་པའི་མིང་ཙམ་ཡོད་སྲིད་ཀྱང་མདོའི་དགོངས་པ་གྲུབ་མཐའ་གཉིས་ཐ་དད་དུ་བཀྲལ་ནས་གཞུང་འཛུགས་[1]པ་ནི། སྔར་བསྟན་པ་ཁོ་ན་ལྟར་བཟུང་སྟེ་གཞན་དུ་ན་ཀླུ་སྒྲུབ་ཐོགས་མེད་སོགས་ཀྱི་སྔོན་དུ་ཐེག་ཆེན་གྱི་སྲོལ་བཏོད་པའི་བཀའི་དགོངས་འགྲེལ་གྱི་བསྟན་བཅོས་དང་སློབ་དཔོན་གང་ཡིན་པ་བསྟན་དགོས་ན་དེ་ཡང་རྙེད་པ་མ་ཡིན་ནོ།།

དེ་ལྟར་དེ་བཞིན་གཤེགས་པས་ལུང་བསྟན་པའི་སློབ་དཔོན་དེ་གཉིས་དུས་ཅི་ཙམ་ནས་བྱུང་ཞེ་ན། [6b]

འཕགས་པ་ཀླུ་སྒྲུབ་ནི། རྩ་རྒྱུད་དུ།

ང་ནི་མྱ་ངན་འདས་འོག་ཏུ། །ལོ་ནི་བཞི་བརྒྱ་ལོན་པ་ན།།

ཞེས་འབྱུང་ལ། དགོངས་འགྲེལ་གྱི་འགྲེལ་ཆེན་བམ་པོ་བདུན་ཅུ་རྩ་ལྔ་ལས།

> དེ་ནས་སངས་རྒྱས་མྱ་ངན་ལས་འདས་ནས་ལོ་ཉིས་བརྒྱ་ལོན་པའི་འོག་ཏུ་བྱང་ཆུབ་སེམས་དཔའ་ཀླུ་སྒྲུབ་ཀྱིས་མདོ་སྡེ་ཤེས་རབ་ཀྱི་ཕ་རོལ་ཏུ་ཕྱིན་པ་ལ་བརྟེན་ནས་བསྟན་བཅོས་རྣམས་མཛད་དེ། འདི་ལྟ་སྟེ་ཤེས་རབ་ཀྱི་ཕ་རོལ་ཏུ་ཕྱིན་པའི་འགྲེལ་པ་དང་། དབུ་མ་ལ་སོགས་པའོ། །དེ་དག་ལས་རྣམ་པར་བརྟགས་པའི་ངོ་བོ་ཉིད་སྤངས་པས་མཚན་ཉིད་མེད་པའི་ཚུལ་རབ་ཏུ་བསྟན་ཏོ། །དེ་ནས་འཕགས་པའི་ལྷ་ལ་སོགས་པས་གཞུང་དེ་ཡང་དག་པར་བླངས་ཏེ། གཅིག་ནས་གཅིག་ཏུ་བརྒྱུད་ཅིང་སྤེལ་ཏེ།[2] སངས་རྒྱས་མྱ་ངན་ལས་འདས་ནས་ལོ་དགུ་བརྒྱ་ལོན་པ་ན་བྱང་ཆུབ་སེམས་དཔའ་བྱམས་པས་མདོ་སྡེ་དགོངས་པ་ཟབ་མོ་ངེས་པར་འགྲེལ་པ་ལ་སོགས་པ་ལ་བརྟེན་ནས་བསྟན་བཅོས་རྣམས་མཛད་དེ་རྣལ་འབྱོར་སྤྱོད་པའི་ས་དང་དབུས་དང་མཐའ་རྣམ་པར་འབྱེད་པ་ལ་སོགས་པའོ། །སློབ་དཔོན་ཐོགས་མེད་དང་དབྱིག་གཉེན་གྱིས་གཞུང་དེ་ཡང་དག་པར་བླངས་ནས་རབ་ཏུ་སྤེལ་ཏེ། དེའི་ཚེ་སངས་རྒྱས་ཀྱི་ཆོས་རོ་གཅིག་པས་སྟོང་པ་དང་ཡོད་པར་སྨྲ་བ་ལ་རྩོད་པ་མེད་དོ། །དེའི་ཕྱིར་སློབ་དཔོན་ཉི་བའི་འོད་ན་རེ།

---

[1] *gpung 'dzags* O,P. [2] *spel te→spel bstan te→°to?*

ལོ་སྟོང་གི་མདུན་རོལ་དུ་ནི་སངས་རྒྱས་ཀྱི་ཆོས་རོ་གཅིག་གོ །དེ་རྒྱུན་ཆད་ནས་ནི་དྲན་པ་དང་ཤེས་
རབ་ཁད་ཀྱིས་འགགས་[1123]པས་སྟོང་པ་དང་ཡོད་པར་སྨྲ་བ་རྣམས་འཇིག་རྟེན་ན་རྒྱས་པར་གྱུར་ཏོ།
།ཞེས་བཤད་དོ་ཞེའོ།།

ཞེས་སོ།།

[Chapter Two]

འོ་ན་དེ་ལྟ་བུའི་སེམས་ཙམ་གྱི་གྲུབ་པའི་མཐའ་ལས་འབྱུང་བའི་ཀུན་གཞི་[7a]དང་ཉོན་ཡིད་དེ་ཇི་ལྟ་བུ་ཞེ་ན།

མཚན་ཉིད་སྒྲུབ་པར་བྱེད་པ་དང་། །དགུ་དང་གཅིག་ཕྱུར་འདོད་པ་དགག །དོན་རྣམ་བཞི་ཡིས་
ཀུན་གཞི་དང་། །ཉོན་མོངས་ཅན་ཡིད་ཤེས་པར་བྱ།།

མཚན་ཉིད་གཏན་ལ་དབབ་པ་དང་། དེའི་སྒྲུབ་བྱེད་དང་། རྣམ་ཤེས་ཚོགས་དགུར་འདོད་པ་དང་། ཚོགས་གཅིག་ཏུ་འདོད་པ་དགག་པ་སྟེ་དོན་བཞི་ཡིས་ཀུན་གཞི་དང་ཉོན་ཡིད་ཤེས་པར་བྱའོ། །ཞེས་མདོར་བསྟན་ནོ།།

རྒྱས་པར་བཤད་པ་ལ་བཞི་ལས། དང་པོ་མཚན་ཉིད་ལ། ཀུན་གཞི་དང་ཉོན་ཡིད་ཀྱི་མཚན་ཉིད་གཏན་ལ་དབབ་པ་གཉིས་ལས་ཀུན་གཞི་ལ་རྟེན་དུ་གྱུར་པ་རྣམ་སྨིན་གྱི་ཀུན་གཞི་དང་། བརྟེན་པ་ས་བོན་གྱི་ཀུན་གཞིའི་མཚན་ཉིད་གཉིས་ཡོད་ཅེས་སྟོན་པ་ནི།།

མཚན་ཉིད་གཉིས་ལས་ཀུན་གཞི་ནི། །རྟེན་དང་བརྟེན་པའི་དབྱེ་བ་ཡིས། །མཚན་ཉིད་རྣམ་པ་
གཉིས་སུ་འདོད།།

རྟེན་དུ་གྱུར་པའི་ཀུན་གཞིའི་མཚན་ཉིད་ཇི་ལྟ་བུ་ཞེ་ན།

དེ་ལ་རྟེན་གྱུར་ཀུན་གཞི་ནི། །དོན་དང་སེམས་ཅན་བག་ཆགས་ལ། །རྣམ་པར་རིག་པ་མ་རིག་པ།།
ལུང་དུ་མ་བསྟན་རིག་ལ་སོགས། །ལྔ་ཉིད་དང་ལྡན།

ཞེས་པས་སྟོན་ཏོ།།

དེ་ཡང་། དམིགས་པ། རྣམ་པ། ངོ་བོ། གྲོགས་ཇི་བཞིན་རིག་པར་བྱ་སྟེ། དམིགས་ཡུལ་གཟུགས་སྒྲ་དྲི་རོ་རེག་བྱ་སྟེ་དོན་ལྔ། མིག་རྣ་བ་སྣ་ལྕེ་ལུས་ཀྱི་དབང་པོ་ལྔའི་སེམས་ཅན་དང་། བདག་དང་ཆོས་ཀུན་བཏགས་པའི་ངོ་བོ་ཉིད་ལ་མངོན་པར་ཞེན་པའི་བག་ཆགས་དང་གསུམ་ལ་དམིགས། རྣམ་པ་སྣོད་བཅུད་དེ་དག་སྣང་ཡང་རང་གིས་ཀྱང་མི་ངེས་ལ་རྗེས་སུ་ངེས་པ་ཡང་འདྲེན་མི་ནུས་པ། ངོ་བོ་མ་བསྒྲིབས་ལ་ལུང་དུ་མ་བསྟན་[7b]ཅིང་། འཁོར་ཚོར་བ། འདུ་ཤེས། སེམས་པ། རེག་པ། ཡིད་ལ་[1124]བྱེད་པ་སྟེ་སེམས་བྱུང་ལྔ་འཁོར་ན

དང་མཚུངས་པར་ལྡན་པའོ། །དེ་སྐད་དུའང་།

དོན་དང་སེམས་ཅན་དུ། །སྣང་བའི་རྣམ་པར་ཤེས་པ་ནི། །རབ་ཏུ་སྐྱེའོ

ཞེས་དང་། སུམ་ཅུ་པ་ལས།

དེ་ནི་ལེན་པ་དག་དང་གནས། །རྣམ་པར་རིག་པ་མི་རིག་པ། །རྟག་ཏུ་རེག་དང་ཡིད་བྱེད་དང་།
།རིག[1] དང་འདུ་ཤེས་སེམས་པར་ལྡན། །དེ་ལ་ཚོར་བ་བཏང་སྙོམས་ཏེ། །དེ་ནི་མ་བསྒྲིབས་ལུང་
མ་བསྟན། །རེག་ལ་སོགས་པའང་དེ་བཞིན་ནོ།།

ཞེས་སོ།།

རྣམ་སྨིན་དང་དེ་ཉིད་དང་གཞན་དུ་བརྗོད་དུ་མེད་པའི་བག་ཆགས་རྣམ་སྨིན་གྱི་དམིགས་པར་ཇི་ལྟར་འགྱུར་ཞེ་ན།

ས་བོན་གྱི། །དབང་གིས་གནས་དོན་ལུས་སུ་ནི། །སྣང་ཕྱིར་དམིགས་པ་དག་ཏུ་འདོད།།

ས་བོན་དེ་སྣང་ནས་ཡུལ་དུ་མི་འགྱུར་ཀྱང་དེའི་དབང་གིས་ཀུན་གཞི་རྣམ་སྨིན་དེ་གནས་དབང་རྟེན་དང་། ལུས་དབང་པོ་དང་། དོན་ཡུལ་ལྔའི་སྣོད་བཅུད་དུ་སྣང་བར་འགྱུར་བས་ན་དམིགས་པར་བཞག་སྟེ། དཔེར་ན་ཡུལ་གྱི་དབང་གིས་ཤེས་པ་དེའི་རྣམ་པ་ཅན་དུ་བྱུང་བས་ཡུལ་དེ་མི་སྣང་ཡང་དམིགས་པར་འདོད་པ་བཞིན་ནོ།།

འོ་ན་གཟུགས་མེད་ཀྱི་ཀུན་གཞི་ལ་ཡང་སྣོད་བཅུད་སྣང་ངམ་ཞེ་ན།

ཀུན་གཞིའི་གཟུང་ཆ་དག་ལ་ནི། །རྣམ་ཤེས་ལྔ་ཡིས་འཛིན་བྱེད་ཅིང་། །དྲུག་པས་ཐ་སྙད་འདོགས་
པས་ན། །ཁམས་གཉིས་དག་ཏུ་ངེས་པ་སྟེ། །དེ་ལྟ་མིན་ན་གཟུགས་མེད་པ། །གཟུགས་ཀྱི་འདུ་ཤེས་
མ་འདས་དང་། །གཟུགས་ཅན་ས་རུ་ཐལ་འགྱུར་ཏེ། །ཤེས་ལ་གཟུགས་སུ་སྣང་བ་ལས། །མ་
གཏོགས་ཕྱི་རོལ་མེད་ཕྱིར་རོ།།

ཀུན་གཞི་ལ་དོན་དུ་[8a]དངོས་སུ་སྣང་བ་ལ་དབང་ཤེས་ལྔས་འཛིན་ཅིང་ཡིད་ཤེས་ཀྱིས་དབང་དོན་གཉིས་ཅར[2]ལ་ཐ་སྙད་འདོགས་པས་ན་གཟུགས་མེད་ཀྱི་ཀུན་གཞི་ལ་སྣོད་བཅུད་མི་སྣང་སྟེ་གཟུགས་མེད་ཀྱི་ཡིད་ཤེས་ཀྱིས[3] གཟུགས་ལ་ཐ་སྙད་འདོགས་པ་མི་སྲིད་དོ། །དེའི་ཕྱིར་རྟེན་གཅིག་གི་ཀུན་གཞི་ལ་དངོས་སུ་སྣང་བའི་དོན་ལྔ་ནི་རྟེན་དེའི་དབང་ཤེས་ལ[4][1125]ལྐོག་ཏུ་གྱུར་པ་མ་ཡིན་ནོ།།

འོ་ན་གཟུང་བྱ་གཅིག་ཉིད་རྣམ་ཤེས་གཉིས་ཀྱི་གཟུང་ཆར་འགྱུར་ལ་འདོད་ན། ཤེས་པ་ལ་གང་སྣང་བ་དེའི་བདག་ཉིད་ཡིན་པའི་ཕྱིར་ཤེས་པ་གཉིས་རྫས་གཅིག་ཏུ་འགྱུར་བས་ན་གཟུང་ཆ་ཐུན་མོང་བ་མི་སྲིད་དོ་ཞེ་ན། སྐྱོན་མེད་དེ་ཤེས་པ་ལ་གང་སྣང་བ་དེའི་བདག་ཉིད་དམ། དེ་ལས་གཅིག་དང་ཐ་དད་གང་དུ་ཡང་མ་གྲུབ

[1] *rigs* D,O, P. [2] *char* P. *gnyis car*→°*ka*? [3] *gzugs med kyis* (D,O,P) *yid shes kyi* N. [4] *las* M,N.

ཅེས་པ་ནི་རྣམ་པར་དཔྱད་པ་ན་ཡིན་གྱི་,དེའི་ཚེ་ནི་ཐུན་མོང་བ་ཁས་མི་ལེན་ལ་མ་བརྟགས་མ་དཔྱད་པའི་ངོ་ན་[1] གཟུང་ཆ་ཐུན་མོང་བ་འདོད་ཀྱང་དེ་ཤེས་པའི་བདག་ཉིད་དུ་མི་འདོད་དེ་,གཞན་དུ་ན་ཕུང་པོ་ལྔའི་རྣམ་གཞག་འཇིག་པ་དང་། སྐྲ་ཤད་དང་། དུང་གི་སེར་པོ་སོགས་དང་། རྨི་ལམ་གྱི་ཡུལ་རྣམས་རྫས་སུ་གྲུབ་པར་འགྱུར་པ་དང་། གཟུགས་སྒྲ་སོགས་མྱོང་བའི་ངོ་བོར་ཐལ་བའི་ཕྱིར་རོ། །གལ་ཏེ་གཟུགས་མེད་ཀྱི་ཀུན་གཞི་ལ་སྣོད་བཅུད་སྣང་ན་གཟུགས་མེད་ཀྱི་སེམས་ཅན་རྣམས་གཟུགས་ཀྱི་འདུ་ཤེས་ལས་མ་འདས་པར་འགྱུར་ཏེ། གཟུགས་ཅན་གྱི་སྣོད་བཅུད་རང་གི་ཤེས་པ་ལ་དངོས་སུ་སྣང་བའི་ཕྱིར་རོ། །འདོད་པར་མི་ནུས་ཏེ།

ཐོགས་པའི་འདུ་ཤེས་ཀྱང་ནུབ། སྣ་ཚོགས་པའི་འདུ་ཤེས་ཀྱང་ནུབ།།

ཅེས་གསུངས་པའི་ཕྱིར་རོ།།

གཞན་ཡང་[8b]གཟུགས་མེད་པ་གཟུགས་ཅན་གྱི་ས་རུ་འགྱུར་ཏེ། དང་པོའི་ཀུན་གཞི་ལ་གཟུགས་ཅན་གྱི་སྣོད་བཅུད་མཚན་ཉིད་པ་དངོས་སུ་སྣང་བའི་ཕྱིར་རོ། །མ་ངེས་པ་ཡང་མ་ཡིན་ཏེ། ཁམས་གོང་མ་གཉིས་ནའང་ཤེས་པ་ལ་གཟུགས་སུ་སྣང་བ་ཙམ་མ་གཏོགས་པའི་ཕྱི་རོལ་གྱི་གཟུགས་མ་གྲུབ་པའི་ཕྱིར་རོ། །དེས་ན་གཟུགས་མེད་ཀྱི་སྙོམས་འཇུག་བསྒོམས་པའི་མཐུས་ཀུན་གཞི་ལ་ཡོད་པའི་གཟུགས་ཅན་སྣང་བར་འགྱུར་པའི་ས་བོན་ལ་གནོད་པ་བྱས་པས་རེ་ཞིག་གཟུགས་མེད་དུ་གནས་ཀྱི་བར་དུ་གཟུགས་ཅན་སྣང་མི་ནུས་ཏེ། དཔེར་ན་འདུ་ཤེས་མེད་པའི་སྙོམས་འཇུག་བསྒོམས་པའི་མཐུས་ཀུན་གཞི་ལ་ཡོད་པའི་ཚོགས་དྲུག་གི་ས་བོན་ལ་གནོད་པ་བྱས་པས་སྙོམས་འཇུག་དེ་ལས་ཇི་སྲིད་མི་ལྡང་གི་བར་དུ་ཚོགས་[1126]དྲུག་མི་འབྱུང་བ་བཞིན་ནོ།།

དེ་ལྟ་ན་གཟུགས་མེད་ཀྱི་[2]ཀུན་གཞི་ལ་དམིགས་པ་མེད་པར་འགྱུར་ཏེ། གཟུགས་ཅན་གྱི་སྣོད་བཅུད་ནི་མི་སྣང་ལ་བག་ཆགས་དམིགས་པར་འཇོག་པའི་དོན་ཡང་མེད་པའི་ཕྱིར་རོ། །འདོད་ན་དམིགས་པ་དང་བྲལ་བའི་ཤེས་པ་ཁས་བླངས་པར་འགྱུར་རོ་ཞེ་ན། །ཉེས་པ་མེད་དེ། ཐེག་པ་ཆེན་པོ་བསྡུས་པ་ལས།

འདས་སོགས་དེ་བཞིན་རྨི་ལམ་དང་། །གཟུགས་བརྙན་རྣམ་པ་གཉིས་ལ་ཡང་།[3] །དམིགས་པ་ཡོད་
པ་མ་ཡིན་པས། །དེ་ལ་[4] དམིགས་པར་རུང་ཕྱིར་རོ།།

ཞེས་གསུངས་པ་ལྟར་ཤེས་པ་ཐམས་ཅད་དམིགས་པ་ཡོད་པ་ལ་བལྟོས་མི་དགོས་ཀྱི་,བྱེ་བྲག་ཏུ་ཀུན་གཞི་ནི། སྔོན་གྱི་དགེ་མི་དགེའི་ལས་ཀྱིས་བདེ་འགྲོ་དང་ངན་འགྲོའི་གཞིར་འཕངས་ནས་[ཅི་→]ཇི་སྲིད་མ་ཤིའི་བར་དུ་སྐད་ཅིག་ཀྱང་མི་ལྡོག་པས་ན་འཕེན་བྱེད་ཀྱི་ལས་ཀྱི་སྟོབས་ཀྱིས་འཇུག་གི་,སྣང་བའི་དམིགས་པ་ལ་བལྟོས་ནས་

---

[1] *don* O,P. [2] *gzugs med kyi gzugs kun gzhi la* D,O,P. This is syntactically forced and there would be a mere repetition of what was already said earlier. [3] *gnyis po→gnyis la* (Lamotte 1938:31). [4] *ni* D,O,P.

ནི་མ་ཡིན་ནོ། །དེ་ལྟ་ན་གཟུགས་མེད་དུ་དོན་དང་དབང་པོ་མེད་པའི་ཕྱིར་དམིགས་པ་གསུམ་ལས་བག་ཆགས་དམིགས་པ་ཡིན་ལ། དེ་ཡང་བག་ཆགས་དམིགས་[9a]པར་འགྱུར་པའི་དོན་དངོས་སུ་མེད་ཀྱང་དེའི་མཐུས་གནས་དོན་ལུས་སུ་སྣང་རུང་ཡིན་པས་དམིགས་པར་འགྱུར་ཏེ། དཔེར་ན་སྤྲིང་ན་གནས་པའི་ས་བོན་དེ་རྐྱེན་དང་ཕྲད་ན་མྱུ་གུ་བསྐྱེད་རུང་ཡིན་པས་མྱུ་གུའི་རྐྱེན་བྱེད་ཅེས་བརྗོད་པ་བཞིན་ནོ། །དེ་ལྟར་བྱས་ན་གཟུགས་མེད་ཀྱི་ཀུན་གཞི་ལ་གཟུགས་ཅན་གྱི་སྣོད་བཅུད་སྣང་ཞེས་ཁ་ཅིག་འདོད་པ་བསླུན་པ་ཉིད་དུ་གྱུར་ཏོ།།

གཟུགས་མེད་དུ་དེ་ལྟ་ཡིན་ན་ཁམས་འོག་མ་གཉིས་སུའང་ཀུན་གཞི་གཅིག་ལ་སྣོད་བཅུད་ཀྱི་རྫས་ཐམས་ཅད་སྣང་ངམ་ཞེ་ན།

འོག་ནའང་སེམས་ཅན་གཅིག་གི་ནི། །ཀུན་གཞི་ལ་ནི་སྣོད་དང་བཅུད། །ཐམས་ཅད་སྣང་ན་གཟུགས་
ཁམས་ཀྱི། །ལྷ་ལའང་དམྱལ་སྣང་འབྱུང་བ་དང་། །དམྱལ་བ་ལ་ཡང་ལྷ་རྣམས་ཀྱི། །སྣོད་བཅུད་སྣང་
བ་འབྱུང་བ་དང་། །ཐ་མལ་རྣམས་ལའང་བསྐལ་པ་ཡི། །ཡུལ་སྣ་ཚོགས་པ་སྣང་བར་[1127]འགྱུར།།

ཁམས་འོག་མ་གཉིས་ལའང་ཀུན་གཞི་གཅིག་ལ་སྣོད་བཅུད་ཀྱི་རྫས་ཐམས་ཅད་སྣང་ན་གཟུགས་ཁམས་ཀྱི་ལྷ་ལའང་ལྟུགས་བསྲེགས་འབར་བ་སོགས་དམྱལ་བའི་སྣང་བ་རྣམས་འབྱུང་བར་འགྱུར་རོ། །འདོད་ན་དེ་དག་ལ་སྡུག་བསྔལ་གྱི་གདུང་བ་ཡོད་པར་འགྱུར་ཏེ། དེ་དག་གི་ཀུན་གཞིའི་སྟེང་གི་དམྱལ་སྣང་མཚན་ཉིད་པ་སྣང་བའི་ས་བོན་སད་པའི་ཕྱིར་རོ། །མ་གྲུབ་པ་མ་ཡིན་[1] ཏེ། དམྱལ་སྣང་དེ་ཀུན་གཞི་ལ་དངོས་སུ་སྣང་ལ་དེ་ཡང་བག་ཆགས་སད་པ་ལ་བལྟོས་པའི་ཕྱིར་རོ། །མ་ངེས་པ་ཡང་མ་ཡིན་ཏེ། ས་བོན་གྱི་མཐུས་དེ་དག་དངོས་སུ་སྣང་ན་ཕན་གནོད་དུ་འགྱུར་ཏེ། དཔེར་ན་རྨི་ལམ་གྱི་དུས་སུ་ཡིད་དུ་འོང་མི་འོང་[2] གི་ཡུལ་སྣང་བས་ཕན་གནོད་[9b]དུ་འགྱུར་བ་བཞིན་ནོ།།

འགྲོ་བ་རིགས་མཐུན་པའི་སྣོད་ནི་སྣང་འགྱུར་དང་སྤྱོད་འགྱུར་གཉིས་ཀའི་ལས་ལས་གྲུབ་པས་ཕན་གནོད་དུ་འགྱུར་ཡང་རིགས་མི་མཐུན་གྱི་སྣོད་རྣམས་སྣང་འགྱུར་གྱི་ལས་ལས་གྲུབ་ལ་སྤྱོད་འགྱུར་གྱི་ལས་ལས་མ་གྲུབ་པས་ཕན་གནོད་དུ་མ་འགྱུར་ཞེས་ཀྱང་བརྗོད་པར་མི་ནུས་ཏེ། གཟུགས་སྒྲ་སོགས་ཀྱི་ཡུལ་འགའ་ཞིག་རིགས་མཐུན་པའི་འགྲོ་བ་འགའ་ཞིག་ལ་ཡང་ཁ་ཅིག་ལ་ཕན་པར་མཐོང་ལ་ཁ་ཅིག་ལ་གནོད་པར་མཐོང་བའི་ཕྱིར་དང་། ནང་གི་ཤེས་པ་ལ་གཟུགས་སུ་སྣང་བ་ཙམ་ལས་མ་གཏོགས་པའི་སྣོད་ཀྱང་མི་འདོད་པས་ན་ཡིད་དུ་འོང་བ་དང་ཡིད་དུ་མི་འོང་བ་རང་མཚན་པར་སྣང་བའི་ཡུལ་སྣང་བ་ཙམ་གྱིས་ཕན་གནོད་དུ་འགྱུར་གྱི་, སྤྱོད་འགྱུར་ལ་མི་བལྟོས་ཏེ། དཔེར་ན་སྒྲུ་མའི་གཤིན་རྗེ་ལ་གཤིན་རྗེ་རང་མཚན་པར་སྣང་བ་ན་འཇིགས་པ་བསྐྱེད་པ་དང་། སྒྲུ་མའི་ན་ཆུང་ལ་ན་ཆུང་རང་མཚན་པར་སྣང་བ་ན་དེ་ཙམ་གྱིས་ཆགས་པ་སྐྱེད་པ་བཞིན་ནོ།།

---

[1] *yin* N,O; *min* P. [2] *mi 'ong* omit M.

གཞན་ཡང་མི་ལྟ་བུའི་ཀུན་གཞི་ལ་དམྱལ་བ་སྣང་བ་དེ་དམྱལ་བ་པ་ལ་ཇི་ལྟར་སྣང་བ་ལྟར་སྣང་ངམ་མི་སྣང་། དང་པོ་ལྟར་ན། དམྱལ་སྣང་དེ་དམྱལ་བ་པ་ཁོ་ནའི་ལས་དབང་གིས་སྣང་བ་དེ་མ་ཡིན་པར་ཐལ་ལོ། །འདོད་ན།

ལྕགས་བསྲེགས་[1128]ས་གཞི་སུ་ཡིས་བྱས། །མོ་ཚོགས་དེ་དག་ཅི་ལས་བྱུང་། །དེས་ན་དེ་དག
ཐམས་ཅད་ནི།[1] །སྡིག་སེམས་བྱུང་བར་ཐུབ་པས་གསུངས།།

ཞེས་པས་གནོད་དོ། །ཡང་མིའི་ཀུན་གཞི་ལ་སྣོད་ཇི་ལྟར་སྣང་བ་ལྟར་དམྱལ་བའི་ཀུན་གཞི་ལ་ཡང་སྣང་བར་ཁས་ལེན་དགོས་ལ། དེ་ལྟ་ན། ཇི་སྐད་དུ།

ཡི་དྭགས་དུད་འགྲོ་མི་རྣམས་དང་། །ལྷ་རྣམས་ཇི་ལྟར་རིགས་རིགས་སུ། །དངོས་གཅིག་ཡིད་
[10a]ནི་ཐ་དད་ཕྱིར། །དོན་མ་གྲུབ་པར་འདོད་པ་ཡིན།།

ཅེས་ཕྱི་རོལ་གྱི་དོན་མ་གྲུབ་པའི་རིགས་པ་གསུངས་པ་རྣམས་བོར་བར་ཡང་འགྱུར་རོ།།

གལ་ཏེ་དེ་ནི་སེམས་ཅན་དེ་དག་གི་དབང་ཤེས་ལ་དེ་ལྟར་སྣང་བ་ཡིན་ལ་དེ་དང་ཀུན་གཞིའི་སྣང་བ་གཉིས་མི་གཅིག་གོ་ཞེ་ན། དབང་ཤེས་ལ་དོན་ལྔར་སྣང་བ་དེ་གཉིས་ཀ་ཀུན་གཞིའི་གཟུང་ཆ་ཉིད་ཡིན་ཏེ། "དོན་དུ་སྣང་བའི་རྣམ་པར་ཤེས་ལ་སྐྱེའོ"[2] ཞེས་པའི་ལུང་དང་། "རྣམ་ཤེས་ལྔ་ཡིས་འཛིན་བྱེད་ཅིང་" ཞེས་སོགས་ཀྱིས་བསྟན་ཟིན་ཏོ།།

གཉིས་པ་ལྟར་ན་དམྱལ་བ་པ་ལ་ཇི་ལྟར་སྣང་བ་ལྟར་མི་སྣང་ཡང་དམྱལ་སྣང་མཚན་ཉིད་པ་སྣང་བར་འདོད་ན་ཏ་ཙང་ཐལ་བར་འགྱུར་ཏེ། བདེ་འགྲོའི་བདེ་བ་ཐམས་ཅད་ལ་ཡང་སྣང་བར་འགྱུར་རོ། །རྐང་པ་ལྷག་མ་བཞི་ཡང་རིགས་པ་འདིས་དཔགས་ལ་ཤེས་པར་བྱའོ།།

དེའི་ཕྱིར་མངོན་པ་བ་འགའ་ཞིག་ཀུན་གཞི་གཅིག་ལ་བསམ་གཏན་བཞི་པ་མན་ཆད་མནར་མེད་པ་ཡན་ཆད་སྣང་ཞེས་འདོད་ལ། ཁ་ཅིག་བསམ་གཏན་བཞི་པ་ནི་ཐུན་མོང་མ་ཡིན་པའི་ལས་[3]ལས་གྲུབ་པས་མི་སྣང་ལ་གཞན་སྣང་ཞེས་འདོད་པ་དང་། གཞན་དག་ཕྱི་བཤད་ལས།

འདིའི་དམིགས་པ་དང་རྣམ་པ་ཡོངས་སུ་བཅད་པར་མི་ནུས་སོ།།

ཞེས་པའི་དོན་དུ་བསམས་ནས་ཚད་ཀྱིས་བཅད་མི་ནུས་པའི་སྣོད་བཅུད་ཀྱི་རྫས་ཐམས་ཅད་སྣང་བར་འདོད་པ་ལ་ནི་སྒྲུབ་པར་བྱེད་པ་མེད་ལ། གནོད་པར་བྱེད་པ་ཡོད་དོ།།

མ་ཡིན་ཏེ། ལུང་འདི་ཉིད་གནོད་བྱེད་དོ་ཞེ་ན། ལུང་དེའི་དོན་ནི་ཚད་ཀྱིས་བཅད་མི་ནུས་པའི་སྣོད་

---

[1] Bhattacharya (1960:54) gives the Tibetan as *de 'dra de dag thams cad kyang//.* [2] At 7b1 the passage reads *don...du snangs ba'i rnam par shes pa ni rab tu skye'o*. [3] *lam* N, O,P.

བཅུད་ཐམས་ཅད་སྣང་[1129]བར་སྟོན་པ་མིན་གྱི ,དམིགས་པ་འདི་ལྟ་བུ་ཞིག་ལ་རྣམ་པ་འདི་འདྲ་བ་ཞིག་གིས་[10b]བཟུང་ངོ་ཞེས་ཀུན་གཞི་རང་ཉིད་ཀྱིས་ཀྱང་གསལ་བར་བཅད་མི་ནུས་ལ་རྗེས་སུ་ངེས་པ་ཡང་འདྲེན་མི་ནུས་པའི་དོན་ཡིན་ཏེ། གཞན་དུ་ན་སྔར་ལྟར་གྱི་གནོད་བྱེད་འཇུག་གོ།

འོ་ན་ཁམས་འོག་མ་གཉིས་ན་སྣོད་བཅུད་ཇི་ལྟ་བུ་ཞིག་སྣང་ཞེ་ན།

དངོས་སུ་རང་གི་དབང་དོན་ནོ། །བརྒྱུད་ནས་དེ་ཡི་ཚོགས་དྲུག་གི །ཡུལ་དུ་སྣང་བར་གང་ནུས་པ།
།ཀུན་གཞིའི་ཡུལ་དུའང་འཇོག་པ་ཡིན།།

དངོས་སུ་དམིགས་པ་ནི་རང་རྒྱུད་ཀྱི་དབང་པོ་དེ་ལ་སྣང་བའི་ཡུལ་རྣམས་ཡིན་ལ་བརྒྱུད་ནས་ནི་རྟེན་དེའི་ཚོགས་དྲུག་གི་ཡུལ་དུ་སྣང་བར་གང་ནུས་པ་རྟེན་དེའི་ཀུན་གཞིའི་ཡུལ་དུའང་འཇོག་གོ།

འོ་ན་སེམས་ཅན་ཞེས་པའི་འགྲེལ་པར།

སེམས་ཅན་ནི་བདག་དང་གཞན་གྱི་རྒྱུད་ལ་དབང་པོ་ལྟར་སྣང་བ་གང་ཡིན་པའོ་

ཞེས་པས་གནོད་དོ་ཞེ་ན།

དེ་ནི་ཀུན་གཞི་ལ་སྣང་བའི་དབང་པོ་ལ་བདག་གཞན་གྱི་རྒྱུད་ཀྱི་དབང་པོ་ལྟའོ་ཞེས་སྟོན་གྱི ,ཀུན་གཞི་གཅིག་ལ་བདག་གཞན་གྱི་དབང་པོ་ལྟ་དངོས་སུ་སྣང་ཞེས་སྟོན་པ་མིན་ནོ། །དེ་ལྟར་མ་ཡིན་ཏེ་རང་གི་ཀུན་གཞི་ལ་དངོས་སུ་སྣང་བའི་གཞན་གྱི་དབང་པོ་དེ་གཞན་རྒྱུད་ཀྱི་དབང་པོ་མཚན་ཉིད་པ་ཡིན་ན་འགྲོ་བ་རྣམས་རྒྱུད་གཅིག་ཏུ་འགྱུར་ཏེ། ལུས་དང་ལུས་ཅན་གྱི་རྣམ་རིག་རྣམས་ནི་མངོན་བརྗོད་ཀྱི་བག་ཆགས་ལས་འབྱུང་ལ ,བག་ཆགས་དེ་ཡང་རང་གི་ཀུན་གཞི་ལ་གཞན་རྒྱུད་ཀྱི་ཤེས་པས་གནོད་མི་ནུས་པའི་ཕྱིར་རོ།།

གལ་ཏེ་ཚོགས་དྲུག་གི་ཡུལ་ཐམས་ཅད་ཀུན་གཞིའི་ཡུལ་ཡིན་ན་ཡིད་ཤེས་ཀྱི་ཡུལ་གསུང་རབ་ཡན་ལག་བཅུ་གཉིས་ལྟ་བུ་དང་། འདས་སོགས་སྒྲོ་བཏགས་རྣམས་ཀྱང་ཀུན་གཞིའི་ཡུལ་དུ་འགྱུར་རམ་ཞེ་ན།

དབང་དོན་ལས་གཞན་དྲུག་[11a]པའི་ཡུལ། །ཀུན་གཞིའི་ཡུལ་དུ་མི་འགྱུར་ཏེ། །དྲུག་པ་བཏགས་
པའི་ཡུལ་ཅན་དང་། །ཀུན་གཞི་བཀྲར་འཛིན་གྱིས་དབེན་ཕྱིར།།

དབང་དོན་བག་ཆགས་གསུམ་ལས་གཞན་པའི་ཡིད་ཤེས་ཀྱི་ཡུལ་ཡན་[1130]ལག་བཅུ་གཉིས་ལྟ་བུ་དང །འདས་སོགས་སྒྲོ་བཏགས་རྣམས་ནི་ཀུན་གཞིའི་ཡུལ་དུ་མི་འགྱུར་ཏེ། དེ་དག་ནི་ཡིད་ཤེས་ཀྱིས་སྒྲོ་བཏགས་ནས་ཡུལ་དུ་བྱས་པ་ཙམ་ཡིན་ཅིང་ཀུན་གཞིའི་ཡང་ཐ་སྙད་འདོགས་པའི་འདུ་ཤེས་བཀྲ་བར་འཛིན་པ་དང་བྲལ་བའི་ཕྱིར་རོ།།

ཀུན་གཞི་དེ་དགེ་མི་དགེ་ལ་མི་འཇོག་པར་མ་བསྒྲིབས་ལུང་མ་བསྟན་ཁོ་ནར་ངེས་པ་ཅི་ཞེ་ན།

བག་ཆགས་བསྒོ་གཞི་ཡིན་ཕྱིར་དང་། །དགེ་དང་མི་དགེ་མངོན་གྱུར་དང་། །རྒྱུད་གཅིག་ལ་ནི་འཇུག

པའི་ཕྱིར། །མ་བསྒྲིབས་ལུང་མ་བསྟན་དུ་གྲུབ།།

ཀུན་གཞི་དེ་དགེ་མི་དགེའི་བག་ཆགས་བསྒོ་བའི་གཞི་ཡིན་པའི་ཕྱིར་དང་། དགེ་མི་དགེའི་སེམས་མངོན་གྱུར་དང་རྒྱུད་གཅིག་ལ་དུས་གཅིག་ཏུ་འཇུག་པའི་ཕྱིར་མ་བསྒྲིབས་ལུང་མ་བསྟན་དུ་གྲུབ་སྟེ་དགེ་བ་དང་ཉོན་མོངས་ཅན་བག་ཆགས་ཀྱི་གཞིར་མི་རུང་བའི་ཕྱིར་རོ།།

རིག་ལ་སོགས། །ལྔ་ཉིད་དང་ལྡན་ཞེས་གང་སྨྲས་པ་འཁོར་སེམས་བྱུང་ལྔར་ངེས་པ་ཅི་ཞེ་ན།

ལུང་མ་བསྟན་དང་མ་གསལ་ཕྱིར། །རིག་སོགས་ལྔར་ངེས།

མ་བསྒྲིབས་ལུང་མ་བསྟན་ཡིན་པའི་ཕྱིར་དགེ་བ་བཅུ་གཅིག་དང་རྩ་ཉོན་ཉེ་ཉོན་རྣམས་མི་འབྱུང་ལ་ཡུལ་བྱེ་བྲག་ཏུ་གསལ་བར་གཅོད་མི་ནུས་པའི་ཕྱིར་ཡུལ་ངེས་ལྔ་མི་འབྱུང་ངོ་། །གཞན་དུ་འགྱུར་བ་བཞི་ཡང་གདགས་གཞི་མི་འབྱུང་[11b]བའི་ཕྱིར་དེ་དག་གང་ཡང་ལྡན་པ་མ་ཡིན་ནོ། །ཀུན་ཏུ་འགྲོ་བ་ལྔ་དང་ནི་མཚུངས་པར་ལྡན་ཏེ། རེག་པ་ནི་སེམས་བྱུང་ཀུན་གྱི་རྒྱུ་ཡིན་པའི་ཕྱིར་དང་།[1]སེམས་ཐམས་ཅད་ལ་མྱོང་བ་རྣམ་པ་གསུམ་ལས་གང་ཡང་རུང་བ་གཅིག་དམིགས་པའི་ཕྱིར་དང་། ཡུལ་གྱི་སྒྲ་རིས་གཅོད་པ་ཙམ་དང་། ཡུལ་ལ་གཡོ་བ་ཙམ་དང་། རང་གི་དམིགས་པ་ལ་སེམས་གཏོད་པ་ཙམ་སེམས་ཐམས་ཅད་ལ་ཡོད་པའི་ཕྱིར་རོ།།

ཀུན་གཞིའི་འཁོར་གྱི་ཚོར་བ་དེ་མྱོང་བ་གསུམ་གང་ཞེ་ན།།

ཚོར་བ་ནི། །བར་མའོ།

ཚོར་བ་ནི་བདེ་བ་དང་གདུང་བ་གཉིས་ཀའི་ངོ་བོར་མ་གྱུར་པ་,བར་མར་[1131]ཉམས་སུ་མྱོང་བ་བཏང་སྙོམས་པ་ཡིན་ཏེ། འདི་ལ་ཚོར་བ་ནི་དམིགས་ལ་བདེ་བ་དང་གདུང་བ་གང་ཡང་མེད་པའི་ཕྱིར། ཇི་ལྟར་ཞེ་ན། གལ་ཏེ་ཚོར་བ་བདེ་བ་དང་ལྡན་ན་བསམ་གཏན་བཞི་པ་ཡན་ཆད་ཀྱང་ཚོར་བ་བདེ་བའི་སར་འགྱུར་ལ། དམྱལ་བ་ན་ཡང་རྣམ་སྨིན་གྱི་བདེ་བ་ཡོད་པར་འགྱུར་རོ། །དེ་སྟེ་སྡུག་བསྔལ་དང་ལྡན་ན་བསོད་ནམས་དང་མི་གཡོ་བའི་ལས་ཀྱི་རྣམ་པར་སྨིན་པ་སྡུག་བསྔལ་འཕེན་པར་འགྱུར་བ་དང་། གཟུགས་མེད་པ་ལྟ་བུ་ཡང་ཚོར་བ་གདུང་བའི་སར་འགྱུར་བ་སོགས་རྒྱ་ཆེའོ།།

ཅིའི་ཕྱིར་རྟེན་དུ་གྱུར་པ་རྣམ་པར་སྨིན་པའི་རྣམ་ཤེས་དེ་ལ་ཀུན་གཞི་ཞེས་བྱ་ཞེ་ན།

འདི་ལ་བདག་ཏུ་ནི། །སྦྱོར་བའི་ཕྱིར་ན་ཀུན་གཞིའོ།།

འགྲོ་བ་ལྔའི་སེམས་ཅན་རྣམས་འདིར་ཉོན་མོངས་ཀྱིས་བདག་ཏུ་སྦྱོར་བའི་ཕྱིར་ཀུན་གཞི་ཞེས་བྱ་སྟེ་ཉོན་ཡིད་ཀྱིས་བདག་ཏུ་ལྟ་བའི་ཡུལ་ནི་ཀུན་གཞིའི་རྣམ་སྨིན་གྱི་ཆ་ཡིན་པའི་ཕྱིར་རོ།།

---

[1] In M *dang* and the shad have been dropped and the words *sems thams cad la myong ba rnam pa gsum las gang yang rung ba gcig dmigs pa'i phyir dang* have been accidentally repeated twice.

དེ་ལྟ་བུའི་རྣམ་སྨིན་གྱི་ཆ་དེ་དུས་གང་བར་དུ་འཇུག་ཅིང་ལྡོག་ཅེ་ན།

ལྷག་མ་མེད་དང་རྡོ་རྗེ་ལྟའི། །བར་དུ་རྒྱུན་མི་འཆད་[12a]དུ་འཇུག།

ཐེག་དམན་གྱི་ལྷག་མེད་ཀྱི་མྱང་འདས་དང་། ཐེག་ཆེན་གྱི་རྡོ་རྗེ་ལྟ་བུའི་ཏིང་ངེ་འཛིན་གྱི་རྗེས་སུ་ལྡོག་ཅིང་དེའི་སྔོན་དུ་རྒྱུན་མི་འཆད་དུ་འཇུག་གོ །དེ་ཡང་ཇི་སྐད་དུ།

ལས་ཀྱི་བག་ཆགས་འཛིན་གཉིས་ཀྱི། །བག་ཆགས་བཅས་པ་སྔ་མ་ཡི། །རྣམ་པར་སྨིན་པ་ཟད་ནས་
གཞན། །རྣམ་སྨིན་བསྐྱེད་པ་དེ་ཡིན་ནོ།།

ཞེས་གསུངས་པ་ལྟར་ཚེ་སྔ་མའི་དགེ་སྡིག་ལས་ཀྱིས་འཕངས་པའི་ཀུན་གཞིའི་རྣམ་སྨིན་དེ་ཚེ་འདིར་ཇི་སྲིད་མ་ཤིའི་བར་དུ་འཇུག་ཅིང་། ལས་དེའི་ནུས་པ་ཟད་པའི་ཚེ་དེ་ལོག་ནས་ཡང་ལས་ཕྱི་མས་བསྐྱེད་པའི་རྣམ་སྨིན་[1] འཇུག་པས་རྒྱུན་མི་འཆད་དོ།།

འདིར་ཅིའི་ཕྱིར་རྟེན་དུ་གྱུར་པའི་རྣམ་པར་ཤེས་པ་ཁོ་ན་ལ་རྣམ་པར་སྨིན་པ་ཞེས་བྱ། མིག་སོགས་དབང་པོ་ལྔ་ཡང་རྣམ་པར་སྨིན་པ་མ་ཡིན་ནམ་ཞེ་ན།

ཉེས་པ་མེད་དེ་འདི་ལྟར་རྣམ་པར་སྨིན་པ་ནི་མ་བསྒྲིབས་ལ་ལུང་དུ་མ་བསྟན་པ་དང་། ཚེ་ཇི་སྲིད་ཀྱི་བར་དུ་རྒྱུན་མ་ཆད་དུ་[1132]འཇུག་པ་དང་། སྔོན་གྱི་དགེ་བའམ་མ་དགེ་བས་འཕངས་པའི་འབྲས་བུ་ཡིན་པ་སྟེ་ཁྱད་པར་གསུམ་དང་ལྡན་པ་ཞིག་དགོས་པ་ལས་དེ་ཀུན་གཞི་འཁོར་བཅས་ལས་གཞན་པ་ལ་མི་རུང་བའི་ཕྱིར་ཏེ། མ་བསྒྲིབས་ལུང་མ་བསྟན་དེ་དགེ་མི་དགེའི་རྣམ་སྨིན་དུ་འགལ་བ་མེད་ལ་དགེ་བ་དང་མི་དགེ་བ་ནི་རིམ་པ་བཞིན་མི་དགེ་བ་དང་དགེ་བའི་རྣམ་སྨིན་དུ་འགལ་ཏེ་དེ་གཉིས་མི་མཐུན་པ་དང་གཉེན་པོ་ཡིན་པའི་ཕྱིར་རོ།།

གལ་ཏེ་དགེ་བ་ཉིད་དགེ་བའི་རྣམ་སྨིན་དང་མི་དགེ་བ་ཉིད་མི་དགེ་བའི་རྣམ་སྨིན་དུ་འགལ་བ་མེད་པས་རྣམ་སྨིན་ལུང་མ་བསྟན་ཁོ་ནར་མ་ངེས་སོ་ཞེ་ན།

དེ་ལྟ་ན་[12b]ཀུན་ནས་ཉོན་མོངས་པ་ལྡོག་པ་མེད་པའི་སྐྱོན་དུ་འགྱུར་ཏེ། འདི་ལྟར་རྣམ་སྨིན་ནི་ཚེ་རབས་ཐམས་ཅད་དུ་ཇི་སྲིད་འཚོའི་བར་དུ་རྒྱུན་མི་འཆད་དུ་འཇུག་པ་ན་རྣམ་སྨིན་དགེ་བ་ཡིན་ན་དགེ་སེམས་སྐད་ཅིག་ཀྱང་རྒྱུན་མི་འཆད་དུ་འཇུག་པས་ཀུན་ནས་ཉོན་མོངས་པ་སྐྱེ་བའི་སྐབས་མེད་ལ་སྐྱེ་བ་མེད་པའི་ཕྱིར་དེ་སྔོན་དུ་འགྲོ་བའི་འགག་པའང་མེད་དོ། །རྣམ་སྨིན་གྱི་མི་དགེ་བ་ཡིན་ན་མི་དགེ་བའི་སེམས་རྒྱུན་མི་འཆད་པའི་, གཉེན་པོ་སྐྱེ་བའི་སྐབས་མེད་ལ་དེ་མེད་པའི་ཕྱིར་ཀུན་ནས་ཉོན་མོངས་པ་ལོག་པར་མི་འགྱུར་རོ། །གཞན་ཡང་དགེ་རྩ་ཆད་པའི་གང་ཟག་ལ་དགེ་སེམས་མངོན་གྱུར་དུ་ཡོད་པ་སོགས་མཐའ་ཡས་སོ། །དེའི་ཕྱིར་

[1] *rmi lam 'jug* O,P.

མ་བསྒྲིབས་ལུང་མ་བསྟན་ཁོ་ནར་ངེས་སོ། །དེ་སྐད་དུ།

ཅིའི་ཕྱིར་དགེ་བ་དང་མི་དགེ་བའི་ཆོས་རྣམས་ཀྱི་རྣམ་པར་སྨིན་པ་མ་བསྒྲིབས་ལ་ལུང་དུ་མ་བསྟན་པའི་རྣམ་པར་སྨིན་པ་ཞེས་བྱ་ཞེ་ན། འདི་ལྟར་མ་བསྒྲིབས་ལ་ལུང་དུ་མ་བསྟན་པ་[1] ནི་དགེ་བ་དང་མི་དགེ་བ་དང་འགལ་བ་མེད་དེ། དགེ་བ་དང་མི་དགེ་བ་ནི་ཕན་ཚུན་མི་མཐུན་ནོ། །རྣམ་པར་སྨིན་པ་ཡང་དགེ་བ་དང་མི་དགེ་བར་གྱུར་ན་ནི་ཀུན་ནས་ཉོན་མོངས་པ་ལོག་པར་མི་འགྱུར་རོ[2]།དེ་ལྟ་བས་ན་རྣམ་པར་སྨིན་པའི་རྣམ་པར་ཤེས་པ་ནི་མ་བསྒྲིབས་ལ་ལུང་དུ་མ་བསྟན་པ་ཉིད་དོ།།

ཞེས་སོ། །ཡང་ཐེག་བསྡུས་སུ།

རྣམ་པར་སྨིན་པའི་རྣམ་པར་ཤེས་པ་རྒྱུན་ [1133]ཆད་པ་ནི་ཉིང་མཚམས་སྦྱོར་བ་མ་གཏོགས་པ་གཞན་དུ་མངོན་པར་འགྲུབ་པ་མེད་པའི་ཕྱིར།

ཞེས་འབྱུང་བས་རྣམ་སྨིན་ཇི་སྲིད་འཚོའི་བར་དུ་འཇུག་དགོས་པ་ཡིན་པའི་ཕྱིར་མ་ཤིའི་བར་དུ་འབྱུང་དགོས་ལ་མིག་ལ་སོགས་པ་ནི་མ་ཤིའི་གོང་དུ་ཡང་ལྡོག་པ་མཐོང་པའི་ཕྱིར་དེ་དག་རྣམ་སྨིན་མཚན་ཉིད་པ་མ་[13a]ཡིན་ནོ།།

ཀུན་ལས་བཏུས་སུ་ཡང་།

རྣམ་པར་སྨིན་པ་གང་ཞེ་ན། ཀུན་གཞི་རྣམ་པར་[3] ཤེས་པ་མཚུངས་པར་ལྡན་པ་དང་བཅས་པའོ་

ཞེས་འབྱུང་ངོ་། །དེས་ན་རྟེན་དུ་གྱུར་པའི་རྣམ་ཤེས་ཁོ་ན་རྣམ་སྨིན་ཡིན་ནོ།།

དེ་དག་གིས་རྟེན་གྱི་མཚན་ཉིད་བཤད་ཟིན་ཏོ།།

[Chapter Three]

བརྟེན་པ་ས་བོན་གྱི་ཀུན་གཞིའི་མཚན་ཉིད་དེ་ཇི་ལྟ་བུ་ཞེ་ན།

བརྟེན་པ་ས་བོན་ཀུན་གཞི་ནི། །སྒོ་བར་བྱེད་པས་བསྒོ་གཞི་ལ། །འགག་ལ་མངོན་དུ་ཕྱོགས་པའི་ཚེ།
།བཞག་པའི་ནུས་པའོ།

སྒོ་བྱེད་ཚོགས་བདུན་གྱིས་[4] སྒོ་གཞི་ལ་རང་ཉིད་འགག་པ་ལ་མངོན་དུ་ཕྱོགས་པའི་ཚེ་དགེ་མི་དགེ་ལུང་མ་བསྟན་གསུམ་གྱི་[5] ས་བོན་བཞག་པའི་ནུས་པ་ཞིག་གོ །དེ་ཡང་ཚོགས་དྲུག་གིས་ནི་དགེ་མི་དགེ་ལུང་མ་བསྟན་གསུམ་ཆར་གྱི་ས་བོན་འཇོག་སྟེ་དེ་དག་ལ་དགེ་སོགས་གསུམ་ཆར་ཡོད་པས་སོ། །ཉོན་ཡིད་འཁོར་བཅས་ཀྱིས་ནི་ལུང་མ་བསྟན་གྱི་ས་བོན་ཁོ་ན་བསྒོ་སྟེ། དེ་ནི་རྟག་ཏུ་ལུང་མ་བསྟན་གྱི་ངོ་བོར་གནས་པའི་ཕྱིར་རོ།།

---

[1] Delete *'di* (Lamotte 1938:24). [2] For *log par mi 'gyur ro* Lamotte (1938:24) reads *ldog par mi rung ngo.* [3] O and P add *rmin par.* [4] *gyi* D,O,P. [5] *gyis* D,O,P.

སྒོ་བར་བྱེད་པ་ཚོགས་བདུན་འཁོར་བཅས་སུ་ཇི་ལྟར་ངེས་ཤེ་ན།

འཇུག་ཤེས་རྣམས་དང་ཀུན་གཞི་གཉིས་ཉིད་ཕན་ཚུན་འབྲས་བུའི་དངོས་པོ་དང་རྒྱུའི་དངོས་པོར་རྟག་ཏུ་སྦྱོར་ཏེ་འདི་ལྟར་འཇུག་པའི་ཤེས་པ་རྣམས་ཀྱིས་ས་བོན་རྙིང་བ་གསོ་བས་[1]ཀུན་གཞི་ས་བོན་གྱི་ཆའི་བདག་རྐྱེན་བྱེད་ལ། ས་བོན་གསར་པ་འཇོག་པས་དེའི་རྒྱུའི་རྐྱེན་བྱེད་དེ་ཇི་སྐད་དུ།

རྣམ་པར་ཤེས་པ་གཉིས་ནི་གཅིག་གི་རྐྱེན་གཅིག་ཡིན་ཏེ། ཆོས་མངོན་པའི་མདོ་ལས་

> ཆོས་ཀུན་རྣམ་པར་ཤེས་ལ་སྦྱར། །དེ་དག་ལ་ཡང་དེ་དེ་བཞིན། །ཕན་ཚུན་འབྲས་བུའི[13b]
> དངོས་པོ་དང་། །རྒྱུ་ཡི་དངོས་པོར་རྟག་ཏུ་སྦྱར།།

ཞེས་སོ། །དུས་མཉམ་པའི་རྒྱུ་འབྲས་ཀྱི་དབང་[1134]དུ་བྱས་ནས་དེ་སྐད་བཤད་ཀྱི།[2]མི་མཉམ་པའི་དབང་དུ་བྱས་ན། ཚེ་ཕྱི་མའི་ཀུན་གཞིའི་རྣམ་སྨིན་ཆ་འགྲུབ་པའི་ས་བོན་ཡང་འཇོག་པར་བྱེད་དོ།།

དེ་ཡང་རྟེན་དེ་དང་སྒོ་བ་པོ་རང་ཉིད་སྐྱེ་འགག་ལྷན་ཅིག་ཏུ་བྱས་པས་སྒོ་བར་བྱེད་དེ། དཔེར་ན་ཏིལ་དང་སྣ་མ་གཉིས་ལྷན་ཅིག་ཏུ་གནས་ཏེ་སྐྱེ་འགག་བྱས་པས་ཕྱིས་མེ་ཏོག་དེ་མེད་ཀྱང་ཏིལ་ལ་མེ་ཏོག་གི་དྲི་རྗེས་སུ་འཇུག་པ་བཞིན་ནོ། དེ་སྐད་དུ་ཡང་།

> དེ་ལ་འཇུག་པའི་རྣམ་པར་ཤེས་པ་ནི་ཀུན་གཞི་རྣམ་པར་ཤེས་པ་ལ་རྣམ་པར་གཉིས་ཀྱིས་རྐྱེན་བྱེད་དེ། མཐོང་བའི་ཆོས་ལ་ས་བོན་ཡོངས་སུ་གསོ་བ་དང་། ཚེ་ཕྱི་མ་ལ་དེ་མངོན་པར་འགྲུབ་པར་བྱ་བའི་ཕྱིར་ས་བོན་ཡོངས་སུ་འཛིན་པ་འཇོག་པའི་སྒོ་ནས་སོ།། དེའི་ཕྱིར་མཐོང་བའི་ཆོས་ལ་ས་བོན་ཡོངས་སུ་རྒྱས་ན་ཇི་ལྟ་ཇི་ལྟར་ཀུན་གཞི་རྣམ་པར་ཤེས་པ་ལ་བརྟེན་པའི་དགེ་བ་དང་མི་དགེ་བ་དང་། ལུང་དུ་མ་བསྟན་པ་འབྱུང་བ་དེ་ལྟ་དེ་ལྟར་རང་གི་རྟེན་ལ་ལྷན་ཅིག་འབྱུང་བ་དང་འགག་པས་སྒོ་བར་བྱེད་དོ།།[3]

ཞེས་སོ།།

བསྒོ་གཞི་དེ་ལ་ཇི་ལྟ་བུ་ཞིག་དགོས་ཤེ་ན།

> བསྒོ་གཞི་ནི། །བརྟན་[4] ལུང་མ་བསྟན་བསྒོ་བྱ་བ། །སྒོ་བར་བྱེད་དང་འབྲེལ་བ་དང་། །མཐའ་གཅིག་རྟེན་
> དུ་གྱུར་པ་སྟེ། །ཁྱད་པར་ལྔ་དང་ལྡན་པའོ།།

ཁྱད་པར་ལྔ་དང་ལྡན་པ་ཞིག་བསྒོ་གཞིར་འཇོག་གོ །ལྔ་གང་ཞེ་ན། བརྟན་པ་ནི་ཏིལ་ལ་སོགས་པ་ལྟར་རྒྱུད་རྒྱུན་ཆགས་པ་ཞིག་དགོས་ཀྱི, སྒྲ་གློག་ལྟ་བུའི་མི་བརྟན་པ་ནི་སྒོ་གཞིར་མི་རུང་སྟེ་དེ་དག་ལ་བག་ཆགས་འཆགས་སུ་མི་འདོད་ཅིང་ཆགས་ཀྱང་ཆུད་ཟོས་པ་ཉིད་དུ་འགྱུར་རོ། །འདིས་ནི་ཚོགས་[14a]བདུན་དང་

---

[1] *ba'i* D,O,P. [2] *kyis* D,O,P. [3] This quotation is similar to MSam (Nagao 1982:23). [4] *bstan* N,O,P.

གཟུགས་བསྒོ་གཞིར་མི་རུང་བར་བསྟན་ཏེ། དེ་དག་ནི། ཇི་སྐད་དུ།

ཡིད་ཀྱི་རྣམ་ཤེས་འབྱུང་བ་ནི། །རྟག་ཏུའོ་འདུ་ཤེས་མེད་པ་པ། །སྙོམས་པར་འཇུག་པ་རྣམ་
གཉིས་དང་། །སེམས་མེད་གཉིད་དང་བརྒྱལ་མ་གཏོགས།།

ཞེས་དང་།

འཇིག་རྟེན་འདས་པའི་ལམ་ན་མེད། །འགོག་པའི་སྙོམས་པར་འཇུག་ནའང་མེད།།

ཅེས་འབྱུང་བ་ལྟར་རྒྱུན་འཆད་པའི་ཕྱིར་དང་གཟུགས་[1135]ཀྱང་གཟུགས་མེད་དུ་མེད་པའི་ཕྱིར་རོ།།

དེ་ལྟ་ན་ཀུན་གཞི་ཡང་བསྒོ་གཞིར་མི་རུང་སྟེ།

དགྲ་བཅོམ་ཉིད་ནས་དེ་ལྡོག་གོ།

ཞེས་པ་ལྟར་རྒྱུན་འཆད་པའི་ཕྱིར་རོ། །ཞེ་ན། ཉེས་པ་མེད་དེ་ཇི་སྲིད་སྒོ་བྱེད་ཡོད་ཀྱི་བར་དུ་རྒྱུན་མི་འཆད་པས་ཆོག་པའི་ཕྱིར་རོ།།

ལུང་དུ་མ་བསྟན་པ་ནི་སྒོག་སྐྱ་དང་ཙནྡ་ལྟ་བུ་དྲི་མ་མི་མཉམ་པ་ལ་ས་བོན་ཐམས་ཅད་བསྒོད་མི་ནུས་ཀྱི་, ཏིལ་ལྟ་བུའི་དྲི་མཉམ་པ་ལ་ནུས་པས་ན་དྲི་མཉམ་པ་ལྟ་བུའི་ལུང་མ་བསྟན་ནི་དགེ་བ་དང་མི་དགེ་བའི་སེམས་ཏ་ཅང་གསལ་བ་དང་མི་མཐུན་པ་མེད་པའི་ཕྱིར་རོ། །འདིས་ནི་དགེ་བ་དང་ཉོན་མོངས་ཅན་བསྒོ་གཞིར་མི་རུང་བར་བསྟན་ཏོ།།

བསྒོ་བྱ་བ་ནི། བསྒོ་བར་ནུས་པ་སྟེ་མི་རྟག་པ་ལ་བསྒོད་ཀྱི་,རྟག་པ་ལ་མི་ནུས་སོ་ཞེས་པས་འདུས་མ་བྱས་བསྒོ་གཞིར་མི་རུང་བར་བསྟན་ཏོ།།

སྒོ་བར་བྱེད་དང་འབྲེལ་བ་ནི། །སྒོ་བྱེད་དང་བསྒོ་གཞི་སྐྱེ་འགག་དུས་གཅིག་ལ་བྱས་པའི་འབྲེལ་བ་དང་ལྡན་པ་ཞིག་དགོས་སོ། །འདིས་ནི་རྒྱུད་ཐ་དད་དང་དུས་མི་མཉམ་པའི་ཆོས་རྣམས་བསྒོ་བྱ་སྒོ་བྱེད་དུ་མི་རུང་བར་བསྟན་ཏོ།།

མཐའ་གཅིག་ཏུ་རྟེན་དུ་གྱུར་པ་ནི། རྣམ་གྲངས་ཀྱིས་མ་[14b]ཡིན་པར་མཐའ་གཅིག་རྟེན་དུ་གྱུར་པའོ།། འདིས་ནི་ཀུན་གཞིའི་འཁོར་གྱི་རིག་པ་སོགས་བསྒོ་གཞི་ཡིན་པ་སེལ་ཏེ་དེ་དག་ནི་གཙོ་བོ་སེམས་ཀུན་གཞི་རྣམ་ཤེས་ལ་བརྟེན་པས་ན་མཐའ་གཅིག་ཏུ་བརྟེན་[1]པ་མ་ཡིན་ནོ།།

འོ་ན་རིག་སོགས་དེ་དག་གིས་རང་འགྲུབ་པའི་ས་བོན་ཀུན་གཞི་ལ་བསྒོད་དམ་མི་བསྒོད། དང་པོ་ལྟར་ན། ཚོགས་བདུན་ལས་གཞན་པའི་སྒོ་བྱེད་ཡོད་པར་འགྱུར་རོ། །གཉིས་པ་ལྟར་ན་དེ་དག་རྒྱུ་མེད་དུ་འགྱུར་རོ། །ཞེ་ན།

[1] *brten*→*rten* (?) cp. 13b5.

"འདི་ལ་རྒྱུ་མེད་དུ་འགྱུར་པའི་ཕྱིར་བསྒོད་དགོས་"ཞེས་པ་དང་། "དེ་དག་ཤིན་ཏུ་མི་གསལ་བའི་ལུང་མ་བསྟན་ཡིན་པའི་ཕྱིར་མི་བསྒོད་དོ། །འོན་ཀྱང་སྡོན་ལས་ཀྱི་རྣམ་སྨིན་ཡིན་པས་མ་ཤིའི་བར་དུ་འཕན་པས་འཇུག་"ཅེས་འདོད་པས་གཉིས་བཤད་ཀྱང་,ཕྱི་མ་ལེགས་ཏེ་གཞན་དུ་ན་ཀུན་གཞི་ཉིད་ཀྱིས་ཀྱང་བསྒོད་དགོས་པས་བསྒོ་གཞི་མ་རྙེད་པའི་སྐྱོན་[1136]དུ་འགྱུར་རོ།།

དེ་ལྟ་བུའི་བག་ཆགས་དེ་ལ་དབྱེ་བ་དུ་ཞིག་ཅེ་ན། དྲུག་ཏུ་དབྱེ་བ། གསུམ་དུ་དབྱེ་བ། བཞི་ཚན་གཉིས་སུ་དབྱེ་བ་དང་བཞིའོ། །དང་པོ་དྲུག་ཏུ་དབྱེ་བ་ནི།

ཕྱི་དང་ནང་དང་མི་གསལ་བ། །གཉིས་དང་ཀུན་རྫོབ་ཉིད་དང་ནི། །དམ་པའི་དོན་ཏེ་དེ་དག
ཀུན། །ས་བོན་རྣམ་པ་དྲུག་ཏུ་འདོད།།

ཕྱིའི་ས་བོན་ནི་ནས་དང་ཨུཏྤ་ལའི་རྩ་བ་ལྟ་བུའོ། །ནང་གི་ས་བོན་ནི་ཀུན་གཞིའི་ས་བོན་གྱི་ཆའོ། །མི་གསལ་བ་གཉིས་ནི། །མི་གསལ་བ་ནི་ལུང་མ་བསྟན་པ་ཡིན་ཏེ་དེ་ལ་ནི། ཀུན་ནས་ཉོན་མོངས་དང་རྣམ་བྱང་གི་མི་གསལ་བའམ། དགེ་བ་དང་མི་དགེ་བ་གཉིས་མི་གསལ་བའི་ཕྱིར་རོ། །གཉིས་ནི་ཕྱིའི་ས་བོན་དང་ནང་གི་ས་བོན་ནོ། །ཐེག་བསྡུས་ཀྱི་ཊཱི་ཀ་བྱེད་ཁ་[15a]ཅིག་གི་ལུགས་ཀྱིས་ནི། གཉིས་སུ་མི་གསལ་ཞེས་འདོན་པ་ལྟར་ན། ཀུན་ནས་ཉོན་མོངས་དང་རྣམ་བྱང་ངམ། དགེ་མི་དགེར་དཔྱད་ན་དེ་དག་གང་དུ་ཡང་མི་གསལ་བ་ལུང་དུ་མ་བསྟན་པའོ།

ཡང་ན་གཉིས་ཞེས་པ་ཀུན་གཞི་རྣམ་ཤེས་དེ་ཉིད་ཉོན་མོངས་པའི་ཆོས་རྣམས་ཀྱི་ས་བོན་ཅན་ཡིན་པས་ཀུན་ནས་ཉོན་མོངས་པའི་ཆོས་རྣམས་འབྱུང་བས་དེ་དག་དང་རྒྱུ་འབྲས་དང་། རྣམ་བྱང་གི་ཆོས་རྣམས་ཀྱི་ས་བོན་ཀྱང་གནས་སམ། རྟེན་གྱི་དངོས་པོ་བྱས་པས་དེ་དག་དང་རྒྱུ་འབྲས་སུ་གྱུར་པ་གཉིས་སོ། །དེ་ལྟར་ཡང་དོན་གསང་དུ།

མི་གསལ་བ་གཉིས་ཞེས་པ་ནི། དགེ་བ་དང་མི་དགེ་བ་གཉིས་སམ་ཀུན་ནས་ཉོན་མོངས་པ་དང་། རྣམ་པར་བྱང་བ་གཉིས་མི་གསལ་ཞིང་ཡོངས་སུ་མི་གསལ་བ་སྟེ། ལུང་དུ་མ་བསྟན་པ་ཞེས་བྱ་བའི་ཐ་ཚིག་གོ །ཁ་ཅིག་ནི་གཉིས་སུ་ཞེས་འདོན་ཏེ་ས་བོན་ནི་དགེ་བ་དང་མི་དགེ་བ་གཉིས་སུ་དཔྱད་དམ། ཀུན་ནས་ཉོན་མོངས་པའམ་རྣམ་པར་བྱང་བ་གཉིས་སུ་དཔྱད་ན་མི་གསལ་ཏེ་ལུང་དུ་མ་བསྟན་ཏོ་ཞེས་བྱ་བའི་དོན་ནོ། །དེ་ལ་ཕྱིའི་ས་བོན་ནི་ལུང་དུ་མ་བསྟན་པ་སྟེ་ལུང་དུ་མ་བསྟན་པ་ཉིད་ཀྱིས་མི་གསལ་བ་ཡིན་ནོ།[1] །ནང་གི་ཡང་དགེ་བ་ལ་སོགས་པའི་ངོ་བོར་མི་དམིགས་པའི་ཕྱིར་མི་གསལ་བ་ཡིན་ནོ།།

---

[1] *ba'o→ba yin no* P5553:69.1.4.

ཞེས་དང་། [1137]བཤད་སྦྱར་ལས་ཀྱང་།

> མི་གསལ་བ་ནི་ལུང་དུ་མ་བསྟན་པའོ། །གཉིས་ནི་ཕྱི་དང་ནང་གིའོ། །ཡང་ན་འབྲས་བུ་དང་རྒྱུ་སྟེ་དེ་
> གཉིས་ཀྱི་རྒྱུ་མཚན་ཀུན་གཞི་རྣམ་པར་ཤེས་པ་ཡང་གཉིས་སོ། །དེ་ལ་རྒྱུ་དང་གཞིའི་[1] དངོས་པོས་
> ཀུན་ནས་ཉོན་མོངས་པ་དང་རྣམ་པར་བྱང་[15b]བའི་ཆོས་འབྱུང་བའི་ཕྱིར...

ཞེས་སོ།།

ཀུན་རྫོབ་པའི་ས་བོན་ནི་ཕྱིའི་ས་བོན་ཏེ་ཐ་སྙད་པའི་ཤེས་པའི་ཡུལ་ཙམ་ཡིན་པའི་ཕྱིར་རོ། །དོན་དམ་པའི་ས་བོན་ནི་ནང་གི་ས་བོན་ཏེ་རྣམ་པར་དཔྱད་པ་ན་ཡང་ཁས་ལེན་དགོས་པའི་ཕྱིར་རོ། །དོན་གསང་དང་བཤད་སྦྱར་གྱི་བཤད་པ་སྔ་མ་ལྟར་ན་དང་པོ་དང་གསུམ་པ་ལྔ་པ་རྣམས་ཞར་ལ་བྱུང་བ་ཙམ་ཡིན་ལ་བཤད་སྦྱར་གྱི་བཤད་པ་གཉིས་པ་ལྟར་ན་ཞར་བྱུང་ངོ་། །དེ་སྐད་དུ་ཡང་ཐེག་ཆེན་བསྡུས་པ་ལས།

> ཕྱི་དང་ནང་དང་མི་གསལ་བ། །གཉིས་དང་[2] ཀུན་རྫོབ་ཉིད་དང་ནི། །དམ་པའི་དོན་ཏེ་དེ་དག་
> ཀུན། །ས་བོན་རྣམ་པ་དྲུག་ཏུ་འདོད།[3] །བརྟན་ལུང་མ་བསྟན་བསྒོ་བྱ་བ། །སྒོ་བར་བྱེད་དང་
> འབྲེལ་བ་ལ།[4] །སྒོ་བྱེད་དེ་ལས་གཞན་ནི་[5] མིན། །དེ་ནི་བག་ཆགས་མཚན་ཉིད་དོ།།

ཞེས་སོ།།

> གཉིས་པ་གསུམ་དུ་དབྱེ་བ་ནི།།
> གཞན་ཡང་སྡོན་བརྗོད་བདག་ལྟ་དང་། །སྲིད་པའི་ཡན་ལག་བག་ཆགས་གསུམ།།
> དེ་ཡང་ཇི་སྐད་དུ།
> ཀུན་གཞི་རྣམ་པར་ཤེས་པ་འདིའི་[6] རབ་ཏུ་དབྱེ་བ་གང་ཞེ་ན། མདོར་བསྡུས་ན་རྣམ་པ་གསུམ་དང་། རྣམ་པ་བཞིར་བལྟ་བར་བྱའོ། །དེ་ལ་བག་ཆགས་རྣམ་པ་གསུམ་གྱི་བྱེ་བྲག་གིས་རྣམ་པ་གསུམ་སྟེ། མངོན་པར་བརྗོད་པའི་བག་ཆགས་ཀྱི་བྱེ་བྲག་དང་། བདག་ཏུ་ལྟ་བའི་བག་ཆགས་ཀྱི་བྱེ་བྲག་དང་། སྲིད་པའི་ཡན་ལག་གི་བག་ཆགས་ཀྱི་བྱེ་བྲག་གིས་སོ།།

ཞེས་པ་ལྟར་གསུམ་མོ། །དེ་ལ་བག་ཆགས་དང་པོ་ནི། ཀུན་གཞིའི་སྟེང་གི་ས་བོན་གཟུགས་ནས་རྣམ་མཁྱེན་གྱི་བར་གྱི་ཆོས་རྣམས་ཀྱི་མིང་དང་མཚན་མའི་རྣམ་པར་འབྱུང་ཞིང་མདོར་ན་ཐ་སྙད་སྣ་ཚོགས་འདོགས་པའི་ཡིད་ཤེས་ཀྱི་རྒྱུའི་རྐྱེན་ནོ། [16a]།འདི་ལ་སྦྱོས་པའི་བག་ཆགས་ཞེས་ཀྱང་ཟེར་ཏེ། ཡིད་ཤེས་ཡུལ་སྣ་[1138]

---

[1] *'bras bu'i→gzhi'i* Lamotte (1938:vol. 2, 38). [2] *ni* Lamotte (1938:12). [3] An additional śloka separates the two verses in the original (Lamotte 1938:12, Nagao I,22): སྐད་ཅིག་པ་དང་ལྡན་ཅིག་འབྱུང་། །དེ་ནི་རྒྱུན་ཆགས་འབྱུང་བར་འདོད། །ངེས་དང་རྐྱེན་ལ་ལྟོས་པ་དང་། །རང་གི་འབྲས་བུས་བསྒྲུབས་པའོ།། [4] *dang→la* Lamotte (1938:12). [5] *du→ni* Ibid. [6] *pa'i→'di'i* (Lamotte 1938:22).

ཚོགས་ལ་འགྲོ་བའི་ས་བོན་ཡིན་པའི་ཕྱིར་རོ། །མངོན་བརྗོད་ཀྱི་བག་ཆགས་ཞེས་ཀྱང་ཟེར་ཏེ་མིག་མིག་ཅེས་དང་། གཟུགས་གཟུགས་ཞེས་པའི་བརྗོད་པའི་རྣམ་པ་ཅན་གྱི་ཡིད་ཤེས་ཀྱི་ས་བོན་ཡིན་པའི་ཕྱིར་རོ།།

དེ་ལྟ་ན་ཐེག་ཆེན་བསྡུས་པར།

དེ་ལ་ལུས་དང་ལུས་ཅན་དང་ཟ་བ་པོའི་རྣམ་པར་རིག་པ་གང་ཡིན་པ་དང་། དེས་ཉེ་བར་དསྤྱད་པར་བྱ་བའི་རྣམ་པར་རིག་པ་གང་ཡིན་པ་དང་། དེ་ལ་ཉེ་བར་སྤྱོད་པའི་རྣམ་པར་རིག་པ་གང་ཡིན་པ་དང་། དུས་དང་གྲངས་དང་ཡུལ་དང་ཐ་སྙད་ཀྱི་རྣམ་པར་རིག་པ་གང་ཡིན་པ་དེ་ནི་མངོན་པར་བརྗོད་པའི་བག་ཆགས་ཀྱི་ས་བོན་ལས་འབྱུང་བའི་ཕྱིར་རོ།།

ཞེས་གསུངས་པ་ཇི་ལྟར་དྲང་ཞེ་ན།

ཉེས་པ་མེད་དེ་ཡིད་ཤེས་ཀྱི་ས་བོན་ཞེས་སྨྲར་བརྗོད་པ་ནི་གཙོ་བོའི་དབང་དུ་བྱས་ལ། འདིར་བསྟན་པ་ནི། གཞན་དབང་དེ་ཀུན་གཞིའི་ས་བོན་ཅན་ཡང་དག་པ་མ་ཡིན་པའི་ཀུན་ཏུ་རྟོག་པས་བསྡུས་པའི་རྣམ་རིག་ཡིན་ལ་དེ་ལ་ཡང་ལུས་ཞེས་པ་ནས་ཐ་སྙད་པའི་བར་གྱི་རྣམ་རིག་རྣམས་ནི་བག་ཆགས་གསུམ་དུ་ཕྱེད་པ་ན་མངོན་བརྗོད་ཀྱི་བག་ཆགས་ལས་འབྱུང་སྟེ། གཞན་གཉིས་ལས་མི་འབྱུང་ལ་འདི་དག་ཀྱང་ཡིད་ཤེས་ཀྱི་མངོན་པར་བརྗོད་པར་བྱ་བའི་ཆོས་ཡིན་པའི་ཕྱིར་རོ། །སྙམ་དུ་བསམས་སོ། །དེས་ན་མངོན་པར་བརྗོད་པར་བྱ་བའི་དབང་དུ་བྱས་ན། དེའི་བག་ཆགས་དེ་འཇོག་པ་ཡང་ཡིད་ཤེས་འཁོར་བཅས་ཁོ་ནས་འཇོག་ལ། བསྐྱེད་པ་ཡང་ཐ་སྙད་འདོགས་པའི་ཡིད་ཤེས་ཉིད་བསྐྱེད་དོ།།

གཉིས་པ་བདག་ལྟའི་བག་ཆགས་ནི། ཉོན་ཡིད་མཚུངས་[16b]ལྡན་དང་བཅས་པས་བཞག་པ་བདག་དང་གཞན་དུ་སྣང་བའི་རྣམ་རིག་འབྱུང་བའི་ས་བོན་ཏེ། ཇི་སྐད་དུ།

བདག་དང་གཞན་གྱི་བྱེ་བྲག་གི་རྣམ་པར་རིག་པ་གང་ཡིན་པ་དེ་ནི། བདག་ཏུ་ལྟ་བའི་བག་ཆགས་ཀྱི་ས་བོན་ལས་འབྱུང་བའི་ཕྱིར་རོ།།

ཞེས་སོ། །འདི་ལ་འཇིག་ཚོགས་ལ་ལྟ་བའི་བག་ཆགས་ཞེས་ཀྱང་ཟེར་ཏེ་འཇིག་ལྟའི་ས་བོན་ཡིན་པའི་ཕྱིར་རོ།།

གསུམ་པ་སྲིད་པའི་ཡན་ལག་གི་[1139]བག་ཆགས་ནི། འཛུག་ཤེས་དགེ་བའམ་མི་དགེ་བས་གཞག་པ་སྲིད་པ་བདེ་འགྲོའམ་ངན་འགྲོ །འཆི་འཕོ་དང་སྐྱེ་བར་སྣང་བའི་ས་བོན་ཏེ། ཇི་སྐད་དུ།

བདེ་འགྲོ་དང་ངན་འགྲོ་དང་འཆི་འཕོ་བ་དང་སྐྱེ་བའི་རྣམ་པར་རིག་པ་གང་ཡིན་པ་དེ་ནི། སྲིད་པ་ཡན་ལག་གི་བག་ཆགས་ཀྱི་ས་བོན་ལས་འབྱུང་བའི་ཕྱིར་རོ།།

ཞེས་སོ། །འདི་ལ་རྣམ་སྨིན་གྱི་བག་ཆགས་ཞེས་ཀྱང་བྱ་སྟེ་འདི་ཡོངས་སུ་སྨིན་པ་རྣམ་སྨིན་གྱི་ངོ་བོར་གྱུར་པ་ཡིན་པའི་ཕྱིར་རོ།།

དབང་པོ་དང་དོན་འདི་དག་ལ་འདིར་རྣམ་པར་རིག་པ་ཞེས་པ་དེ་དག་ཤེས་རིག་གི་ངོ་བོར་གྱུར་པས་དེ་སྐད་བརྗོད་པ་ཡིན་ནམ་ཞེ་ན་མ་ཡིན་ནོ། །འོ་ན་ཇི་ལྟ་བུ་ཞེ་ན།

དབང་པོ་ལྔ་དང་གཟུགས་སྒྲ་སོགས་དོན་ལྔར་སྣང་བ་འདི་དག་ལ་དཔྱད་པ་ན་ཕྱི་རོལ་ལྟ་བུར་ཀུན་ཏུ་ཆད་པར་སྣང་ལ་དེའི་ཚེ་ནི་དེ་དག་ཤེས་པའི་ངོ་བོར་མི་འདོད་དེ་འཇིག་རྟེན་ན་གྲགས་པ་དང་མ་དག་པའི་བློ་ལ་ཇི་ལྟར་སྣང་བ་ལྟར་རྣམ་གཞག་བྱེད་དོ། །བརྟགས་ཤིང་དཔྱད་པ་ན་དེ་ལྟར་སྣང་བ་དེ་ཤེས་པ་དང་དེ་ཉིད་དང་གཞན་དུ་བརྗོད་དུ་མེད་པ་ཡིན་ཏེ་ཀུན་བཏགས་པ་ཡིན་པའི་ཕྱིར་རོ། །དེས་ན་དོན་དུ་སྣང་བར་ནི་དམིགས་ལ་མུ་སྟེགས་ལྟར་གྱི་བདག་དང་གཙོ་བོ་སོགས་དང་། རང་སྡེ་འོག་མ་ལྟར་གྱི་རྡུལ་ཕྲན་[17a]དུ་བཏགས་པ་རྣམས་ནི་མ་གྲུབ་སྟེ་དེ་དག་སྣང་བར་མི་རིགས་ལ་,གཟུང་འཛིན་རིགས་པས་ཁེགས་ཀྱང་སྔོ་བ་རྫས་སུ་དམིགས་པའི་ཕྱིར་ནང་གི་ཤེས་པ་ཉིད་དེ་ལྟར་སྣང་བ་ཡིན་ཞིང་དེ་ལ་ཡིད་ཀྱིས་སྒྲོ་བཏགས་པ་ཡིན་ནོ། །དེ་སྐད་དུ་ཡང་ཐེག་ཆེན་བསྡུས་པར།

> རྣམ་པར་རིག་པ་འདི་རྣམས་ཀྱིས་ཁམས་དང་འགྲོ་བ་དང་སྐྱེ་གནས་[1]དང་ཀུན་ནས་ཉོན་མོངས་པ་ཐམས་ཅད་བསྡུས་པ་གཞན་གྱི་དབང་གི་[2] མཚན་ཉིད་ཀྱི་ཡང་དག་པ་མ་ཡིན་པའི་ཀུན་ཏུ་རྟོག་པར་བསྟན་པ་ཡིན་ནོ། །རྣམ་པར་རིག་པ་འདི་རྣམས་ཀྱི་རྣམ་པར་རིག་པ་ཙམ་ཉིད་ཡང་དག་པ་མ་ཡིན་པའི་ཀུན་ཏུ་རྟོག་པས་བསྡུས་པ་ཡོད་པ་མ་ཡིན་པ་དང་། ནོར་བའི་དོན་སྣང་བའི་གནས་གང་ཡིན་པ་འདི་ནི་གཞན་གྱི་དབང་གི་མཚན་ཉིད་དོ།།

> དེ་ལ་ཀུན་བཏགས་པའི་[1140]མཚན་ཉིད་གང་ཞེ་ན། གང་དོན་མེད་ཀྱང་རྣམ་པར་རིག་པ་ཙམ་དེ་དོན་ཉིད་དུ་སྣང་བའོ། །དེ་ལ་ཡོངས་སུ་གྲུབ་པའི་མཚན་ཉིད་གང་ཞེ་ན། གང་གཞན་གྱི་དབང་གི་མཚན་ཉིད་དེ་ཉིད་ལ་དོན་གྱི་མཚན་ཉིད་དེ་གཏན་མེད་པ་ཉིད་དོ།།

ཞེས་དང་།

> རྣམ་པར་རིག་པ་འདི་དག་ནི་དོན་མེད་པའི་ཕྱིར་རྣམ་པར་རིག་པ་ཙམ་མོ་ཞེས་བྱ་བ་འདི་ལ་དཔེ་ཅི་ཡོད་ཅེ་ན།

> རྨི་ལམ་ལ་སོགས་པ་ནི་དཔེར་བལྟ་བར་བྱའོ། །དཔེར་ན་རྨི་ལམ་ན་དོན་མེད་པར་ཡང་རྣམ་པར་ཤེས་པ་ཙམ་ཉིད་དུ་གཟུགས་དང་སྒྲ་དང་དྲི་དང་རོ་དང་རེག་བྱ་དང་། ཁང་ཁྱིམ་དང་ནགས་ཚལ་དང་ས་དང་རི་ལ་སོགས་པའི་དོན་སྣ་ཚོགས་ཀྱི་རྣམ་པར་སྣང་གི་,དེ་ན་དོན་ནི་ཅི་ཡང་མེད་དོ། །དཔེ་འདིས་ནི་ཐམས་ཅད་དུ་ཡང་རྣམ་པར་རིག་པ་ཙམ་ཉིད་དུ་ཁོང་དུ་ཆུད་པར་བྱའོ།[3] །སོགས་པ་ཞེས་བྱ་བ་སྨོས་

---

[1] MSam (Lamotte 1938:25) adds *dang kun nas nyon mongs pa* after *skye gnas.* [2] *gis* D,O,P. [3] P179.3.8-4.1.reads *khong du chud par sogs pa.*

པས་ནི་སྒྱུ་མ་དང་སྨིག་རྒྱུ་[17b]དང་རབ་རིབ་རྣམས་དཔེར་རིག་པར་བྱའོ།།

ཞེས་སོ།།

གསུམ་པ་བཞི་ཚན་དང་པོར་དབྱེ་བ་ནི།

ཐུན་མོང་ཐུན་མོང་མ་ཡིན་དང་། །ཚོར་དང་བཅས་དང་ཚོར་མེད་པ། །ས་བོན་རྣམ་བཞི།

དེ་ཡང་ས་བོན་ཐུན་མོང་བ་ནི། ཀུན་གཞིའི་སྣང་གི་སྣོད་ཀྱི་འཇིག་རྟེན་འགྲུབ་པའི་ས་བོན་ནོ། །ཐུན་མོང་མ་ཡིན་པ་ནི། བཅུད་ཀྱི་འཇིག་རྟེན་འགྲུབ་པའི་ས་བོན་ནོ། །དེ་གཉིས་རིམ་པ་བཞིན་ཚོར་བ་མེད་པ་འབྱུང་བའི་ས་བོན་དང་། ཚོར་བ་དང་བཅས་པ་འབྱུང་བའི་ས་བོན་ཞེས་ཀྱང་བྱ་སྟེ་སྣོད་ནི་སེམས་ཀྱིས་མ་ཟིན་པས་བདེ་སྡུག་གི་རྟེན་དུ་མི་སྣང་ལ་བཅུད་ནི་དེ་ལས་བཟློག་པས་སོ། །དེ་སྐད་དུ་ཡང་།

དེ་ལ་མཚན་ཉིད་ཀྱིས་རབ་ཏུ་དབྱེ་བ་གང་ཞེ་ན། གང་དེ་ཉིད་ཐུན་མོང་གི་མཚན་ཉིད་དང་། ཐུན་མོང་མ་ཡིན་པའི་མཚན་ཉིད་དང་། ཚོར་བ་མེད་པ་འབྱུང་བའི་ས་བོན་གྱི་མཚན་ཉིད་དང་། ཚོར་བ་དང་བཅས་པ་འབྱུང་བའི་ས་བོན་གྱི་མཚན་ཉིད་དེ། །ཐུན་མོང་ནི་[1] སྣོད་ཀྱི་འཇིག་རྟེན་གྱི་ས་བོན་གང་ཡིན་པའོ། །ཐུན་མོང་མ་ཡིན་པ་ནི་སོ་སོ་རང་[1141]གི་སྐྱེ་མཆེད་ཀྱི་ས་བོན་གང་ཡིན་པའོ། །ཐུན་མོང་གང་ཡིན་པ་དེ་ནི་ཚོར་བ་མེད་པ་འབྱུང་བའི་ས་བོན་ནོ། །ཐུན་མོང་མ་ཡིན་པ་གང་ཡིན་པ་དེ་ནི་ཚོར་བ་དང་བཅས་པ་འབྱུང་བའི་ས་བོན་ཏེ།།

ཞེས་སོ།།

བཞི་པ་བཞི་ཚན་གཉིས་པར་དབྱེ་བ་ནི།

གནས་ངན་ལེན། །ཤིན་ཏུ་སྦྱངས་དང་སྨྱུད་ཟིན་དང་། །མ་ཟིན་པ་དང་བཞི་རུའང་གསུངས།།

དེ་ལ་གནས་ངན་ལེན་གྱི་ས་བོན་ནི་འདོད་ཆགས་དང་ཞེ་སྡང་སོགས་རྩ་ཉོན་དང་ཁྲོ་བ་དང་ཁོན་དུ་འཛིན་པ་སོགས་ཉེ་བའི་ཉོན་མོངས་པ་རྣམས་ཀྱི་ས་བོན་ནོ། །ཤིན་ཏུ་སྦྱངས་པའི་ས་བོན་ནི། འཇིག་རྟེན་པའི་ཆོས་དགེ་བ་རྣམས་[18a]ཀྱི་ས་བོན་ནོ། །སྨྱུད་ཟིན་པའི་ས་བོན་ནི། དགེ་མི་དགེའི་ས་བོན་བདེ་འགྲོ་དང་ངན་འགྲོའི་རྣམ་སྨིན་གྱི་ངོ་བོར་རྣམ་པར་སྨིན་ཟིན་པ་ཡིན་ཏེ་དེ་ནི་གཡོས་སུ་བྱས་པའི་ཁ་ཟས་དང་འདྲ་བར་སླར་ཡང་རྣམ་པར་སྨིན་པར་མི་འགྱུར་བའི་ཕྱིར་རོ། །སྨྱུད་མ་ཟིན་པའི་ས་བོན་ནི། མངོན་བརྗོད་ཀྱི་བག་ཆགས་ཏེ་དེ་ནི་ཐོག་མ་མེད་པ་ནས་འབྱུང་བའི་ཕྱིར་ཏེ། སེམས་ཅན་རྣམས་སྐྱེས་ཙམ་ནས་ཆེད་དུ་མ་བསློས་པར་གཟུང་བ་དང་འཛིན་པའི་སྤྲོས་པ་དུ་མ་རྒྱུད་ལ་འཇུག་པའི་ཕྱིར་རོ། །དེ་སྐད་དུའང་།

ཡང་གནས་ངན་ལེན་གྱི་མཚན་ཉིད་དང་། ཤིན་ཏུ་སྦྱངས་པའི་མཚན་ཉིད་དོ། །གནས་ངན་ལེན་གྱི་

[1] *gi* D,O,P.

མཚན་ཉིད་ནི། ཉོན་མོངས་པ་དང་ཉེ་བའི་ཉོན་མོངས་པའི་ས་བོན་གང་ཡིན་པའོ། །ཤིན་ཏུ་སྦྱངས་པའི་མཚན་ཉིད་ནི། ཟག་པ་དང་བཅས་པའི་དགེ་བའི་ཆོས་ཀྱི་ས་བོན་གང་ཡིན་སྟེ།།

ཞེས་དང་།

ཡང་སྤྱད་ཟིན་པ་དང་མ་སྤྱད་པའི་མཚན་ཉིད་དོ། །སྤྱད་ཟིན་པའི་མཚན་ཉིད་ནི་གང་དགེ་བ་དང་མི་དགེ་བའི་ས་བོན་གྱི་རྣམ་པར་སྨིན་པ་རྣམ་པར་སྨིན་ཟིན་པའོ། །མ་སྤྱད་པའི་མཚན་ཉིད་ནི། གང་མངོན་པར་བརྗོད་པའི་བག་ཆགས་ཀྱི་ས་བོན་དེ་ཐོག་མ་མེད་པའི་དུས་ནས་སྤྲོས་པ་འབྱུང་བས་[1] ས་བོན་ཡིན་པའི་ཕྱིར་རོ།།

ཞེས་སོ། དེས་ན་ཁ་ཅིག་ཐེག་བསྡུས་ལས་སྤྱད་ཟིན་མ་ཟིན་གཉིས་གསུངས་པ་ནི། རིམ་པ་ལྟར་མྱུ་གུ་སྐྱེས་པ་ན་ས་[1142]བོན་གྱི་སྙིང་པོ་འགགས་པ་ལྟར། བདེ་འགྲོ་ངན་འགྲོའི་རྣམ་སྨིན་གྱི་བག་ཆགས་རྣམ་སྨིན་གྱི་ངོ་བོར་སྨིན་ཟིན་པ་ནི་མེད་པའི་ཕྱིར་གསོ་བར་བྱ་བ་མིན་པ་དང་། འབྲས་བུ་མ་བྱུང་བའི་བག་ཆགས་རྣམས་ནི་བག་ཆགས་གསར་པས་གསོ་བར་བྱ་བ་དང་གཉིས་[18b]ཡིན་ཞེས་བཞེད་པ་ནི་ཐེག་བསྡུས་ཀྱི་དགོངས་པ་མ་ཡིན་ནོ།།

དེ་ལྟ་བུའི་བག་ཆགས་དེ་དག་རང་གི་རྟེན་དུ་གྱུར་པའི་རྣམ་ཤེས་དང་རྫས་གཅིག་གམ་ཐ་དད་ཅེ་ན།

བག་ཆགས་དེ་ཡང་རྟེན་ལས་ནི། །རྫས་གཅིག་ཐ་དད་གང་ཡང་མིན།།

ཇི་ལྟར་ན་གཅིག་མ་ཡིན་ཞེ་ན།

ས་བོན་དམིགས་རྣམ་ཡོད་པ་དང་། །འགྲོ་བ་ལྔ་ཡི་ས་བོན་རྣམས། །འཆོལ་བ་ཉིད་དུ་
འགྱུར་བ་དང་། །ཁམས་ཀྱང་འཆོལ་ཕྱིར་གཅིག་ཉིད་མིན།།

ས་བོན་དང་ཀུན་གཞི་རྣམ་ཤེས་གཉིས་རྫས་གཅིག་མ་ཡིན་ཏེ། གཞན་དུ་ན་ཀུན་གཞི་ས་བོན་ཆ་དེ་ལ་དམིགས་རྣམ་ཡོད་པར་འགྱུར་རོ། །འདོད་ན།

ས་བོན་ལ་ནི་དམིགས་པ་དང་རྣམ་པ་མེད་དོ་

ཞེས་བཤད་པ་དང་འགལ་ལོ།།

ཡང་འགྲོ་བ་ལྔའི་ས་བོན་རྣམས་འཆོལ་བ་ཉིད་དུ་འགྱུར་ཏེ། འགྲོ་བ་ལྔའི་ས་བོན་རྣམས་རྫས་གཅིག་ཏུ་ཁས་ལེན་དགོས་པའི་ཕྱིར་རོ། །ཇི་ལྟར་ཞེ་ན། རྟེན་གཅིག་ལ་འགྲོ་བ་ལྔའི་ས་བོན་ཡོད་པ་དེ་དུས་མཉམ་དུ་ནི་ཡོད་དགོས་ལ་དེ་དག་ཀྱང་རྟེན་དེའི་ཀུན་གཞིའི་[2] རྣམ་ཤེས་སྐད་ཅིག་མ་གཅིག་དང་རྫས་གཅིག་པར་ཁས་ལེན་དགོས་ཤིང་སྐད་ཅིག་དེ་ལ་ཆ་ཤས་མེད་པས་ན་ས་བོན་ལྔ་པོ་དེ་རྫས་ཆ་ཤས་མེད་པ་གཅིག་ཏུ་འགྱུར་

---

[1] *ba'i* M.N. [2] *kun gzhi* D.

ཏེ། ཤེས་པ་ཆ་མེད་གཅིག་གི་རང་བཞིན་ཡིན་པའི་ཕྱིར་རོ།[1] །ཇི་ལྟར་ཞེ་ན། རྟེན་གཅིག་ལ་འགྲོ་བ་ལྔའི་ས་བོན་ཡོད་པ་དེ་དུས་མཉམ་དུ་ནི་ཡོད་དགོས་ལ་དེ་དག་ཀྱང་རྟེན་དེའི་ཀུན་གཞི་རྣམ་ཤེས་སྐད་ཅིག་མ་གཅིག་དང་རྫས་གཅིག་པར་ཁས་ལེན་དགོས་ཤིང་སྐད་ཅིག་དེ་ལ་ཆ་ཤས་མེད་པས་ན་ས་བོན་ལྔ་པོ་དེ་རྫས་ཆ་ཤས་མེད་པ་གཅིག་ཏུ་འགྱུར་ཏེ། ཤེས་པ་ཆ་མེད་གཅིག་གི་རང་བཞིན་[19a]ཡིན་པའི་ཕྱིར་རོ།[2] །དེ་འདོད་ན། བདེ་འགྲོའི་རྣམ་སྨིན་གྱི་ས་བོན་དེ་འཇོག་བྱེད་མི་དགེ་བས་བཞག་པར་ཐལ། ངན་འགྲོའི་རྣམ་སྨིན་གྱི་ས་བོན་ཡིན་པའི་ཕྱིར་རོ། །ཡང་ངན་འགྲོའི་རྣམ་སྨིན་གྱི་ས་བོན་དེ་འཇོག་བྱེད་དགེ་བས་བཞག་པར་ཐལ། བདེ་འགྲོའི་རྣམ་སྨིན་གྱི་ས་བོན་ཡིན་པའི་ཕྱིར་རོ།།

དེ་ལ་བློ་གྲོས་ཀྱི་འཇུག་པ་ཡངས་པའི་རིགས་པ་ལ་མ་འབད་ཅིང་སྒྲའི་སྤྱི་ཙམ་ཤར་བ་ཁ་ཅིག་འགྲོ་བ་ལྔའི་ས་བོན་རྣམས་ཕན་ཚུན་[1143]ཡིན་མི་དགོས་ཏེ། དངོས་པོ་དང་གཟུགས་གཞན་ནོ་སྙམ་དུ་སེམས་ན། འདི་དཔྱད་དེ། ཅི་གཟུགས་དང་རྫས་གཅིག་པའི་དངོས་པོ་དེ་གཟུགས་ཀྱི་རྫས་ཡིན་ནམ་མ་ཡིན། དང་པོ་ལྟར་ན་ཁྱོད་ཀྱི་འདོད་པ་མི་འགྲུབ་སྟེ། ཁྱོད་ནི་གཟུགས་དང་རྫས་གཅིག་པའི་དངོས་པོ་དེ་སྒྲ་དང་དྲི་རོ་ལྟ་བུ་དང་ཡང་རྫས་གཅིག་པར་འདོད་ལ་གཟུགས་ཀྱི་རྫས་ཡིན་ན་དེ་དག་ལ་རྫས་སུ་འགྲོ་བ་མེད་དོ། །གཟུགས་ཀྱི་རྫས་མ་ཡིན་ན་རྫས་གཅིག་པའང་ཡིན་ལ་རྫས་གཞན་པའང་ཡིན་པ་འདི་ནི་སྨྱོན་པའི་ཚིག་སྟེ་ཁོ་བོ་ཅག་སྨྱོན་པ་དང་ལྷན་ཅིག་མི་རྩོད་དོ།།

ཆོས་ཀྱི་རྗེས་[3] ཀྱང་།

ཤིང་མིན་ལས་ལྡོག་དངོས་པོ་སྟེ། །ཤ་པ་ཡིན་ན་གཞན་ཤིང་མིན། །གཞན་ཤིང་ཡིན་ན་ཤ་
པ་མིན། །དེ་ཡི་རང་བཞིན་གཞན་མིན་ཕྱིར།།

ཞེས་ཤིང་མ་ཡིན་ལས་ལྡོག་པའི་དངོས་པོ་དེ་ཤ་པ་དང་རྫས་གཅིག་གམ་ཐ་དད། །དང་པོ་ལྟར་ན་ཤ་པ་ལས་གཞན་པའི་ཤིང་གི་གསལ་བ་རྣམས་ཤིང་མ་ཡིན་པར་འགྱུར་ལ། གཉིས་པ་ལྟར་ན་ཤ་པ་ཤིང་མ་ཡིན་པར་འགྱུར་ཏེ། ཤིང་མིན་ལས་མ་ལོག་པའི་ཕྱིར་རོ། །གལ་ཏེ་ཤ་པ་ལས་གཞན་ཡང་ཤིང་དང་རྫས་གཅིག་ཏུ་འདོད་ན། ཤ་པ་ཤིང་[19b]མ་ཡིན་ཏེ། "རྫས་རྣམས་ཕན་ཚུན་ལ་འདྲེས་པར་གནས་པའི་ཕྱིར་" ཞེས་གསུངས་པའི་རིགས་པ་དང་རྗེས་སུ་མཐུན་ནོ། །དེས་ན་ཇི་སྲིད་གསལ་བ་རྣམས་ལས་མ་གཏོགས་པའི་སྤྱི་རྫས་སུ་གྲུབ་པར་འདོད་པ་དེ་སྲིད་དུ་རྫས་གཅིག་དང་ཐ་དད་བརྟགས་པའི་སྐྱོན་གཉིས་པོ་སྤོང་མི་ནུས་སོ།།

གཞན་ཡང་རྫས་གཅིག་ཏུ་ཁས་བླངས་ནས་ཆ་གཉིས་འདོད་པ་ལ་འགལ་བ་མེད་ན་ཡན་ལག་དང་ཡན་

---

[1] D reads *shes pa cha shas gnyis gcig gi rang bzhin yin pa'i phyir.* [2] In O, 18b5-19a1 (from *ji ltar zhe na* to *rang bzhin yin pa'i phyir ro*) is an accidental repetition by the blockcutter. [3] *chos kyi rdzas* O.

ལག་ཅན་གཉིས་རྫས་གཅིག་པ་སངས་རྒྱས་ཀྱིས་ཀྱང་དགག་པར་མི་ནུས་སོ།།

ཡང་ཁམས་ཀུང་འཚོལ་པ་ཉིད་དུ་འགྱུར་ཏེ། འདི་ལྟར་གཟུགས་ཁམས་ཀྱི་ལྷའི་[1] སྙོམས་འཇུག་བསྒོམ་པའི་མཐུས་གཟུགས་ཀྱི་ལྷའི་རྣམ་སྨིན་འགྲུབ་པའི་ས་བོན་འདོད་པའི་ཀུན་གཞི་ལ་བསྒོས་[2] པ་དེ་ཀུན་གཞི་རྣམ་ཤེས་དེ་དང་རྫས་གཅིག་ཏུ་འདོད་དགོས་པའི་ཕྱིར་དང་། ས་བོན་དེ་འདོད་བའི་སར་གཏོགས་ [1144] པ་ཁོ་ནར་འགྱུར་ཏེ། གསར་དུ་བཞག་པའི་ས་བོན་དེ། འདོད་ཁམས་ཀྱི་ཀུན་གཞིའི་རྣམ་ཤེས་ཡིན་པའི་ཕྱིར་རོ། །དེས་ན་རྫས་གཅིག་པ་ལ་འདི་ལྟ་བུའི་རིགས་པ་མཐའ་ཡས་སོ།།

རྫས་ཐ་དད་ཇི་ལྟར་མ་ཡིན་ཞེ་ན།

རྟེན་གཅིག་ལ་ནི་ཀུན་གཞི་གཉིས། །ཡོད་པར་འགྱུར་པས་སོ་སོ་མིན།།

རྫས་ཐ་དད་ན། གཟུགས་དང་ལྡན་མིན་དང་ཚོགས་བདུན་གང་ཡང་མིན་ཏེ། རྫས་སུ་གྲུབ་པ་དང་གཟུགས་མེད་ནའང་ཡོད་པ་དང་། ཚོགས་བདུན་མེད་པའི་ཚེ་ཡང་འབྱུང་བའི་ཕྱིར་རོ། །དེས་ན་ཀུན་གཞི་རྣམ་ཤེས་གཉིས་པོ་གཅིག་ཏུ་འགྱུར་དགོས་ལ། དེ་འདོད་ན། རྟེན་གཅིག་ལ་ཀུན་གཞི་རྣམ་ཤེས་གཉིས་ཡོད་པའི་ཕྱིར་རྒྱུད་དུ་མ་ཉིད་དུ་འགྱུར་རོ།།

མ་ངེས་ཏེ། སེམས་གཅིག་གི་འཁོར་དུ་སེམས་བྱུང་དུ་མ་འབྱུང་བ་དང་ཀུན་གཞི་དང་ཚོགས་བདུན་ལྡན་ཅིག [20a] འཇུག་ཀྱང་རྒྱུད་དུ་མར་མི་འགྱུར་པ་བཞིན་ནོ་ཞེ་ན། མི་མཚུངས་ཏེ། སེམས་གཅིག་ལ་བལྟོས་ཏེ་འཇུག་ལ་ཚོགས་བདུན་ཀུན་གཞི་གཅིག་ལ་རག་ལས་ཏེ་འཇུག་ཅིང་ཀུན་གཞི་གཉིས་ཡོད་ན་གཅིག་གཅིག་ལ་མི་བལྟོས་ཏེ་གཉིས་ཀ་བརྟན་པ་རང་དབང་ཅན་གྱི་རྣམ་ཤེས་ཡིན་པའི་ཕྱིར་སྐྱོན་སོ་ན་གནས་སོ།།

འོ་ན་བག་ཆགས་དེ་ཇི་ལྟ་བུ་ཞིག་ཏུ་གནས་ཤེ་ན།

དེས་ན་རྟེན་ལས་དེ་ཉིད་དང་། །གཞན་དུ་བརྗོད་དུ་མེད་པ་སྟེ། །བཏགས་ཡོད་ཙམ་དུ་གནས་ཕྱིར་རོ།།

རྫས་གཅིག་དང་ཐ་དད་གང་ཡང་མིན་པ་དེའི་ཕྱིར། རྟེན་གྱི་རྣམ་ཤེས་དེ་ལས་གཅིག་དང་ཐ་དད་གང་དུ་ཡང་མ་གྲུབ་པ་རྣམ་ཤེས་དེའི་ནུས་པ་བག་ལ་ཉལ་གྱི་ངོ་བོར་བཏགས་ཡོད་ཙམ་དུ་གནས་ཏེ། ཇི་སྐད་དུ།

ཀུན་གཞིའི་རྣམ་པར་ཤེས་པ་ལ་[3] ཀུན་ནས་ཉོན་མོངས་པའི་ཆོས་[4] ཀྱི་ས་བོན་དེ་དག་ཅི་རྫས་སུ་[5]སོ་སོ་ཐ་དད་དམ། འོན་ཏེ་ཐ་དད་པ་མ་ཡིན་པར་གནས་ཤེ་ན། དེ་ལ་གནས་པ་དེ་དག་དང་རྫས་སུ་ཐ

---

[1] *lhas* M,D. [2] *dgos* N,O,P. [3] *dang* /→*la* Lamotte (1938:10). [4] *thams cad* omit Ibid. [5] *rdzas su* Ibid.

དད་པ་ཡང་མ་ཡིན་།[1] ཐ་མི་དད་པ་ཡང་མ་ཡིན་མོད་ཀྱི་, གང་དེ་འབྱུང་བའི་མཐུའི་ཁྱད་པར་ཅན་ཀུན་གཞི་རྣམ་པར་ཤེས་པ་དེ།[2] དེ་བཞིན་དུ་འབྱུང་བ་ལ་ས་བོན་ [1145] ཐམས་ཅད་པ་ཞེས་བྱའོ།།

ཞེས་དང་། དེའི་འགྲེལ་པ་དོན་གསང་དུ།

དེ་ལྟར་ཕྱོགས་གཉིས་ཀ་ལ་ཡང་ཉེས་པ་གཉིས་[3]སྣང་བས་དེ་ལ་གནས་པ་དེ་དག་དང་རྫས་སུ་ཐ་དད་པ་ཡང་མ་ཡིན་ཞེས་བྱ་བ་ལ་སོགས་པ་སྨོས་ཏེ། ཀུན་གཞི་རྣམ་པར་ཤེས་པ་ལས་དེ་ཉིད་དང་གཞན་ཉིད་དུ་བརྗོད་པར་བྱ་བ་མ་ཡིན་པ་རྣམས་ཡིན་ནོ་ཞེས་བྱ་བའི་དོན་ཏེ་

ཞེས་དང་། ཡང་དེའི་[4] འགྲེལ་པ་བཤད་སྦྱར་ལས་ཀྱང་།

དེ་དག་དང་རྫས་སུ་ཐ་དད་པ་ཡང་མ་ [20b] ཡིན་ཐ་མི་དད་པ་ཡང་མ་ཡིན་མོད་ཀྱི་ཞེས་བྱ་བ་ནི། ཐ་དད་པ་དང་ཐ་དད་པ་མ་ཡིན་པ་ལས་ཡང་དག་པར་འདས་པའི་ཚུལ་གྱིས་ཀུན་གཞི་རྣམ་པར་ཤེས་པ་ལ་བག་ཆགས་རྣམས་གནས་པར་བརྗོད་དེ་ནུས་པའི་ཁྱད་པར་གྱི་རང་བཞིན་ཡིན་པའི་ཕྱིར་རོ། །བག་ཆགས་ཞེས་བྱ་བ་ནི་ནུས་པའི་ཁྱད་པར་ཏེ་ནུས་པ་ཡང་ནུས་པ་ཅན་དང་[5] དེ་ཉིད་དམ་གཞན་ཞེས་བརྗོད་པར་བྱ་བ་མ་ཡིན་ནོ། །དེ་དག་དང་ཕན་ཚུན་ཐ་དད་དམ་ཐ་དད་པ་མ་ཡིན་ཞེས་འདྲི་བ་འདི་ཚུལ་གཞན་མ་ཡིན་པ་སྟེ་ནུས་པ་ཅན་བསྒྱུར་[6] བྱས་ནས་བཏགས་པའི་ཕྱིར་རོ།།

ཞེས་བཀྲལ་བས་ན་སློབ་དཔོན་འདི། ནུས་པ་བཏགས་ཡོད། ནུས་པ་ཅན་རྫས་ཡོད་དུ་བཞེད་པའི་ཕྱིར་བག་ཆགས་དང་ཀུན་གཞིའི་རྣམ་ཤེས་གཉིས་རྫས་ཐ་དད་མ་ཡིན་ལྡོག་པ་གཅིག་མ་ཡིན་ཅེས་བཀྲལ་ནས་དེ་ཉིད་རྫས་གཅིག་ལྡོག་པ་ཐ་དད་དུ་འདོད་པ་ནི་གཞུང་ལུགས་གཞན་གྱི་ཆོས་སྐད་འཕྱུགས་པས་ན་རང་སྐད་མ་ཐོན་པ་ཡིན་ནོ།།

གཞན་ཡང་མཛོད་ཀྱི་གནས་གཉིས་པའི་འགྲེལ་བཤད་དུ། སློབ་དཔོན་དབྱིག་གཉེན་གྱི་རང་ལུགས་འགྲེལ་པ་ནི། ས་བོན་དང་ནུས་པ་དང་བག་ཆགས་ཞེས་བྱ་བ་ནི་དོན་གཅིག་གོ །ས་བོན་ནི་བཏགས་པའི་ཡོད་པ་ཡིན་གྱི་,རྫས་སུ་ཡོད་པ་ནི་མ་ཡིན་ནོ།།ཞེས་འབྱུང་བས་སྐུ་མཆེད་དགོངས་པ་གཅིག་གོ །དེས་ན་བསྒོས་པའི་ས་བོན་འདི་ནི། འདུ་བྱེད་ཀྱི་ཕུང་པོའི་ཕྱོགས་གཅིག་ལྡན་མིན་འདུ་བྱེད་ཀྱི་ཐོབ་པ་ཡིན་ཏེ། འདུས་བྱས་ཡིན་ལ་གཟུགས་སེམས་སེམས་བྱུང་གང་ཡང་མིན་པའི་ཕྱིར་དང་། ཀུན་ལས་བཏུས་སུ།

ལྡན་ [1146] པ་གང་ཞེ་ན། མཚན་ཉིད་ཀྱིས་ནི་སྔ་མ་བཞིན་ནོ། །རབ་ཏུ་དབྱེ་བ་ནི་གསུམ་སྟེ། ས་བོན་དང་ལྡན་པ་དང་། [21a] དབང་དང་ལྡན་པ་དང་། ཀུན་འབྱུང་བ་དང་ལྡན་པའོ།།

---

[1] add *te* D,O,P. [2] *shes pa de bzhin du* D,O,P. [3] *gnyis* omit D,O and P. [4] *de'i* omit M. [5] *dang* omit M. [6] *rgyur byas nas*→*bsgyur byas nas* P.

ཞེས་གསུངས་པའི་ཕྱིར་རོ།།

དེ་ལྟ་ན་

བག་ཆགས་རྣམ་པ་གསུམ་གྱི་བྱེ་བྲག་གིས་[1] རྣམ་པ་གསུམ་སྟེ་

ཞེས་གོང་དུ་དྲངས་པ་དང་། དོན་གསང་དུ་ཡང་ཀུན་གཞི་རྣམ་པར་ཤེས་པ་ཡང་ས་བོན་དང་རྣམ་པར་སྨིན་པའི་བྱེ་བྲག་གིས་རྣམ་པ་གཉིས་སུ་དབྱེ་སྟེ་ཞེས་གསུངས་པ་རྣམས་ཇི་ལྟར་དྲངས་ཤེ་ན།

ཉེས་པ་མེད་དེ། སྤྱིར་ཀུན་གཞི་ས་བོན་ལ་ཡང་རྣམ་ཤེས་ཀྱི་སྒྲས་བསྟན་པ་ནི། ས་བོན་དང་རྣམ་སྨིན་མ་ཕྱེ་བའི་རགས་[2] བཤད་ཡིན་ཏེ། ཕྱེ་ནས་ས་བོན་དང་རྣམ་ཤེས་རྫས་གཅིག་ཐ་དད་དྲིས་པ་ན་གང་ཡང་མ་ཡིན་པས་[3] བསྟན་པའི་ཕྱིར་རོ། །བྱེ་བྲག་ཏུ་དོན་གསང་ལས་དེ་ལྟར་བསྟན་པ་ནི། གོང་གི་འཕྲོས་བཙལ་ན་བསྡུས་པའི་རྒྱུས་བཤད་དུ་འདུག་པ་དང་། སོ་སོ་ཐ་དད་དམ་ཞེས་པའི་ཐད་དུ་འགྲེལ་པ་གཉིས་ཀས་ཞལ་འཆམ་པར་བཀྲལ་པའི་ཕྱིར་དང་། དོན་གསང་དུ་

ས་བོན་སྔ་མའི་རྒྱུན་འཇུག་པས་ས་བོན་ཕྱི་མའི་དུས་ཐ་དད་པ་ཁོ་ནའི་རྒྱུའི་རྐྱེན་ཡིན་ནོ། །བདག་པོའི་རྐྱེན་ནི་མ་ཡིན་ཏེ་སྐལ་བ་མཉམ་པ་མངོན་པར་འགྲུབ་པའི་རྒྱུ་ཡིན་པའི་ཕྱིར་རོ། །མཚུངས་པ་དེ་མ་ཐག་པའི་རྐྱེན་ཡང་མ་ཡིན་ཏེ། སེམས་དང་[4] སེམས་ལས་བྱུང་བའི་ངོ་བོ་ཉིད་མ་ཡིན་པའི་ཕྱིར་རོ། །དམིགས་པའི་རྐྱེན་ཡང་མ་ཡིན་ཏེ། ས་བོན་ལ་དམིགས་པ་མེད་པའི་ཕྱིར་རོ།།

ཞེས་པ་དང་། བཤད་སྦྱར་དུ།

བག་ཆགས་ཙམ་ནི་ཀུན་གཞི་རྣམ་པར་ཤེས་པ་མ་ཡིན་གྱི་

ཞེས་འབྱུང་པའི་ཕྱིར་ཡི་གེ་ཙམ་མཐོང་བས་འཁྲུལ་བར་མི་རིགས་སོ།།

གལ་ཏེ་ས་བོན་དངོས་པོར་འདོད་ལ་རྫས་སུ་མི་འདོད་ན། སྟོན་མེད་པའི་ལུགས་སོ་ཞེ་ན།

དེ་ལ་ཡང་ཉེས་པ་མེད་དེ། སློབ་དཔོན་འདི་[21b]སྐུ་མཆེད་དངོས་པོ་ལ་རྫས་བཏགས་གཉིས་སུ་འབྱེད་དེ། ལྡན་མིན་འདུ་བྱེད་འདུས་བྱས་སུ་བཞེད་ལ་རྫས་སུ་མི་བཞེད་པའི་ཕྱིར་རོ། །དེ་ཉིད་ཀྱི་ཕྱིར་ཡང་སློབ་དཔོན་སོ་སོའི་ལུགས་མ་འདྲེས་པར་འབྱེད་པ་[1147]ནི་མཁས་པ་མཛངས་པ་གསལ་བ་ཡིད་གཞུངས་པའོ།།

བག་ཆགས་དེ་དག་དགེ་བ་དང་མ་དགེ་བ་ལུང་དུ་མ་བསྟན་པ་གསུམ་ལས་གང་ཞེ་ན།

འཇོག་བྱེད་དགེ་སོགས་གང་ཡིན་ཀྱང་། །བཞག་པའི་བག་ཆགས་ལུང་མ་བསྟན།།

མ་བསྒྲིབས་ལ་ཞེས་པ་ནི་ལྷག་མའོ།།

དེ་ནི་མི་རིགས་ཏེ། ལུང་དང་རིགས་པ་དང་འགལ་བའི་ཕྱིར་ཏེ། འདི་ལྟར། ཀུན་ལས་བཏུས་སུ།

---

[1] *gi* D,O,P. [2] *rigs→rags* P. [3] *par* D,O,P. [4] *sems dang* supplied from P5553:67,4.4.

རྗེས་སུ་འབྲེལ་པའི་དགེ་བ་གང་ཞེ་ན། དེ་དག་ཉིད་ཀྱི་བག་ཆགས་གང་ཡིན་པའོ།།

ཞེས་དང་།

རྗེས་སུ་འབྲེལ་པའི་མི་དགེ་བ་གང་ཞེ་ན། དེ་དག་ཉིད་ཀྱི་བག་ཆགས་གང་ཡིན་པའོ།།

ཞེས་བག་ཆགས་དགེ་མི་དགེ་གསུངས་པའི་ཕྱིར་དང་། གལ་ཏེ་བསྒོས་པའི་བག་ཆགས་ཐམས་ཅད་ལུང་མ་བསྟན་དུ་འདོད་ན་རྣམ་སྨིན་གྱི་རྒྱུ་མི་བྱེད་པར་ཐལ་བ་དང་། འདུག་ཤེས་དགེ་མི་དགེ་ལུང་མ་བསྟན་བསྐྱེད་པའི་ས་བོན་གྱིས་རྒྱུ་མཐུན་གྱི་འབྲས་བུ་མི་བསྐྱེད་པར་ཐལ་བ་དང་། སྡོམ་པ་ཐོབ་ནས་ཇི་སྲིད་མ་བཏང་བར་དུ་དགེ་བ་རྒྱུན་ཆགས་སུ་མི་འབྱུང་བར་ཐལ་བར་འགྱུར་ཏེ། རྣམ་སྨིན་འཕེན་པ་ལ་དགེ་མི་དགེ་གང་རུང་ཞིག་དགོས་པའི་ཕྱིར་དང་། རྒྱུ་མཐུན་གྱི་འབྲས་བུ་དེ་རྒྱུ་དང་[1]རིགས་མཐུན་ཞིག་དགོས་པའི་ཕྱིར་དང་། ཚོགས་དྲུག་འགགས་པའི་ཚེ་ན་ཡོད་མཛོན་གྱུར་དུ་ནི་མེད་ལ་ས་བོན་ཡོད་ཀྱང་ལུང་མ་བསྟན་དུ་འདོད་པའི་ཕྱིར་རོ་ཞེ་ན།

དེ་ནི་དེ་ལྟ་མ་ཡིན་ནོ། །འོ་ན་ཇི་ལྟ་བུ་ཞེ་ན།

དགེ་དང་མི་དགེ་མཚན་ཉིད་པས། །འདོད་ལ་སྒྲུབ་པ་བྱེད་པ་མེད།། [22a]

ཅེ་སྙེ་སྡར་ཀྱི་ལུང་རིགས་དེ་ཉིད་དོ་ཞེ་ན། འདི་ནི་བག་ཆགས་དགེ་མི་དགེ་མཚན་ཉིད་པའི་སྒྲུབ་པར་བྱེད་པ་ཡང་དག་པ་མ་ཡིན་ནོ། །ཇི་ལྟར་ཞེ་ན། འདི་ལ་ལུང་སྒྲུབ་བྱེད་དུ་མི་འགྲོ་བར་བསྟན་པ་དང་། རིགས་པ་སྒྲུབ་བྱེད་དུ་མི་འགྲོ་བར་བསྟན་པ་གཉིས་སོ།།

དང་པོ་ནི། རྗེས་སུ་འགྲེལ་བ་ཞེས་སོགས་ཀྱི་ལུང་ཡོད་པས་བག་ཆགས་དགེ་མི་དགེ་མཚན་ཉིད་པར་གྱུར་ན། དེ་ལྟ་ན་གཟུགས་མེད་དུ་ཡང་གཟུགས་མཚན་ཉིད་པ་ཞིག་ཡོད་པར་འགྱུར་ཏེ། རྗེས་སུ་འབྲེལ་བའི་གཟུགས་སུ་བཤད་[1148]པ་དེ་དོན་[2] མཚན་ཉིད་པ་ཡོད་པའི་ཕྱིར་ཏེ་གཟུགས་ཀྱི་ས་བོན་ཡོད་པའི་ཕྱིར་རོ། །ཁམས་གོང་མ་གཉིས་ན་མི་དགེ་བ་མཚན་ཉིད་པ་ཡོད་པར་ཡང་འགྱུར་རོ།།

གཉིས་པ་ལ་གསུམ་ལས། དང་པོ་རྣམ་སྨིན་གྱི་རྒྱུ་མི་བྱེད་པར་ཐལ་ཞེས་པ་ནི། རྣམ་སྨིན་འཕེན་བྱེད་མ་ཡིན་པར་ཐལ་བ་ནི་འདོད་པ་སྟེ། བག་ཆགས་དེ་འཇོག་བྱེད་དགེ་མི་དགེས་འཕངས་ཟིན་པ་ཡིན་པའི་ཕྱིར་འཇོག་བྱེད་ཉིད་འཕེན་བྱེད་ཡིན་པས་སོ། །རྣམ་སྨིན་མི་བྱེད་པར་ཐལ་བ་ལ་ནི་ཁྱབ་པ་མེད་དེ། གཞན་དུ་ན་ཀུན་གཞི་རྣམ་ཤེས་ཀྱི་སྐད་ཅིག་མ་ཐ་མ་ཡང་ལུང་དུ་མ་བསྟན་པར་[མི]་འགྱུར་རོ།།[3]

---

[1] N omits *dang*. [2] *de na* M,R. [3] The context obviously requires the emendation *lung du ma bstan par 'gyur ro*→*°mi 'gyur ro*. Ke'u tshang (227.3-4) says *'dir dka' 'grel gyi dpe rnams las "gzhan du...'gyur ro" zhes 'byung ba ni dgag tshig chad par gsal te/ de lung ma bstan du 'dod pas de mi 'dod pa'i thal ba 'phangs pas ci zhig bya? pha rol pos kyang 'dod pa'i len 'deps pa'i phyir ro.*

གཉིས་པ་རྒྱུ་མཐུན་མི་རུང་བར་ཐལ་ཞེས་པས་ཀྱང་མི་གནོད་དེ། འཇོག་བྱེད་དང་རྒྱུ་མཐུན་པ་ཡིན་ལ་དེ་ཙམ་གྱིས་རྒྱུ་མཐུན་པའི་དོན་ཚང་བའི་ཕྱིར་རོ།།

གསུམ་པ་སྨོན་པ་རྒྱུན་ཆགས་སུ་མི་འབྱུང་བར་ཐལ་ཞེས་པས་ཀྱང་མི་གནོད་དེ། ཇི་སྲིད་བསླབ་བྱ་དང་འགལ་བའི་ཆོས་རྒྱུད་[1] ལ་ཉེ་བ་ན་ངོ་ཚ་ཁྲེལ་ཡོད་དང་དྲན་ཤེས་རྣམས་བསྐྱེད་ནས། འཆལ་[2] ཁྲིམས་ཀྱི་རྒྱུན་སྨོན་པའི་ནུས་པ་ཡོད་ན་དེ་ཙམ་གྱིས་སྔར་བླངས་པའི་[22b]སྨོན་པ་ཡོད་པར་འཇོག་ནུས་ལ་དེ་ཡང་དེའི་ཚེ་རྗེས་སུ་འཇུག་པའི་ཕྱིར་རོ། །གཞན་ཡང་མི་གསལ་བ་ཞེས་པའི་འགྲེལ་པ་གཉིས་ཀར་ལུང་མ་བསྟན་དུ་བཀྲལ་བའི་ཕྱིར་ལུང་མ་བསྟན་དུ་གྲུབ་བོ།།

འོ་ན་དོན་གསང་དུ།

ནང་གི་ཡང་ཙུང་ཟད་ཅིག་མི་གསལ་ཏེ། ནང་གི་དགེ་བ་དང་མི་དགེ་བའི་ཆོས་ཀྱིས་བསྐྱེད་པ་གང་ཡིན་པ་དེ་ནི་དགེ་བ་དང་མི་དགེ་བ་ཡིན་པའི་ཕྱིར་རོ།།

ཞེས་དང་།

ས་བོན་རྣམས་ཀྱང་མ་བསྒྲིབས་ལ་ལུང་དུ་མ་བསྟན་པ་ཡིན་པའི་ཕྱིར་མ་བསྒྲིབས་ལུང་དུ་མ་བསྟན་པའི་ཆོས་ཉིད་འབྱུང་བ་ཁོ་ནར་འགྱུར་གྱི་མ་བསྒྲིབས་ལུང་དུ་མ་བསྟན་གྱི་[3] ལས་དགེ་བ་དང་མི་དགེ་བའི་ཆོས་འབྱུང་བར་ནི་རུང་བ་མ་ཡིན་ནོ་

ཞེས་པ་རྣམས་དང་མི་འགལ་ལམ་ཞེ་ན།

ཕྱི་མ་ནི་ཕྱོགས་སྔ་མར་བཀོད་པ་ཙམ་ཡིན་གྱི་,ངེས་པ་མ་ཡིན་ཏེ། གཞན་དུ་ན་ལུང་མ་བསྟན་གྱི་སེམས་ཀྱིས་དགེ་བ་དང་མི་དགེ་བའི་སེམས་ཀྱི་དེ་མ་[1149]ཐག་རྐྱེན་བྱེད་པ་མེད་པར་འགྱུར་རོ།།

ལུང་སྔ་མ་ནི། མི་གསལ་བ་ཞེས་པ་ལ་བཤད་པའི་ན་ཡམས་ཙམ་བྱས་པ་ཡིན་གྱི་རང་ལུགས་ནི་སྔར་དྲངས་པའི་ན་ཡམས་སྔ་མ་ཉིད་ཡིན་ཏེ། ཚེ་གུའི་རྗེའི་དཔེ་བསྟན་པའི་ཐད་ཀྱི་དོན་གསང་དུ།

བག་ཆགས་ནི་ཀུན་གཞི་རྣམ་པར་ཤེས་པ་རྒྱུར་བྱས་ནས་འཇུག་པའི་ཕྱིར་ཐ་དད་པ་མ་ཡིན་ཞིང་། དགེ་བ་དང་མི་དགེ་བ་ཉིད་དུ་མི་དམིགས་པའི་ཕྱིར་སྣ་ཚོགས་མ་ཡིན་ལ་

ཞེས་བག་ཆགས་ཀྱི་དུས་ན་ཐ་དད་པ་མི་ཡིན་ཞིང་སྣ་ཚོགས་པ་མ་ཡིན་ཞེས་ཕྱོགས་སྔ་མ་དང་རང་ལུགས་གཉིས་ཀར་ཁས་བླངས་པ་ལ་དེ་ལྟར་དུ་བཀྲལ་བའི་ཕྱིར་རོ།།

གལ་ཏེ་བག་ཆགས་ཀུན་གཞི་ལས་ཐ་དད་པ་མ་ཡིན་ཞིང་། དགེ་མི་དགེ་སྣ་ཚོགས་སུ་མི་སྣང་བ་ལས།

[1] *rgyu* P. [2] *'dul* M; *'tshul* O,P; *tshul* N; *'chal* D. [3] *pa* M.

འབྲས་[23a]བུ་རང་གི་མཚན་ཉིད་ཐ་དད་པ་དང་དགེ་མི་དགེ་ལ་སོགས་སྣ་ཚོགས་སུ་འབྱུང་བ་མི་འཐད་དེ། རྒྱུ་ཐ་དད་པ་མ་ཡིན་པ་ལས་འབྲས་བུ་ཐ་དད་པ་མི་རིགས་པའི་ཕྱིར་རོ་ཞེ་ན།

ཉེས་པ་མེད་དེ། ཐེག་ཆེན་བསྡུས་པ་ལས།

> བག་ཆགས་ཐ་དད་པ་མ་ཡིན་ཞིང་སྣ་ཚོགས་མ་ཡིན་པ་ཆོས་ཐ་དད་པ་སྣ་ཚོགས་དག་གི་རྒྱུར་ཇི་ལྟར་རུང་ཞེ་ན། དཔེར་ན་ཆི་གུའི་རྩི་སྣ་ཚོགས་ཀྱིས་བསྒྱུར་བའི་རས་སྣ་ཚོགས་སུ་མི་སྣང་བ་གང་གི་ཚེ་ཚོན་གྱི་སྣོད་དུ་བཅུག་པ་དེའི་ཚེ་རས་ལ་ཚོན་རྣམས་ཀྱི་དབྱེ་བ་ཐ་དད་པ་རྣམ་པ་སྣ་ཚོགས་དུ་མ་སྣང་བ་དེ་བཞིན་དུ། ཀུན་གཞི་རྣམ་པར་ཤེས་པ་བག་ཆགས་སྣ་ཚོགས་ཀྱིས་བསྒོས་པ་ཡང་བག་ཆགས་ཀྱི་དུས་ན་སྣ་ཚོགས་མ་ཡིན་ཀྱང་འབྲས་བུ་མངོན་པར་འགྲུབ་པའི་ཚོན་གྱི་སྣོད་དུ་མངོན་པར་ཕྱོགས་ན་ཆོས་སྣ་ཚོགས་ཚད་མེད་པ་དག་སྣང་ཏེ། འདི་ནི་ཐེག་པ་ཆེན་པོ་ལ་ཕྲ་བ་མཆོག་ཏུ་ཟབ་པའི་རྟེན་ཅིང་འབྲེལ་བར་འབྱུང་བའོ།།

ཞེས་པ་ལྟར་གོ་བར་བྱའོ།།

[Chapter Four]

བག་ཆགས་དེ་དག་གདོད་མ་ནས་ཀུན་གཞི་ལ་གནས་པ་ཞིག་གམ། འོན་ཏེ་གསར་དུ་བསྒོས་པ་ཞིག་ཡིན་ཞེ་ན།

> བག་ཆགས་འཇོག་པའི་ཚུལ་ལ་གསུམ། །ཆོས་ཉིད་ཀྱིས་[1] གནས་ཐོན་མེད་སྐྱེད། །དེ་དག་
> གཉིས་ཀར་འདོད་པའོ།།

བག་ཆགས་[1150]འཇོག་ཚུལ་ལ། རྣལ་འབྱོར་སྤྱོད་པའི་སློབ་དཔོན་རྣམས་ཀྱི་ལུགས་གསུམ་མོ། །གང་ཞེ་ན། སྒོ་བྱེད་ལ་མི་ལྟོས་པར་ཆོས་ཉིད་ཀྱིས་གནས་པར་འདོད་པ་དང་། སྒོ་བྱེད་ཀྱིས་[2] ཐོན་མེད་གསར་དུ་བཞག་པ་དང་སྔར་[3]བཞག་པ་བསྒོ་བྱེད་ཀྱིས་གསོ་བར་འདོད་པ་དང་། ཆོས་ཉིད་ཀྱིས་གནས་པ་གསོ་བ་དང་ཐོན་མེད་[23b]གསར་དུ་བཞག་པར་འདོད་པའི་ལུགས་གསུམ་དོན་གསང་དུ་བཀོད་ནས་ཕན་ཚུན་སྐྱོན་བརྗོད་པ་དང་། དེའི་འགལ་སྤོང་རྒྱས་པར་བྱས་ཤིང་ལུགས་དང་པོ་འཐད་ཕྱོགས་སུ་ཁས་བླངས་ཀྱང་འདིར་ནི་ཕྱོགས་གསུམ་པ་གཟུང་ངོ་།།

དེ་ཡང་ཟག་མེད་ཀྱི་ས་བོན་དང་། རྒྱུ་མཐུན་གྱི་ས་བོན་དང་། རྣམ་སྨིན་གྱི་ས་བོན་གསུམ་དུ་བྱས་ནས

---

[1] *kyi* O,P. [2] *kyi* N,O,P. [3] *gsar du* N,O,P.

དཔྱད་པར་བྱའོ།།

> དེ་ལ་དང་པོ་ནི་རང་བཞིན་གནས་པའི་རིགས་ཡིན་པས་ཆོས་ཉིད་ཀྱིས་གནས་པ་ཡིན་ཏེ། བྱང་ས་ར། དེ་ལ་རང་བཞིན་དུ་གནས་པའི་རིགས་ནི། བྱང་ཆུབ་སེམས་དཔའ་རྣམས་ཀྱི་སྐྱེ་མཆེད་དྲུག་གི་ཁྱད་པར་གང་ཡིན་པ་སྟེ་དེ་ནི་གཅིག་ནས་གཅིག་ཏུ་བརྒྱུད་འོངས་པ་ཐོག་མ་མེད་པ་བའི་དུས་ཅན་ཆོས་ཉིད་ཀྱིས་ཐོབ་པ་དེ་ལྟ་བུ་ཡིན་ནོ།།

ཞེས་འབྱུང་བའི་ཕྱིར་རོ།།

རྒྱུ་མཐུན་དང་རྣམ་སྨིན་གྱི་ས་བོན་གཉིས་ནི། རིམ་པ་བཞིན་འཇུག་ཤེས་དགེ་མི་དགེ་ལུང་མ་བསྟན་རྣམས།[1] ཀུན་གཞི་དང་སྐྱེ་འགག་ལྷན་ཅིག་ཏུ་བྱས་པས་མ་འོངས་པ་ན་འཇུག་ཤེས་རིགས་འདྲ་འགྲུབ་པའི་ས་བོན་འཇོག་པའི་ཕྱིར་དང་། རྣམ་སྨིན་འཕེན་བྱེད་དགེ་བའམ་མི་དགེ་བ་མངོན་གྱུར་དུ་སྐྱེས་པས་རྣམ་སྨིན་གྱི་ས་བོན་བཞག་དགོས་པའི་ཕྱིར་དེ་གཉིས་གསར་དུ་བཞག་པའོ། །འདི་ནི་རེ་ཞིག་འཇོག་བྱེད་ལ་ལྟོས་མ་ལྟོས་ལ་ཆོས་ཉིད་ཀྱིས་གནས་པ་དང་གསར་དུ་བཞག་པའི་དབང་དུ་བྱས་པ་ཡིན་ནོ།།

ཐོག་མ་ཡོད་མེད་ལ་བྱེད་ན། རིགས་ནི་ཐོག་མ་ཡང་མེད་ལ་འཇོག་བྱེད་ལ་ཡང་མ་ལྟོས་པ་ཡིན་ཞིང་། ཕྱི་མ་གཉིས་ལ་ནི་གཉིས་ཀ་ཡོད་དེ། འདི་ལྟར་རྒྱུ་མཐུན་གྱི་ས་བོན་གསར་དུ་སྣོད་མཁན་དེ་ཡང་རྒྱུ་མཐུན་གྱི་ས་བོན་སྔ་མ་ཞིག་ལས་འབྱུང་བ་ས་[24a]བོན་དེ་ཡང་རྒྱུ་མཐུན་འཇོག་[1151]བྱེད་དེའི་སྔ་མ་ཞིག་གིས་གཞག་དགོས་པས་ཐོག་མ་མེད་དོ།།

རྒྱུ་མཐུན་གྱི་ཁྱད་པར་འགའ་ཞིག་ལ་ཡང་ཐོག་མ་མེད་ན་ད་ལྟ་སྐྱེས་པའི་སེམས་དགེ་མི་དགེས་མ་འོངས་པ་ན་རིགས་མཐུན་འགྲུབ་པའི་ས་བོན་མ་བཞག་པར་འགྱུར་བ་དང་། རྣམ་སྨིན་གྱི་ས་བོན་ལ་ཐོག་མ་ཡོད་ན་འཁོར་བ་ལ་ཐོག་མ་ཡོད་པར་འགྱུར་ལ། ཁྱད་པར་འགའ་ཞིག་ལ་ཡང་ཐོག་མ་མེད་ན་བསོད་ནམས་དང་བསོད་ནམས་མ་ཡིན་པའི་ལས་འཕྲལ་དུ་སྤྱད་པས་རྣམ་སྨིན་གྱི་བག་ཆགས་མ་བཞག་པར་འགྱུར་རོ།།

> གང་ཡང་ཐོས་པའི་བག་ཆགས་ཆུང་ངུ་གསར་དུ་བཞག་པ་དེ་ཕྱིས་ཐོས་པས་གསོ་ན་རྒྱུ་མཐུན་དང་ཟག་མེད་ཀྱི་ས་བོན་གསར་པ་གསོ་བར་འགྲུབ་ཅིང་ཐོས་པའི་བག་ཆགས་ཆོས་ཉིད་ཀྱིས་གནས་ན་འགྲོ་བ་ཀུན་ཐར་པའི་རིགས་སད་པར་ཐལ་ཏེ། དེ་འདྲ་བའི་ཐོས་པའི་བག་ཆགས་ནི་བསྒྲུབས་པའི་རིགས་ཡིན་པའི་ཕྱིར་རོ།།

ཞེས་གསུངས་པ་ནི། དཔྱད་དགོས་པ་ཞིག་སྟེ། འདི་ལྟར་ཐོས་པའི་བག་ཆགས་ནི་འཇོག་བྱེད་ཀྱིས་གསར་དུ་བཞག་པ་མིན་ལ་ཐོས་བསམ་སྒོམ་གསུམ་གྱིས་ཀྱང་དེ་རྟས་པར་བྱེད་པ་ཙམ་ཞིག་གོ །གཞན་དུ་ན་རང་བཞིན་

[1] *rnams kun gzhi dang / skye* O,P.

དུ་གནས་པར་མི་འགྱུར་རོ། །དེའི་ཕྱིར་ཐོས་པའི་བག་ཆགས་གསར་དུ་ཐོས་པས་བཞག་པ་ནི་མེད་ལ་ཆོས་ཉིད་ཀྱིས་གནས་པའི་བག་ཆགས་ཙམ་ནི་བསྒྲུབས་པའི་རིགས་མ་ཡིན་པས་དེ་ཙམ་ཞིག་ཡོད་པས་རིགས་སད་པར་ཐལ་བ་ཅི་ཞིག་དགོས།

འདིར་རང་བཞིན་དུ་གནས་པ་དང་རྒྱས་པའི་རིགས་གང་ཞི་ན།

རང་བཞིན་དུ་གནས་པའི་རིགས་ནི་འཇིག་བྱེད་ [24b]ལ་མ་བལྟོས་པར་ངོ་བོ་ཉིད་ཀྱིས་གནས་པ་ཟག་པ་མེད་པའི་ཆོས་རྣམས་ཀྱི་ས་བོན། གཞན་གྱི་སྒྲ་དང་ཚུལ་བཞིན་ཡིད་བྱེད་ཀྱི་རྐྱེན་དང་ཕྲད་ན་ཐོས་པ་དང་བསམ་པ་དང་སྒོམ་པ་འཕེལ་བར་འགྱུར་པའི་གནས་སུ་གྱུར་པ་ཞིག་གོ།

ཅིའི་ཕྱིར་རང་བཞིན་དུ་གནས་པའི་རིགས་ཞེས་བྱ་ཞི་ན། འཇིག་བྱེད་ཀྱིས་གསར་དུ་བཞག་པ་མིན་པར་གདོད་མ་ནས་ཆོས་ཉིད་ཀྱིས་གནས་པའི་ཕྱིར་རོ།།

ཅི་ཕྱིར་ཐོས་པའི་བག་ཆགས་ཞེས་བྱ་ [1152]ཞི་ན། སངས་རྒྱས་དང་བྱང་ཆུབ་སེམས་དཔའ་རྣམས་དང་ཕྲད་ནས་ཆོས་ཀྱི་དབྱིངས་ཤིན་ཏུ་རྣམ་པར་དག་པའི་རྒྱུ་མཐུན་པ་གསུང་རབ་ཡན་ལག་བཅུ་གཉིས་ལྟ་བུ་རྣམས་ཐོས་པའི་གནས་སུ་གྱུར་པའི་ཕྱིར་རོ།།

ཅི་ཕྱིར་སྐྱེ་མཆེད་དྲུག་གི་ཁྱད་པར་ཅན་ཞེས་བྱ་ཞི་ན། རང་ཉིད་གང་གི་རྒྱུད་ལ་ལྡན་པའི་དེའི་སྐྱེ་མཆེད་དྲུག་གཞན་ལས་ཁྱད་པར་དུ་བྱེད་པའི་ཕྱིར་རོ།།

རྒྱས་པའི་རིགས་ནི་རང་བཞིན་དུ་གནས་པའི་རིགས་དེ་ཉིད་གཞན་གྱི་སྒྲ་དང་ནང་གི་ཚུལ་བཞིན་ཡིད་བྱེད་ཀྱི་རྐྱེན་དང་ཕྲད་དེ་ཐོས་བསམ་སྒོམ་གསུམ་གྱིས་བརྟས་པར་བྱས་པས་ནུས་པ་མཐུ་ཅན་དུ་སོང་བ་ཉིད་ལ་འཇོག་སྟེ། འདི་གཉིས་ཀ་ཡང་རྣམ་སྨིན་གྱི་རྣམ་ཤེས་ལ་གནས་པའི་ས་བོན་ཡིན་པའི་ཕྱིར་དང་། ཟག་མེད་ཀྱི་ས་བོན་དེ་ཡང་ཐོས་བསམ་སྒོམ་གསུམ་གྱིས་རྟས་པར་བྱེད་པ་ཙམ་མིན་གྱི, གསར་དུ་བཞག་པ་མིན་པར་གསུངས་པའི་ཕྱིར་དང་། བསྒྲུབས་པའི་རིགས་ཆོས་ཉིད་ཀྱིས་ནི་མི་གནས་ལ་གསར་དུ་རིགས་འཇོག་པ་ཡང་མི་འདོད་པའི་ཕྱིར་རོ། །དེ་ལྟར་ཡང་དོན་གསང་དུ།[1]

ས་བོན་གྱི་བདག་ཉིད་དེ་ཡང་རྣམ་པ་གཉིས་ཏེ། རང་བཞིན་དུ་གནས་ [25a]པ་དང་རྐྱེན་གྱིས་ཡང་དག་
པར་བླངས་པའོ།།

ཞེས་འབྱུང་བའི་ཕྱིར་རོ།།

ཅིའི་ཕྱིར་འདི་ལ་ཡང་དག་པར་བསྒྲུབས་པའམ། རྒྱས་པའམ། རྐྱེན་གྱིས་ཡང་དག་པར་བླངས་པ་

[1]The reading at P5553:51.4.2 *sa bon gyi bdag nyid kyang de yang rnam pa gnyis ste / rang bzhin du gnas pa dang yang dang yang dag par blangs pa dang rkyen gyis bsgrubs pa dang rnam pa gnyis te* appears to be corrupt.

ཞེས་བྱ་ཞེ་ན། ཆོས་ཉིས་ཀྱིས་གནས་པའི་ས་བོན་དེ་ཉིད་ཐོས་བསམ་སྒོམ་པའི་རྐྱེན་གྱིས་ནུས་པ་མཐུ་ཅན་དུ་བསྒྲུབས་པའམ། རྒྱས་པར་བྱས་པའམ། ཆུང་ངུ་ལས་འབྲིང་། འབྲིང་ལས་ཆེན་པོར་བླངས་པའི་ཕྱིར་རོ།།

དེས་ན་ས་བོན་དེ་ཉིད་ཆོས་ཉིད་ཀྱིས་གནས་པའི་ཆ་ནས་རང་བཞིན་དུ་གནས་པའི་རིགས་སུ་འཇོག་ལ། རྐྱེན་གྱིས་ཡང་དག་པར་བླངས་པའི་ཆ་ནས་རྒྱས་པའི་རིགས་སུ་འཇོག་གོ།

དེ་ལྟར་བྱས་ན་སྔར་གྱི་དོན་གསང་གི་ལུང་དང་། འཕགས་པ་རྣམ་གྲོལ་སྡེས་སེམས་ཙམ་པའི་འདོད་པ་བརྗོད་པ་ན།

གཞན་དག་རིགས་ནི་སྐྱེ་མཆེད་དྲུག་གི་ཁྱད་པར་ཡིན་ལ། དེ་ཡང་རྐྱེན་གྱིས་ཡང་དག་ [1153]པར་བླངས་
པ་དང་། རང་བཞིན་དུ་གནས་པ་གཉིས་ཡོད་ཟེར་རོ།།

ཞེས་འབྱུང་བ་དང་འགྲིག་པར་ཡང་འགྱུར་རོ།།

དེས་ན་སློབ་དཔོན་ཐོགས་མེད་ཀྱི་བཞེད་པས་རིགས་མཚན་ཉིད་པ་ནི། སྔར་བསྟན་པ་ལྟར་ཡིན་ལ་སློབ་དཔོན་འདི་ཡི་གཞུང་འགའ་ཞིག་ཏུ་ཆོས་ཉིད་རྟེན་དང་ཆོས་ཉིད་རིགས་ཡིན་ནོ་ཞེས་འབྱུང་བ་དེ་ཡང་ཁམས་བྱང་ཆུབ་ཡོན་ཏན་འཕྲིན་ལས་བཞི་འབྲས་བུ་དཀོན་མཆོག་གསུམ་མངོན་དུ་བྱེད་པའི་རྟེན་ཙམ་དུ་འགྱུར་བ་ལ་རིགས་སུ་འདོགས་པ་བཞིན། ཆོས་ཉིད་དེ་ལ་དམིགས་ནས་ལམ་ལ་འབད་པས་ཐེག་པ་གསུམ་གྱི་ཡོན་ཏན་འབྱུང་བར་འགྱུར་བ་ཙམ་ལ་རྟེན་རིགས་ཀྱི་ཐ་སྙད་འདོགས་པ་ཡིན་ཏེ། གཞན་དུ་ན་རིགས་ [25b]ལ་དངོས་པོ་ཐ་དད་པ་གསུམ་དུ་མི་བྱེད་པ་དང་། ཉན་ཐོས་ཀྱི་རིགས་ལྷག་མ་མེད་ཀྱི་ཚེ་ལྡོག་པར་མི་སླ་བར་གྱུར་པ་དང་། ཐེག་པ་ཆེན་པོ་བསྡུས་པར་ཀུན་གཞི་མེད་ན་འཇིག་རྟེན་ལས་འདས་པའི་རྣམ་བྱང་མི་རུང་སྟེ། འཇིག་རྟེན་ལས་འདས་པའི་སེམས་ཀྱི་ས་བོན་དེ་ཀུན་གཞི་ལས་གཞན་པ་ལ་གནས་སུ་མི་རུང་བར་བསྟན་པ་རང་ལུགས་ཐུན་མོང་མ་ཡིན་པར་མི་འགྱུར་བ་ལ་སོགས་པའི་སྐྱོན་མང་པོ་འཇུག་གོ།

གལ་ཏེ་དེ་ལྟ་ན་རྒྱས་རིགས་ཐོབ་ནས་རང་བཞིན་དུ་གནས་པའི་རིགས་མེད་པར་འགྱུར་བ་དང་། ངོ་བོ་ཉིད་ཀྱི་སྐུའི་རྒྱུ་འདུས་བྱས་སུ་འགྱུར་ཏེ། ཟག་མེད་ཀྱི་ས་བོན་དེ་ཉིད་རྐྱེན་གྱིས་བརྟས་པར་བྱས་པ་ཙམ་ཞིག་རྒྱས་རིགས་ཡིན་ལ་དེ་གཉིས་ཀྱང་རྒྱུར་ཡོད་ལ་འབྲས་བུར་མེད་པར་བཤད་པའི་ཕྱིར་དང་། རང་བཞིན་དུ་གནས་པའི་རིགས་ངོ་བོ་ཉིད་ཀྱི་སྐུའི་རྒྱུར་བཤད་པས་ན་ཁྱོད་ཀྱི་ལུགས་དེ་ཡང་རྫ་མེད་པ་མ་ཡིན་ནོ་ཞེ་ན།

འདི་ལ་བརྗོད་པར་བྱ་སྟེ། ཉེས་པ་དང་པོས་གནོད་པར་མི་ནུས་ཏེ། ཟག་མེད་ཀྱི་ས་བོན་རྐྱེན་གྱིས་བརྟས་པར་བྱས་པའི་ཚེ་ཡང་ཐོས་པ་ལན་མང་དུ་བྱས་པས་ཆུང་ངུ་དང་། དེ་ཉིད་བསམ་པ་ལན་མང་དུ་བྱས་པས་འབྲིང་དང་། དེ་ཉིད་སྒོམ་པ་ལན་མང་དུ་བྱས་པས་ཆེན་པོར་འཕེལ་བ་ཙམ་ཡིན་ལ་ས་བོན་གྱིས

དངོས་པོ་དེ་ [1154]ཉིད་གསར་དུ་སྐྱེད་པ་མིན་གྱི་རྟས་བྱེད་ཀྱི་ལྷན་ཅིག་བྱེད་རྐྱེན་དང༌། ས་བོན་རིགས་འདྲ་སྔ་མས་རྒྱུ་རྐྱེན་བྱས་པའི་མཐུས་གོང་ནས་གོང་དུ་འཕེལ་བས་ན་དེའི་ཚེ་ཡང་ཆོས་ཉིད་ཀྱིས་གནས་པ་དང་རྐྱེན་གྱིས་ཡང་དག་པར་བླངས་པ་གཉིས་ཀ་ཡིན་པའི་ཕྱིར་དང༌། རྒྱུར་ཡོད་པ་ལ་འབྲས་བུར་མེད་པར་གསུངས་པ་ཡང་རྐྱེན་དང་མ་ཕྲད་པའི་དབང་དུ་མཛད་པའི་ [26a]ཕྱིར་རོ།།

ཉིས་པ་གཉིས་པས་ཀྱང་མ་གནོད་དེ། ཐེག་བསྡུས་སུ། ཟག་མེད་ཀྱི་ས་བོན་ཆོས་ཀྱི་སྐུའི་ས་བོན་དུ་གསུངས་ལ་ཆོས་ཀྱི་སྐུ་ཡང་སྒྲིབ་གཉིས་བག་ཆགས་དང་བཅས་པ་སྤངས་པའི་དེ་བཞིན་ཉིད། སྟོབས་སོགས་ཀྱི་ཡོན་ཏན་གྱི་ཆོས་ཀྱི་རྟེན་དུ་གྱུར་པ་ཡིན་པར་འགྲེལ་པ་གཉིས་ཀས་བཀྲལ་བའི་ཕྱིར་དང༌། རིགས་དང་པོ་ངོ་བོ་ཉིད་ཀྱི་སྐུའི་རྒྱུར་གསུངས་པ་དེར་ཡང་མཉམ་བཞག་མི་རྟོག་ཡེ་ཤེས་ཆོས་སྐུའི་རྒྱུ་དང༌། རྗེས་ཐོབ་གཟུགས་སྐུའི་རྒྱུར་གསུངས་པའི་ཕྱིར་དང༌། སྐབས་གཞན་དུ་ཡང་ཚོགས་གཉིས་རིམ་པ་བཞིན་སྐུ་གཉིས་ཀྱི་རྒྱུར་གསུངས་པའི་ཡང་ཕྱིར་རོ།།

འདུས་མ་བྱས་ཀྱི་སྐུ་དང་འདུས་བྱས་ཀྱི་སྐུ་གཉིས་ཡོད་པ་ལྟར་དེ་དག་རིགས་ལ་ཡང་དེ་ལྟར་དགོས་ན། འདུས་བྱས་ལ་ཡང་ལོངས་སྤྲུལ་མཚན་ཉིད་ཐ་དད་པ་གཉིས་ཡོད་པས་དེ་གཉིས་ཀྱི་རིགས་མཚན་ཉིད་ཐ་དད་པ་གཉིས་དགོས་པས་རིགས་གཉིས་སུ་མ་ངེས་པར་གསུམ་དུ་ཡང་འགྱུར་རོ། །མི་འགྱུར་ཏེ་དེ་གཉིས་ཀ་ཡང་རྒྱས་རིགས་སུ་གཅིག་པས་སོ་ཞེས་ཀྱང་བརྗོད་པར་མི་ནུས་ཏེ། སྔ་མ་ལས་མ་འདས་པའི་ཕྱིར་ཏེ། འདི་ལྟར་ངོ་བོ་ཉིད་སྐུ་དང་གཟུགས་སྐུ་མཚན་ཉིད་ཐ་དད་པའི་དེའི་རིགས་ཀྱང་འདུས་བྱས་འདུས་མ་བྱས་གཉིས་སུ་འདོད་དགོས་ཞེས་པ་ཙམ་དུ་ཟད་པའི་ཕྱིར་རོ།།

གཞན་ཡང་ཆོས་ཉིད་ལ་རིགས་སུ་འདོད་པ་ཡང་རྟེན་ཆོས་ཀྱིས་[1]ཐ་དད་དུ་འབྱེད་པས་རིགས་ལ་དངོས་པོ་ཐ་དད་གསུམ་དུ་མི་བྱེད་པའི་སྐྱོན་དུ་མི་འགྱུར་ཞེས་ཀྱང་བརྗོད་པར་མི་ནུས་ཏེ། དེ་ནི་ཐེག་གསུམ་དྲང་དོན་དུ་འདོད་པ་ལ་རུང་གི་, མཐར་ཐུག་ཐེག་གསུམ་དུ་འདོད་པ་ལ་མི་འཐད་ [1155]དེ། དེ་ [26b]དག་གི་གཞུང་དུ་ཡང་

> ཁམས་ཐ་དད་དང༌། མོས་པ་ཐ་དད་དང༌། ངེས་པར་སྒྲུབ་མི་སྒྲུབ་དང༌། ས་བོན་གྱི་འབྲས་བུ་ཐ་དད་
> དག་གསུམ་དམིགས་པས་ན་རིགས་ཐ་དད་པ་གསུམ་ཡོད་དོ་

ཞེས་འབྲས་བུའི་སྒོ་ནས་རྒྱུ་ཐ་དད་ཉིད་དུ་དཔགས་ཀྱི། རྟེན་ཐ་དད་པས་རིགས་ཐ་དད་པར་མ་བསྟན་པའི་ཕྱིར་རོ།།

---

[1] Although the manuscripts have *rten chos* (=*āśraya-* or *ādhāra-dharma*) I suspect the original reading to have been *brten chos*, as in AA1.39.

དེ་དག་གི་དེ་བཞིན་ཐོབ་པ་དང་

ཞེས་པའི་འགྲེལ་པར་ཡང་བྱང་ས་ལྟར་སྐྱེ་མཆེད་དྲུག་གི་ཁྱད་པར་ལ་བཤད་པའི་ཕྱིར་རོ།།

དེ་ལྟར་རྣམ་སྨིན་གྱི་རྣམ་ཤེས་ལ་གནས་པའི་ཟག་མེད་ཀྱི་ས་བོན་དེ་ཀུན་གཞིའི་གཉེན་པོ་ཡིན་པས། ཀུན་གཞི་མ་ཡིན་པ་དང་། ཐོས་བསམ་སྒོམ་གསུམ་གྱིས་ལན་མང་དུ་གསོས་བཏབ་པས་རྣམ་བྱང་གི་ས་བོན་འཕེལ་ཀུན་ཉོན་གྱི་ས་བོན་འགྲིབས་ནས། ངང་བས་འོ་མ་དང་ཆུ་ཐ་དད་དུ་མི་དམིགས་པ་འོ་མ་རེལ་གྱིས་བླངས་ནས་ཆུ་གསལ་བར་འགྱུར་བ་དང་འདྲ་བར་ས་བོན་ཀྱང་ཀུན་གཞི་དང་ཐ་དད་དུ་མི་དམིགས་པར་འཇུག་ཀྱང་ཀུན་ཉོན་ཀྱི་ས་བོན་འགྲིབས་རྣམ་བྱང་གི་ཕྱོགས་རྣམས་རྒྱས་ནས་གནས་གྱུར་ཏེ་སྐུ་གསུམ་མངོན་དུ་འགྱུར་བ་ཡིན་ཏེ། ཐེག་ཆེན་བསྡུས་པར།

དེ་ལྟ་བས་ན་[1] འཇིག་རྟེན་ལས་འདས་པའི་རྣམ་པར་བྱང་བ་ཡང་ས་བོན་ཐམས་ཅད་པ་རྣམ་པར་སྨིན་པའི་རྣམ་པར་ཤེས་པ་མེད་ན་མི་རུང་སྟེ། དེ་ལ་ཐོས་པའི་བག་ཆགས་ཀྱིས་ནི་དེའི་ས་བོན་ཡོངས་སུ་འཛིན་པར་མི་རིགས་པའི་ཕྱིར་རོ།།

གལ་ཏེ་[2] ས་བོན་ཐམས་ཅད་པ་རྣམ་པར་སྨིན་པའི་རྣམ་པར་ཤེས་པ་ནི་ཀུན་ནས་ཉོན་མོངས་པའི་རྒྱུ་ཡིན་ན་དེའི་གཉེན་པོ་འཇིག་རྟེན་ལས་འདས་པའི་སེམས་ཀྱི་ས་བོན་དུ་ཇི་ལྟར་རུང་། འཇིག་རྟེན་ལས་འདས་པའི་སེམས་ནི་མ་འདྲིས་པ་སྟེ་དེ་བས་ན་[3]དེའི་བག་ཆགས་ནི་མེད་པ་ཉིད་དོ། །བག་ཆགས་ [27a] དེ་མེད་ན་ས་བོན་གང་ལས་འབྱུང་བ་བརྗོད་དགོས་སོ་ཞེ་ན།

ཆོས་ཀྱི་དབྱིངས་ཤིན་ཏུ་རྣམ་པར་དག་པའི་རྒྱུ་མཐུན་པ་ཐོས་པའི་བག་ཆགས་ཀྱི་ས་བོན་ལས་དེ་འབྱུང་ངོ་།།

ཐོས་པའི་བག་ཆགས་གང་ཡིན་པ་དེ་ཡང་ཅི་ཀུན་གཞི་རྣམ་པར་ཤེས་པའི་ངོ་[1156]བོ་ཉིད་ཡིན་ནམ། འོན་ཏེ་མ་ཡིན། གལ་ཏེ་ཀུན་གཞི་རྣམ་པར་ཤེས་པའི་ངོ་བོ་ཉིད་ཡིན་ན་ནི། ཇི་ལྟར་དེའི་གཉེན་པོའི་ས་བོན་དུ་རུང་། ཅི་སྟེ་དེ་ཡི་ངོ་བོ་ཉིད་མ་ཡིན་ན་ནི། དེས་ན་[4] ཐོས་པའི་བག་ཆགས་ཀྱི་ས་བོན་དེ་ཡི་གནས་ཇི་ཞིག་ཡིན་པར་བལྟ་ཞེ་ན།

སངས་རྒྱས་རྣམས་ཀྱི་བྱང་ཆུབ་ལ་བརྟེན་ནས་ཐོས་པའི་བག་ཆགས་འཇུག་པར་འགྱུར་[5]གང་ཡིན་པ་གནས་གང་ལ་འཇུག་པ་དེ་ལྷན་ཅིག་འཇུག་[6] པའི་ཚུལ་གྱིས་རྣམ་པར་སྨིན་པའི་རྣམ་པར་ཤེས་པ་ལ་འཇུག་སྟེ། འོ་མ་དང་ཆུ་བཞིན་ནོ། །དེ་ནི་ཀུན་གཞི་རྣམ་པར་ཤེས་པ་མ་ཡིན་ཏེ། དེའི་གཉེན་པོའི་

---

[1] *de lta ma yin na* D,O,P. [2] *gal te* omit Lamotte (1938:19). [3] *ma 'dres bas na* D,O,P. Lamotte reads *'dris pa.* [4] *na* omit Lamotte. [5] *bag chags su gyur pa* D,M,N,O,P. [6] *'dus pa'i* D,M,N,O,P.

ས་བོན་ཉིད་ཡིན་པའི་ཕྱིར་རོ། །བག་[1] ཆགས་ཆུང་ངུ་ལ་བརྟེན་ནས་བག་ཆགས་འབྲིང་པོར་འགྱུར་རོ། །བག་ཆགས་འབྲིང་པོ་ལ་བརྟེན་ནས་བག་ཆགས་ཆེན་པོར་འགྱུར་ཏེ། ཐོས་པ་དང་བསམ་པ་དང་སྒོམ་པ་ལན་མང་དུ་བྱ་བ་དང་ལྡན་པའི་ཕྱིར་རོ། །དེ་ལ་ཐོས་པའི་བག་ཆགས་ཀྱི་ས་བོན་ཆུང་ངུ་དང་འབྲིང་དང་ཆེན་པོ་ཡང་ཆོས་ཀྱི་སྐུའི་ས་བོན་དུ་བལྟ་སྟེ། ཀུན་གཞིའི་རྣམ་པར་ཤེས་པའི་གཉེན་པོ་ཡིན་པ་དང་[2] ཀུན་གཞི་རྣམ་པར་ཤེས་པའི་ངོ་བོ་ཉིད་མ་ཡིན་པས།[3] འཇིག་རྟེན་པ་ཡིན་ཀྱང་འཇིག་རྟེན་ལས་འདས་པའི་ཆོས་ཀྱི་དབྱིངས་ཤིན་ཏུ་རྣམ་པར་དག་པའི་རྒྱུ་མཐུན་པ་ཡིན་པས། འཇིག་རྟེན་ལས་འདས་པའི་སེམས་ཀྱི་[27b]ས་བོན་དུ་འགྱུར་བའོ། །དེ་ནི་འཇིག་རྟེན་ལས་འདས་པའི་སེམས་མ་བྱུང་དུ་ཟིན་ཀྱང་། ཉོན་མོངས་པའི་ཀུན་ནས་དཀྲིས་པའི་གཉེན་པོ་དང་། ངན་སོང་གི་འགྲོ་བའི་གཉེན་པོ་དང་། ཉེས་པར་བྱས་པ་ཐམས་ཅད་དེངས་[4] པོར་བྱེད་པའི་གཉེན་པོ་ཡིན་ནོ། །སངས་རྒྱས་དང་བྱང་ཆུབ་སེམས་དཔའ་དང་ཕྲད་པའི་རྗེས་སུ་མཐུན་པའོ། །བྱང་ཆུབ་སེམས་དཔའ་ལས་དང་པོ་པ་རྣམས་ཀྱི་འཇིག་རྟེན་པ་ཡིན་ཀྱང་ཆོས་ཀྱི་སྐུར་བསྡུས་པ་དང་། ཉན་ཐོས་དང་རང་སངས་རྒྱས་རྣམས་ཀྱི་རྣམ་པར་གྲོལ་བའི་ལུས་སུ་བསྡུས་པར་ཡང་བལྟའོ། །དེ་ནི་ཀུན་གཞི་རྣམ་པར་ཤེས་པ་མ་ཡིན་གྱི་,ཆོས་ཀྱི་སྐུ་དང་རྣམ་པར་གྲོལ་བའི་ལུས་སུ་བསྡུས་པ་སྟེ། ཆུང་ངུ་[1157]དང་འབྲིང་དང་ཆེན་པོ་ཇི་ལྟ་ཇི་ལྟར་རིམ་གྱིས་འཕེལ་བ་སྟེ་དེ་ལྟ་དེ་ལྟར་རྣམ་པར་སྨིན་པའི་རྣམ་པར་ཤེས་པ་ཡང་འབྲི་ཞིང་གནས་ཀྱང་འགྱུར་རོ། །གནས་རྣམ་པ་ཐམས་ཅད་དུ་གྱུར་ན་རྣམ་པར་སྨིན་པའི་རྣམ་པར་ཤེས་པ་ས་བོན་ཐམས་ཅད་པ་ཡང་ས་བོན་མེད་པར་གྱུར་པ་དང་། རྣམ་པ་ཐམས་ཅད་དུ་སྤངས་པ་ཡང་ཡིན་ནོ།།

ཡང་ཇི་ལྟར་ན་ཀུན་གཞི་རྣམ་པར་ཤེས་པ་དང་ཀུན་གཞི་རྣམ་པར་ཤེས་པ་མ་ཡིན་པ་ཆུ་དང་འོ་མ་བཞིན་དུ་[5] ལྷན་ཅིག་གནས་པ་རྣམ་པ་ཐམས་ཅད་དུ་འགྲིབ་པར་འགྱུར་ཞེ་ན།

ངང་པས་ཆུ་ལས་འོ་མ་འཐུངས་པ་ལྟ་བུ་དང་། འཇིག་རྟེན་པའི་འདོད་ཆགས་དང་བྲལ་བ་ན། མཉམ་པར་བཞག་པ་མ་ཡིན་པའི་སའི་བག་ཆགས་འགྲིབས་ཏེ། མཉམ་པར་བཞག་པའི་སའི་བག་ཆགས་འཕེལ་ནས་གནས་གྱུར་པ་བཞིན་ནོ།།

ཞེས་སོ།།

ཆོས་ཀྱི་དབྱིངས་ཤིན་ཏུ་[28a]རྣམ་པར་དག་པའི་རྒྱུ་མཐུན་པ་དང་། སངས་རྒྱས་ཀྱི་བྱང་ཆུབ་ལ་བརྟེན་ནས་ཞེས་པ་དང་། ཆོས་ཀྱི་སྐུ་དང་། རྣམ་པར་གྲོལ་བའི་ལུས་ཀྱི་ཁྱད་པར་དང་། གནས་གྱུར་ལ་དཔེ་གཉིས

---

[1] D,M,N,O,P add *de la* before *bag*. [2] *yin pa'i phyir* D,O,P. [3] *ma yin par bsdus pa* D,O,P. [4] *dngos* D,O,P. [5] Schmithausen (1987: note 580); D,M,N,O,P add *gnas*.

སློས་པ་གང་ཞི་ན།

དང་པོ་ནི། བཤད་སྦྱར་ལས།

སངས་རྒྱས་རྣམས་ཀྱི་ཆོས་ཀྱི་དབྱིངས་ཤིན་ཏུ་རྣམ་པར་དག་པ་གློ་བུར་གྱི་སྒྲིབ་པ་དང་བྲལ་བ་གང་ཡིན་པ་དེའི་རྒྱུ་མཐུན་ནི་བསྟན་པའི་ཆོས་ཏེ་དེ་རྒྱུ་ལས་བྱུང་བར་གྱུར་ན་འདྲ་བའི་ཕྱིར་རོ། །དེ་མཉན་པ་ནི་ཐོས་པའོ། །དེའི་བག་ཆགས་གང་ཡིན་པ་དེ་ནི་འཇིག་རྟེན་ལས་འདས་པ་ཟག་པ་མེད་པའི་སེམས་ཀྱི་ས་བོན་ཏེ། ཀུན་གཞི་རྣམ་པར་ཤེས་པ་ནི་མཐུན་པ་མ་ཡིན་པའི་ཕྱིར་རོ།

ཞེས་སོ།།

གཉིས་པ་ནི། དེ་ཉིད་ལས།

སངས་རྒྱས་རྣམས་ཀྱི[1] བྱང་ཆུབ་ལ་བརྟེན་ནས་ཤེས་བྱ་བ་ནི་ཡེ་ཤེས་དྲི་མ་མེད་ཅིང་ཐོགས་པ་མེད་པ་མདོའི་སྡེ་ལ་སོགས་པ་བསྟན་པའི་ཆོས་ཐོས་པའི་བག་ཆགས་ཀྱི་གནས་ཡིན་གྱི་ཀུན་གཞི་རྣམ་པར་ཤེས་པ་ནི་གནས[2] མ་ཡིན་ཏེ། དེ་དང་ལྷན་ཅིག་ནི་འཇུག་གོ།

ཞེས་སོ། །དེ་ཡང་འཕེལ་བའི་གནས་བསྟན་པའི་ཆོས་ཐོས་པ་ལྟ་བུ་ཡིན་ལ་རྟེན་པའི་གནས་ཀུན་[1158]གཞིའོ།།

གསུམ་པ་ནི། དེ་ཉིད་ལས།

དེ་ལ་ཆོས་ཀྱི་སྐུ་དང་རྣམ་པར་གྲོལ་བའི་ལུས་ཀྱི་ཁྱད་པར་ནི་འདི་ཡིན་ཏེ། རྣམ་པར་གྲོལ་བ་ནི་ཉོན་མོངས་པའི་བཅིངས་པ་དང་བྲལ་བ་ཙམ་དུ[3]ཟད་དེ། དཔེར་ན་གྲོང་མི་ཞིག་ལྕགས་སྒྲོག་ལ་སོགས་པའི་བཅིངས་པ་དང་བྲལ་བ་ཙམ[4]ན་སྡུག་བསྔལ་དེ་ལོག་པ་ལ།[5]འབྲས་བུ་ཙམ་དུ་ཟད་ཀྱི་དེ་ལས་ལྷག་པའི་དབང་ཕྱུག་གི་ཁྱད་པར་དང་ལྡན་པ་མ་ཡིན་པ་ལྟ་བུའོ། །ཆོས་ཀྱི་སྐུ་ནི་བག་ཆགས་དང་བཅས་པའི་[6]ཉོན་མོངས་[28b]པ་དང་ཤེས་བྱའི་སྒྲིབ་པ་ལས་རྣམ་པར་གྲོལ་བ་སྟོབས་དང་མི་འཇིགས་པ་ལ་སོགས་པ་ངོ་མཚར་གྱི་ཡོན་ཏན་དུ་མས་བརྒྱན་པ་འགྲོ་བ་ཐམས་ཅད་ཀྱི་གནས་ཇི་ལྟར་འདོད་པ་བཞིན་དུ་སྤྱོད་པས་རང་དབང་མཆོག་ཐོབ་པ་སྟེ། དཔེར་ན་རྒྱལ་པོའི་བུ་བཅིངས་པ་དང་བྲལ་མ་ཐག་ཏུ་སྤྱི་བོ་ནས་དབང་བསྐུར་བ་དང་། དབང་ཕྱུག་ཕུན་སུམ་ཚོགས་པ་མཆོག་དང་ལྡན་པ་ལྟ་བུའོ།།

ཞེས་སོ།།

བཞི་པ་ནི། ངང་བའི་དཔེ་ནི་འཇིག་རྟེན་ན་གྲགས་པ་ཡིན་ལ། ཆགས་བྲལ་གྱི་དཔེ་ནི་བསྟན་བཅོས་ལ་གྲགས་པའི་དབང་དུ་བྱས་པར་མངོན་ནོ།།

དེ་ལྟར་བྱས་ན་མཁས་པ་ཁ་ཅིག་ཟག་མེད་ཀྱི་ས་བོན་ཀུན་གཞིར་འདོད་པ་ནི་རྩིངས་པར་མངོན་ཏེ། ལུང་

---

[1] *kyis* O,P. [2] *de* O,P. [3] *cung* O,P. [4] *omit* D,M. [5] *la/*omit D,O,P. [6] *bag chags dang bcas pa'i* omit D,O,P.

འདི་ལས་ཕྱི་རོལ་དུ་གྱུར་པའི་ཕྱིར་རོ།།

སྤྲོས་པ་བཏང་ལ་དཀྲུས་མ་ཉིད་བཤད་དེ། ཀུན་གཞི་ས་བོན་གྱི་ཆ་དེ་ལ་ཅི་ཕྱིར་ཀུན་གཞི་ཞེས་བྱ་ཞེ་ན།

> ཀུན་ནས་ཉོན་མོངས་ཆོས་ཐམས་ཅད། །རྒྱུ་འམ་འབྲས་བུའི་དངོས་པོ་རུ། །སྦྱོར་བའི་
> ཕྱིར་ན་ཀུན་གཞིའོ།།

ཇི་སྐད་དུ།

> ཅི་ཕྱིར་དེ་ལ་ཀུན་གཞི་རྣམ་པར་ཤེས་པ་ཞེས་བྱ་ཞེ་ན། སྐྱེ་བ་ཅན་ཀུན་ནས་ཉོན་མོངས་པའི་ཆོས་ཐམས་ཅད་འབྲས་བུའི་དངོས་པོར་དེར་སྦྱོར་བའམ། དེ་ཡང་རྒྱུའི་དངོས་པོར་དེ་དག་ཏུ་སྦྱོར་བའི་ཕྱིར་ཀུན་གཞི་རྣམ་པར་ཤེས་པའོ། །ཡང་ན་སེམས་ཅན་དག་དེའི་བདག་ཏུ་སྦྱོར་བས་[1] ཀུན་གཞི་རྣམ་པར་ཤེས་པའོ།།

ཞེས་གསུངས་པ་ལྟར་[1159]བཤད་པར་བྱའོ། །དེ་ལ་འདིར་ངེས་ཚིག་གསུམ་ཆོས་གཅིག་གི་ངེས་ཚིག་ལྟར་གསུངས་པ་ནི་ས་བོན་དང་རྣམ་སྨིན་མ་ཕྱེ་བའི་དབང་དུ་བྱས་པ་ཡིན་པས། རྣམ་པར་དབྱེ་སྟེ་བཤད་དོ།།

དེ་ཡང་འདིར། སྤྱིར་ཀུན་གཞི་ཞེས་འབྱུང་བའི་དོན་ནི་[29a]འདིར་ཆོས་ཀུན་སྦྱོར་བའི་ཕྱིར་ཡིན་ལ་བྱེ་བྲག་ཏུ་ཀུན་གཞི་ས་བོན་གྱི་ཆ་ལ་ཀུན་གཞི་ཞེས་པ་ནི། ཚོགས་བདུན་གྱིས་བསྡུས་པའམ། ཉོན་མོངས་པ་དང་ལས་དང་སྐྱེ་བའི་ཀུན་ནས་ཉོན་མོངས་པའི་ཆོས་རྣམས་ཀྱི་རྒྱུའི་རྐྱེན་ཡིན་པས་དེ་དག་འདིའི་འབྲས་བུར་འདིར་སྦྱོར་བའམ། ཡང་ན་ཀུན་གཞི་དེ་ཉིད་ཆོས་དེ་དག་གི་རྒྱུའི་དངོས་པོར་འདིར་སྦྱོར་བའི་ཕྱིར་ན་ཀུན་གཞིའོ།།

ཀུན་གཞི་རྣམ་སྨིན་གྱི་ཆ་ནི་འགྲོ་བ་ལྔའི་སེམས་ཅན་ཀུན་འདིར་ཉོན་ཡིད་ཀྱིས་བདག་ཏུ་སྦྱོར་བའི་ཕྱིར་ཀུན་གཞིའོ།།

དེ་ལྟ་བུའི་ས་བོན་གྱི་ཆ་དེའི་ལྡོག་དུས་གང་ཞེ་ན།

> དེ་ཕྱིར་དབང་ཐོབ་དགྲ་བཅོམ་ལ། །ཀུན་གཞི་ཡོད་པ་མ་ཡིན་ཏེ། །འཇོག་བྱེད་གཉིས་པོ་
> མེད་ཕྱིར་རོ།།

གང་གི་ཕྱིར་ཀུན་ནས་ཉོན་མོངས་པའི་ཆོས་རྣམས་འབྲས་བུའི་དངོས་པོར་རམ། ས་བོན་གྱི་ཀུན་གཞི་དེ་ཉིད་དེ་དག་གི་རྒྱུའི་དངོས་པོར་སྦྱོར་བའི་ཕྱིར་དང་། ཉོན་ཡིད་ཀྱིས་བདག་ཏུ་སྦྱོར་བའི་ཕྱིར་ན་ཀུན་གཞིར་བཞག་པ་དེའི་ཕྱིར་དབང་ཐོབ་པའི་བྱང་ཆུབ་སེམས་དཔའ་ས་བརྒྱད་པ་ཡན་ཆད་དང་། ཉན་ཐོས་དང་རང་སངས་རྒྱས་དགྲ་བཅོམ་པ་རྣམས་ལ་བྱེ་བྲག་ཏུ་ཀུན་གཞི་ས་བོན་གྱི་ཆ་མེད་ལ་སྤྱིར་ཀུན་གཞི་རྣམ་ཤེས་མེད་

---

[1] *ba'i phyir* D,M,N,O,P.

དེ། ཉོན་མོངས་པ་མ་ལུས་པར་སྤངས་པས་ཀུན་གཞིར་འཇོག་བྱེད་གཉིས་པོ་གང་ཡང་མེད་པའི་ཕྱིར་རོ། །མ་གྲུབ་པ་མིན་[1] དེ། ཐེག་བསྡུས་ལས།

ཉན་ཐོས་དང་བྱང་ཆུབ་སེམས་དཔའ་སློབ་པ་རྣམས་ཀྱི་[2] ནི་ཕྱོགས་གཅིག་གནོན་པའི་[3] མཚན་ཉིད་དོ། །དགྲ་བཅོམ་པ་དང་རང་སངས་རྒྱས་དང་། དེ་བཞིན་གཤེགས་པ་རྣམས་ཀྱི་ནི་ཉོན་[29b] མོངས་པའི་སྒྲིབ་པ་མཐའ་དག་གནོན་པའི་མཚན་ཉིད་དང་།[4] ཉོན་མོངས་པ་དང་། ཤེས་བྱའི་སྒྲིབ་པ་མཐའ་དག་གནོན་པའི་མཚན་ཉིད་དེ་ཅི་[1160] རིགས་སུ་སྦྱོར་

ཞེས་སོ།།

བྱེ་བྲག་ཏུ། བག་ཆགས་གསུམ་གྱི་ལྡོག་དུས་ནི། དོན་གསང་ལས།

སྲིད་པའི་ཡན་ལག་གི་བག་ཆགས་ཀྱི་ས་བོན་ནི་རྣམ་པར་སྨིན་པའི་འབྲས་བུ་མ་བྱུང་གི་བར་དུའོ། །འཇིག་ཚོགས་ལ་ལྟ་བའི་ས་བོན་དང་ཉོན་མོངས་པ་ཅན་གྱི་སྨྲས་པའི་བག་ཆགས་ཀྱི་ས་བོན་ནི། གཉེན་པོ་མ་བྱུང་གི་བར་དུའོ། །དགེ་བ་དང་ལུང་དུ་མ་བསྟན་པའི་སྨྲས་པའི་བག་ཆགས་ཀྱི་ས་བོན་ཡང་ཉན་ཐོས་དང་རང་སངས་རྒྱས་དག་གི་ཡོངས་སུ་མྱ་ངན་ལས་མ་འདས་ཀྱི་བར་དུའོ། །དེ་བཞིན་གཤེགས་པའི་ནི་རྡོ་རྗེ་ལྟ་བུའི་བར་དུ་རྒྱུན་འཇུག་པ་ཙམ་གྱིས་རྒྱུན་ཆགས་སུ་འབྱུང་ངོ་།།

ཞེས་པ་ལྟར་རོ།།

གལ་ཏེ་ཀུན་གཞི་རྣམ་ཤེས་དབང་ཐོབ་པ་དང་དགྲ་བཅོམ་པ་དག་ལ་མེད་ན། དེ་དག་གི་རྒྱུད་ལ་རྣམ་ཤེས་བརྒྱད་པོ་ཁས་ལེན་དགོས་སམ་མི་དགོས། དགོས་ན་ཀུན་གཞི་རྣམ་ཤེས་ཡོད་པར་འགྱུར་ཏེ། གཞན་དུ་ན་རྣམ་ཤེས་ཚོགས་བརྒྱད་དུ་མ་གདོགས་པའི་རྣམ་ཤེས་ཡོད་པར་འགྱུར་རོ། །མི་དགོས་ན་རྣམ་སྨིན་ནི་རྡོ་རྗེ་ལྟ་བུ་དང་། ལྷག་མེད་ཀྱི་བར་དུ་འཇུག་པ་ཉམས་སོ་ཞེ་ན།

ཉེས་པ་མེད་དེ། ཀུན་གཞི་རྣམ་ཤེས་ལ་རྣམ་སྨིན་གྱིས་ཁྱབ་ཀྱང་རྣམ་སྨིན་གྱི་རྣམ་ཤེས་ལ་ཀུན་གཞིས་མ་ཁྱབ་སྟེ། དབང་ཐོབ་པ་དང་དགྲ་བཅོམ་པ་ལ་རྣམ་སྨིན་གྱི་རྣམ་ཤེས་ཡོད་ཀྱང་ཀུན་གཞིའི་དོན་མེད་པའི་ཕྱིར་སྐྱོན་གཉིས་པ་མི་འབྱུང་ལ། ཚོགས་བརྒྱད་དུ་སྟོན་པ་ན་ཀུན་[30a] གཞི་རྣམ་ཤེས་དང་བརྒྱད་དུ་བྱེད་པ་ནི་རིགས་ལ་སེམས་ཀྱི། རྫས་ལ་མ་ཡིན་ཏེ། གཞན་དུ་དགྲ་བཅོམ་པ་དང་ས་བརྒྱད་པ་ཡན་གྱི་བྱང་སེམས་འགོག་པ་ལ་ཞུགས་པ་འཇུག་ཤེས་དང་ཀུན་གཞི་གཉིས་ཀ་མེད་པའི་སྐུར་གསུངས་པ་མི་རིགས་པར་འགྱུར་རོ།།

---

[1] *yin* O,P. [2] *kyis* D,M,N,O,P. [3] Surprisingly D,M,N,O,P all read *ston pa*. [4] Cp. Lamotte (1938: vol. 2, 86) who reads *mtshan nyid do*.

ཀུན་གཞི་ས་བོན་གྱི་ཆ་མེད་པའོ་ཞེས་ཀྱང་མི་རིགས་ཏེ། རྣམ་སྨིན་གྱི་ཆ་ཀུན་གཞིར་འཇོག་པ་ཡང་ཉོན་ཡིད་ཀྱིས་བདག་ཏུ་སྒྲོར་བའི་དོན་དུ་གསུངས་པའི་ཕྱིར་རོ། །དེ་ལྟར་ཡང་དོན་གསང་ལས།

> རྣམ་པར་སྨིན་པའི་རྣམ་པར་ཤེས་པ་ལ་འཇུག་སྐྱེ་ཞེས་བྱ་བ་ལ་ཀུན་གཞི་རྣམ་པར་ཤེས་པ་ལ་ [1161]སྒྲོས་པ་ནི་མ་ཁྱབ་པའི་ཕྱིར་ཏེ། འདི་ལྟར་དེ་ནི་ས་བརྒྱད་པ་ལ་སོགས་པ་ལ་གནས་པའི་བྱང་ཆུབ་སེམས་དཔའི་རྒྱུད་དང་། དགྲ་བཅོམ་པ་དང་རང་སངས་རྒྱས་རྣམས་ཀྱི་རྒྱུད་ལ་མེད་ཀྱི་, རྣམ་པར་སྨིན་པའི་རྣམ་པར་ཤེས་པ་ནི་ཡོད་དོ།།

ཤེས་པ་དང་། རྣམ་པར་གཏན་ལ་དབབ་པ་བསྡུ་བར་ཡང་མུ་བཞི་གསུངས་ཏེ། ཀུན་གཞི་ཡོད་ལ་འཇུག་ཤེས་མེད་པའི་མུ་ནི་སེམས་མེད་པའི་གནས་སྐབས་ལྔའོ། །བཟློག་བ་ནི་སེམས་ཡོད་པའི་གནས་སྐབས་ཀྱི་མི་སློབ་པ་དང་ཕྱིར་མི་ལྡོག་པའི་བྱང་ཆུབ་སེམས་དཔའ་འོ། །གཉིས་ཀ་ཡོད་པ་ནི་དེ་དག་ལས་གཞན་པའི་གནས་སྐབས་སེམས་ཡོད་པའི་དུས་སོ། །གཉིས་ཀ་མེད་པ་ནི་མི་སློབ་པ་དང་ཕྱིར་མི་ལྡོག་པའི་བྱང་ཆུབ་སེམས་དཔའ་འགོག་པ་ལ་ཞུགས་པ་དང་ཕུང་པོ་ལྷག་མེད་ཀྱི་མྱང་འདས་ཞེས་གསུངས་པ་དང་། སུམ་ཅུ་པར་ཡང་།

> དགྲ་ [30b]བཅོམ་ཉིད་ན་དེ་ལྡོག་གོ།

ཞེས་གསུངས་པས་ན། སྔར་ཁོ་བོས་བསྟན་པའི་ཀུན་གཞི་མེད་པའི་ས་མཚམས་རྒྱ་མེད་པར་གཟུང་བར་བྱའོ།།

དེས་ན་དབང་ཐོབ་པའི་སེམས་དཔའ་དང་། དགྲ་བཅོམ་པའི་རྒྱུད་ཀྱི་རྣམ་ཤེས་བརྒྱད་པོ་དེ་ལ་རྣམ་སྨིན་གྱི་རྣམ་ཤེས་དང་། བསམ་གྱིས་མི་ཁྱབ་པའི་འཆི་འཕོ་བ་ཡོད་པས་ལེན་པའི་རྣམ་ཤེས་ཞེས་ཟེར་གྱི་, ཀུན་གཞི་ཞེས་མི་བརྗོད་དོ།།

> དེ་ལྟར་ན་དབང་ཐོབ་པ་དང་། དགྲ་བཅོམ་པ་ལ་སེམས་ཀྱང་མེད་པར་འགྱུར་ཏེ། ཇི་སྐད་དུ།
> ཅིའི་ཕྱིར་སེམས་ཞེས་ཀྱང་བྱ་ཞེ་ན། ཆོས་ཀྱི་བག་ཆགས་ཀྱི་ས་བོན་སྣ་ཚོགས་རྣམས་ཀྱིས་ཀུན་ཏུ་བསགས་པའི་ཕྱིར་རོ།[1]

ཅེས་གསུངས་པས་སོ་ཞེ་ན།།

མི་མཚུངས་ཏེ། དེའི་དོན་ནི། མདོ་ལས་ "སེམས་ཡིད་རྣམ་པར་ཤེས་པ་" ཞེས་ཡིད་དང་རྣམ་ཤེས་ལས་ཐ་དད་པའི་སེམས་ཀྱི་ལུས་གསུམ་པོ་གསུངས་ལ། དེ་ནི་ཀུན་གཞི་རྣམ་ཤེས་ལ་མ་གཏོགས་པ་གཞན་ལ་བཞག་ཏུ་མེད་དེ། འདི་ལྟར་སེམས་ཀྱི་དོན་ནི་སྐབས་དེར་བསགས་པ་ལ་འཆད་དགོས་ལ་ཀུན་གཞི་ནི་བག་ཆགས་ཐམས་ཅད་བསགས་པ་ཡིན་ཞིང་དོན་དེ་ཡིད་དང་རྣམ་ཤེས་ལ་མ་ཚང་ [1162]བས་སོ་སྙམ་

---

[1] *phyi rol* D,M,N,O,P.

ད་བསམ་པས་ན་ཡིད་དང་རྣམ་ཤེས་ལས་ཐ་དད་པའི་བག་ཆགས་བསགས་པ་དེ་དག་ན་མེད་ཀྱང་།

དེ་ལ་དོན་མཐོང་རྣམ་པར་ཤེས།

ཞེས་པའི་དོན་ཚང་བའི་སེམས་ནི་ཡོད་དེ་སེམས་ཀྱི་དོན་བག་ཆགས་བསགས་པ་ཁོ་ནར་མ་ངེས་པའི་ཕྱིར་དང་། ཀུན་གཞིར་འཇོག་བྱེད་གསུམ་མམ་གཉིས་ལས་གཞན་མ་གསུངས་པའི་ཕྱིར་རོ། །དེ་ལྟར་ཡང་། ཐེག་ཆེན་བསྡུས་པར།

ཀུན་གཞི་ [31a]རྣམ་པར་ཤེས་པ་མ་གཏོགས་པར་སེམས་ཀྱི་ལུས་[1] གསུམ་པ་མི་དམིགས་ཏེ། དེ་ལྟ་བས་ན་ཀུན་གཞི་རྣམ་པར་ཤེས་པ་ནི་སེམས་ཉིད་ཡིན་པར་གྲུབ་

ཅེས་སོ།།

ད་ནི་འདི་དཔྱད་དེ། མཁས་པ་འགའ་ཞིག་རྣམ་སྨིན་གྱི་ཆ་ཐེག་དམན་གྱི་ལྷག་མེད་ནས་ལྡོག་པར་ཐེག་དམན་པ་དག་འདོད་གསུངས་། ཅི་གྲུབ་མཐའ་དམན་པ་བྱེ་བྲག་སྨྲ་བ་དང་མདོ་སྡེ་པ་རྣམས་འདོད་པ་ཡིན་ནམ། ཐེག་པ་དམའ་བ་ཉན་རང་གི་ལམ་ལ་གནས་པ་རྣམས་བཞེད་བརྟག་གྲང་། དང་པོ་ནི་མི་རིགས་ཏེ། གྲུབ་མཐའ་སྨྲ་བ་དེ་གཉིས་རྣམ་ཤེས་ཚོགས་དྲུག་ལས་གཞན་པའི་རྣམ་ཤེས་ཁས་མི་ལེན་པའི་ཕྱིར་རོ། །གཉིས་པ་ཡང་མི་རུང་སྟེ། དེ་དག་གིས་ཀུན་གཞིའི་འཇུག་ལྡོག་གཏན་ལ་འབེབས་པའི་རྣམ་གཞག་མཛད་པ་བསྟན་དགོས་ན་དེ་ཡང་རྙེད་པ་མ་ཡིན་ནོ།།

འོ་ན་སུའི་ལུགས་ཤེ་ན། འདིའི་འཇུག་པ་དང་ལྡོག་པའི་རྣམ་བཞག་རྒྱས་པར་ནི་རྣལ་འབྱོར་སྤྱོད་པའི་གཞུང་ལས་འབྱུང་ངོ་།།

དེ་ལྟ་ན་ཐེག་ཆེན་གྱི་ལུགས་ལ་ཐེག་དམན་གྱིས་ཤེས་སྒྲིབ་ཟད་པར་སྤངས་པ་ཞིག་སྲིད་དེ། དེའི་ལྷག་མེད་ནས་རྣམ་སྨིན་གྱི་ཆ་ལྡོག་པའི་ཕྱིར་རོ། །ཞེ་ན།

ཉེས་པ་མེད་དེ། འདི་ལྟར་ལྷག་མེད་ཀྱི་ཚེ་ན། ཐེག་དམན་གྱི་ལམ་གྱིས་ཤེས་སྒྲིབ་ནུས་ཆུང་དུ་རིམ་གྱིས་བཏང་བའི་མ་ལུས་པར་སྤངས་པ་མེད་ཀྱང་ཤེས་སྒྲིབ་རྒྱུན་ཆད་པའི་ལྡོག་པ་ཡོད་དེ། ཕུང་པོ་ལྔའི་རྒྱུན་ལྡོག་པའི་ཕྱིར་རོ།།

མ་གྲུབ་པ་མ་ཡིན་ཏེ། ལྷག་མེད་ཀྱི་ཚེ་ན་དགྲ་བཅོམ་པ་ཚེའི་འདུ་བྱེད་བཏང་བ་ཡིན་ལ། དེ་ཤི་བའི་འོག་ཏུ་རིག་པ་འབྱུང་བ་ལ་ནི། སྐྱེ་[31b]བ་ལེན་[1163]དགོས་ན། ལས་དང་ཉོན་མོངས་པ་མ་ལུས་པར་སྤངས་པའི་ཕྱིར་དང་། དེས་བསྐྱེད་པའི་རྣམ་སྨིན་གྱི་ཕུང་པོ་ཡང་ལོག་པའི་ཕྱིར་ལས་ཉོན་གྱི་དབང་གིས་སྐྱེ་བ་ཡང་མེད་ལ་,ལས་ཉོན་གྱི་རྣམ་པས་ལུས་འགྲུབ་པར་ཡང་མི་ནུས་ཏེ། འདི་ཞི་བ་ཕྱོགས་གཅིག་པ་ཡིན་

1 D,M read *sems kyi mu*; N,O,P *sems kyis mu*.

པའི་ཕྱིར་དང་། རྟེན་ལོག་པའི་ཕྱིར་རོ། །དེས་ན་འདིར་ནི་སྤྲོས་པ་ཉེ་བར་ཞི་བ་འདུས་བྱས་ཀྱི་འཇུག་པ་རྒྱུན་ཆད་པའི་མཚན་མ་མེད་པའི་དབྱིངས་འབབ་ཞིག་གོ།

དེ་ལྟ་ན་ཐེག་པ་ཆན་པོའི་མཚན་མ་མེད་པའི་དབྱིངས་དང་ཁྱད་མེད་པར་འགྱུར་རོ་ཞེ་ན།།

མི་འགྱུར་ཏེ། འདི་ན་འདུས་བྱས་ཀྱི་འཇུག་པ་ཉེ་བར་ཞི་བ་ཙམ་ཡིན་གྱི་, ཞི་བའི་དབྱིངས་ནས་གཞན་དོན་བྱེད་པའི་སྐུ་མི་ལྡང་སྟེ། གཞན་དོན་དུ་ལམ་[1]ལ་གོམས་པར་མ་བྱས་པའི་ཕྱིར་རོ། །གཞན་ཡང་རྣམ་པར་གདན་ལ་དབབ་པ་བསྡུ་བར། འཇུག་ཤེས་དང་ཀུན་གཞི་གཉིས་ཀ་མེད་པའི་སྐུ། ལྷག་མེད་ཀྱི་མྱང་འདས་ལ་གསུངས་པའི་ཕྱིར་ཡང་སྔར་ལྟར་ཡིན་ནོ། །འདི་ཉན་ཐོས་དང་སློ་བསྟུན་ཅེས་ཀྱང་བརྗོད་མི་ནུས་ཏེ། ཀུན་གཞི་ཡོད་ན་གདན་ལ་འབེབས་པའི་སྐབས་ཡིན་པའི་ཕྱིར་རོ།།

དེས་ན་བྱེ་བྲག་སྨྲ་བ་ནི། ལྷག་མེད་ཀྱི་ཚེ་འདུས་བྱས་རྒྱུན་ཆད་པའི་སོ་སོར་བརྟགས་འགོག་ནི་རྫས་སུ་གྲུབ་པའི་འདུས་མ་བྱས་ཤིག་ཡོད་པར་འདོད་ལ། མདོ་སྡེ་པ་ནི། འདུས་བྱས་འགགས་པའི་མེད་དགག་ཙམ་མེད་པ་ཞིག་ཏུ་འདོད་དེ། ཕུང་པོ་དང་བྲལ་བར་ནི་འདོད་ལ། འདུས་མ་བྱས་རྫས་སུ་མི་འདོད་པའི་ཕྱིར་རོ། །གཉིས་ཀས་ཀྱང་།

ལུས་ཞིག་ཚོར་བ་བསིལ་བར་གྱུར། །འདུ་ཤེས་འགགས་ཤིང་འདུ་བྱེད་ཞི། །རྣམ་པར་ཤེས་པ་
ནུབ་གྱུར་པ། །འདི་འདྲ་དེ་ནི་སྡུག་བསྔལ་མཐའ།།

ཞེས་[32a]པའི་མདོའི་དོན་ཡིན་པར་སེམས་ཤིང་། བྱེ་བྲག་ཏུ་མདོ་སྡེ་པས།

མར་མེ་ཤི་བར་གྱུར་པ་ལྟར། །དེ་ཡི་སེམས་ནི་རྣམ་པར་ཐར།།

ཞེས་དགྲ་བཅོམ་པའི་སེམས་ཀྱི་རྣམ་པར་གྲོལ་བ་མར་མེ་ཤི་བ་ལྟར་གསུངས་པ་དང་། རང་གི་གྲུབ་མཐའ་
[1164]མཐུན་པར་འདོད་དོ།།

རྣལ་འབྱོར་སྤྱོད་པ་ནི། བེམ་རིག་གི་འཇུག་པ་ཐམས་ཅད་ཉེ་བར་ཞི་བའི་དེ་བཞིན་ཉིད། ཚོར་བའི་བདེ་བ་མེད་ཀྱང་སྡུག་བསྔལ་གདན་བྲལ་བའི་བདེ་བ་ཡོད་པ། མེད་དགག་ཙམ་མེད་ཀྱང་མིན་ལ། རྫས་གྲུབ་ཀྱི་ཡོད་པ་ཡང་མིན་པ། རྟག་པ་འགྱུར་མེད་དུ་ཡོད་པ་ཡིན་པར་འདོད་དོ། །དེའི་ཕྱིར་ལྷག་བཅས་ཕན་ཆད་དུ་ཐེག་ཆེན་དུ་འཇུག་སྲིད་ལ། འདིར་སོན་ནས་འཇུག་པར་མི་འདོད་དེ། རྣམ་པར་གདན་ལ་དབབ་པ་བསྡུ་བར།

ཉན་ཐོས་བྱང་ཆུབ་ཡོངས་སུ་འགྱུར་བ་ཅི་ཕུང་པོ་ལྷག་མ་དང་བཅས་པའི་མྱང་ངན་ལས་འདས་པའི་

---

[1] *las* D,O,P.

དབྱིངས་ལ་གནས་ཤིང་བླ་ན་མེད་པ་ཡང་དག་པར་རྫོགས་པའི་བྱང་ཆུབ་སྒྲུབ་པར་བྱེད་དམ། འོན་ཏེ་ཕུང་པོ་ལྷག་མ་མེད་པའི་མྱ་ངན་ལས་འདས་པའི་དབྱིངས་ལ་གནས་ཤིང་བྱེད་ཅེ་ན།

ཕུང་པོའི་ལྷག་མ་དང་བཅས་པའི་མྱ་ངན་ལས་འདས་པའི་དབྱིངས་ལ་གནས་ཤིང་བྱེད་དེ། འདི་ལྟར་ཕུང་པའི་ལྷག་མ་མེད་པའི་མྱ་ངན་ལས་འདས་པའི་དབྱིངས་ལ་གནས་པ་ནི། རྩོམ་པ་ཐམས་ཅད་དང་བྲལ་ཞིང་འབད་པ་ཐམས་ཅད་རྒྱུན་བཅད་པ་ཡིན་པའི་ཕྱིར་རོ།།

ཞེས་སོ། །དེ་ལྟ་བུའི་འདོད་ཚུལ་རྣམས་མ་ཕྱེད་པར་དབུ་སེམས་ཕྱོགས་གཅིག་ཏུ་བཟུང་ནས་རྣམ་སྨིན་གྱི་རྣམ་ཤེས་ཐེག་དམན་གྱི་ལྷག་མེད་དུ་འགའ་ཞིག་ལྡོག་པར་འདོད། འགའ་[32b]ཞིག་ལྷག་མེད་ནས་ཀྱང་ཐེག་ཆེན་དུ་འཇུག་དགོས་པས་མི་ལྡོག་ཅེས་ངལ་ཞིང་དུབ་པའི་མཐའ་ལ་བརྟེན་[1]པར་བྱེད་དོ།།

འདིར་བསྟན་པ་ལྟར་རྒྱས་པར་ཕུང་པོ་དང་བཅས་པ་དང་། ཕུང་པོ་མེད་པའི་རྣམ་པར་གཏན་ལ་དབབ་པའི་སྒོམ་གྱི་འགྲེལ་པ་དང་། བརྒྱད་སྟོང་འགྲེལ་ཆེན་གྱི་

ཡུལ་ངེས་པ་དང་ཁྱབ་པ་དང་།

ཞེས་པའི་འགྲེལ་པར་སེམས་ཙམ་པའི་འདོད་པ་བཀོད་པ་ལས་ཤེས་པར་བྱའོ།།

སྐབས་འདིར། ཐེག་པ་གསུམ་དུ་གསུངས་པ་དང་། གཅིག་ཏུ་གསུངས་པའི་མདོ་ལ་ངོ་བོ་ཉིད་མེད་པར་སྨྲ་བ་དང་། རྣམ་པར་ཤེས་པ་སྨྲ་བ་གཉིས་དྲང་ངེས་སུ་[1165]འདོད་ཚུལ་དེ་དག་གི་སྒྲུབ་བྱེད་དང་བཅས་ཏེ་གཞུང་ལུགས་ཆེན་པོ་རྣམས་སུ་འབྱུང་བ་རྣམས་སྦྱོར་ནུས་མོད། ཚིག་མང་ན་དབང་པོ་རྟུལ་པོ་རྣམས་མགོ་འཁྱུས་པར་འགྱུར་བས་རེ་ཞིག་བཞག་གོ།

དེ་དག་གིས་རྣམ་སྨིན་དང་ས་བོན་གྱི་ཀུན་གཞིའི་དཀའ་བའི་གནས་ཐམས་ཅད་དཔྱིས་ཕྱིན་པར་བཤད་ཟིན་ཏོ།།

[Chapter Five]

ཉོན་ཡིད་ཀྱི་མཚན་ཉིད་དེ་ཇི་ལྟ་བུ་ཞིག་ཅེ་ན།

> ཉོན་མོངས་ཅན་ཡིད་མཚན་ཉིད་ནི། །ཀུན་གཞི་རྣམ་སྨིན་ཆ་ཉིད་ལ། །བདག་ལྟ་བསྒྲིབས་
> ལ་ལུང་མ་བསྟན། །རེག་དང་ཆགས་སོགས་དགུ་པོ་ན།།

དེ་ལ་དམིགས་པ་ནི་ས་བོན་དང་རྣམ་སྨིན་གྱི་ཆ་གཉིས་ལས་ཕྱི་མ་སྟེ་འདིའི་དམིགས་པ་ལ་བདག་དང་ཆོས་མཚུངས་པ་ཞིག་དགོས་པའི་ཕྱིར་རོ།།

---

[1] *brten* D,M,N,O→*bsten* P.

> རྣམ་པ་ནི་དམིགས་པ་དེ་ལ་བདག་ཏུ་རློམ་སེམས་པའོ། །དེ་ཡང་དོན་གསང་དུ།
> བདག་གི་རྣམ་པར་སྐྱེ་བའི་སྒོ་ནས་ཡིན་གྱི་,རང་གི་ངོ་བོ་འཛིན་པའི་སྒོ་ནས་ནི་མ་ཡིན་ནོ།།

ཞེས་གསུངས་པས་ན་རྣམ་སྨིན་གྱི་རྗེས་དེ་ཉིད་སྣང་ནས་ཉོན་ཡིད་ཀྱི་[33a]ཡུལ་དུ་མི་འགྱུར་ཡང་རྣམ་སྨིན་གྱི་རྣམ་ཤེས་དེའི་མཐུས་རང་ཉིད་ལ་བདག་ཏུ་འཁྲུལ་བ་ཙམ་ལ་ཡུལ་དུ་འཛིན་གོ།

ངོ་བོ་ནི་བསྒྲིབས་ལ་ལུང་དུ་མ་བསྟན་པའོ།།

བསྒྲིབས་པ་དང་མ་བསྒྲིབས་པའི་དོན་གང་ཞེ་ན། བསྒྲིབས་པ་ཞེས་པ་ནི་ཉོན་མོངས་པས་རྙོག་རྙོག་པོར་བྱས་པ་ཡིན་ལ་ཡིད་འདི་ཡང་ཆ་བའི་ཉོན་མོངས་པ་བཞིས་རྙོག་རྙོག་པོར་བྱས་པའི་ཕྱིར་རོ། །མ་བསྒྲིབས་པ་ཞེས་པ་ནི་ཉོན་མོངས་པས་དྲི་མ་ཅན་དུ་མ་བྱས་པ་དབང་པོ་ལྔ་དང་དད་པ་སོགས་བཅུ་གཅིག་ལྟ་བུའོ།།

དོན་འདི་ལ་འགའ་ཞིག །ཉོན་ཡིད་འཕགས་པའི་མཉམ་བཞག་ན་མེད་པ་དང་། ཀུན་གཞི་ཡོད་པ་ལ་བསམས་ནས་མཉམ་བཞག་ལ་བསྒྲིབ་མི་བསྒྲིབ་ཏུ་འདོད་པ་དང་། ཉོན་སྒྲིབ་མ་ལུས་པར་མ་སྤངས་པར་ཐར་པ་མི་ཐོབ་པ་ལ་བསམས་ནས་ཐར་པ་ལ་བསྒྲིབ་མི་བསྒྲིབ་ཏུ་འདོད་པ་ནི་སྒྲིབ་པ་དང་མི་སྒྲིབ་པའི་རང་གི་ངོ་བོ་མ་ཤེས་ཤིང་དེ་གཉིས་ཀྱི་ཀུན་གཞི་[1166]ཉོན་ཡིད་གཉིས་ཁོ་ན་ལ་འཛིན་པས་ན་བསམ་བློ་རྒྱ་ཆུངས་པར་འདུག་སྟེ། འདི་ལྟར། དེ་གཉིས་ཀྱི་དོན་ཆོས་རང་ཉིད་བསྒྲིབས་པའམ་མ་བསྒྲིབས་པ་དཔྱོད་པ་ཡིན་གྱི་, དེས་གཞན་ལ་བསྒྲིབས་མི་བསྒྲིབས་མ་ཡིན་ཏེ། གཞན་དུ་ན་འཕགས་པ་རྣམས་ཀྱི་ཡིད་དགེ་བ་དང་ལུང་དུ་མ་བསྟན་གཡེང་བའི་ཆར་གྱུར་པ་རྣམས་ཀྱང་མཉམ་བཞག་ལ་གེགས་བྱེད་པའི་ཕྱིར་བསྒྲིབས་པར་འགྱུར་བ་དང་། ཡང་སྲིད་འཕེན་ངེས་ཀྱི་ཀུན་འབྱུང་མ་ལུས་པར་མ་སྤངས་པར་ཐར་པ་གསུམ་པོ་གང་ཡང་མི་ཐོབ་པའི་ཕྱིར་བསོད་ནམས་དང་མི་གཡོ་བའི་ལས་སྲིད་པ་འཕེན་ངེས་རྣམས་ཀྱང་བསྒྲིབས་པར་ཐལ་ལོ།།

དེ་དག་[33b]ལས་ཀྱི་ཀུན་ཉོན་ཡིན་པས་བསྒྲིབས་པའོ་ཞེས་ཀྱང་བརྗོད་པར་མི་ནུས་ཏེ། སྒྲིབ་པ་ནི་ཉོན་མོངས་པའམ། དེས་ཀུན་ནས་བསླངས་པའི་ལུས་ངག་གི་མི་དགེ་བ་ལ་གསུངས་པའི་ཕྱིར་དང་། དགེ་བ་དང་ཚེའི་ཀུན་ཉོན་མ་བསྒྲིབས་པ་རྣམས་ཀྱང་བསྒྲིབ་པར་འགྱུར་བའི་ཕྱིར་རོ། །དེ་སྐད་དུའང་། ཀུན་ལས་བཏུས་སུ།

> མི་དགེ་བ་དང་བསྒྲིབས་ལ་ལུང་དུ་མ་བསྟན་པ་ནི་ཉོན་མོངས་པ་ཅན་ནོ། །བསྒྲིབས་ལ་ལུང་དུ་མ་བསྟན་པ་ནི། ཀུན་ཏུ་འགྲོ་བའི་ཡིད་དང་མཚུངས་པར་ལྡན་པའི་ཉོན་མོངས་པ་དང་། ཡིད་ཀྱི་རྣམ་པར་ཤེས་པ་དང་མཚུངས་པར་ལྡན་པའི་ལྷན་ཅིག་སྐྱེས་པའི་འཇིག་ཚོགས་ལ་ལྟ་བ་དང་།[1] མཐར་འཛིན་པར་ལྟ་བ་དང་། གཟུགས་དང་གཟུགས་མེད་པ་དང་མཚུངས་པར་ལྡན་པའོ།།

---

[1] *la lta ba* omit D,M.

ཞེས་དང་།

དགེ་བ་དང་མ་བསྒྲིབས་ལ་ལུང་དུ་མ་བསྟན་པ་ནི་ཉོན་མོངས་པ་ཅན་མ་ཡིན་པའོ།

ཞེས་དང་། ཐེག་ཆེན་བསྡུས་པར་ཡང་།

ཡིད་ནི་ཉོན་མོངས་པ་ཅན་ཡིན་པའི་ཕྱིར་བསྒྲིབས་ལ་ལུང་དུ་མ་བསྟན་པ་སྟེ། སྒྲིབ་པའི་ཉོན་མོངས་པ་རྣམ་པ་བཞི་དང་རྟག་ཏུ་མཚུངས་པར་ལྡན་པའོ། །གཟུགས་དང་གཟུགས་མེད་པ་ན་སྤྱོད་པའི་ཉོན་མོངས་པ་བཞིན་དུ་འདི་ནི་བསྒྲིབས་ལ་ལུང་དུ་མ་བསྟན་པ་ཉིད་དོ།[1] གཟུགས་དང་གཟུགས་མེད་པ་ན་སྤྱོད་པའི་ཡིད་[2] ནི་ཞི་གནས་ཀྱིས་འཁྲུད་པ་ཡིན་ལ། ཡིད་ནི་དུས་[1167]ཐམས་ཅད་དུ་ལྡན་པའི་ཕྱིར་རོ།།

ཞེས་སོ།།

བསྒྲིབས་པའི་དོན་དེ་ལྟར་ཡིན་ན་ལུང་མ་བསྟན་ཁོ་ནར་ངེས་པ་ཅི་ཞེ་ན།

ཉོན་ཡིད་འདི་ཉོན་མོངས་པ་ཅན་ཡིན་པས་དགེ་བ་མིན་ལ། དགེ་བའི་སེམས་དང་རྒྱུད་གཅིག་ལ་དུས་གཅིག་ཏུ་མངོན་གྱུར་དུ་འཇུག་པའི་ཕྱིར་མི་དགེ་བ་མིན་ནོ། །གཞན་དུ་ན་དགེ་བའམ་མི་དགེ་བའི་སེམས་མངོན་གྱུར་སོ་སྐྱེ་ལ་སྐྱེ་མི་སྲིད་པར་འགྱུར་ཏེ། ཡིད་འདི་འཕགས་[34a]ལམ་མ་སྐྱེས་བར་དུ་རྟག་ཏུ་མངོན་གྱུར་དུ་འཇུག་པའི་ཕྱིར་རོ།།

འཁོར་ནི་རེག་པ་ལ་སོགས་པ་ལྔ་དང་། འདོད་ཆགས། མ་རིག་པ། ང་རྒྱལ། བདག་ལྟ་བཞི་སྟེ་དགུ་པོ་ན་འབྱུང་སྟེ། དོན་གསང་དུ།

དེ་ལ་ཉོན་མོངས་པ་བཞི་དང་། སྔར་བསྟན་པའི་ཀུན་ཏུ་འགྲོ་བ་ལྔ་དང་མཚུངས་པར་ལྡན་པའི་ཕྱིར་འདིའི་སེམས་ལས་བྱུང་བ་ནི་དགུ་པོ་ནའོ།།

ཞེས་དང་། སུམ་ཅུ་པ་ལས།

དེ་ལ་གནས་པ་རབ་འབྱུང་ཞིང་། །དེ་ལ་དམིགས་པ་ཡིད་ཅེས་བྱ། །རྣམ་སེམས་ང་ར་སེམས་བདག་ཉིད་ཅན། །བསྒྲིབས་ལ་ལུང་དུ་མ་བསྟན་པའི། །ཉོན་མོངས་བཞི་དང་རྟག་ཏུ་འགྲོགས། །བདག་ཏུ་ལྟ་དང་བདག་ཏུ་རྨོངས། །བདག་རྒྱལ་བདག་ཏུ་ཆགས་པ་སྟེ། །གང་དུ་སྐྱེས་པ་དེའི་འོ་གཞན། །རེག་སོགས་ཀྱང་སྟེ།

ཞེས་འབྱུང་བའི་ཕྱིར་རོ།།

འདིའི་འཁོར་གྱི་ཚོར་བ་དེ་གང་ཞེ་ན། ཚོར་བ་ནི་བཏང་སྙོམས་འབའ་ཞིག་ཡིན་ཏེ། བདེ་བ་ཡིན་ན་

[1] *de* D,M,N. [2] Lamotte emends to *nyon mongs pa* on the basis of Paramārtha's Chinese commentary.

ཡིད་བདེ་ཡིན་དགོས་ལ་དེ་ལྟ་ན་ཡིད་བདེ་མངོན་གྱུར་དུ་རྟག་ཏུ་འབྱུང་བའི་ཕྱིར་སོ་སྐྱེ་ལ་ཡིད་མི་བདེ་གདན་མི་འབྱུང་བར་ཐལ་བ་དང་། བསམ་གཏན་བཞི་པ་ཡན་ཆད་ཀྱང་ཚོར་བ་བདེ་བའི་སར་འགྱུར་བ་དང་། མནར་མེད་པ་ལ་ཡང་ཡིད་བདེ་མངོན་གྱུར་རྟག་ཏུ་འཇུག་པར་འགྱུར་རོ། །མ་ངེས་པ་ཡང་མ་ཡིན་ཏེ། འདིའི་འཁོར་ལ་ཁམས་གསུམ་གར་མང་ཉུང་མི་འབྱུང་སྟེ། བརྟན་པའི་རྣམ་ཤེས་ཡིན་པས་གཙོ་བོ་དང་འཇུག་ལྡོག་གི་དུས་གཅིག་ཡིན་པའི་ཕྱིར་རོ། །སྡུག་བསྔལ་གྱི་ཚོར་བ་ཡང་མི་འབྱུང་བ་རིགས་པ་[1168]དེས་དཔག་པར་བྱའོ།།

དེས་ན་ཉོན་ཡིད་ཀྱི་དགའ་བའི་རྣམ་པ་ནི་ཚོར་བའི་དགའ་རྣམ་མ་ཡིན་གྱི་,[34b]འདོད་ཆགས་ཀྱི་དགའ་རྣམ་ཡིན་ཏེ། སུམ་ཅུ་པ་ལས། ཀུན་གཞིའི་འཁོར་གྱི་རིག་སོགས་ལྔ་པོ་ཉིད་ཡིད་ཀྱི་འཁོར་དུའང་བཤད་ཅིང་ཚོར་བ་ལ་བྱེ་བྲག་ཏུ་མ་བྱས་པའི་ཕྱིར་རོ། །དེ་ལྟར་ཡང་དོན་གསང་ལས།

> དགའ་བའི་རྣམ་པ་ཅན་ཉིད[1] ཡིན་ཀྱང་སེམ[2] པའི་ཚོར་ཅན་ནི་མ་ཡིན་ཏེ།
> གང་དུ་སྐྱེ་པ་དེའི་འོ་གཞན།།
>
> ཞེས་འབྱུང་བའི་ཕྱིར་རིག་པ་ལ་སོགས་པ་ཇི་ལྟར་སྐབས་སུ་བབ་པ་དག་ཁོ་ན་བསྒྲིས་པའི་ཕྱིར་རོ། །འོན་ཏེ་ཚོར་བ་གཞན་ཡང་ཡོད་ན་ནི་ཁྱད་པར་དུ་བྱས་པར་འགྱུར་རོ་

ཞེས་དང་།

> འོ་ན་བདང་སྙོམས་པ་ཡིན་ན་ཇི་ལྟར་དགའ་བའི་རྣམ་པ་ཅན་ཡིན་ཞི་ན། བདག་ལ་ཆགས་པ་དང་བཚུངས་པར་ལྡན་པའི་ཕྱིར་རོ་

ཞེས་སོ།།

ཅིའི་ཕྱིར་འདིའི་འཁོར་དགུར་ངེས། ངའོ་སྙམ་པ་ལ་བདགས་པའི་རྣམ་གཡེང་། འདོད་ཆགས་དང་གཏི་མུག་ལ་བདགས་པའི་བག་མེད། འདོད་ཆགས་ལ་བདགས་པའི་རྒོད་པ། གཏི་མུག་གི་ཆ་ལ་བདགས་པའི་མ་དད་པ། ལེ་ལོ། རྨུགས་པ་སྟེ་དྲུག་འབྱུང་བས་ན་འཁོར་བཅོ་ལྔར་འགྱུར་བ་མ་ཡིན་ནམ་ཞི་ན།

དེ་དག་འབྱུང་བར་བཤད་ཀྱང་དགུར་གྲངས་ངེས་ཏེ། དྲུག་པོ་དེ་དག་གདགས་གཞི་ཉོན་མོངས་པ་བཞི་པོ་དེའི་རྫས་ཡིན་པས་ན་དེ་བཞི་ལས་གུད་ན་མེད་དོ། །རྫས་དགུ་པོ་འདི་ལས་སེམས་བྱུང་གཞན་མི་འབྱུང་བ་ནི། རྒྱས་པར་དོན་གསང་རྣམ་པར་ཕྱེ་བ་བསྟུས་ཏེ་བཤད་པ་ལས་ཤེས་པར་བྱ་སྟེ། འདིར་ནི་ཚིག་མངས་སུ་དོགས་པ་དང་། དཀའ་བའི་གནས་མ་ཡིན་པས་མ་བྲིས་སོ།།

ལྔ་པ་ས་དཔྱད་པ་ནི། ཅི་ཉོན་ཡོད་འདི་གང་གི་རྒྱུད་ལ་ཡོད་པ་རྟེན་དེ་གང་དུ་སྐྱེས་པའི་ས་དེ་ཡིན་ནམ་

---

[1] *nyid* omit D,O,P. [2] *sems* D,O,P.

མ་ཡིན། དང་པོ་ལྟར་ན་འདོད་པའི་སོ་སྐྱེ་ཞིག་གིས་འདོད་པ་ལ་ཆགས་པ་དང་[35a]བྲལ་བ་ན་ཉོན་ཡིད་མི་ལྡོག་པས་འདོད་པའི་ཉོན་མོངས་མངོན་གྱུར་དུ་རྒྱུད་ལ་འཇུག་པར་འགྱུར་རོ། །གཉིས་པ་ལྟར་ན་རྟེན་དེའི་ཀུན་གཞི་ལ་ཉོན་[1169]ཡིད་འཁོར་བཅས་ཀྱིས་བདག་ཏུ་སྲིད་པས་རེས་སུ་བཅད་པས་འདོད་པའི་ཉོན་མོངས་རྣམས་རྒྱས་པར་མི་འགྱུར་རོ་ཞེ་ན།

"གང་དུ་སྐྱེས་པ་དེའི་འོ་" ཞེས་འབྱུང་བ་དང་། ཇི་སྐད་བཤད་པའི་སྐྱོན་དུ་འགྱུར་བའི་ཕྱིར་ཕྱོགས་གཉིས་པ་ཁས་མི་ལེན་ནོ།།

དེ་ལྟ་ན་ཕྱོགས་དང་པོ་ལ་ཡང་སྐྱོན་བརྗོད་པ་མ་ཡིན་ནམ་ཞེ་ན།

ཉེས་པ་མེད་དེ། འདོད་པའི་སོ་སྐྱེ་འདོད་པ་ལ་ཆགས་པ་དང་བྲལ་ཞེས་པ་ནི། གཙོ་བོར་འཁྲིག་པ་ལ་ཆགས་པ་དང་བྲལ་བ་དང་། ཞི་གནས་ཀྱི་ལམ་ཐོབ་པ་ཡིད་མི་བདེའི་གདུང་བ་མེད་པ་དང་། འདོད་ཡོན་ལྔ་ལ་ཆགས་པ་མངོན་གྱུར་པ་རྒྱུད་གདུང་བར་བྱེད་པ་མེད་བས་ན། ཁ་ཕྱིར་བལྟས་ཀྱི[1] ཆགས་སྤང་འགའ་ཞིག་ཙམ་སྤངས་པ་ཡིན་གྱི, ཉོན་ཡིད་འདི་ནི་བདག་ལྟ་ལྷན་སྐྱེས་དང་མཚུངས་ལྡན་ཡིན་པས་འདི་གཉེན་པོའི་མཐུས་ལྡོག་པས[2] ཟག་མེད་ཀྱི་ཤེས་རབ་བསྐྱེད་དགོས་པ་ཡིན་པའི་ཕྱིར་རོ།།

དེ་ལྟ་བུའི་ཡིད་འདི་འཇུག་ལྡོག་གི་དུས་གང་ཞེ་ན།

འགོག་པ་མཉམ་བཞག་གནས་སྐབས་དུས། །དབང་ཐོབ་དགྲ་བཅོམ་མཐར་ཐུག་གོ།

འདི་ལ་གནས་སྐབས་རེས་འགའ་བའི་ལྡོག་དུས་དང་། མཐར་ཐུག་གཏན་ལྡོག་པའི་དུས་གཉིས་སོ། །དང་པོ་ནི། ས་བརྒྱད་པ་ལ་མི་སློབ་བའི་ལམ་མ་ཐོབ་པའི་དུས་ཀྱི་འགོག་པ་ལ་ཞུགས་པའི་ཚེ་དང་། འཕགས་པ་རྣམས་ཀྱི་མཉམ་བཞག་གི་དུས་སོ། །གཉིས་པ་ནི་དབང་ཐོབ་པའི་བྱང་ཆུབ་སེམས་དཔའ་[35b]ས་བརྒྱད་པ་ཡན་ཆད་དང་། ཉན་རང་དགྲ་བཅོམ་པ་རྣམས་སོ། །དེ་ལྟར་ཡང་སུམ་ཅུ་པ་ལས།

> དགྲ་བཅོམ་མེད། །འགོག་པའི་སྙོམས་པར་འཇུག་ན་མེད། །འཇིག་རྟེན་འདས་པའི་ལམ་ན་
> མེད། །འདི་ནི་གྱུར་པ་གཉིས་པའོ།།

ཞེས་དང་། ཀུན་ལས་བཏུས་སུ་ཡང་།

> ཡིད་གང་ཞེ་ན། གང་དུས་རྟག་ཏུ་ཀླམ་སེམས་པའི་བདག་ཉིད་དང་། ཀུན་གཞི་རྣམ་པར་ཤེས་པ་ལ་
> དམིགས་པ་དང་། ཉོན་མོངས་པ་བཞི་པོ་བདག་ཏུ་ལྟ་བ་དང་། བདག་ལ་ཆགས་པ་དང་། ངའོ་སྙམ་
> པའི་ང་རྒྱལ་དང་། མ་རིག་པ་མཚུངས་པར་ལྡན་པ་[1170]སྟེ། དེ་ཡང་ལམ་མངོན་དུ་གྱུར་པ་དང་།
> འགོག་པའི་སྙོམས་པར་ཞུགས་པ་དང་། མ་སློབ་པའི་ས་མ་གཏོགས་པར་དགེ་བ་དང་མི་དགེ་བ་དང་

[1] *ltas kyis* D,O,P. [2] *pa la* D,O,P.

> ལུང་དུ་མ་བསྟན་པ་ཐམས་ཅད་དུ་འགྲོ་བ་དང་། གང་ཡང་རྣམ་པར་ཤེས་པ་དྲུག་པོ་རྣམས་འགགས་
> མ་ཐག་པའི་རྣམ་པར་ཤེས་པའོ་

ཞེས་འབྱུང་བའི་ཕྱིར་རོ།།

དེ་ལྟར་བྱས་ན་ཡིད་ནི་གཉིས་ཏེ། ང་ར་སེམས་པའི་ཡིད་དང་། དེ་མ་ཐག་པའི་ཡིད་དོ། །དེ་གཉིས་ལ་རིམ་པ་ལྟར་དོན་དམ་པའི་ཡིད་དང་། ཀུན་རྫོབ་པའི་ཡིད་ཅེས་ཀྱང་བྱ་སྟེ། རྣམ་ཤེས་གཞན་ལ་མ་ལྟོས་པར་རང་རྒྱུ་ཐུབ་པའི་རྫས་སུ་ཡོད་པ་དང་། ཚོགས་དྲུག་ལས་གུད་ན་གཞག་ཏུ་མེད་པའི་ཕྱིར་རོ། །དེ་ལ་དང་པོས་ནི་ཚོགས་དྲུག་མཚན་མ་ལ་འཆིང་བའི་གནས་བྱས་ནས་ཀུན་ནས་ཉོན་མོངས་པ་ཟག་པ་དང་བཅས་པར་བྱེད་ལ། གཉིས་པ་ནི་ཚོགས་དྲུག་གི་དེ་མ་ཐག་རྐྱེན་བྱས་ནས་རང་འགགས་སྟོབས་ཀྱིས་རྣམ་ཤེས་ཀྱི་ཕྱི་མ་སྐྱེ་བའི་གོ་འབྱེད་པ་ཡིན་ཏེ། ཇི་སྐད་དུ།

> དེ་ལ་ཡིད་ནི་རྣམ་པ་གཉིས་ཏེ་དེ་མ་ཐག་པའི་རྐྱེན་བྱེད་པས་གནས་སུ་གྱུར་པའི་ [36a]ཕྱིར་རྣམ་པར་ཤེས་
> པ་འགགས་མ་ཐག་པའི་ཡིད་ཅེས་བྱ་བ་རྣམ་པར་ཤེས་པ་སྐྱེ་བའི་གནས་དང་། གཉིས་པ་ཉོན་མོངས་
> པ་ཅན་གྱི་ཡིད་ཉོན་མོངས་པ་བཞི་པོ་འཇིག་ཚོགས་ལ་ལྟ་བ་དང་། ངའོ་སྙམ་པའི་ང་རྒྱལ་དང་། བདག་
> ལ་ཆགས་པ་དང་། མ་རིག་པ་དང་རྟག་ཏུ་མཚུངས་པར་ལྡན་པ་སྟེ་དེ་ནི་རྣམ་པར་ཤེས་པ་ཀུན་ནས་
> ཉོན་མོངས་པའི་གནས་སོ། །རྣམ་པར་ཤེས་པ་ནི་གང་གནས་གཅིག་པོས་ནི་བསྐྱེད་ལ། གཉིས་པས་ནི་
> ཉོན་མོངས་པ་ཅན་དུ་བྱས་པ་སྟེ། ཡུལ་ལ་རྣམ་པར་རིག་པའི་ཕྱིར་རྣམ་པར་ཤེས་པའོ། །དེ་མ་ཐག་
> པ་དང་ང་ར་སེམས་པའི་ཕྱིར་ཡིད་ནི་རྣམ་པ་གཉིས་སོ་

ཞེས་སོ།།

གལ་ཏེ་དབང་ཐོབ་པའི་སེམས་པ་དང་། དགྲ་བཅོམ་པ་དང་། འཕགས་པའི་མཉམ་གཞག་ན་ཉོན་ཡིད་མེད་ན། དེ་དག་ན་ཡིད་ཤེས་ཀྱང་མེད་པར་འགྱུར་ཏེ་ཡིད་ཤེས་ཀྱི་བདག་རྐྱེན་ཉོན་ཡིད་མེད་པའི་ཕྱིར་རོ། །ཡང་ [1171] དབང་ཐོབ་པ་དང་། དགྲ་བཅོམ་པས་མཉམ་ཉིད་ཡེ་ཤེས་ཐོབ་པར་འགྱུར་ཏེ། ཇི་སྐད་དུ།

> ཉོན་མོངས་ཅན་ཡིད་གནས་གྱུར་པས། །མཉམ་ཉིད་ཡེ་ཤེས་བརྗོད་པར་བྱ།།

ཞེས་པ་ལྟར་ཉོན་ཡིད་ལྡོག་པའི་ཕྱིར་ཞེ་ན།

> ཉོན་མོངས་ཅན་དུ་འཇོག་བྱེད་པའི། །གང་ཟག་འཛིན་པ་ལོག་གྱུར་ཀྱང་། །དེའི་རིགས་
> ཅམ་ཡོད་ཕྱིར་དང་།[1] ། ཆོས་འཛིན་སྐྱེད་ནུས་མ་ལོག་ཕྱིར། །ཡིད་ཤེས་མེད་དང་མཉམ་
> པ་ཉིད། །ཐོབ་པའི་སྐྱོན་གཉིས་རིང་དུ་སྤངས།།

[1] For a brief discussion of alternate readings see note to translation.

འདིའི་ལན་ལ། མཉམ་གཞག་ན་ཡིད་ཡོད་མེད་དང་། ཡིད་དེ་ཟག་པ་དང་བཅས་མ་བཅས་དཔྱད་པའོ།།

དང་པོ་ནི། མཉམ་[36b]གཞག་གི་ཚེ་ཡང་། ཡིད་ཀྱི་རྗེས་རྒྱུན་ཆད་པའི་ལོག་པ་ནི་མེད་དེ། དགོངས་འགྲེལ་ལས། ཀུན་གཞི་དེ་ཉུང་ཡང་རྣམ་ཤེས་གཅིག་ཡིད་དང་ལྷན་ཅིག་འཇུག་པར་བསྟན་པའི་ཕྱིར་དང་། མཉམ་གཞག་གི་ཚེ། དམིགས་པ་ཀུན་གཞི་ཉེ་ཞིང་། རྒྱུའི་རྐྱེན་ཡང་ཀུན་གཞི་ལས་འབྱུང་ལ་ཚོགས་དྲུག་ལྟར་རེས་གཟུགས་ལ་ལྟའོ་རེས་སྒྲ་མཉན་ནོ་སྙམ་པ་ལྟ་བུའི་མྱོང་བ་རིགས་མི་མཐུན་མེད་པ་འཁོར་བ་ཇི་སྲིད་པ་རིགས་གཅིག་ཏུ་འཇུག་པའི་ཕྱིར་རོ། །འདི་ལྟར་ཡང་དོན་གསང་དུ།

> འཇིག་རྟེན་ལས་འདས་པའི་སྙོམས་པར་འཇུག་པ་སློབ་པའི་གནས་སྐབས་ཀྱི་ཡིད་ཀྱི་རྣམ་པར་ཤེས་པས་མ་ངེས་པ་ཡང་མ་ཡིན་ཏེ། དེའི་ཚེ་ཡང་ཡིད་གྱུར་པ་གནས་པའི་ཕྱིར་རོ། །དགོངས་པ་ངེས་པར་འགྲེལ་བའི་མདོ་ལས།
>
> > རེས་འགའ་ནི་གཅིག་དང་སྐྱེ་གང་གི་ཚེ་ཡིད་དང་
>
> ཞེས་འབྱུང་བའོ།།
>
> > རེས་འགའ་ནི་གཉིས་དང་སྐྱེ་ཡིད་དང་[1] ཡིད་ཀྱི་རྣམ་པར་ཤེས་པ་དང་
>
> ཞེས་འབྱུང་བའི་ཕྱིར་རོ། །གལ་ཏེ་ཡང་དེའི་ཚེ་གྱུར་པ་ཡང་ཡིད་མ་ཡིན་པ་ཞིག་ཏུ་གྱུར་ན་ནི། འདི་[2] ཡང་ཡིད་མ་ཡིན་པར་འགྱུར་ལ་འདི་སྐད་དུ
>
> > རེས་འགའ་ནི་གཅིག་དང་སྐྱེ་གང་གི་ཚེ་ཡིད་ཀྱི་རྣམ་པར་ཤེས་པ་དང་
>
> ཞེས་ཀྱང་བཤད་པར་འགྱུར་རོ། །གཞན་ཡང་
>
> > བརྒྱལ་བ་ལ་སོགས་པ་ལ་འཇུག་པའི་རྣམ་པར་ཤེས་པའི་ཚོགས་ཡུལ་ལ་རག་ལས་ཏེ་སྐྱེ་བ་རྣམས་དེ་མི་ཉེ་[1172]བའི་ཕྱིར་རྒྱུན་ཆད་དོ་
>
> ཞེས་བྱ་བ་ནི། རིགས་ནི་[3] ཡིད་འཁོར་བ་ཇི་སྲིད་བར་རིགས་གཅིག་པ་དང་།[4] དམིགས་པ་[5] ཉེ་བ་ཀུན་གཞི་རྣམ་པར་ཤེས་པ་ལས་འབྱུང་བ་གོ་ཇི་ལྟར་རྒྱུན་ཆད།

ཅེས་སོ།།

གཉིས་པ་ཡིད་དེ་ཟག་བཅས་ཟག་མེད་དཔྱད་པ་ལ་རྣལ་འབྱོར་སྤྱོད་པའི་སློབ་དཔོན་གཉིས་ཀྱི་ལུགས་ [37a] ལས། ལུགས་དང་པོ་ནི་མཉམ་གཞག་གི་ཚེའི་ཡིད་དེ། དེ་ཟག་མེད་ཡིན་ཏེ། ཉོན་མོངས་པ་དང་ཟག་མེད་ཀྱི་ཤེས་པ་རྒྱུད་གཅིག་ལ་དུས་གཅིག་ཏུ་འཇུག་པ་མི་སྲིད་ལ། ཡིད་རྒྱུན་ཆད་པ་ཡང་མིན་ཞིང་། འཇིག་ལྟ་སོགས་བཞི་དེའི་ཚེ་ས་བོན་ཙམ་གྱི་ངོ་བོར་གནས་པའི་ཕྱིར་རོ། །དེ་ཡང་། བདག་མེད་པ་མངོན་སུམ་དུ

---

[1] *yid dang* omit D,O,P. [2] *'di la* D,O,P. [3] *rigs ni* omit D,O,P. [4] *dang/* omit D,O,P. [5] *par* O,P.

མཐོང་བའི་ཡིད་ཤེས་མཉམ་གཞག་གི་ཚེ་ཟག་མེད་དུ་འགྱུར་བ་ཀུན་གཞི་ལ་རང་གི་ཟག་མེད་ཀྱི་ས་བོན་གནས་པ་ལས་གྱུར་པ་བཞིན་དུ། དེའི་ཚེ་ཡིད་ཀྱང་ཟག་མེད་ཀྱི་ས་བོན་ཆོས་ཉིད་ཀྱིས་གནས་པ་ལས་ཀུན་གཞི་དང་ལྷན་ཅིག་ཏུ་ཟག་མེད་དུ་འཇུག་གོ །དེ་ལས་ལངས་ནས། ཟག་བཅས་ཀྱི་སེམས་པ་དགེ་བ་ལྟ་བུ་མངོན་གྱུར་པ་ན་ཉོན་མོངས་བཞིའི་ས་བོན་ལས་ཕྲ་ཉེན་བཞི་མངོན་དུ་གྱུར་ནས་ཡིད་དེ་ཉོན་མོངས་པ་ཅན་དུ་བྱེད་དོ། །དེ་ལྟར་ཡང་། དོན་གསང་ལས།

> ཡིད་དེ་ཡང་ཁ་ཅིག་ན་རེ། གནས་སྐབས་དེ་ན་ཟག་པ་མེད་པ་ཡིན་ཏེ། འདི་ལྟར་ཉོན་མོངས་པ་ཅན་གང་ཡིན་པ་དེ་ནི་འཕགས་པའི་ལམ་ལ་སྙོམས་པར་འཇུག་པས་རྒྱུན་ཀུན་ཏུ་མི་འབྱུང་བས་[1] ས་བོན་གྱི་གནས་སྐབས་པར་འཇོག་གོ་ཞེས་ཟེར་རོ། །ཟག་པ་མེད་པ་ནི་ཐོག་མ་མེད་པའི་རང་གི་རིགས་ལ་བདག་མེད་པ་མངོན་སུམ་དུ་བྱས་པའི་འཕགས་པའི་ལམ་བཞིན་དུ། ཀུན་གཞི་རྣམ་པར་ཤེས་པ་དང་འབྱུང

ཞེས་སོ། །དེ་ལྟར་ན་འདིའི་ལུགས་ཀྱིས་ཀྱང་མཉམ་གཞག་ན་ཉོན་མོངས་པ་བཞི་མངོན་གྱུར་དུ་མེད་པས་དེས་དྲི་མ་ཅན་དུ་བཏགས་པའི་ཉོན་ཡིད་མེད་ཀྱང་། ཡིད་དེ་བཞི་དང་བྲལ་བའི་ཟག་མེད་དུ་གྱུར་པ་འདོད་པས་ན་བདག་རྒྱུན་ཡོད་པར་འདོད་དོ།།

ལུགས་གཉིས་པ་ནི། མཉམ་གཞག་ན་ཡིད་ནི་[1173]ཡོད་ལ། དེ་ཡང་ཟག་བཅས་[37b]སུ་ཡོད་པར་འདོད་དེ། འོ་ན་ཉོན་མོངས་པའི་ཟག་པ་ཡོད་དམ་ཞེ་ན་མེད་དོ། །གཞན་དུ་ན་ཇི་ལྟར་ཟག་པ་དང་བཅས་ཤེ་ན། བདུན་ཡིད་འདི་ལ་ཀུན་གཞི་ལར་[2] བདག་ཏུ་བལྟས་ནས་ཉོན་མོངས་བསྐྱེད་པའི་ནུས་པ་གཅིག་དང་། ཐ་སྙད་སྣ་ཚོགས་འདོགས་པའི་ཡིད་ཤེས་ཀྱི་ལྷན་ཅིག་སྐྱེ་བའི་རྟེན་བྱས་ནས་ཆོས་སུ་འཛིན་པ། ཤེས་སྒྲིབ་བསྐྱེད་པའི་ནུས་པ་གཅིག་དང་གཉིས་ཡོད་ལ་དེ་ལ

དང་པོ་ནི། ཡིད་ཉོན་མོངས་ཅན་དུ་འཇོག་བྱེད་ཡིན་ཅིང་། དེ་ཡང་ཇི་སྲིད་ཉོན་མོངས་མ་ལུས་པར་མ་སྤངས་པ་དེ་སྲིད་དུ་འཇུག་ལ་མ་རིག་པ་དང་ལྟ་བ་ལོག་པ་ན་ལྡོག་པའི་ཕྱིར་བརྒྱད་པ་ཡན་དང་། དགྲ་བཅོམ་པ་རྣམས་ཀྱིས་ཕྲ་བ་དང་ཉེ་བའི་ཉོན་མོངས་པ་མ་ལུས་པར་སྤངས་པས་ན་གང་ཟག་ཏུ་འཛིན་པ་སྐྱེད་པའི་ནུས་པ་ལོག །དེ་ལོག་པས་དེས་ཉོན་མོངས་ཅན་དུ་གཞག་པ་ཡང་མེད་པས་ཉོན་ཡིད་ལོག་གོ །འོན་ཀྱང་ཡིད་དེ་ཆོས་སུ་འཛིན་པ་བསྐྱེད་པའི་ནུས་པ་མ་ལོག་པ་དང་། ཡིད་དེའི་གསལ་རིག་གི་རྫས་ཙམ་ནི་རྒྱུན་ཆད་པ་མེད་དེ་དེའི་ཕྱིར་ཡིད་ཤེས་ཀྱི་བདག་རྒྱུན་མེད་པས་ཡིད་ཤེས་མེད་པའི་སྐྱོན་ཡང་མེད་ཅིང་མཉམ་པ་ཉིད་ཀྱི་ཡེ་ཤེས་དྲི་མ་མཐའ་དག་དང་བྲལ་བ་ལས་ཐོབ་པའི་ཕྱིར་ཆོས་སུ་འཛིན་པ་མ་བཅོམ་པར་ཡེ་ཤེས་དེ་ཐོབ་པར་ཡང་མི་འགྱུར་རོ།།

---

[1] *pa'i* D,O,P. [2] *la nga→lar* O,P.

འདི་ཉིད་ནི་རིགས་ཏེ། རྣམ་ཤེས་རྒྱུན་སོ་སོར་ངེས་པ་ཆང་བ་ལས་སྐྱེ་བར་ནི་འདོད་པའི་ཕྱིར་དང་། བདུན་ཡིད་ནི་ཉོན་མོངས་པ་བཞིའི་གཞན་སྟོབས་ཀྱིས་ཉོན་མོངས་ཅན་དུ་གྱུར་པ་ཡིན་ལ། རང་གི་ངོ་བོ་ཉིད་ཀྱིས་ནི་མ་ཡིན་པས་འཁོར་ཉོན་མོངས་ཅན་དེ་དག་ཉོན་སྒྲིབ་སྤངས་པ་ན་ལྡོག་པ་རིགས་ལ,ཡིད་རང་གི་ངོ་བོ་ཡི་མེད་དུ་ལྡོག་པ་མི་རིགས་པའི་ཕྱིར་ཏེ། གནས་[38a]གྱུར་གྱི་དོན་གློ་བུར་གྱི་ཉེས་པ་རྣམས་ལམ་གྱི་མཐུས་ཟད་པར་བྱས་ནས་རང་གི་རང་བཞིན་གསལ་བར་འགྱུར་བར་འདོད་པའི་ཕྱིར་རོ། །དེ་སྐད་དུ་དོན་གསང་ལས།

ཁ་ཅིག་ན་རེ་ཟག་པ་དང་བཅས་པ་སྟེ། འདི་ལྟར་ནུས་པ་[1174]གཉིས་དང་ལྡན་པའི་ཕྱིར་རོ་ཞེས་ཟེར་རོ་

ཞེས་སོ།།

ཡང་ལུགས་ཕྱི་མ་འདི་ལ་ཞིབ་ཏུ་དཔྱད་པ་འདི་ཡོད་དེ། འདས་ལམ་མ་སྐྱེས་གོང་དུ་དུས་གཅིག་ཏུ་གང་ཟག་དང་ཆོས་སུ་འཛིན་པ་འབྱུང་ལ་འདས་ལམ་སྐྱེས་ན་ནི། ཉན་ཐོས་འཕགས་པ་ཞིག་ཡིན་ན་མཉམ་གཞག་གི་ཚེ་ཡིད་དེ་གང་ཟག་ཏུ་སྒྲོ་འདོགས་པ་མེད་པ་དང་། གང་ཟག་གི་བདག་མེད་ཀྱི་དོན་ལ་གསལ་བར་འཇུག་ལ། ཆོས་རྣམས་ལ་སྒྲོ་འདོགས་དང་མ་བྲལ་ཞིང་མི་གསལ་བར་འཇུག་གོ །དེ་ཡང་མ་རིག་པ་ལྟ་བ་ང་རྒྱལ་དང་འདོད་ཆགས་ཉོན་མོངས་པ་ཅན་མ་ཡིན་པ་བཞི་དང་མཚུངས་པར་ལྡན་ལ་དེ་དག་ཀྱང་ཉོན་མོངས་ཅན་མ་ཡིན་པས་ཉན་ཐོས་ཀྱི་འབྲས་བུ་ཐོབ་པ་ལ་གེགས་མི་བྱེད་ཅིང་དགེ་བ་ཡང་མིན་ནོ།།

གལ་ཏེ་བྱང་སེམས་འཕགས་པ་ཞིག་ཡིན་ན་མཉམ་གཞག་གི་ཚེ་བདག་མེད་པ་གཉིས་ཀ་མངོན་སུམ་དུ་མཐོང་བས་བདག་མེད་བ་གཉིས་མཐོང་བ་ལ་གེགས་བྱེད་པའི་གང་ཟག་ཏུ་འཛིན་པ་དང་ཆོས་སུ་འཛིན་པ་གཉིས་ཆར་མངོན་དུ་མི་འགྱུར་བས་ཟག་པ་མེད་པ་ཡིན་ནོ། །དེ་ལྟར་ཡང་དོན་གསང་ལས།

ཅིག་ཅར་བདག་མེད་པ་གཉིས་ཀ་མཐོང་བའི་གེགས་[1] སུ་གྱུར་པའི་མ་རིག་པ་གང་ཡིན་པ་དེ་ལ་བརྟེན་ནས་ཐག་པའི་སྲིད་ཀྱི་དབྱིབས་ལ་རྟོག་པ་སྔོན་དུ་འགྲོ་བ་ཅན་གྱི་སྦྲུལ་དུ་རབ་ཏུ་རྟོག་པ་བཞིན་དུ། ཉོན་མོངས་པ་ཅན་གྱི་ཡིད་དང་མཚུངས་པར་ལྡན་པའི་ལྟ་བ་ཅིག་[38b]ཅར་ཆོས་དང་གང་ཟག་ཏུ་རབ་ཏུ་རྟོག་པར་བྱེད་པ་འབྱུང་ངོ་། །འཇིག་རྟེན་ལས་འདས་པའི་ལམ་སྐྱེས་ན་ནི། འཕགས་པ་ཉན་ཐོས་གང་ཟག་ལ་བདག་མེད་པ་མཐོང་བའི་ཕྱིར་གང་ཟག་ཏུ་སྒྲོ་འདོགས་པ་མེད་བར་ཡིད་དེ་ཆོས་རྣམས་ལ་མི་གསལ་བ་དང་། སྒྲོ་འདོགས་པའི་ངོ་བོ་ཉིད་གཏི་མུག་དང་ལྟ་བ་དང་མཚུངས་པར་ལྡན་པར་འབྱུང་ངོ་། །ཉོན་མོངས་པ་ཅན་མ་ཡིན་པ་དེ་ཡང་ཉན་ཐོས་ཀྱི་འབྲས་བུ་ལ་གེགས་མི་བྱེད་པའི་ཕྱིར་དང་། འདོད་པའི་འབྲས་བུའི་རྒྱུ་ཡིན་པའི་ཕྱིར་དང་། མྱ་ངན་ལས་འདས་པ་ཐོབ་པར་བྱེད་པ་ཡིན་པའི་ཕྱིར་ཏེ།[1175]

---

[1] *gnas su gyur*D,O,P.

དོན་དམ་པ་མ་ཡིན་པའི་ཕྱིར་[1] དགེ་བ་ནི་མ་ཡིན་ནོ་

ཞེས་དང་།

ཆོས་ཉོན་མོངས་པ་ཅན་མ་ཡིན་པ་ལ་ཆགས་པ་དང་ང་རྒྱལ་དག་དང་ཡང་མཚུངས་པར་ལྡན་ནོ་

ཞེས་དང་།

བྱང་ཆུབ་སེམས་དཔའ་བྱང་ཆུབ་ཏུ་ཡོངས་སུ་བསྔོ་བའམ་ངེས་པའི་རིགས་ཅན་ཞིག་ཡིན་པར་གྱུར་ན་ནི་གནས་སྐབས་དེ་ན་[2] བདག་མེད་པ་གཉིས་མངོན་སུམ་པའི་ཟག་པ་མེད་པ་ཁོ་ན་འབྱུང་ངོ་།།

ཞེས་སོ།།

འོ་ན་སངས་རྒྱས་ཀྱི་ས་ལ་ཡིད་ཤེས་ཀྱི་བདག་རྐྱེན་ཇི་ལྟ་བུ་ཞེ་ན། དོན་གསང་དུ།

མི་ལོང་ལྟ་བུའི་ཡེ་ཤེས་ལ་བག་ཆགས་སྣོད་དམ་མི་སྣོད། སྣོད་ན་སངས་རྒྱས་སྔ་མ་རྣམས་བག་ཆགས་བསྒོ་ཡུན་རིང་བས་དེ་དག་མཐུ་ཆེ་ལ་སངས་རྒྱས་ཕྱི་མ་རྣམས་ཡུན་ཐུང་བས་མཐུ་ཆུང་བར་འགྱུར་བ་དང་། བག་ཆགས་བསྒོ་གཞི་ལུང་མ་བསྟན་ཁོ་ནར་མ་ངེས་པར་འགྱུར་རོ། །མི་སྣོད་ན་སྟོབས་དང་མི་འཇིགས་པ་སོགས་ཀྱི་ཡོན་ཏན་དཔག་ཏུ་མེད་པ་འབྱུང་བ་རྣམས་རྒྱུ་མེད་དུ་འགྱུར་

ཞེས་པའི་ལན་ལ།

རྡོ་རྗེ་ལྟ་བུའི་ཏིང་ངེ་འཛིན་གྱི་ཚེ་ཟག་མེད་ཀྱི་ས་བོན་ཐམས་ཅད་ཅིག་ཅར་ནུས་པ་མཐར་ཐུག་ཏུ་རྒྱས་པས་ན་བག་ཆགས་གསར་པ་ལ་མ་ལྟོས་པར་རྒྱུན་ཆགས་སུ་འབྱུང་

ཞེས་པ་ལྟར་རྒྱུན་མཐའི་རྗེས་སུ་ཡིད་[39a]ཤེས་ཟག་མེད་སྐྱེས་པ་དེ་ཉིད་ནུས་པ་མཐར་ཐུག་པའི་ངོ་བོ་ཉིད་དུ་སོན་པས་རྒྱུན་ཆགས་སུ་འཇུག་པར་ཐལ་ལོ་ཞེས་པའམ། ཡང་ན་རྣམ་ཤེས་གང་གནས་གྱུར་པའི་ཡེ་ཤེས་དེ་དག་ཕན་ཚུན་རྐྱེན་དང་རྐྱེན་ཅན་དུ་འགྱུར་པར་ཤེས་པར་བྱའོ།།

གོང་གི་ཚུལ་དེ་ལྟར་བྱས་ནས་དགུ་པར་ཡང་ཡིད་ཤེས་གནས་གྱུར་པར་གསུངས་པ་ཡང་སོ་སོ་ཡང་དག་པར་རིག་པ་བཞི་ཐོབ་ཡེ་ཤེས་ལ་དབང་བར་འགྱུར་པའི་ཕྱིར་དང་། སྒོམ་སྤངས་ཆུང་ངུའི་ཆུང་ངུ་ཙམ་ལུས་པའི་ཕྱིར་རགས་པ་ཙམ་ལ་དགོངས་ཀྱི ,ཡིད་ཤེས་མ་ལུས་པར་གནས་ན་སྤྲོས་པའི་བག་ཆགས་མ་ལུས་པར་སྤངས་ཕྱུང་བའི་ཕྱིར་མིང་དང་མཚན་མའི་རྣམ་པར་འབྱུང་བའི་ཤེས་པ་མེད་པའི་ཕྱིར་ཤེས་སྒྲིབ་མ་ལུས་པར་སྤངས་པར་འགྱུར་རོ།།

དེས་ན་ས་བརྒྱད་པ་ནས་མི་རྟོག་ཡེ་[1176]ཤེས་རྒྱུན་མི་འཆད་དུ་འབྱུང་བ་དང་། འབད་རྩོལ་ཞི་བའི་འཕྲིན་ལས་ལྷུན་གྲུབ་འབྱུང་བར་བཤད་པ་ནི་བདག་གིས་མཉམ་པར་བཞག་པའོ། །བདག་གིས་སེམས་ཅན་

---

[1] *te/ don dam pa ma yin pa'i phyir* omit D,O,P. [2] *don* O,P.

གྱི་དོན་བསྒྲུབ་པོ་སྐམ་པའི་གང་ཟག་ཏུ་ཞེན་པའི་རྟོག་པའི་འབད་རྩོལ་ཞི་བ་ལ་དགོངས་པ་ཡིན་གྱི་,ཤེས་སྒྲིབ་ཐ་སྙད་སྣ་ཚོགས་འདོགས་པའི་ཡིད་ཀྱི་འགྱུ་བ་མེད་པ་མ་ཡིན་ནོ། །དེ་ལྟར་བྱས་ན་དབང་ཐོབ་པ་དང་དགྲ་བཅོམ་པ་ལ་ཡིད་ཀྱི་གསལ་རིག་གི་རྗེས་དེ་ཡོད་ཀྱང་ཉོན་ཡིད་དུ་མི་བརྗོད་པ་དང་། རྣམ་སྨིན་གྱི་རྣམ་ཤེས་ཡོད་ཀྱང་ཀུན་གཞི་ཞེས་མི་བརྗོད་པ་ནི་དེ་དག་གི་དོན་མ་ཚང་བའི་ཕྱིར་རོ།།

འདི་དག་ལ་བརྗོད་པར་བྱ་བ་མང་དུ་ཡོད་མོད་ཀྱི་སྤྲོས་པས་ཆོག་གོ།

དེ་དག་གིས་ཉོན་ཡིད་ཀྱི་མཚན་ཉིད་གཏན་ལ་དབབ་པ་བཤད་ཟིན་ཏོ། །ཡིད་དང་ཀུན་གཞིའི་དཀའ་བའི་གནས་རྒྱ་ཆེར་འགྲེལ་པ་ལེགས་[39b]པར་བཤད་པའི་རྒྱ་མཚོ་ཞེས་བྱ་བ་ལས་མཚན་ཉིད་གཏན་ལ་དབབ་པ་སྟེ་ལེའུ་དང་པོའོ།།

[Chapter Six]

གཉིས་པ་ཡིད་དང་ཀུན་གཞིའི་སྒྲུབ་པར་བྱེད་པ་སྟོན་པ་ནི།

གལ་ཏེ་རྣམ་ཤེས་དྲུག་ལས་ཐ་དད་པའི་[1] ཀུན་གཞི་དང་ཡིད་ཁས་ལེན་ན། དེ་དག་ཡོད་པར་གང་གིས་ཤེས་ཤེ་ན།།

ཡིད་ཆེས་ལུང་དང་རིགས་པ་ཡིས། །རྣམ་ཤེས་དྲུག་ལས་ཐ་དད་པའི། །ཡིད་དང་ཀུན་
གཞི་རྣམ་པར་ཤེས། །ཡོད་པར་ཁོང་དུ་ཆུད་པར་བྱ།།

འདི་ལ་ལུང་དང་རིགས་པའི་སྒྲུབ་བྱེད་གཉིས་སོ། །དང་པོ་ལ་འང་ཀུན་གཞི་དང་། ཉོན་ཡིད་ཀྱི་ལུང་གཉིས་ལས། དང་པོ་ནི། ཆོས་མངོན་པ་ཐེག་པ་ཆེན་པོའི་མདོ་ལས།

ཐོག་མ་མེད་པའི་དུས་ཀྱི་དབྱིངས། །ཆོས་རྣམས་ཀུན་གྱི་གནས་ཡིན་ཏེ། །དེ་ཡོད་པས་ན་
འགྲོ་ཀུན་དང་། །མྱ་ངན་འདས་པའང་ཐོབ་པར་འགྱུར།།

ཞེས་དང་།

ཆོས་ཀུན་ས་བོན་ཐམས་ཅད་པའི། །རྣམ་པར་ཤེས་པ་ཀུན་གཞི་སྟེ། །དེ་བས་ཀུན་གཞི་
རྣམ་ཤེས་ཏེ། །དམ་པ་དག་ལ་ངས་བཤད་དོ།།

ཅེས་དང་། དགོངས་འགྲེལ་ལས་ཀྱང་།

ལེན་པའི་རྣམ་པར་ཤེས་པ་[1177]ཟབ་ཅིང་ཕྲ། །ས་བོན་ཐམས་ཅད་ཆུ་བོའི་རྒྱུན་བཞིན་འབབ།
།བདག་ཏུ་རྟོག་པར་འགྱུར་ན་མི་རུང་ཞེས། །འདི་ནི་བྱིས་པ་རྣམས་ལ་ངས་མ་བསྟན།།

ཞེས་དང་། འཕགས་པ་ལང་ཀར་གཤེགས་པ་ལས་ཀྱང་།

[1] *na*/D,O,P.

སེམས་ནི་ཀུན་གཞི་རྣམ་ཤེས་ཏེ། །ང་ར་སེམས་པ་ནི་ཡིད་ཡིན་ནོ། །ཡུལ་ལ་རྣམ་པར་
རིག་པ་གང་། །དེ་ནི་འཇུག་པའི་རྣམ་ཤེས་འདོད།།

ཅེས་སོགས་མཐའ་ཡས་པ་ཐེག་པ་ཆེན་པོའི་མདོ་སྡེ་རྣམས་ལས་འབྱུང་ངོ་།།

གཉིས་པ་ཉོན་ཡིད་ཀྱི་ལུང་ནི། དགོངས་འགྲེལ་ལས།

རེས་འགའ་ནི་ཀུན་གཞི་རྣམ་པར་ཤེས་པ་འདི་རྣམ་པར་ཤེས་པ་[40a]གཅིག་དང་ལྷན་ཅིག་འཇུག་སྟེ་ཡིད་དང་། རེས་འགའ་ནི་གཉིས་དང་སྟེ་ཡིད་དང་ཡིད་ཀྱི་རྣམ་པར་ཤེས་པ་དང་ངོ་། །རེས་འགའ་ནི་འཇུག་པའི་རྣམ་པར་ཤེས་པ་བདུན་ག་དང་ལྷན་ཅིག་འཇུག་སྟེ་

ཞེས་དང་། གསེར་འོད་དམ་པ་བམ་པོ་བཅུ་པ་ལས།

ཀུན་གཞི་ལ་གནས་པའི་ཡིད་སྦྱངས་པས་ནི་ལོངས་སྤྱོད་རྫོགས་པའི་སྐུ་ཐོབ་བོ་

ཞེས་དང་། གཞན་ཡང་རྒྱན་སྟུག་ལང་གཤེགས་སོགས་སུ་རྣམ་ཤེས་བརྒྱད་དུ་གསུངས་པ་རྣམས་འདིའི་སྒྲུབ་བྱེད་དོ།།

གཉིས་པ་རིགས་པ་ལ་ཀུན་གཞིའི་རིགས་པ་དང་། ཉོན་ཡིད་ཀྱི་རིགས་པ་གཉིས་ལས། དང་པོ་ནི།

རྣལ་འབྱོར་སྤྱོད་པའི་གཞུང་ལུགས་ནས། །སྒྲུབ་བྱེད་རིགས་པ་མཐའ་ཡས་པ། །གསུངས་
ཀྱང་ལེན་དང་དང་པོ་གསལ། །ས་བོན་ལས་དང་ལུས་ཚོར་དང་། །སྙོམས་འཇུག་འཆི་
འཕོ་མི་རུང་བ། །བརྒྱད་དུ་འདུས་ཕྱིར་འདི་བཤད་བྱ།།

ཐེག་བསྡུས་སུ་ཉོན་མོངས་པའི་དང་། ལུས་ཀྱི་དང་། སྐྱེ་བའི་ཀུན་ནས་ཉོན་མོངས་པ་མི་རུང་བ་གསུམ་དང་། འཇིག་རྟེན་པ་དང་འཇིག་རྟེན་ལས་འདས་པའི་རྣམ་བྱང་མི་རུང་བ་གཉིས་ཏེ་ལྔ་དང་[1] འཕྲོས་པ་དང་བཅས་པ་རྒྱ་ཆེན་པོ་དང་། ཕུང་པོ་ལྔའི་རབ་ཏུ་བྱེད་པར་རིགས་པ་བཞི་དང་། སའི་སྟོད་འགྲེལ་དུ་ལུང་གི་སྒྲུབ་བྱེད་བཅུ་བདུན་དང་། རིགས་པའི་སྒྲུབ་བྱེད་དང་། རྟེན་འབྲེལ་མདོ་འགྲེལ་དུ། [1178] ཐེག་བསྡུས་ཀྱི་རིགས་པ་འགའ་ཞིག་དང་། ཀུན་ལས་བཏུས་བཀོད་ནས་བསྒྲུབ་པ་ནི་རྣམ་པར་ངེས་པ་བསྡུ་བར།

ལེན་དང་དང་པོ་གསལ་བ་དང་། །ས་བོན་ལས་དང་ལུས་ཚོར་དང་། །སེམས་མེད་སྙོམས་པར་
འཇུག་པ་དང་། །དེ་བཞིན་འཆི་འཕོ་མི་རུང་འགྱུར།།

ཞེས་གསུངས་པ་ཀུན་ལས་[40b] བཏུས་ཀྱི་འགྲེལ་པར་

རྣམ་པ་བརྒྱད་ཀྱིས་ཀུན་གཞི་རྣམ་པར་ཤེས་པ་ཡོད་པ་ཉིད་དུ་རྟོགས་པར་བྱ་སྟེ། འདི་ལྟར་ཀུན་གཞི་རྣམ་པར་ཤེས་པ་མེད་ན་ལུས་ཉེ་བར་ལེན་པ་མི་སྲིད་པ་དང་། གཟོད་མ་འབྱུང་བ་མི་སྲིད་པ་དང་།

[1] O and P have a shad after *dang*.

གསལ་བར་འབྱུང་བ་མི་སྲིད་པ་དང་། ས་བོན་ཉིད་མི་སྲིད་པ་དང་། ལས་མི་སྲིད་པ་དང་། ལུས་ཀྱི་མྱོང་བ་མི་སྲིད་པ་དང་། སེམས་མེད་པའི་སྙོམས་པར་འཇུག་པ་མི་སྲིད་པ་དང་། རྣམ་པར་ཤེས་པ་འཆི་འཕོ་བ་མི་སྲིད་པའི་ཕྱིར་རོ་

ཞེས་བཀོད་པའི་རིགས་པ་བརྒྱད་དུ་ཕལ་ཆེར་འདུས་པས་དེའི་ཕྱིར་འདི་བརྒྱད་བཤད་པར་བྱའོ།།

དེ་ལ་རིགས་པ་དང་པོ་ནི། ཀུན་གཞི་མེད་ན་ལུས་ཉེ་བར་[1] ལེན་པ་ཇི་ལྟར་མི་རུང་ཞེ་ན། གལ་ཏེ་ཀུན་གཞི་མི་འདོད་ན་ཉོན་ཡིད་ཀྱང་མེད་པས་ན་ཚོགས་དྲུག་གིས་ལུས་ལེན་དགོས་ལ་དེ་ནི་རྒྱུ་ལྔས་ལུས་ལེན་བྱེད་དུ་མི་རུང་སྟེ། འདི་ལྟར།

ཀུན་གཞི་ནི་ཚེ་སྔ་མའི་ལས་ཀྱི་རྣམ་སྨིན་ཡིན་པས་ན་ལས་ཀྱི་མཐུས་འཇུག་པས་ཉིང་མཚམས་སྦྱོར་བ་ན་ཡང་ཡོད་པས་ལུས་ལེན་པར་རུང་ཡང་། ཚོགས་དྲུག་ནི་མདོ་ལས་ནང་གི་དབང་པོ་དང་ཕྱིའི་ཡུལ་དང་ལྟ་འདོད་ལ་སོགས་པའི་ཡིད་བྱེད་ཀྱི་དབང་གིས་སྐྱེ་བར་གསུངས་པའི་ཕྱིར་དང་ལུས་གྲུབ་ཟིན་ཚེ་འདིའི་ད་ལྟ་བའི་རྐྱེན་ལས་འབྱུང་བས་ཉིང་མཚམས་སྦྱོར་བ་མེད་པའི་ཕྱིར་དང་།

འཇུག་ཤེས་སྔོན་ལས་ཀྱི་རྣམ་སྨིན་དང་། ཡིད་ཤེས་ཉིང་མཚམས་སྦྱོར་བ་ན་ཡང་ཡོད་པས་ཚོགས་དྲུག་ལུས་ལེན་པར་སྨྲ་བར་ཡང་མི་ནུས་ཏེ། རྣམ་སྨིན་མཚན་ཉིད་པ་དང་། ཉིང་མཚམས་སྦྱོར་བའི་རྣམ་ཤེས་ཡིན་ན་སྐྱེ་གནས་ཀྱི་དང་པོར་མཚམས་སྦྱོར་བ་རྣམ་སྨིན་ཡིན་པས་མཐའ་གཅིག་ཏུ་ལུང་དུ་མ་[1179]བསྟན་པ་དགོས་པ་ལས། དེ་དག་དགེ་མི་དགེར་ཡང་མཐོང་བའི་ཕྱིར་དང་།

གལ་ཏེ་དེ་[41a] དྲུག་ལ་དགེ་མི་དགེ་ཡོད་ཀྱང་མ་བསྒྲིབས་ལུང་མ་བསྟན་ཀྱང་ཡོད་ལ་དེ་རྣམ་སྨིན་ཡིན་པས་ཉེས་པ་མེད་དོ་ཞེས་ཀྱང་སྨྲ་མི་ནུས་ཏེ། ལུང་མ་བསྟན་རྣམ་སྨིན་གྱི་ཆར་གྱུར་པ་ནི་ཚེ་ཇི་སྲིད་ཀྱི་བར་དུ་རྒྱུན་མི་འཆད་དུ་འཇུག་ན་ཚོགས་དྲུག་ནི་ཇི་སྲིད་དུ་བར་མ་ཆད་དུ་འཇུག་པ་མེད་པའི་ཕྱིར་དང་།

ཡང་ཚོགས་དྲུག་གིས་ལུས་ལེན་ན་ལུས་ལེན་བྱེད་ཀྱི་ཤེས་རྒྱུན་གྱིས་མ་ཁྱབ་ན་གང་མ་ཁྱབ་པ་དེ་ཤེས་པས་མ་ཟིན་པས་རོ་ལྟར་འགྱུར་བས། ཚོགས་དྲུག་གནས་སོ་སོར་ངེས་པའི་ཕྱིར་གནས་གང་[2] དུ་རྣམ་ཤེས་འབྱུང་བ་དེ་ཉིད་ཟིན་པར་འགྱུར་གྱི་,ལུས་ལྷག་མ་མ་ཟིན་པས་དེ་ལྟར་འགྱུར་ཏེ། འཇུག་ཤེས་ལ་དུས་གཅིག་ཏུ་ལུས་ཐམས་ཅད་ལ་ཁྱབ་པར་སྐྱེ་བའི་ནུས་པ་མེད་པའི་ཕྱིར་རོ།།

གལ་ཏེ་འདུ་ཤེས་ཀྱི་གནས་ལུས་དབང་གིས་ལུས་ཀུན་ལ་ཁྱབ་བས་གནས་རང་ཉིད་ཀྱིས་ཟིན་ནོ་ཞེ་ན། མི་རུང་སྟེ་རང་ཉིད་ཤེས་པ་དང་བྲལ་བས་མ་ཟིན་པའི་ཕྱིར་དང་། ཡང་དེ་དྲུག་གིས་ལུས་ལེན་ན་ཚེ་གཅིག་ལ་ལུས་ལེན་མང་པོ་ལེན་པའི་སྐྱོན་དུ་ཡང་འགྱུར་ཏེ། དེ་དག་རེས་འབྱུང་རེས་མི་འབྱུང་བའི་ཕྱིར་རོ། །དེས་

---

[1] *mdo na°* M; *med na lus te bar* D. [2] *gnas 'gyur* O,P.

ན་ཀུན་གཞི་མེད་ན་ཚོགས་དྲུག་གིས་ལུས་ལེན་པར་འདོད་དགོས་ལ་དེ་དག་རྒྱུ་ལྡས་མི་རུང་བའི་ཕྱིར་དང་། ལུས་ལེན་པ་དམིགས་པའི་ཕྱིར་ལུས་ལེན་བྱེད་ཀུན་གཞི་རྣམ་ཤེས་ཁས་བླང་བར་བྱའོ། །དེ་སྐད་དུ་ཡང་།

> ཅིའི་ཕྱིར་ལུས་ཉེ་བར་ལེན་པ་མི་རུང་ཞེ་ན།
>
> སྨྲས་པ་རྣམ་པ་ལྔ་སྟེ། འདི་ལྟར་ཀུན་གཞི་རྣམ་པར་ཤེས་པ་ནི་སྔོན་གྱི་འདུ་བྱེད་ཀྱི་རྒྱུ་ལས་བྱུང་བའོ། །མིག་ལ་སོགས་པ་འཇུག་པའི་རྣམ་པར་ཤེས་པ་ནི་དེ་ལྟར་གྱི་རྐྱེན་ལས་བྱུང་བ་ཇི་སྐད་དུ "དབང་པོ་དང་ཡུལ་དང་ཡིད་ལ་བྱེད་པའི་དབང་གིས་རྣམ་པར་ཤེས་པ་རྣམས་འབྱུང་བར་འགྱུར [41b] རོ་" ཞེས་རྒྱ་ཆེར་གསུངས་པ་ལྟ་བུ་སྟེ་འདི་ནི་གནད་ཚིགས་དང་པོའོ། །ཡང་རྣམ་པར་ཤེས་པའི་ཚོགས་དྲུག་ནི་དགེ་བ་དང་མི་དགེ་བར་དམིགས [1180] ཏེ་འདི་ནི་གནད་ཚིགས་གཉིས་པའོ། །ཡང་རྣམ་པར་ཤེས་བའི་ཚོགས་དྲུག་པོ་དག་ལ་ཡང་ལུང་དུ་མ་བསྟན་པ་རྣམ་པར་སྨིན་པས་བསྡུས་པར་གྱུར་པ་གང་ཡིན་པའི་རྣམ་པ་མི་དམིགས་ཏེ་འདི་ནི་གནད་ཚིགས་གསུམ་པའོ། །ཡང་རྣམ་པར་ཤེས་པའི་ཚོགས་དྲུག་འབྱུང་བ་ནི་གནས་སོ་སོར་ངེས་པ་སྟེ། གནས་གང་དང་གང་ལས་རྣམ་པར་ཤེས་པ་གང་དང་གང་འབྱུང་བ་དེ་དང་དེ་ནི་དེས་ཟིན་པར་འགྱུར་གྱི, ལྷག་མ་ནི་མ་ཟིན་པར་འགྱུར་ཏེ་མི་རུང་ངོ་། །ཟིན་པར་ཡང་མི་རུང་སྟེ་རྣམ་པར་ཤེས་པ་མེད་པའི་ཕྱིར་འདི་ནི་གནད་ཚིགས་བཞིའོ། །ཡང་དང་ཡང་ལུས་འཛིན་པའི་ཉེས་པར་འགྱུར་ཏེ། འདི་ལྟར་མིག་གི་རྣམ་པར་ཤེས་པ་རེས་འགའ་ནི་འབྱུང་རེས་འགའ་ནི་མི་བྱུང་ངོ་། ལྷག་མ་རྣམས་ཀྱང་དེ་བཞིན་ཏེ་འདི་ནི་གནད་ཚིགས་ལྔ་པའོ།།

ཞེས་སོ།།

རིགས་པ་གཉིས་པ་ནི། །ཁ་ཅིག་ན་རེ་ཀུན་གཞི་ཡོད་པར་འདོད་པ་ལ་ཡང་སྐྱོན་ཡོད་དེ། འདི་ལྟར་རྣམ་ཤེས་གཉིས་ཅིག་ཅར་འབྱུང་བར་འགྱུར་ཏེ། ཀུན་གཞི་རྒྱུན་དུ་འཇུག་ལ་འཇུག་ཤེས་ཀྱང་རེས་འགའ་འབྱུང་བའི་ཕྱིར་རོ་ཞེ་ན། ཁྱོད་ནི་ཉེས་པ་མེད་པ་ལ་ཉེས་པར་འཛིན་པ་ཞིག་སྟེ་འདི་ནི་ཁོ་བོ་འདོད་པ་ཡིན་ནོ།།

གལ་ཏེ་རྣམ་ཤེས་གཉིས་ཅིག་ཅར་མི་འབྱུང་ན། གང་ཟག་ཁ་ཅིག་ཡུལ་དྲུག་ལ་མཐོང་བར་འདོད་པ་ནས་རྣམ་པར་ཤེས་པའི་བར་དུ་འདོད་པ་སྟེ་ཡུལ་དྲུག་སོ་སོ་ལ་ཡིད་བྱེད་རིམ་སུ་མ་ཆད་པར་དྲུག་ག་ལ་ཉེ་རིང་མེད་པ་ན་ཐོག་མར་རྣམ་ཤེས་བྱེ་བྲག་པ་གཅིག་ཀྱང་མི་སྐྱེ་བར་འགྱུར་ཏེ་འཇུག་ཤེས་དེ་དག་ཡུལ་[1] དབང་ཡིད་བྱེད་ [42a] ཀྱི་རྒྱུ་རྣམས་ཡོད་པར་ཁྱད་པར་མེད་པའི་ཕྱིར་རོ།།

མཐོང་འདོད་ཉན་འདོད་ཀྱི་རྟོག་པ་གཉིས་ཅིག་ཅར་སྐྱེ་བ་མི་སྲིད་པས་ཡུལ་དྲུག་ག་ལ་ཡིད་བྱེད་དྲུག་དུས་མཉམ་དུ་ཡོད་པ་ལྟར་གསུངས་ཀྱང་། ཡུལ་སོ་སོ་ལ་རིམ་སུ་མ་ཆད་པར་ཉེ་རིང་མེད་པ་གང་ཡང་འབྱུང་

---

[1] *lus* D,O,P→*yul* as in ASBh ... *viṣayo 'pi* quoted below 42b2.

རྟུང་གཅིག་ལ་བྱའོ།།

གལ་ཏེ་རེས་སུ་མ་ཆད་པའི་ཡིད་བྱེད་ཀྱང་སྟེ། ཡུལ་དབང་ཡང་ཉེ་བའི་ཚེ་རྣམ་ཤེས་དྲུག་ལས་འདི་དང་པོར་སྐྱེའོ་ཞེས་མི་ངེས་ཀྱང་ [1181]གང་རྟུང་གཅིག་སྐྱེས་པ་ན་དེ་དང་དུས་མཉམ་པར་ཤེས་པ་གཞན་མི་སྐྱེ་སྟེ། ཡིད་བྱེད་གཅིག་གིས་ཤེས་པ་རིགས་མཐུན་གཉིས་ཅིག་ཅར་སྐྱེ་བའི་སྐབས་འབྱེད་པ་མི་སྲིད་པའི་ཕྱིར་རོ་ཞེ་ན།

ཡུལ་གཟུགས་ལྟ་བུ་ལ་ལྟ་འདོད་ལྟ་བུའི་ཡིད་བྱེད་ངེས་པར་རྒྱུར་དགོས་ན་རྟོག་པ་གཉིས་ཅིག་ཅར་མི་སྲིད་པས་ཁྱེད་བདེན་མོད། འོན་ཀྱང་རྐྱེན་བཞི་འཚོགས་ན་འབྲས་བུ་རྣམ་ཤེས་སྐྱེས་པས་ན་ཤེས་པ་གཉིས་ཅིག་ཅར་འབྱུང་སྟེ། འདི་ལྟར་ཚོགས་དྲུག་གའི་རྒྱུའི་རྐྱེན་དང་ཡུལ་དང་དབང་པོ་ཡང་དུས་མཉམ་དུ་ཡོད་ཅིང་། དེ་མ་ཐག་རྐྱེན་ཀྱང་རང་གི་སྔ་རོལ་ཏུ་འགགས་པས་བྱེད་པའི་ཕྱིར་རོ།།

འོ་ན་

རྣམ་པར་ཤེས་པ་གཉིས་ཅིག་ཅར་འབྱུང་བ་ནི་གནས་མ་ཡིན་ཅིང་སྐབས་མེད་དོ།།

ཞེས་གསུངས་པ་དང་འགལ་ལོ་ཞེ་ན།

མི་འགལ་ཏེ་ཤེས་པ་རིགས་མཐུན་གཉིས་ལ་དགོངས་སོ། །དེ་ལྟར་ཡང་།

ཅིའི་ཕྱིར་གཟོད་མའི་འཇུག་པ་མི་རྟུང་ཞེ་ན།

གལ་ཏེ་ལ་ལ་ཞིག་འདི་སྐད་དུ། ཅི་སྟེ་ཀུན་གཞི་རྣམ་པར་ཤེས་པ་ཡོད་ན། དེའི་ཕྱིར་རྣམ་པར་ཤེས་པ་གཉིས་ཅིག་ཅར་འབྱུང་བར་འགྱུར་རོ་ཞེས་ཟེར་ན། དེ་ལ་འདི་སྐད་བརྗོད་པར་བྱ་སྟེ་ཉེས་པ་མེད་པ་ལ་ཁྱོད་ཉེས་པར་འདུ་ཤེས་སུ་ཟད་ཀྱི, འདི་ལྟར་རྣམ་པར་ཤེས་པ་གཉིས་ཅིག [42b] ཅར་འབྱུང་བ་ཉིད་དོ། །དེ་ཅིའི་ཕྱིར་ཞེ་ན། འདི་ལྟར་ཁ་ཅིག་ཅིག་ཅར་མཐོང་བར་འདོད་པ་ནས་རྣམ་པར་ཤེས་པའི་བར་དུ་འདོད་པ་ལ། ཐོག་མར་རྣམ་པར་ཤེས་པ་གང་ཡང་རྟུང་བ་ཞིག་འབྱུང་དུ་མི་རྟུང་སྟེ། འདི་ལྟར་དེ་ནི་ཡིད་ལ་བྱེད་པ་དང་། དབང་པོ་དང་ཡུལ་ཡང་ཡོད་པར་བྱེ་བྲག་མེད་པའི་ཕྱིར་རོ།།

ཞེས་སོ།།

རིགས་པ་གསུམ་པ་ནི། གལ་ཏེ་རྣམ་ཤེས་གཉིས་ཅིག་ཅར་མི་འབྱུང་ན་ཡིད་ཀྱི་རྣམ་པར་ཤེས་པ་གསལ་བར་མི་འཇུག་གོ །དེ་ཇི་ལྟར་ཞེ་ན། འདི་ལྟར་དབང་ཤེས་ཀྱིས་གཟུང་བའི་ཡུལ་ལ་རྗེས་སུ་རྟོག་པའི་ཡིད་ཤེས་ཀྱིས་འཇུག་པ་ལ་རྒྱུ་བ་[1] གསལ་བ་ཞིག་ནི་དམིགས་ལ་དབང་ཤེས་ཀྱིས་སྔར་མྱོང་ཟིན་པའི་འདས་པའི་ཡུལ་དྲན་པའི་ཡིད་ཀྱི་རྒྱུ་བ་ནི་མི་གསལ་བའི་ [1182] ཕྱིར་ད་ལྟ་བའི་དབང་ཤེས་ཀྱི་ཡུལ་ལ་རྒྱུ་བ་ཉིད་གསལ་

[1] *rgyu ba la* O,P.

བར་འདོད་དགོས་པས་ཤེས་པ་གཉིས་ཅིག་ཅར་འབྱུང་བ་དང་ཡིད་ཀྱི་རྒྱུ་བ་གསལ་བར་ཡང་རུང་ངོ་། །དེ་ལྟར་མ་ཡིན་ན་རྗེས་སུ་རྟོག་པའི་ཡིད་ཤེས་དེ་དག་ལ་གསལ་བ་དང་མི་གསལ་བ་མི་རུང་ངོ་།།

གལ་ཏེ་དབང་ཤེས་དང་དུས་མི་མཉམ་ཡང་ད་ལྟར་བའི་ཡུལ་ཅན་ཡིད་ནི་གསལ་ལ། འདས་པ་ལྟ་བུ་མི་གསལ་བ་ཡིན་ནོ་ཞེ་ན། མི་རུང་སྟེ་ཡིད་ཤེས་དེ་གཉིས་ཀ་ཡང་ཡུལ་ལ་འཇུག་པ་ན་ཡུལ་རྣམས་ཀྱི་རང་གི་མཚན་ཉིད་ནི་མི་སྣང་ལ་འདས་པ་མེད་ཅིང་དུས་མཉམ་པའི་ཡུལ་གསལ་བར་འཛིན་པའི་ཤེས་པ་ཡང་མེད་པའི་ཕྱིར་རོ། །དེ་ལྟར་ཡང་།

> རྣམ་པར་ཤེས་པ་ཅིག་ཅར་འབྱུང་བ་མེད་ན་ཅིའི་ཕྱིར་མིག་ལ་སོགས་པའི་རྣམ་པར་ཤེས་པ་དང་ལྷན་ཅིག་རྗེས་སུ་འཇུག་པ་ཡིད་ཀྱི་རྣམ་པར་ཤེས་པ་གསལ་བར་མི་འགྱུར་ཞེ་ན། འདི་ལྟར་གང་གི་ཚེ་འདས་པའི་ཡུལ་མྱོང་བ་རྗེས་སུ་དྲན་[43a]པ་དེའི་ཚེ་ཡིད་ཀྱི་རྣམ་པར་ཤེས་པ་རུང་བ་ནི་གསལ་བ་མ་ཡིན་ལ། དེ་ལྟར་ཀྱི་ཡུལ་ལ་རྒྱུ་བའི་ཡིད་ནི་དེ་ལྟར་མི་གསལ་བ་མ་ཡིན་ཏེ་དེའི་ཕྱིར་ཡང་ཅིག་ཅར་འབྱུང་བ་དང་། ཡིད་ཀྱི་རྣམ་པར་ཤེས་པ་གསལ་བར་ཡང་རུང་ངོ་།།

ཞེས་སོ།།

རིགས་པ་བཞི་པ་ནི། དགེ་མི་དགེ་ལ་སོགས་པའི་ས་བོན་མེད་པར་ཐལ། ཀུན་གཞི་མེད་པའི་ཕྱིར། མ་ངེས་པ་མ་ཡིན་ཏེ། ཀུན་གཞི་ཁོ་ན་བག་ཆགས་སོགས་པའི་གཞི་ཡིན་པའི་ཕྱིར་རོ།།

གས་ཏེ་ཚོགས་དྲུག་པོ་ས་བོན་གྱི་རྟེན་ཡིན་སྐྱོན་མེད་དོ་ཞེ་ན། མི་རིགས་ཏེ་ས་བོན་བསྒོད་པ་ལ་སྒོད་བྱེད་དང་བསྒོ་གཞི་སྐྱེ་འགག་དུས་གཅིག་ཏུ་བྱེད་དགོས་ན་དེ་དག་དགེ་བའི་འོག་ཏུ་མི་དགེ་བ་དང་། བཀློག་པ་དང་། དེ་བཞིན་དུ་འཇིག་རྟེན་པའི་སེམས་ཀྱི་འོག་ཏུ་འཇིག་རྟེན་ལས་འདས་པའི་སེམས་རྣམས་འབྱུང་བའི་ཕྱིར་རོ། །གཞན་ཡང་ཚོགས་དྲུག་རྒྱུན་ཆད་པའི་དུས་སུ་བག་ཆགས་ཀྱི་རྟེན་མེད་པ་དེ་ཡང་རྒྱུན་ཆད་པར་འགྱུར་ལ་དེ་ལྟ་ན་ཕྱིས་འབྱུང་བའི་སེམས་རྣམས་རྒྱུ་མེད་པར་འགྱུར་རོ། །དེ་ལྟར་ཡང་།

> ཅིའི་ཕྱིར་[1183]རྣམ་པར་ཤེས་པའི་ཚོགས་དྲུག་པོ་དག་ཕན་ཚུན་ས་བོན་ཉིད་མ་ཡིན་ཞེ་ན།
>
> འདིར་དགེ་བའི་འོག་ཏུ་མི་དགེ་བ་འབྱུང་ལ། མི་དགེ་བའི་འོག་ཏུ་དགེ་བ་དང་། དེ་གཉིས་ཀའི་འོག་ཏུ་ལུང་མ་བསྟན་པ་དང་། ཁམས་ངན་པའི་འོག་ཏུ་ཁམས་བར་མ་དང་། ཁམས་བར་མའི་འོག་ཏུ་ཁམས་བཟང་པོ་དང་། དེ་བཞིན་དུ་ཁམས་བཟང་པོའི་འོག་ཏུ་ཁམས་ངན་པ་དང་། ཟག་པ་དང་བཅས་པའི་འོག་ཏུ་ཟག་པ་མེད་པ་དང་། ཟག་པ་མེད་པའི་འོག་ཏུ་ཟག་པ་དང་བཅས་པ་དང་། འཇིག་རྟེན་པའི་འོག་ཏུ་འཇིག་རྟེན་ལས་འདས་པ་དང་། འཇིག་རྟེན་ལས་འདས་པའི་འོག་ཏུ་འཇིག་རྟེན་པ་འབྱུང་སྟེ་དེ་[43b]དག་ནི་དེ་ལྟར་ས་བོན་ཉིད་དུ་མི་རུང་ངོ་། །རྒྱུད་ཀྱི་རྒྱུན་ཆད་ནས་ཡུན་རིང་དུ་ལོན་པ་ཡང་ཡུན་རིང་ཞིག་ནས

འབྱུང་བས་དེའི་ཕྱིར་ཡང་མི་རུང་ངོ་

ཞེས་སོ། །འདིས་ནི་ཐེག་བསྡུས་ཀྱི་རིགས་པ་ལྔ་བཤད་དོ།།

རིགས་པ་ལྔ་པ་ནི། རྣམ་ཤེས་དུ་མ་ཅིག་ཅར་མི་འབྱུང་ན། སྣོད་ལམ་འཕྲང་ལྟ་བུའི་རྣམ་རིག་དང་། གནས་རྐང་པ་འདེགས་འཇོག་ལྟ་བུའི་རྣམ་རིག ངའོ་སྙམ་པའི་རྣམ་རིག ཡུལ་ལམ་གྱི་དྲུང་གི་ས་རྡོ་སོགས་ཀྱི་རྣམ་རིག་རྣམས་དུས་གཅིག་ཏུ་མི་འབྱུང་བར་ཐལ་ལོ། །འདོད་ན་མགྱོགས་པར་འགྲོ་བ་སོགས་ཀྱི་ཚེ་དེ་དག་དམིགས་པས་གསལ་ལོ་ཞེས་གསུངས་སོ། །རྣམ་པ་གཅིག་ཏུ་ན། སྣོད་ཀྱི་རྣམ་རིག་ནི། བརྟན་པ་ཕྱིའི་འཇིག་རྟེན་དུ་སྣང་བའོ། །གནས་ཀྱི་རྣམ་རིག་ནི། སེམས་ཅན་གྱི་རྫས་སྐྱེ་མཆེད་དྲུག་གཞི་དང་བཅས་པ་གཡོ་བའི་འཇིག་རྟེན་དུ་སྣང་བའོ། །ངའོ་སྙམ་པའིརྣམ་རིག་ནི། ཁ་ནང་དུ་བལྟས་ཏེ་རྟག་ཏུ་ངའོ་སྙམ་དུ་འཛུག་པའོ། །ཡུལ་གྱི་རྣམ་རིག་ནི། གཟུགས་སྒྲ་སོགས་སུ་སྣང་བའོ། །དེས་ན་ཕྱི་ནང་དུ་སྣང་བ་དང་།[1]ངར་འཛིན་པ་དང་། ཡུལ་དྲུག་གང་རུང་ལ་འཛིན་པ་རྣམས་དུས་གཅིག་ཏུ་དམིགས་པའི་ཕྱིར་རྣམ་ཤེས་དུ་མ་ཅིག་ཅར་འབྱུང་སྟེ། ཤེས་པ་གཅིག་ལ་ངོ་བོ་ཐ་དད་པའི་ལས་འདི་ལྟ་བུ་མི་རུང་བའི་ཕྱིར་རོ།།

བཞི་པོ་འདི་ལ་ལས་ཞེས་པ་ཅི་ཞེ་ན། འདི་ནི་བྱེད་པ་[2] དང་ལས་ཀྱི་དབང་དུ་བྱས་པའི་ལས་སུ་མངོན་ཏེ། བདག་བདག་གི་བར་སྣང་བའི་ཕྱིར་རོ།། **[1184]**

དེ་ལྟར་བཞི་པོ་དེ་ཀུན་གཞི་མི་འདོད་པ་ལ་མི་རིགས་ཀྱི་,ཀུན་གཞི་ཁས་ལེན་པ་ལ་ནི་རིགས་ཏེ། ཕྱི་ནང་དུ་སྣང་བ་དོན་དང་སེམས་ཅན་དུ་སྣང་བའི་རྣམ་རིག་ཀུན་གཞི་ཉིད་དོ། །བདག་ཏུ་སྣང་བ་ནི་བདག་གི་རྣམ་རིག་ཉོན་ཡིད་དོ། །ཡུལ་དུ་སྣང་བ་ནི།

གསུམ་པ་ཡུལ་རྣམས་དྲུག་པོ་ལ །དམིགས་པ་གང་ཡིན་དེ་དག་སྟེ།

ཞེས་ **[44a]** པ་ལྟར་ཚོགས་དྲུག་གོ །དེ་ལྟར་ཡང་

རྣམ་པར་ཤེས་པ་གཉིས་ཅིག་ཅར་འབྱུང་བ་མེད་ན་ཅིའི་ཕྱིར་ལས་མི་སྲིད་ཅེ་ན།

འདི་ལྟར་མདོར་བསྡུས་ན་ལས་རྣམ་པ་བཞི་སྟེ། སྣོད་ཀྱི་རྣམ་པར་རིག་པ་དང་། གནས་ཀྱི་རྣམ་པར་རིགས་པ་དང་། ངའོ་སྙམ་པའི་རྣམ་པར་རིག་པ་དང་། ཡུལ་གྱི་རྣམ་པར་རིག་པའོ། །རྣམ་པར་རིག་པ་འདི་དག་ནི་སྐད་ཅིག་སྐད་ཅིག་ལ་ཅིག་ཅར་འབྱུང་བར་དམིགས་ཏེ། རྣམ་པར་ཤེས་པ་གཅིག་གི་སྐད་ཅིག་མ་ནི་ངོ་བོ་ཐ་དད་པའི་ལས་འདི་ལྟ་བུ་འདི་[3]མི་རུང་ངོ་།།

ཞེས་སོ།།

རིགས་པ་དྲུག་པ་ནི། ཀུན་གཞི་མེད་ན་ཚུལ་བཞིན་ནམ་ཚུལ་བཞིན་མ་ཡིན་པའི་སེམས་ལ་སོགས་པའི་

---

[1] *bdag* /D. [2] *byed pa→byed pa po*? [3] *°bu'i 'di*?

སྐབས་ཐམས་ཅད་དུ་ལུས་ལ་ཁྱབ་པར་སྐྱེ་བའི་མྱོང་བ་དེ་མི་སྲིད་པར་འགྱུར་ཏེ། མྱོང་བ་དེ་ལ་རྟེན་སྤྲིན་བའི་སྒོ་ནས་ལུས་ལ་སྐྱེ་བར་འཇུག་པའི་རྟེན་མེད་པས་རྒྱུའི་རྐྱེན་ས་བོན་མེད་པའི་སྐྱོན་དུ་འགྱུར་རོ། །དེ་ལྟར་ཡང་།

ཀུན་གཞི་རྣམ་པར་ཤེས་པ་མེད་ན་ཅིའི་ཕྱིར་ལུས་ཀྱི་མྱོང་བ་མི་རུང་ཞེ་ན།

> འདི་ལྟར་འགའ་ཞིག་ཚུལ་བཞིན་ནམ་ཚུལ་བཞིན་མ་ཡིན་པའི་སེམས་སམ། རྗེས་སུ་རྣམ་པར་རྟོག་གམ། སེམས་མཉམ་པར་བཞག་གམ། སེམས་མཉམ་པར་མ་བཞག་ཀྱང་རུང་སྟེ། རྣམ་པ་སྣ་ཚོགས་མང་པོ་དེ་དག་འབྱུང་བ་དང་། དམིགས་པར་ཡང་མི་རུང་སྟེ། དེའི་ཕྱིར་ཡང་ཀུན་གཞི་རྣམ་པར་ཤེས་པ་ཡོད་དོ།།

ཞེས་སོ།།

རིགས་པ་བདུན་པ་ནི། ཀུན་གཞི་མེད་ན་སྙོམས་འཇུག [1185]གཉིས་མི་རུང་སྟེ། འདི་ལྟར་དེ་མེད་ན་སྙོམས་འཇུག་གཉིས་ལ་ཞུགས་པའི་གང་ཟག་དེ་རྣམ་ཤེས་ཀྱིས་[1] ལུས་བོར་བར་ཐལ། ཚིགས་དྲུག་འགགས་ཤིང་ཀུན་གཞི་མེད་པའི་ཕྱིར། འདོད་ན། དེ་དག་དང་ཤི་བའི་ཁྱད་པར་སྟོན་པ་ནི། དེའི་རྣམ་པར་ཤེས་པ་ལུས་ལས་མ་འདས་ཞེས་གསུངས་པ [44b] དང་འགལ་ལོ།།

གལ་ཏེ་ཡིད་ཀྱི་རྣམ་ཤེས་མ་གསལ་དང་བཅས་པས། རྣམ་ཤེས་དང་བྲལ་བར་མི་འགྱུར་རོ་ཞེ་ན། མི་རུང་སྟེ། རྣམ་པར་ཤེས་པ་ཡོད་ན་གསུམ་འདུས་པའི་རེག་པ། དེ་ཡོད་ན་ཚོར་བ་དང་འདུ་ཤེས་རྣམས་ཡོད་པས་

འདུ་ཤེས་ཚོར་འགོག་གི་[2] སྙོམས་འཇུག

ཅེས་པ་མི་འཐད་པར་འགྱུར་བའི་ཕྱིར་རོ།།

དེ་ལྟ་ན་ཀུན་གཞི་ཡོད་ན་ཡང་། ཚོར་བ་དང་འདུ་ཤེས་ཀུན་འགྲོ་ཡིན་པས་དེའི་ཚེ་ཡང་འདུ་ཤེས་ཚོར་བ་འགོག་མི་འཐད་དོ་ཞེ་ན།

བདེན་ཏེ་འོན་ཀྱང་ཚོགས་དྲུག་འཁོར་གྱི་འདུ་ཤེས་དང་ཚོར་བ་རྒྱུ་བ་རགས་པས་མེད་དགོས་ཤིང་། ཀུན་གཞིའི་འཁོར་གྱི་ཚོར་འདུ་ནི་དམིགས་རྣམ་ཤིན་ཏུ་ཕྲ་བས་འགོག་སྙོམས་དང་མི་འགལ་བས་ཡོད་ཀྱང་སྐྱོན་མེད་པས་མི་མཚུངས་སོ། །དེ་ལྟར་ཡང་།

ཀུན་གཞི་རྣམ་པར་ཤེས་པ་མེད་ན་ཅིའི་ཕྱིར་སེམས་མེད་པའི་སྙོམས་པར་འཇུག་པ་མི་སྲིད་ཅེ་ན།

> འདི་ལྟར་འདུ་ཤེས་མེད་པའི་སྙོམས་པར་ཞུགས་པ[འམ་འགོག་པའི་སྙོམས་པ་ར་ཞུགས་པ]འི་རྣམ་པར་

[1] *kyi* O,P. [2] *go* O,P.

ཤེས་པ་ཉིད་ལུས་ལས་འདའ་བར་འགྱུར་པའི་རིགས་ན་མ་འདས་ཏེ་དེའི་ཕྱིར་འཆི་བའི་དུས་བྱེད་པ་ཉིད་དུ་འགྱུར་རོ། །ཇི་སྐད་དུ་བཙོམ་ལྡན་འདས་ཀྱིས་ཀྱང་། "དེའི་རྣམ་པར་ཤེས་པ་ལུས་དང་མ་བྲལ་བ་ཡིན་ནོ་" ཞེས་གསུངས་པ་ལྟ་བུའོ།།

ཞེས་སོ།།

རིགས་པ་བརྒྱད་པ་ནི། ཀུན་གཞི་མེད་ན་འཆི་འཕོ་བ་མི་རུང་སྟེ། འདི་ལྟར་རྣམ་ཤེས་ཀྱིས་ལུས་འདོར་བས་འཆི་བར་ནི་འདོད་ན་དེ་ཡང་ཀུན་གཞི་མེད་ན་ཡིད་ཤེས་ཀྱིས་འདོར་དགོས་ལ་དེ་ལྟ་ན། ལུས་ཀྱི་ཏྲོད་རིམ་གྱིས་སྟུད་པ་མི་རུང་སྟེ། འཆི་བའི་སྐད་ཅིག་མ་ཚུན་ཆད་དུ་ཡིད་ཤེས་མི་འབྱུང་བ་མི་སྲིད་པའི་ཕྱིར་རོ།།

འོ་ན་ཀུན་གཞི་ཡང་སློག་འགག་ཚུན་ཆད་རྒྱུན་མི་འཆད་པས་མཚུངས་སོ་ཞེ [1186] ན།

བྱེ་བཤད་དུ།

ཀུན་གཞི་རྣམ་པར་ཤེས་པ་ནི་ཁོག་པ་ཐམས་ཅད་ལ་ཁྱབ་པའོ།། [45a]

ཞེས་གསུངས་པ་ལྟར་ལུས་ཐམས་ཅད་ལ་ཁྱབ་པར་བརྟན་པར་གནས་པའི་ཀུན་གཞི་དེ་ལས་ཀྱི་འཕེན་པའི་ནུས་པ་ཟད་ནས་ལུས་ཀྱི་ཕྱོགས་གང་ནས་ཀུན་གཞི་དེ་གནས་པར་མི་རུང་བར་གྱུར་བའི་ལུས་ཀྱི་ཕྱོགས་དེ་ནས་ཀུན་གཞི་དེ་བསྡུས་པས་དེ་ལ་བརྟེན་བའི་དབང་པོ་རྣམས་འགག་པར་འགྱུར་ཞིང་ཏྲོད་ཡལ་བར་འགྱུར་རོ། །རིམ་པ་འདིས་དབང་པོ་མ་ལུས་པ་བོར་བས་ལུས་རིལ་ཏྲོད་ཡལ་བར་འགྱུར་བས་འཆི་འཕོ་ལ། ཡིད་ཀྱི་ཤེས་པ་ནི་ལུས་ཐམས་ཅད་ལ་ཁྱབ་བར་གནས་ཤིང་ལུས་ཀྱི་ཕྱོགས་ནས་སྡུད་པ་མེད་པའི་ཕྱིར་མི་མཚུངས་སོ།།

དེས་ན་འཆི་བ་ཏྲོད་ཆོར་རིམ་གྱིས་བསྡུས་པས་ལུས་འབོར་བ་ཡིན་ཅིང་། ཤེས་པ་ལས་གཞན་གྱིས་དེ་བྱེད་པར་མི་རིགས་ཏེ་ཤེས་པ་དང་བྲལ་བ་ལ་དེ་ལྟ་བུ་མ་དམིགས་པའི་ཕྱིར་རོ། །ཤེས་པ་ཡིན་ཡང་རེ་ཞིག་སློ་ལྡའི་ཤེས་པས་ནི་ལུས་འབོར་བ་མ་ཡིན་ཏེ། ཡིན་ན་དེ་དག་ལུས་ཀྱི་ཆ་ཤས་ལ་གནས་པས་ན་ལུས་ཀྱི་ཆ་གང་ན་དེ་དག་མེད་པ་དེར་ཏྲོད་ཆོར་མེད་པར་ཐལ་བ་དང་། བརྒྱལ་བ་སོགས་ཀྱི་ཚེ་ཤི་བར་ཡང་འགྱུར་རོ།།

ཡིད་ཤེས་ནི་ལུས་ཀྱི་ཆ་ཤས་ལ་མི་གནས་ཀྱང་ལུས་ཐམས་ཅད་ལ་ཁྱབ་པར་ཀུན་གཞི་ལྟར་ཡང་མི་གནས་ལ་དེ་ཡོད་ཙམ་གྱིས་ལུས་མི་འབོར་ན་སློག་ཐ་མ་ཆད་ཚུན་ཆད་དུ་ཏྲོད་ཆོར་མི་སྡུད་པར་འགྱུར་པ་ལས་དེ་གོང་དུ་ཡང་ཏྲོད་ཆོར་སྡུད་པའི་ཕྱིར་དང་། ཏྲོད་ཆོར་བསྡུས་ཏེ་ལུས་འབོར་བ་ཡང་མཐོང་བའི་ཕྱིར་ལུས་འདོར་བྱེད་ཀུན་གཞི་ཁས་བླང་ངོ་། །དེ་སྐད་དུ་ཡང་།

ཀུན་གཞི་རྣམ་པར་ཤེས་པ་མེད་ན་ཅིའི་ཕྱིར་འཆི་འཕོ་བ་ཡང་མི་རུང་ཞེ་ན།

འདི་ལྟར་འཆི་བའི་རྣམ་པར་ཤེས་པ་ལུས་ཀྱི་སྟོད་དམ། སྨད་དུ་ཏྲོད་ཡལ་བར་བྱེད་ཅིང་འདོར་ན།

ཡིད་ཀྱི་རྣམ་པར་ཤེས་པ་ནི་ནམ་ཡང་མི་འབྱུང་བ་མ་ཡིན་ཏེ། དེའི་ཕྱིར་ཡང་ཀུན་གཞི་རྣམ་པར་ཤེས་པ་ལུས་འཛིན་པ་ཉིད་དང་བྲལ་བའི་ཕྱིར་ལུས་དྲོད་ཡལ་བ་དང་། ལུས་ཚོར་བ་ [1187] མེད་ [45b] པར་ཡང་དམིགས་ཀྱི། ཡིད་ཀྱི་རྣམ་པར་ཤེས་པ་དང་བྲལ་བས་ནི་མ་ཡིན་ཏེ་དེའི་ཕྱིར་ཡང་མི་རིགས་སོ་ཞེས་སོ།།

དེ་ལྟར་བྱས་ན་རིགས་པ་དང་པོ་དང་། བཞི་པ་དང་། དྲུག་པ་དང་། བདུན་པ་དང་། བརྒྱད་པ་སྟེ་ལྔ་ནི་ཀུན་གཞི་མེད་པ་ལ་སྐྱོན་བརྗོད་ནས་ཡོད་པར་སྒྲུབ་པ་དངོས་ཡིན་ལ། ལྷག་མ་གསུམ་ནི་རྗོད་སྦྱོང་དུ་གནས་སོ།།

ཅི་ཀུན་གཞི་རྣམ་ཤེས་དེ་ཐེག་ཆེན་གྱི་མདོ་སྡེ་ལས་གཞན་པ་ཐེག་དམན་གྱི་གཙུག་ལག་རྣམས་ལས་མི་འབྱུང་ངམ་ཞེ་ན།

> དེ་ལྟར་ཀུན་གཞི་རྣམ་ཤེས་ནི། །ཐེག་དམན་གཙུག་ལག་རྣམས་སུ་ཡང་། །ཀུན་གཞི་རྩ་བའི་རྣམ་ཤེས་དང་། །འཁོར་བ་ཇི་སྲིད་ཕུང་པོ་དང་། །སྲིད་པའི་ཡན་ལག་དག་གིས་བསྟན།།

དེ་ལྟར་ཀུན་གཞི་རྣམ་ཤེས་དེ་ཐེག་ཆེན་གྱི་མདོ་སྡེ་རྣམས་ལས་ཤེས་བྱའི་གནས་དང་། ལེན་པའི་རྣམ་ཤེས་ཞེས་སོགས་ཀྱི་ཐ་སྙད་ཀྱིས་བསྟན་ལ་དེར་མ་ཟད་ཐེག་དམན་གྱི་གཙུག་ལག་རྣམས་སུ་ཡང་འདི་རྣམ་གྲངས་ཀྱིས་བསྟན་པ་ཡིན་ཏེ། ཐེག་པ་ཆེན་པོ་བསྡུས་པར།

གཅིག་ལས་འཕྲོས་པའི་ལུང་དེ་བཞིན་གཤེགས་པ་འབྱུང་བའི་ཕན་ཡོན་རྣམ་པ་བཞི་ཡི་མདོ་ལས།

> སྐྱེ་རྒུ་ཀུན་གཞི་ལ་ཀུན་ཏུ་དགའ་བ། ཀུན་གཞི་ལ་དགའ་བ།[1] ཀུན་གཞི་ལས་ཡང་དག་པར་འབྱུང་བ། ཀུན་གཞི་ལ་མངོན་པར་དགའ་བ་ཅན་དག་ལ་ཀུན་གཞི་སྤངས་པའི་ཕྱིར་ཆོས་བསྟན་ན་ཉན་འདོད་ལ་རྣ་བ་གཏོད་དེ། ཀུན་ཤེས་པར་བྱེད་པར་[2] སེམས་ཉེ་བར་འཇོག་ཅིང་ཆོས་ཀྱི་རྗེས་སུ་མཐུན་པའི་ཆོས་སྒྲུབ་སྟེ། དེ་བཞིན་གཤེགས་པ་འཇིག་རྟེན་དུ་བྱུང་ན་ངོ་མཚར་རྨད་དུ་བྱུང་བའི་ཆོས་འདི་ཡང་འཇིག་རྟེན་དུ་འབྱུང་ངོ་

ཞེས་ཇི་སྐད་གསུངས་པ་ལྟ་བུ་སྟེ། །རྣམ་གྲངས་འདིས་ནི། ཀུན་གཞི་རྣམ་པར་ཤེས་པ་ཉན་ཐོས་ཀྱི་ཐེག་པར་ཡང་བསྟན་པ་ཡིན་ནོ། །དགེ་འདུན་ [46a] ཕལ་ཆེན་སྡེའི་ལུང་[3] ལས་ཀྱང་རྩ་བའི་རྣམ་པར་ཤེས་པ་ཞེས་འབྱུང་སྟེ། རྣམ་གྲངས་དེས་ཀྱང་དེ་ཉིད་བསྟན་ཏེ། རྩ་བ་ལ་བརྟེན་པའི་ཤིང་ལྗོན་པ་བཞིན་ནོ། །ས་སྟོན་གྱི་སྡེའི་ལུང་ལས་ཀྱང་། [1188] འཁོར་བ་ཇི་སྲིད་པའི་ཕུང་པོ་རྣམས་ཞེས་འབྱུང་སྟེ། རྣམ་གྲངས་

---

[1] Lamotte (1938:8) reverses the order of the first two compounds. [2] *par*→*pas*(?) cp. Bu ston's *Nyi ma'i 'od zer* 204.2. [3] *rnams* D,O,P.

དེས་ཀྱང་དེ་ཉིད་བསྟན་ཏེ། ལ་ལར་རེས་འགའ་གཟུགས་དང་སེམས་རྒྱུན་ཆད་པར་སྣང་ཡང་ཀུན་གཞི་རྣམ་པར་ཤེས་པ་ལ་དེའི་ས་བོན་ནི་རྒྱུན་མི་འཆད་པའི་ཕྱིར་རོ། །འཕགས་པ་གནས་བརྟན་པ་རྣམས་ཀྱི་ལུང་ལས་ཀྱང་།

སྲིད་པའི་ཡན་ལག་ལྔ་བ་དང་། །ཤེས་པ་དང་ནི་གཏོང་པ་[1] དང་། །གཡོ་[2] བ་དང་ནི་
རྟོགས་པ་དང་། །བདུན་པ་འཇུག་པར་བྱེད་པ་ཡིན།།

ཞེས་འབྱུང་ངོ་། །དེའི་ཕྱིར་གང་ཤེས་བྱའི་གནས་ལ་ཀུན་གཞི་རྣམ་པར་ཤེས་པ་ཉིད་དང་། ལེན་པའི་རྣམ་པར་ཤེས་པ་ཉིད་དང་། སེམས་ཉིད་དང་། ཀུན་གཞི་དང་། རྩ་བའི་རྣམ་པར་ཤེས་པ་ཉིད་དང་།[3] འཁོར་བ་ཇི་སྲིད་པའི་ཕུང་པོ་དང་། སྲིད་པའི་ཡན་ལག་ཏུ་བསྟན་པ་དེ་ནི་ཀུན་གཞི་རྣམ་པར་ཤེས་པ་སྟེ། ཀུན་གཞི་རྣམ་པར་ཤེས་[4] པའི་ལམ་ཆེན་པོ་བཏོད་[5]པ་ཁོ་ན་ཡིན་ནོ་

ཞེས་སོ།།

གལ་ཏེ་ཉན་ཐོས་ཀྱི་ཐེག་པར་ཀུན་གཞི་བསྟན་ན། ཐེག་ཆེན་བསྡུས་པར།

བསྟན་འདི་འདི་ལྟར་གཞན་ལ་མ་མཐོང་ལ། །འདི་དག་བྱང་ཆུབ་མཆོག་གི་རྒྱུར་མཐོང་བས། །གནས་
བཅུ་བསྟན་པས་ཁྱད་ཞུགས་གང་ཡིན་པ། །ཐེག་པ་ཆེན་པོ་སངས་རྒྱས་བཀར་འདོད་དོ།།

ཞེས་གསུངས་པ་ཇི་ལྟར་དྲང་ཞེ་ན།

ཉེས་པ་མེད་དེ། ཉན་ཐོས་ཀྱི་ཐེག་པར་ནི་སྲིད་པའི་ཡན་ལག་ཅེས་སོགས་རྣམ་གྲངས་གཞན་གྱིས་བསྟན་ལ། ཐེག་པ་ཆེན་པོར་ནི་ཀུན་གཞི་རྣམ་ཤེས་ལེན་པའི་རྣམ་ཤེས། ཤེས་བྱའི་གནས་ཞེས་སོགས་སྒྲ་དྲང་པོར་རྫོགས་པར་བསྟན་ཅིང་དེ་ལྟ་བུ་ཉན་ཐོས་ཀྱི་ཐེག་པར་བསྟན་པ་མེད་པའི་ཕྱིར་རོ།། [46b]

ཅིའི་ཕྱིར་ཉན་ཐོས་ཀྱི་ཐེག་པར་དེ་ལྟར་མི་སྟོན་ཞེ་ན།

ཐེག་ཆེན་དུ་བསྟན་པ་ལྟར་ཉན་ཐོས་ཀྱི་ཐེག་པར་སྟོན་དགོས་ཀྱང་མི་དགོས་ལ་བསྟན་ན་ཉེས་པར་ཡང་འགྱུར་རོ། །ཇི་ལྟར་མི་དགོས་ན། འདི་ལྟར་ཀུན་གཞི་སྟོན་པ་ནི་ཤེས་བྱ་ཕྲ་ཞིང་ཕྲ་བ་བརྗོད་བྱར་བསྡུ་བའི་ཕྱིར་ཡིན་ལ་ཉན་ཐོས་ནི་རང་གི་འདོད་པ་གྲུབ་པ་ལ་ཤེས་བྱ་ཕྲ་མོ་ཤེས་མི་དགོས་ཏེ། ཚིག་[1189] བཞིའི་ཚིགས་སུ་བཅད་པ་ཙམ་གྱི་དོན་ལ་སྦྱངས་པས་ཀྱང་ཉོན་སྒྲིབ་སྤངས་པའི་རྣམ་གྲོལ་གྱི་ལུས་མངོན་དུ་བྱེད་ནུས་པའི་ཕྱིར་ཏེ། དགྲ་བཅོམ་པ་ལམ་ཆུང་བ་བཞིན་ནོ།།

བསྟན་ན་ཉེས་པར་ཇི་ལྟར་འགྱུར་ཞེ་ན། ཆོས་ཀུན་གྱི་ས་བོན་གྱི་རྟེན་བྱེད་པས་སྣོད་བཅུད་ཀུན་གྱི་རྒྱུ།

---

[1] *gtod* M,N. *bstod* D,O. *stod* P. [2] *gso* D,O,P. [3] *rtsa ba'i rnam par shes pa nyid dang/* omit D,O,P. [4] *pa ste/ kun gzhi rnam par shes* omit D,O,P. [5] *bstod* D,O,P.

འཁོར་བ་ཇི་སྲིད་དུ་རྒྱུན་མི་འཆད་དུ་འཇུག་པ། བཅིངས་པ་དང་གྲོལ་བའི་གཞིར་གྱུར་པའི་རྣམ་ཤེས་དེ་ཀུན་གཞིའོ་ཞེས་བསྟན་ན་ཉན་ཐོས་ཀྱི་རིགས་ཅན་མི་མཁས་པ་འགའ་ཞིག་བདག་གོ་སྙམ་ནས་བདག་ཏུ་འཛིན་ན་མི་རུང་བའི་ཕྱིར་རོ། །ཐེག་པ་ཆེན་པོར་ནི་བསྟན་དགོས་ཏེ། བྱང་ཆུབ་སེམས་དཔའ་རྣམས་ཤེས་བྱ་ཕྲ་མོ་ལ་མ་སྦྱངས་པར་ཐམས་ཅད་མཁྱེན་པ་ཐོབ་མི་ནུས་པའི་ཕྱིར་དང་། ཀུན་གཞི་དེ་ཊར་ལྟར་བསྟན་ཀྱང་མི་རྟག་གཞན་དབང་ཅན་གྱི་ཆོས་ཙམ་དུ་གོ་བར་འགྱུར་བས་ཉེས་པ་མི་སྐྱེ་བའི་ཕྱིར་རོ། །དེ་སྐད་དུ་ཡང་། ཐེག་ཆེན་བསྡུས་པར།

ཅིའི་ཕྱིར་ཉན་ཐོས་ཀྱི་ཐེག་པར་སེམས་དེ་ཀུན་གཞི་རྣམ་པར་ཤེས་པ་ཞེས་བྱ་བར་རམ། ལེན་པའི་རྣམ་པར་ཤེས་པ་ཞེས་བྱ་བར་མ་བསྟན་ཅེ་ན།

ཤེས་བྱ་ཕྲ་མོ་བསྡུ་བའི་ཕྱིར་ཏེ། ཉན་ཐོས་རྣམས་ནི་ཤེས་བྱ་ཐམས་ཅད་ཤེས་པ་ལ[1] གཏོགས་པ་མ་ཡིན་ནོ། །དེའི་ཕྱིར་དེ་དག་ནི་དེ་བསྟན་པ་མེད་པར་ཡང་ཤེས་པ་རབ་ཏུ [47a] གྲུབ་པའི་ཕྱིར་མ་བསྟན་ཏོ།[2] །བྱང་ཆུབ་སེམས་དཔའ་རྣམས་ནི་ཤེས་བྱ་ཐམས་ཅད་ཤེས་པ་ལ[3] གཏོགས་པ་ཡིན་ནོ། །དེའི་ཕྱིར་དེ་དག་ལ་དེ་བསྟན་ཏེ། དེ་ཤེས་པ་མེད་པར་ནི་ཐམས་ཅད་མཁྱེན་པའི་ཡེ་ཤེས་ཐོབ་པར་སླ་བ་མ་ཡིན་ནོ་

ཞེས་སོ།།

འོ་ན་ཉན་ཐོས་ཀྱི་ཐེག་པར་བསྟན་པའི་སྐྱེ་རྒྱུ་ཀུན་གཞི་ལ་ཞེས་པ་དེ་ཉན་ཐོས་ཀྱི་གྲུབ་མཐའ་སྨྲ་བ་རྣམས་ཀྱིས་མདོའི་དོན་ཇི་ལྟ་བུ་ཞིག་ཏུ་འགྲེལ་ཞེ་ན།

> དེ་ལྟར་གསུངས་པའི་ཀུན་གཞི་ལ། །དབྱིག་བཤེས་མིའུ་ཐུང་དབྱངས་སྒྲོག་གསུམ། །རིམ་
> བཞིན་ཕུང་པོ་ཚོར་བ་དང་། །འཇིག་ལྟ་གསུམ་ལ་དགོངས་ཞེས་འདོད། །

དེ་ལ་བཙུན་པ་དབྱིག་བཤེས་ནི། [1190] མདོ་ཡི་དགོངས་པ་ཉེར་ལེན་གྱི་ཕུང་པོ་ལྔ་ལ་དགོངས་ཏེ། དེ་ནི་སྐྱེ་རྒུ་རྣམས་དགའ་བར་འགྱུར་བའི་གཞི་ཡིན་པའི་ཕྱིར་རོ་ཞེས་ཟེར་རོ། །དེ་བཞིན་དུ་བཙུན་པ་མིའུ་ཐུང་དང་བཙུན་པ་དབྱངས་སྒྲོག་གཉིས་ཀྱང་ཚོར་བ་བདེ་བ་དང་འཇིག་ལྟ་དགོངས་གཞིའོ། །ཞེས་འདོད་དེ། ཐེག་ཆེན་བསྡུས་པར།

ཡང་ཁ་ཅིག་ནི། བཅོམ་ལྡན་འདས་ཀྱིས་སྐྱེ་རྒུ་ཀུན་གཞི་ལ་ཀུན་ཏུ་དགའ་བ་ཞེས་རྒྱ་ཆེར་གང་གསུངས་པ་དེ་ལ་ཉེ་བར་ལེན་པའི་ཕུང་པོ་ལྔ་པོ་དག་ནི་ཀུན་གཞི་ཞེས་བྱའོ་སྙམ་དུ་སེམས་སོ། །གཞན་དག་ནི་བདེ་བའི་ཚོར་བ་འདོད་ཆགས་དང་བཅས་པ་ནི་ཀུན་གཞིའོ་སྙམ་དུ་སེམས་སོ། །གཞན་དག་ནི་འཇིག

---

[1] *ma* D,O,P. [2] D,M,N,O,P read *°grub pas / rnam par grol ba rab tu grub pa'i phyir ma bstan to.* [3] *ma* D,O,P.

ཚོགས་ལ་ལྟ་བ་ཀུན་གཞིའོ་སྙམ་དུ་སེམས་ཏེ། དེ་དག་ནི་ཀུན་གཞི་རྣམ་པར་ཤེས་པ་ལ་མ་རྨོངས་ནས་ལུང་དང་རྟོགས་པས་དེ་སྙམ་དུ་སེམས་སོ།།

ཞེས་སོ།།

འོ་ན་ཅི་མདོ་དེའི་དོན་གྲུབ་མཐའ་སྨྲ་བ་དེ་དག་གིས་བཀྲལ་བ་ལྟར་ཐེག་པ་ཆེན་པོར་ཡང་རུང་ངམ་ཞེ་ན།

ཐེག་པ་འོག་མའི་ལུགས་[47b] ལ་ནི། །ཚུལ་དེ་མི་རུང་མེད་མོད་ཀྱི། །ཐེག་ཆེན་པ་རྣམས་ལུང་དེའི་དོན། །ཀུན་གཞིར་འདོད་པ་ཆེས་བཟང་སྟེ། །གང་ཕྱིར་དགྲིག་བཤེས་སོགས་ཀྱིས་ནི། །བཀྲལ་བ་སྐྱོན་དང་ལྡན་ཕྱིར་རོ།།

ཐེག་པ་འོག་མ་པ་དེ་དག་ནི་ཀུན་གཞི་བསྟན་པའི་སྣོད་མ་ཡིན་ཞིང་དེ་ལ་རྨོངས་པའི་ཕྱིར་ཀུན་གཞིའི་དོན་གཞན་དུ་འཆད་པ་མི་རུང་བ་མེད་པ་སྟེ་མ་ཚང་ཆུང་མེད།[1] འོན་ཀྱང་ཀུན་གཞི་ལ་མ་རྨོངས་པ་ཐེག་ཆེན་པ་རྣམས་ཀྱིས་ཀུན་གཞི་ཞེས་གསུངས་པའི་དོན་ཀུན་གཞི་རྣམ་ཤེས་སུ་འདོད་པ་ཆེས་བཟང་སྟེ། བཙུན་པ་གསུམ་གྱི་འདོད་པ་ནི་སྐྱོན་དང་ལྡན་ལ་ཀུན་གཞི་རྣམ་ཤེས་སུ་འདོད་པ་ནི་ཟླ་མེད་པ་ཡིན་པའི་ཕྱིར་རོ།།

བཙུན་པ་གསུམ་གྱི་འདོད་པ་སྐྱོན་དང་ཇི་ལྟར་ལྡན་ཞེ་ན། ཇི་སྐད་དུ།

ཉན་ཐོས་ཀྱི་ཐེག་པར་རྣམ་པར་བཞག་པའི་ཚུལ་དུ་ན་ཡང་དེ་དག་གི་རྣམ་པར་བཞག་པ་དེ་མི་རུང་བ་མེད་མོད་ཀྱི། དེ་ལ་མ་རྨོངས་པ་རྣམས་ཀྱིས་[2] ཀུན་གཞི་རྣམ་པར་བཞག་པ་དེ་ཀུན་གཞི་རྣམ་པར་ཤེས་པ་ཡིན་པར་[1191]ཡོངས་སུ་བཟུང་ནས་རྣམ་པར་འཇོག་པ་ནི་ཆེས་བཟང་ངོ་།།

ཇི་ལྟར་ཆེས་བཟང་ཞེ་ན། འདི་ལྟར་ཉེ་བར་ལེན་པའི་ཕུང་པོ་ལྔ་པོ་དག་ནི་ཤིན་ཏུ་སྡུག་བསྔལ་བའི་ངན་འགྲོ་རྣམས་སུ་སྐྱེས་པ་དག་དང་མི་མཐུན་པ་ཡིན་ནོ། །དེས་ན་ཤིན་ཏུ་འདོད་པ་མེད་པ་དག་ལ་སྦྱོར་བ་ནི་མི་རིགས་ཏེ། འདི་ལྟར་དེ་དག་ནི་དེ་དང་བྲལ་བ་ཉིད་དུ་འདོད་དོ། །བདེ་བའི་ཚོར་བ་འདོད་ཆགས་དང་བཅས་པ་ཡང་བསམ་གཏན་བཞི་པ་ཡན་ཆད་གོང་མ་ལ་མེད་དེ། དེ་དང་ལྡན་པའི་སེམས་ཅན་རྣམས་དང་མི་མཐུན་པ་ཡིན་པས་དེར་ཡང་དེ་དག་སྦྱོར་བ་མི་རིགས་སོ། །འཇིག་ཚོགས་ལ་ལྟ་བ་ཡང་ཆོས་འདི་པ་བདག་མེད་པ་ལ་མོས་པ་དག་དང་མི་མཐུན་པ་ཡིན་ཏེ། དེའི་ཕྱིར་དེ་ལ་ཡང་[48a]དེ་དག་སྦྱོར་བ་མི་རིགས་སོ།

[ཞེས་སོ།།]

མདོའི་དོན་ཀུན་གཞི་རྣམ་ཤེས་སུ་འདོད་པ་སྐྱོན་མེད་པ་ཇི་ལྟར་ཡིན་ཞེ་ན། ཇི་སྐད་དུ།

---

[1] Possible alternate readings are: a) *ma tshang chung mod*, b) *mtshang chung med*, c) *mtshang chung mod* M,N. [2] *kyi/ de la ma mongs pa rnams* omit D,O,P.

ཀུན་གཞི་རྣམ་པར་ཤེས་པ་ལ་ནང་གི་བདག་གི[1] དངོས་པོར་ཁས་བླངས་པ་ནི། ཤིན་ཏུ་སྡུག་བསྔལ་བའི་འགྲོ་བ་རྣམས་སུ་སྐྱེས་པ་སྡུག་བསྔལ་གྱི་ཕུང་པོ་རྣམ་པར་ཞིག་པར་འདོད་ཀྱང་ཀུན་གཞི་རྣམ་པར་ཤེས་པ་ལ་བདག་ཏུ་ཆགས་པས་བཅིངས་པ་རྣམས། དེ་རྣམ་པར་ཞིག་པར་འདོད་པར་ནི་ནམ་ཡང་མི་འགྱུར་རོ། །བསམ་གཏན་བཞི་པ་ཡན་ཆད་གོང་མར་སྐྱེས་པ་རྣམས་འདོད་ཆགས་དང་བཅས་པའི་བདེ་བ་དང་མི་མཐུན་དུ་ཟིན་ཀྱང་ཀུན་གཞི་རྣམ་པར་ཤེས་པ་ལ་བདག་གི་དངོས་པོར་ཆགས་པའི་རྗེས་སུ་འབྲེལ་བ་ནི་ཡོད་པ་ཉིད་དོ། །དེ་བཞིན་དུ་ཆོས་འདི་པ་བདག་མེད་པ་ལ་མོས་པ་རྣམས་བདག་ཏུ་ལྟ་བ་དང་མི་མཐུན་དུ་ཟིན་ཀྱང་ཀུན་གཞི་རྣམ་པར་ཤེས་པ་ལ་བདག་གི་དངོས་པོར་ཆགས་པའི་རྗེས་སུ་འབྲེལ་བ་ཡོད་པ་ཉིད་དེ། དེ་ལྟ་བས་ན་ཀུན་གཞི་རྣམ་པར་ཤེས་པ་ལ་ཀུན་གཞི་ཉིད་དུ་ཆེས་ལེགས་པར་རྣམ་པར་བཞག་པ་གྲུབ་བོ།།

ཞེས་སོ།།

དེ་དག་གིས་འདི་བསྟན་ཏེ། ཀུན་གཞི་ཞེས་པའི་དོན་སྦྱོར་བ་ཡིན་ཞིང་དེ་ཡང་བདག་ཏུ་མངོན་པར་འདོད་པའི་རྣམ་པས་སེམས་ཅན་རྣམས་དེར་སྦྱོར[1192]བ་ཡིན་པས་ན་ངན་འགྲོ་རྣམས་དང་། ཆོར་བ་བདེ་བ་མེད་པ་བསམ་གཏན་བཞི་པ་ཡན་ཆད་དང་། ཆོས་འདི་པ་བདག་མེད་པ་ལ་མོས་པ་རྣམས་ཀྱང་བདག་ཏུ་མངོན་པར་འདོད་པའི་རྣམ་པས་ཀུན་གཞི་ལ་སྦྱོར་བ་ཡོད་པའི་ཕྱིར་རོ་སྙམ་དུ་བསམས་སོ།།

དེ་ལྟར་བྱས་ན་ཉོན་ཡིད་གནས་གྱུར་ནས་ཀུན་གཞི་རྣམ་ཤེས་མེད་པ་ནི་སློབ[48b]དཔོན་འདི་ཡིས་བཞེད་པ་ཁ་ན་མ་ཐོ་བ་མེད་པ་ཡིན་ནོ།།

ཀུན་གཞི་སྒྲུབ་བྱེད་འཕྲོས་པ་དང་བཅས་པ་བཤད་ཟིན་ཏོ།།

[Chapter Seven]

གཉིས་པ་ཉོན་ཡིད་ཀྱི་རིགས་པ་ནི།

ཉོན་མོངས་ཅན་གྱི་ཡིད་མེད་ན། །མ་འདྲེས་པ་ཡི་མ་རིག་དང་། །ལྔ་པོ་དག་དང་འདྲ་བ་དང་། །སྙོམས་པར་འཇུག་པའི་བྱེ་བྲག་དང་། །ངེས་ཚིག་མེད་པའི་སྐྱོན་དུ་འགྱུར། །འདུ་ཤེས་མེད་པར་སྐྱེས་པའི་རྒྱུན། །ངར་འཛིན་མེད་པའི་སྐྱོན་དུ་འགྱུར། །ངར་འཛིན་པ་དང་ལྡན་པ་ནི། །རྣམ་པ་ཀུན་ཏུ་མི་འཐད་ཕྱིར། །ཉོན་ཡིད་ཡོད་པར་ཤེས་པར་བྱ།།

ཉོན་ཡིད་མེད་ན་གནོད་པ་དྲུག་འབབ་པའི་ཕྱིར་ཉོན་ཡིད་ཡོད་པར་ཁས་བླང་ངོ་།།

ཉོན་ཡིད་མེད་ན་མ་འདྲེས་པའི་མ་རིག་པ་མེད་པར་ཇི་ལྟར་འགྱུར་ཞེ་ན།

---

[1] *nyid*D,O,P.

ཐེག་བསྡུས་སུ།

ཡང་དག་དོན་ལ་འཇུག་པ་ཡི། །སེམས་ཀྱི་གེགས་སུ་རྟག་གྱུར་དང་། །དུས་རྣམས་ཀུན་ཏུ་
འབྱུང་བ་དེ། །མ་འདྲེས་པ་ཡི་མ་རིག་འདོད།།

ཅེས་གསུངས་པ་ལྟར་མ་རིག་པ་དེ་ནི་བདག་མེད་པའི་དོན་མངོན་སུམ་དུ་མཐོང་བ་ལ་རྟག་ཏུ་གེགས་བྱེད་པ་དགེ་མི་དགེ་ལུང་མ་བསྟན་གྱི་སེམས་རྣམས་འབྱུང་བའི་དུས་ཐམས་ཅད་དུ་འབྱུང་བ་ཞིག་ཡིན་ལ། དེ་ཡང་སེམས་བྱུང་ཡིན་པས་གཙོ་བོ་རྣམ་ཤེས་གཅིག་དང་མཚུངས་པར་ལྡན་དགོས་ཤིང་འདི་ཉོན་མོངས་ཡིན་པ་དང་། ཇི་སྲིད་འཕགས་ལམ་མ་སྐྱེས་བར་དུ་རྒྱུན་མི་འཆད་པའི་ཕྱིར་ཀུན་གཞི་དང་ཚོགས་དྲུག་དང་ལྡན་པ་མི་སྲིད་པའི་ཕྱིར་རོ།།

ཅིའི་ཕྱིར་འདི་ལ་མ་འདྲེས་པ་ཞེས་བྱ་ཞེ་ན། བཙུན་པ་ངོ་བོ་ཉིད་མེད་པ་ན་རེ་སངས་རྒྱས་ཀྱི་ཆོས་མ་འདྲེས་པ་ལྟར་རྟེན་ཉོན་ཡིད་ཁོ་ན་ལ་**[1193]**ཡོད་པའི་ཕྱིར། རྟེན་མ་འདྲེས་པ་ལ་འཆད་ལ་དོན་གསང་མཁན་པོས་འདིའི་མཐུས་ཉོན་མོངས་གཞན་འདྲེན་ནུས་ཤིང་གཞན་གྱིས་འདི་འདྲེན་**[49a]**མི་ནུས་པའི་ཕྱིར་མ་འདྲེས་པའམ། མ་བསློས་པའི་རང་དབང་ཅན་ལ་བཤད་དེ། བཤད་སྦྱར་དུ།

དེ་ལྟ་ན་ཡང་འདི་དེ་ལས་གཞན་པ་འཇིག་ཚོགས་ལ་ལྟ་བ་ལ་སོགས་པའི་ཉོན་མོངས་པ་དང་མཚུངས་པར་ལྡན་བའི་ཕྱིར་མ་འདྲེས་པ་མི་འགྲུབ་བོ་ཞེ་ན་མ་ཡིན་ནམ། མི་མཐུན་པར་བཞག་པ་སྙིང་ནི་[1] ཉོན་མོངས་པ་གཞན་དང་མཚུངས་པར་ལྡན་པ་མ་ཡིན་པའི་ཕྱིར་མ་འདྲེས་པ་ཉིད་དུ་འདོད་པ་མ་ཡིན་གྱི་འོ་ན་ཅི་ཞེ་ན། གཞན་མེད་པའི་ཕྱིར་ཏེ་སངས་རྒྱས་ཀྱི་ཆོས་མ་འདྲེས་པ་བཅོ་བརྒྱད་བཞིན་ནོ་ཞེས་སོ། །དོན་གསང་དུ།

མ་འདྲེས་པ་ནི་མ་རིག་པ་རང་དབང་ཅན་ཡིན་གྱི་,རྩ་བའི་ཉོན་མོངས་པ་གཞན་དང་མཚུངས་པར་མི་ལྡན་པས་མ་ཡིན་ཏེ་ཁྲོ་བ་ལ་སོགས་པ་དང་མཚུངས་པར་ལྡན་པ་ཡང་དེར་ཐལ་བར་འགྱུར་དུ་འོང་བས་སོ། །ཉོན་མོངས་པ་དང་ཉེ་བའི་ཉོན་མོངས་པ་ཐམས་ཅད་དང་མཚུངས་པར་མི་ལྡན་པས་དེར་ཐལ་བར་འགྱུར་པ་ཡང་མ་ཡིན་ཏེ་དེ་མེད་པར་ཐལ་བ་ཉིད་དུ་འགྱུར་བས་སོ། །དེ་ལྟ་བས་ན་རྩ་བའི་ཉོན་མོངས་པ་དང་མཚུངས་པར་ལྡན་པ་དང་། དེ་ལས་གཞན་པའི་སེམས་དང་སེམས་ལས་བྱུང་བའི་ཚོགས་ལ་ཡང་རྫས་གཞན་དང་མ་འདྲེས་པའི་ཕྱིར་རང་དབང་ཅན་ནི་མ་འདྲེས་པ་ཡིན་གྱི་,ཐུན་མོང་མ་ཡིན་པའི་དོན་གྱིས་ནི་མ་ཡིན་ཏེ། རྣམ་པར་ཤེས་པ་གཞན་དང་མཚུངས་པར་ལྡན་[2] པས་དེར་ཐལ་བར་འགྱུར་དུ་འོང་བས་སོ

[1] *de ni* O. P reads *steng na* which makes no sense. [2] D,O, and P add *pa yang rnam par shes pa gzhan dang yang mtshung par ldan*

ཞེས། །འདི་མཚུངས་ལྡན་མ་འདྲེས་པར་འདོད་པ་ལ་རྩ་ཉོན་གཞན་དང་མ་འདྲེས་པ་ལ་འཇོག་ན་ཁྲོ་བ་ལྟ་བུ་དང་མཚུངས་ལྡན་གྱི་མ་རིག་པ་ཡང་མ་འདྲེས་པར་[49b]འགྱུར་ལ། རྩ་ཉོན་ཉེ་ཉོན་ཐམས་ཅད་དང་མི་ལྡན་བ་ལ་འདོད་ན་དེ་ལྟ་བུའི་མ་རིག་པ་མི་སྲིད་དོ། །དེས་ན་མ་འདྲེས་པ་ནི་རྫས་གཞན་དང་མ་འདྲེས་པ་རྫས་རང་དབང་ཅན་གྱི་དོན་ཡིན་པས་ན། རྩ་ཉོན་གཞན་དང་[1194]སེམས་སེམས་བྱུང་དེ་ལས་གཞན་པ་དང་ལྡན་པ་ལ་མཚུངས་ལྡན་མ་འདྲེས་པ་མེད་ཀྱང་རྫས་གཞན་དང་མ་འདྲེས་པ་ཡོད་པའི་ཕྱིར་མ་འདྲེས་པ་ཡིན་ཞེས་འདོད་པ་ཙམ་ལས་རང་དབང་ཅན་གྱི་དོན་གཞན་སྐབས་འདིར་མ་བཤད་ཀྱང་། འོག་ཏུ།

> དེ་ནི་ཉོན་མོངས་པ་ཅན་གྱི་ཡིད་ཡིན་ནོ། །དེ་ལ་ནི་མ་རིག་པ་རང་དབང་ཅན་ཡོད་དེ་དེའི་སྟོབས་ཀྱིས་
> དེ་དང་མཚུངས་པར་ལྡན་པའི་འདོད་ཆགས་ལ་སོགས་པ་དྲངས་པའི་ཕྱིར་རོ་

ཞེས་འབྱུང་བའི་ཕྱིར་རོ། །དོན་གསང་མཁན་པོ་རྫས་མ་འདྲེས་པ་ཞེས་བཤད་ཀྱང་མཐུ་མ་འདྲེས་པ་ལ་བཤད་དོ།།

དེ་ལྟར་ལུགས་གཉིས་ཡོད་པ་ལས་མ་ཏ་མ་ཏེ་གཉིས་པ་འཐད་པར་བཞེད་ཀྱང་རང་ལུགས་ལ་རྟེན་མ་འདྲེས་པ་འཐད་པར་མངོན་ཏེ། ཅི་ཙམ་ནས་སྨོངས་པའི་མཐུས་ཆགས་སོགས་གཞན་རྣམས་འཇུག་ཀྱང་དེ་དག་ལ་བརྟེན་ནས་ཀྱང་མ་རིག་པ་འཇུག་པའི་ཕྱིར་དང་། ཉོན་ཡིད་ཀྱི་འཁོར་རྣམས་ཕན་ཚུན་རྒྱུ་འབྲས་ཡིན་པས་འདི་ཁོ་ནས་དྲང་ཞེས་བཞག་ཏུ་མེད་པའི་ཕྱིར་རོ།།

> ཅིའི་ཕྱིར་ཉོན་ཡིད་མེད་ན་ལྔ་པོ་དག་དང་མི་འདྲ་བའི་སྐྱོན་དུ་འགྱུར་ཞེ་ན།།

ཐེག་བསྡུས་སུ།

> ཉོན་མོངས་པ་ཅན་གྱི་ཡིད་དེ་ཡོད་པར་ཅི་མངོན་ཞེ་ན། དེ་མེད་དུ་ཟིན་ན་མ་རིག་པ་མ་འདྲེས་པ་མེད་
> པའི་སྐྱོན་དུ་འགྱུར་རོ། །ལྔ་པོ་དག་དང་འདྲ་བ་མེད་པའི་སྐྱོན་དུ་ཡང་འགྱུར་ཏེ། འདི་ལྟར་རྣམ་པར་
> ཤེས་པ་ལྔའི་ཚོགས་དག་གི་ལྷན་ཅིག་འབྱུང་བའི་གནས་ནི་མིག་ལ་སོགས་པའོ།།

ཞེས་སོ། །འདི་ལ་གཉིས། དོན་གསང་གི་ལུགས་ནི་

> ཡིད་[50a]ཤེས་ནི་རྟེན་འདས་པ་ཁོ་ན་མ་ཡིན་ཏེ་འཇུག་ཤེས་ཡིན་པའི་ཕྱིར་དཔེར་ན་མིག་ཤེས་བཞིན།
> དོན་ནི་དབང་ཤེས་ལྔ་ལ་འདས་པའི་རྟེན་འདས་མ་ཐག་པའི་ཡིད་དེ་དང་ལྷན་ཅིག་པའི་རྟེན་དབང་པོ་
> ལྔ་སྟེ་གཉིས་ཡོད་ལ་ཡིད་ཤེས་ལ་མེད་པ་མི་འཐད་དེ་འཇུག་ཤེས་སུ་ཁྱད་པར་མེད་པའི་ཕྱིར་

ཞེས་པའོ།།

བཤད་སྦྱར་གྱི་ལུགས་ནི། འདི་ནི་རང་ལུགས་ལ་འདོད་པ་མིན་གྱི། གཞན་གྱི་གཞུང་ལས་ལྷན་ཅིག་སྐྱེས་པའི་གནས་མེད་[1195]པའི་རྣམ་པར་ཤེས་པ་ཅི་ཡང་མེད་དོ་ཞེས་འབྱུང་བས་ནི་དེ་སུན་འབྱིན་པའོ། །ཇེ་

ལྟར་ཞི་ན། ཚོགས་དྲུག་ལས་མི་འདོད་པ་དེ་དག་ལ་ཀུན་གཞི་དང་ཉོན་ཡིད་ནི་མེད་པས་ན་ཡིད་ཤེས་མེད་པར་འགྱུར་ཏེ་ལྷན་ཅིག་པའི་རྟེན་མེད་པའི་ཕྱིར་རོ།།

འགྲེལ་པ་གཉིས་ཀ་མ་གྲུབ་སྟེ། སྙིང་གི་ཕྱོགས་བུ་ག་གཅིག་ནས་དགུའི་བར་རྣམས་ཡིན་ནོ་ཞི་ན།

མི་འཐད་དེ་ཡིད་ཤེས་དེ་ངེས་པར་རྟོག་པ་དང་རྗེས་སུ་དྲན་པའི་རྣམ་རྟོག་གིས་རྟོག་བཅས་སུ་མི་འགྱུར་ཏེ་དབང་པོ་གཟུགས་ཅན་རྟེན་དུ་ཡོད་པའི་ཕྱིར་རོ། །དཔེར་ན་དབང་ཤེས་བཞིན། གཞན་ཡང་ཡིད་ཤེས་ཀྱི་ཚོར་བ་རྡུལ་ཕྲ་རབ་བསགས་པ་ལ་བརྟེན་པའི་ཕྱིར་སེམས་ཚོར་བ་མ་ཡིན་པར་འགྱུར་བ་དང་། ཡིད་ནི་ནང་གི་སྐྱེ་མཆེད་དེ་བསྟན་དུ་མེད་པ་ཞེས་པའི་མདོ་དང་འགལ་[གསང་][1] བའི་ཕྱིར་རོ། །ཞེས་པའོ།།

དེ་ལྟར་ལུགས་གཉིས་ཡོད་ཀྱང་། [མཛོད་]

ཐ་མའི་རྟེན་འདས་ལྔ་རྣམས་ཀྱི། །དེ་དང་ལྷན་ཅིག་སྐྱེས་པའང་ཡིན།།

ཞེས་པ་ལྟར་འདོད་པ་རྣམས་ལ་དོན་གསང་ལྟར་སྦྲུབ་དགོས་ལ་ཡིད་ཤེས་ལ་ལྷན་ཅིག་སྐྱེས་པའི་རྟེན་སྙིང་གི་གཟུགས་ཡོད་པར་འདོད་པ་བཤད་སྒྲར་ལྟར་ཡང་བྱའོ།།

ཅིའི་ཕྱིར་ཉོན་ཡིད་མེད་ན་སྙོམས་འཇུག་བྱེ་[50b]བྲག་མེད་པའི་སྐྱོན་དུ་འགྱུར་རོ་ཞི་[གསང་]ན།

ཉོན་ཡིད་མེད་ན་སྙོམས་འཇུག་གཉིས་ཀྱི་ངོ་བོ་ལ་ཁྱད་མེད་པར་འགྱུར་ཏེ། ཚོགས་དྲུག་འགག་པར་ནི་འདྲ་ལ་ཉོན་ཡིད་ཡོད་མེད་ཀྱི་ཁྱད་པར་མེད་པའི་ཕྱིར་རོ། །ཁོ་བོ་ཅག་ལྟར་ན་འདུ་ཤེས་མེད་པའི་སྙོམས་འཇུག་ལ་ངའོ་སྙམ་པའི་ང་རྒྱལ་དང་ང་ར་འཛིན་དང་བདག་ཏུ་ཆགས་པ་རྣམས་ཡོད་པས་མ་ཞི་ལ་འགོག་སྙོམས་དེ་དག་དང་བྲལ་བས་ཞི་བའི་ཕྱིར་[གསང་]རོ།།

གལ་[བཤད་]ཏེ་ས་དང་ཡིད་བྱེད་ཐ་དད་པས་བྱེ་བྲག་མེད་པར་མི་འགྱུར་རོ་ཞི་ན་མ་ཡིན་ཏེ་ཁྱད་པར་དེ་ཙམ་ཡོད་ཀྱང་ཞི་མ་ཞིའི་ངོ་བོའི་ཁྱད་པར་མི་འཐད་པ་སོ་ན་གནས་[སྦྱར་]སོ།།

འོན་[དོན་]ཏེ་འཕགས་པ་དང་སོ་སྐྱེའི་རྒྱུད་ཀྱི་ཁྱད་པར་ཡང་ཡོད་དོ་ཞི་ན། དེ་གཉིས་ཀྱི་ཁྱད་པར་[1196]ཡང་མི་འཐད་དེ་འདི་ལྟར་འཕགས་པ་རྣམས་ཀྱིས་འདུ་ཤེས་མེད་པའི་སྙོམས་འཇུག་ལ་གཡང་སར་འདུ་ཤེས་ནས་སྤོང་བ་ཡིན་ལ་དེ་ཡང་ང་ར་འཛིན་སོགས་མ་ཞི་བས་ཡིན་གྱི་,ཚོགས་དྲུག་འགག་ཙམ་གྱིས་སྤོང་ན་འགོག་སྙོམས་ཀྱང་སྤོང་པར་འགྱུར་རོ། །ཁོ་བོ་ཅག་ལྟར་ན། ཞི་བ་དང་མ་ཞི་བའི་ཁྱད་པར་ཡོད་པས་སྤོང་མི་སྤོང་རིགས་སོ། །དེ་ལྟར་ཡང་ཐེག་ཆེན་བསྡུས་པར།

> འདུ་ཤེས་མེད་པ་དང་འགོག་པའི་སྙོམས་པར་འཇུག་པ་[2] བྱེ་བྲག་མེད་པའི་སྐྱོན་དུ་ཡང་འགྱུར་ཏེ་འདི་ལྟར་འདུ་ཤེས་མེད་པའི་སྙོམས་པར་འཇུག་པ་ནི་ཉོན་མོངས་པ་ཅན་གྱི་ཡིད་ཀྱིས་རབ་ཏུ་ཕྱེ་བ་ཡིན་གྱི,[3]

---

[1] See note to translation for an explanation of such glosses. [2] *'dus shes med pa dang snyoms par 'jug pa gnyis* D,O,P.
[3] *gyis* Lamotte (1938:5).

འགོག་པའི་སྙོམས་པར་འཇུག་པ་ནི་མ་ཡིན་ཏེ། གཞན་དུ་ན་འདི་གཉིས་བྱེ་བྲག་མེད་པ་ཉིད་དུ་འགྱུར་
རོ།།

ཞེས་སོ།།

ཅི་ཉོན་ཡིད་མེད་ན་འདུ་ཤེས་མེད་པ་བར་སྐྱེས་པ་རྣམས་ང་ར་འཛིན་མེད་པའི་སྐྱོན་དུ་འགྱུར་རོ་ཞེ་ན།

འདུ་ཤེས་མེད་པར་སྐྱེས་པའི་དང་པོའི་ཚེ་ཡིད་ཤེས་[51a]ང་ར་འཛིན་དང་བཅས་པར་སྐྱེ་བས་ཉོན་མོངས་ཅན་དང་ང་ར་འཛིན་ཡོད་དུ་ཆུག་ཀྱང་སྐྱེས་ནས་ཇི་སྲིད་འཆི་བའི་སེམས་མ་སྐྱེས་ཀྱི་བར་གྱི་རྒྱུན་དེ་ང་ར་འཛིན་མེད་པར་འགྱུར་ཏེ་ཉོན་ཡིད་ནི་མེད་ལ་ཚོགས་དྲུག་འགག་པའི་ཕྱིར་རོ།།

གལ་[བཤད་]ཏེ་དང་པོའི་སྐྱེས་པའི་ཚེ་ང་ར་འཛིན་ཅན་གྱི་ཡིད་མངོན་དུ་འགྱུར་བ་དེའི་རྗེས་སུ་ང་ར་འཛིན་མངོན་གྱུར་མེད་ཀྱང་བག་ཆགས་ཡོད་པས་ན་ང་ར་འཛིན་དང་བཅས་པའོ་ཞེ་ན།

མི་རུང་སྟེ་ང་ར་འཛིན་གྱི་རྟེན་ཡིད་ཤེས་མེད་ལ་གཟུགས་ཀྱི་ཕུང་པོ་བག་ཆགས་ཀྱི་བསྔོ་གཞིར་མི་རུང་བའི་ཕྱིར་[སྒྲུར་] རོ། །འདུ་ཤེས་མེད་པའི་ལྷ་ལ་ང་ར་འཛིན་མེད་ན་ཉོན་མོངས་པ་ཅན་མ་ཡིན་པར་འགྱུར་རོ། །དེ་འདོད་ན་[དོན་]འཕགས་པ་རྣམས་ཀྱིས་འདུ་ཤེས་མེད་པ་དེ་དག་མི་ཁོམ་པའི་གནས་སུ་གཟིགས་ནས་སྤོང་བར་མི་འགྱུར་རོ། །ཚོགས་དྲུག་ཞི་བ་ཙམ་གྱིས་མི་ཁོམ་པར་མཐོང་ནས་སྤོང་བ་ཡང་མ་ཡིན་ཏེ་འགོག་སྙོམས་བཞིན་ནོ། །ཉོན་ཡིད་ཡོད་ན་ནི་ང་ར་འཛིན་ལ་སོགས་པ་ཀུན་ཏུ་འབྱུང་བ་དང་ཚོགས་དྲུག་ཀྱང་[1197]མེད་པས་ཕྱིན་ཅི་ལོག་གིས་བསྐལ་ཆེན་ལྔ་བརྒྱ་ཙམ་དུ་གནས་དགོས་པས་མི་ཁོམ་པའི་གནས་སུ་འགྱུར་རོ། །དེ་ལྟར་ཐེག་ཆེན་བསྡུས་པར།

གལ་ཏེ་འདུ་ཤེས་མེད་པ་བ་དེ་ན་ང་ར་འཛིན་པ་དང་། ངའོ་སྙམ་པའི་ང་རྒྱལ་མེད་ན་འདུ་ཤེས་མེད་
པར་སྐྱེ་བ་ཐོག་ཐག་[1]ཏུ་ཉོན་མོངས་པ་ཅན་མ་ཡིན་པའི་སྐྱོན་དུ་ཡང་འགྱུར་རོ་

ཞེས་སོ།།

ཉོན་ཡིད་མེད་ན་ངེས་ཚིག་མེད་པའི་སྐྱོན་དུ་ཇི་ལྟར་འགྱུར་ཞེ་ན། ཉོན་ཡིད་མེད་ན་རྟག་ཏུ་ང་ར་སེམས་པའི་ཕྱིར་ཡིད་དོ་ཞེས་པའི་ངེས་ཚིག་འདི་རྣམ་ཤེས་གང་ལ་ཡང་མི་གནས་པར་འགྱུར་ཏེ་ཀུན་གཞི་དང་དབང་ཤེས་ལ་[51b]ང་ར་སེམས་པ་མེད་ལ་ཡིད་ཤེས་འཁོར་བཅས་ལ་རྟག་ཏུ་སེམས་པ་མེད་པའི་ཕྱིར་རོ། །དེ་ལྟར་ཡང་ཐེག་བསྡུས་སུ།

ངེས་པའི་ཚིག་མེད་པའི་སྐྱོན་དུ་ཡང་འགྱུར་རོ་

ཞེས་སོ།།

---

[1] *thob ma thag* M,N.

ཅིའི་ཕྱིར་ཉོན་ཡིད་མེད་ན་ང་ར་འཛིན་པ་རྣམ་པ་ཀུན་ཏུ་འབྱུང་བ་མི་འཐད་ཅེ་ན།

ང་སྦྱིན་པ་བྱེད་ང་སྲོག་བཅོད་ང་ཁྲུས་བྱེད་ཅེས་པ་ལྟར་དགེ་མི་དགེ་ལུང་མ་བསྟན་གྱི་སེམས་ཐམས་ཅད་ལ་ང་ར་འཛིན་དམིགས་ཤིང་དེ་ཡང་ཉོན་ཡིད་ཡོད་ན་རུང་གི ,མེད་ན་མི་རུང་སྟེ་དེ་མེད་ན་ང་ར་འཛིན་མི་དགེ་བའི་སེམས་དང་མཚུངས་པར་ལྡན་པས་ན་དགེ་བ་དང་ལུང་མ་བསྟན་གྱི་སེམས་དང་དུས་གཅིག་ཏུ་མི་འབྱུང་ངོ་། །ཉོན་ཡིད་ཡོད་ན་དེའི་འཁོར་དུ་འབྱུང་ཞིང་དེ་ཡང་ལུང་མ་བསྟན་ཡིན་པའི་ཕྱིར་དགེ་མི་དགེའི་སེམས་དང་ལྡན་ཅིག་ཏུ་འཇུག་པར་མི་འགལ་ལོ། །དེ་སྐད་དུ་ཡང་ཐེག་བསྡུས་སུ།

> དགེ་བ་དང་མི་དགེ་བ་དང་ལུང་དུ་མ་བསྟན་པའི་སེམས་རྣམས་ལ་ཡང་ང་ར་འཛིན་པ་དུས་ཐམས་ཅད་དུ་ཀུན་ཏུ་འབྱུང་བར་དམིགས་པའི་ཡང་ཕྱིར་རོ། །གཞན་དུ་ན་ནི་མི་དགེ་བའི་སེམས་ཁོ་ན་དང་དེ་མཚུངས་པར་ལྡན་པས་ངའོ་སྙམ་པའི་ཉོན་མོངས་པ་ཀུན་ཏུ་འབྱུང་གི ,དགེ་བ་དང་ལུང་དུ་མ་བསྟན་པ་དག་ལ་ནི་མ་ཡིན་ནོ་

ཞེས་སོ།།

> འདི་ལ་ངོ་བོ་ཉིད་མེད་པས་
>
> ང་ར་འཛིན་དུས་ཀུན་ཏུ་འབྱུང་བ་དེ་ཡང་མ་རིག་པ་མེད་ན་མེད་ཅིང་མ་རིག་པ་དེ་ཡང་རྟེན་ཉོན་ཡིད་ཁོ་ན་ལ་[1198]ཡོད་པས་སོ་

ཞེས་འཆད་ལ། དོན་གསང་དུ། ང་ར་འཛིན་དགེ་མི་དགེ་ལུང་མ་བསྟན་གྱི་སེམས་ཐམས་ཅད་ཀྱི་ཚེ་ཡོད་པ་ལྟར་སྣང་བ་ནི་ཆ་ཕྲ་བས་འཁྲུལ་ནས་དགེ་བ་དང་ལུང་དུ་མ་བསྟན་གྱི་སེམས་དང་དུས་མཉམ་པར་བཟུང་བ་ཡིན་ལ། ཉོན་ཡིད་མི་འདོད་ན་མི་དགེ་བའི་སེམས་ཁོ་ན་[52a]ལ་ང་ར་འཛིན་འབྱུང་ཞེས་པ་མི་འཐད་དེ། བྱེ་སྨྲ་ལྟར་ན་འཇིག་ལྟ་བསྒྲིབས་ལ་ལུང་མ་བསྟན་དང་། མདོ་སྡེ་པ་དང་རང་ཉིད་ཀྱི་ལུགས་ལྟར་ན་ཡང་ང་ར་འཛིན་དང་ངའོ་སྙམ་པའི་ང་རྒྱལ་ལྷན་སྐྱེས་རྣམས་བསྒྲིབས་ལ་ལུང་དུ་མ་བསྟན་གྱི་སེམས་ཁོ་ན་ལ་འབྱུང་བར་འདོད་པའི་ཕྱིར་རོ་ཞེ་ན། ཞེས་པའི་རྩོད་པ་གཉིས་བཀོད་ནས་

དང་པོའི་ལན་ལ། ང་ར་འཛིན་དུས་ཐམས་ཅད་དུ་མི་འབྱུང་ན་སོ་སྐྱེའི་དགེ་བ་དང་ལུང་མ་བསྟན་ཇི་ལྟར་ཟག་བཅས་ཡིན། ཟག་པ་ལ་དམིགས་པས་ཟག་པ་རྒྱས་པའི་ཟག་བཅས་སུ་མི་འགྱུར་ཏེ། སེམས་དེ་གཉིས་མངོན་དུ་གྱུར་པའི་ཚེ་རང་རྒྱུད་ཀྱི་ཟག་པ་འགགས་པ་དང་མ་སྐྱེས་ནས་མེད་པས་མེད་པ་ལ་རྒྱས་པར་མི་སྲིད་པའི་ཕྱིར་རོ། །གཞན་གྱི་ཟག་པ་ལ་དམིགས་པས་ཀྱང་མ་ཡིན་ཏེ་ཕྱིའི་དམིགས་པ་མི་འདོད་པས་སོ། །ཟག་པའི་བདག་པོ་ཙམ་གྱིས་ཡིན་ན་ཟག་མེད་ལ་ཡང་ཐལ་ལོ། །ཟག་པའི་ས་བོན་དང་འབྲེལ་བས་ཡིན་ན་ལམ་བདེན་ལ་ཡང་ཐལ་ལོ། །དེས་ན་ཉོན་ཡིད་ཡོད་ན་ཟག་པ་མངོན་གྱུར་དང་ལྷན་ཅིག་འཇུག་པའི་ཕྱིར་ཟག་

བཅས་སུ་རུང་ངོ་ཞེས་དང་།

གཉིས་པའི་ལན་ལ། འབྲས་བུ་མི་འདོད་པ་འབྱིན་པའི་མི་དགེ་བ་མིན་གྱི་དགེ་བའི་མི་མཐུན་པའི་ཕྱོགས་ཙམ་ལ་བྱའོ། །ཞེས་འཆད་དོ།།

ཉོན་ཡིད་ཀྱི་སྒྲུབ་པར་བྱེད་པ་རྣམས་བཤད་ཟིན་ཏོ། །ཡིད་དང་ཀུན་གཞིའི་དཀའ་བའི་གནས་རྒྱ་ཆེར་འགྲེལ་པ་ལེགས་པར་བཤད་པའི་རྒྱ་མཚོ་ཞེས་བྱ་བ་ལས་སྒྲུབ་བྱེད་བཤད་པ་སྟེ་ལེའུ་གཉིས་པའོ།།

[Chapter Eight]

གསུམ་པ་རྣམ་ཤེས་ཚོགས་དགུར་འདོད་པ་དགག་པ་ལ་གཉིས་ལས་ཕྱོགས་སྔ་མ་ནི། [1199]

བདུན་པ་ལེན་པའི་རྣམ་ཤེས་དང་། །ཀུན་གཞི་གསུམ་དུ་འཆད་པ་དང་། །[52b] དགུ་པ་དྲི་
མེད་རྣམ་ཤེས་སུ། །འདོད་པ་ཡང་དག་བདེན་པའི་ལུགས།།

འདིར་ཐེག་པ་ཆེན་པའི་སློབ་དཔོན་རྣམས་རྣམ་ཤེས་གྲངས་མང་ཉུང་དུ་འདོད་པ་རྣམས་རྒྱའི་སློབ་དཔོན་ཞིན་ཆིག་གིས་བཤད་པ་ལྟར་དགོད་དོ། །དེ་ཡང་དགོངས་འགྲེལ་གྱི་འགྲེལ་ཆེན་བམ་པོ་དོན་ལྔ་པ་ལས།[1]

ཉོན་ཐོས་ཀྱི་སྡེ་སྣོད་རྣམས་ལས་རྣམ་པར་ཤེས་པ་ནི་དྲུག་ཁོ་ནའོ་ཞེས་འབྱུང་གི་,བདུན་དང་བརྒྱད་ཅེས་པ་ནི་མི་སྟོན་ཏེ་ཞིབ་ཏུ་ནི་དེ་ཉིད་ལས་བསྟན་པ་བཞིན་ནོ།།

འདིར་ཐེག་པ་ཆེན་པོའི་བསྟན་པ་དང་སྦྱར་ན་བཤད་པ་རྣམ་པ་གཉིས་ཡོད་དེ། དེ་ལ་དང་པོ་ནི་སློབ་དཔོན་ཀླུ་སྒྲུབ་ལ་སོགས་པས།[2] རྣམ་པར་ཤེས་པ་ནི་དྲུག་ཁོ་ནའོ་ཞེས་བཤད་དེ། དེའི་ཕྱིར་སློབ་དཔོན་ཟླ་བྲུས་མཛད་པའི་བསྟན་བཅོས་དབུ་མ་སྙིང་པོའི་ནང་ནས་དེ་ཁོ་ན་ཉིད་ཀྱི་བདུད་རྩི་ལ་འཇུག་པའི་ལེའུ་ལས།

རྣམ་པར་ཤེས་པ་དྲུག་ལས་གུད་ན་གཞན་ཀུན་གཞི་རྣམ་པར་ཤེས་པ་མེད་དེ། མིག་ལ་སོགས་པའི་
རྣམ་པར་ཤེས་པ་དྲུག་གིས་མ་བསྡུས་པའི་ཕྱིར། ནམ་མཁའི་མེ་ཏོག་དང་མཚུངས་སོ།[3]

ཞེས་བཤད་པས།[4]དེའི་ཕྱིར་དེ་དག་གི་གཞུང་གིས་རྣམ་པར་ཤེས་པ་དྲུག་ཁོ་ན་རྣམ་པར་བཞག་པར་རིག་པར་བྱའོ།།

གཉིས་པ་འཕགས་པ་བྱམས་པའི་གཞུང་གིས་ནི། འཕགས་པ་གསེར་འོད་དམ་པའི་མདོ་སྡེ་ལ་སོགས་པ་ལ་བརྟེན་ནས། རྣམ་པར་ཤེས་པ་བརྒྱད་ཚང་བར་འཇོག་པས་གཞུང་འདི[5]ལ་བརྟེན་ནས། རྒྱ་གར་

[1] P5517:103.1.2-4.4=SNṬ. [2] *pa→pas* SNṬ. [3] *pa→so* SNṬ. [4] *do→pas* SNṬ. [5] *pa'i gzhung la brten→pas gzhung 'di la brten* SNṬ.

ཡུལ་པའི་སློབ་དཔོན་རྣམས་རྣམ་པ་གསུམ་དུ་བཤད་དེ།

དང་པོ་ནི་སློབ་དཔོན་བོ་དྷི་ལེའུ་ཅེས་བསྟན་བཅོས་རྣམ་པར་རིག་པ་ཙམ་དུ་གྲུབ་པ་ལ་བརྟེན་ནས། སེམས་རྣམ་པ་གཉིས་རྣམ་པར་འཇོག་གོ །དེ་ལ་དང་པོ་ནི་ཆོས་ཉིད་ཀྱི་སེམས་ཏེ་དེ་ཡང་དེ་བཞིན་ཉིད་ཀྱི་ངོ་བོ་ཉིད་དེ།[1] དེ་བཞིན་ཉིད་ཀྱི་ངོ་བོ་ཉིད་འདི་ཉིད་ལ་སེམས་ཤེས་བྱ་[53a]ཡང་དམིགས་པ་ཅན་ནི་མ་ཡིན་ནོ། །གཉིས་པ་ནི་མཚུངས་པར་ལྡན་པའི་སེམས་ཏེ། དད་པ་དང་འདོད་ཆགས་ལ་སོགས་པའི་སེམས་ལས་[1200]བྱུང་བ་རྣམས་དང་མཚུངས་པར་ལྡན་པའོ། །ཞེས་བཤད་དེ། དེ་ནི་འདི་སྐད་དུ།

རྣམ་པར་རིག་པ་ཙམ་གྱི་ཡིད་ཀྱི་ངོ་བོ་ཉིད་ཡིན་པའི་ཕྱིར་[དང་། རྣམ་པར་རིག་པ་ཙམ་གྱི་ངོ་བོ་ཉིད་ཡིན་པའི་ཕྱིར།][2] ཡིད་དང་རྣམ་པར་ཤེས་པ་ཞེས་བཤད་ཀྱང་འགལ་བ་མེད་དོ། །

ཞེས་བྱ་བའི་ཐ་ཚིག་གོ །

གཉིས་པ་ནི་སློབ་དཔོན་ཡང་དག་བདེན་བས་རྣམ་པར་ངེས་པའི་མཛོད་ཅེས་བྱ་བའི་བསྟན་བཅོས་ལ་བརྟེན་ནས་རྣམ་པར་ཤེས་པ་རྣམ་པ་[3] དགུའི་དོན་འཇོག་སྟེ། རྣམ་པར་ཤེས་པ་རྣམ་པ་[4] དགུའི་ལེའུ་ལས་བསྟན་པ་བཞིན་ནོ། །དེ་ལ་རྣམ་པར་ཤེས་པ་དགུ་ཞེས་བྱ་བ་ཡང་མིག་ལ་སོགས་པའི་རྣམ་པར་ཤེས་པ་དྲུག་ནི་ཕལ་ཆེར་བསྟན་བཅོས་གཞན་དག་ལས་བཤད་པ་དང་མཐུན་ནོ། །བདུན་པ་ནི་ལེན་པའི་རྣམ་པར་ཤེས་པ་སྟེ་བརྒྱད་པ་ལ་བདག་དང་བདག་གིར་འཛིན་པས། ཉོན་མོངས་པ་ཁོ་ནའི་སྒྲིབ་པ་དང་ལྡན་གྱི་ཆོས་ཀྱི་[5] འཛིན་པ་ནི་མེད་དེ། ངེས་པར་སངས་རྒྱས་སུ་མི་འགྲུབ་བོ། །བརྒྱད་པ་ནི་ཀུན་གཞི་རྣམ་པར་ཤེས་པ་སྟེ་འདི་ཡང་རྣམ་པ་གསུམ་མོ། །

ཁ་ཅིག་ན་རེ། དང་པོ་ངོ་བོ་ཉིད་ཀྱི་ཀུན་གཞི་ནི། སངས་རྒྱས་སུ་[6] འགྲུབ་པའི་དོན་དང་ལྡན་པའོ། །གཉིས་པ་རྣམ་པར་སྨིན་པའི་ཀུན་གཞི་ནི་ཁམས་བཅོ་བརྒྱད་པོ་དག་ལ་དམིགས་པ་སྟེ་དེའི་ཕྱིར་བསྟན་བཅོས་དབུས་དང་མཐའ་རྣམ་པར་འབྱེད་པའི་ཚིག་ལེའུར་བྱས་པ་ལས། (འདིར་བསྒྱུར་བ་ལས་མི་སྣང་ཡང་རྒྱ་ནག་ཏུ་འགྱུར་པ་ལ་ཡོད་པར་གསལ།)

དབང་པོ་[7] དོན་དང་བདག་རྣམ་རིག །སྣང་བའི་རྣམ་པར་ཤེས་པ་ལས། །དེ་དང་འདྲ་བར་
རབ་ཏུ་[8] སྐྱེ། །

ཞེས་འབྱུང་བས་བསྟན་བཅོས་འདི་[53b]དག་ལ་སོགས་པ་ལ་བརྟེན་ནས་བརྒྱད་པ་ཁམས་བཅོ་བརྒྱད་

[1] *do→de* SNṬ. [2] Added from SNṬ. [3] *rnam pa* SNṬ. [4] *rnam pa* SNṬ. [5] *gyis* SNṬ. [6] *su* SNṬ. [7] *dang po* SNṬ. [8] *rab tu* omit SNṬ.

ལ་དམིགས་པར་བྱེད་དོ་ཞེས་བཤད་དོ། །གསུམ་པ་ཀུན་ནས་ཉོན་མོངས་པའི་ཀུན་གཞི་འདི་[1] ནི་དེ་བཞིན་ཉིད་ཀྱི་ཡུལ་ལ་དམིགས་ནས་ང་རྒྱལ་རྣམ་པ་བཞི་འབྱུང་སྟེ། དེ་ནི་ཆོས་འཛིན་པ་ཡིན་གྱི་,གང་ཟག་ཏུ་འཛིན་པ་ནི་མིན་ནོ་ཞེས་སློབ་དཔོན་བློ་བརྟན་གྱི་གཞུང་ལ་བརྟེན་ནས་དེ་སྐད་དུ་འཆད་དོ།།

དགུ་པ་ནི་དྲི་མ་མེད་པའི་རྣམ་པར་ཤེས་པ་སྟེ་དེ་བཞིན་[1201]ཉིད་ཀྱི་བདག་ཉིད་དོ། །དེ་བཞིན་ཉིད་ཀྱི་བདག་ཉིད་གཅིག་ལ་དོན་གཉིས་དང་ལྡན་པས་དང་པོ་ནི་དམིགས་པར་བྱ་བའི་ཡུལ་ཏེ་དེ་བཞིན་ཉིད་དང་། ཡང་དག་པའི་མཐའ་ཞེས་བྱ་བ་ལ་སོགས་པའོ། །གཉིས་པ་ནི་དམིགས་པར་བྱེད་པའི་དོན་[2] སྟེ་དེ་ནི་དྲི་མ་མེད་པའི་རྣམ་པར་ཤེས་པ་ཞེས་ཀྱང་བྱ། གཟོད་མ་ནས་རིག་[3] པ་ཞེས་ཀྱང་བྱ་སྟེ་ཞིབ་ཏུ་རྣམ་པར་ཤེས་པ་དགུ་བསྟན་པ་དང་། བསྟན་བཅོས་རྣམ་པར་ངེས་པའི་མཛོད་ཀྱི་ནང་ནས་རྣམ་པར་ཤེས་པ་དགུ་བསྟན་པའི་ལེའུ་ལས་འབྱུང་བ་བཞིན་ནོ་ཞེའོ།།

གསུམ་པ་ནི་སློབ་དཔོན་ཧྱུན་[4] ཙང་གིས་དེ་འཕགས་པ་ལང་ཀར་གཤེགས་པའི་མདོ་[5] ལ་སོགས་པ་དང་། སློབ་དཔོན་ཆོས་སྐྱོང་གི་གཞུང་ལ་བརྟེན་ནས་རྣམ་པར་ཤེས་པ་བརྒྱད་ཁོ་ན་རྣམ་པར་འཇོག་གོ་དགུ་ཞེས་ནི་མི་འཆད་དེ། སློབ་དཔོན་ཟླ་བའི་གཞུང་གཞིག་པའི་ཕྱིར། འདི་སྐད་དུ

> ཚད་མ་རྣམ་པར་གཞག་པ་དེ་ཉིད་ལ་རང་གི་ལུང་དང་འགལ་བའི་སྐྱོན་ཡོད་དེ། འདི་ལྟར་འཕགས་པ་ལང་ཀར་གཤེགས་པ་ལ་སོགས་པའི་མདོ་ཀུན་ལས་བརྒྱད་པ་ནི་ཀུན་གཞི་རྣམ་པར་ཤེས་པའོ།།

ཞེས་གསུངས་པའི་ཕྱིར་རོ།།

གལ་ཏེ་དེ་ལྟར་ན་ཅིའི་ཕྱིར་ཤེས་རབ་ཀྱི་ཕ་རོལ་ཏུ་ཕྱིན་པའི་མདོ་ལེའུ་ཆེན་པོ་ལ་སོགས་པ་ལས། རྣམ་པར་ཤེས་པ་ནི་དྲུག་ཁོ་ནའོ་ཞེས་གསུངས། སློབ་དཔོན་ཆོས་སྐྱོང་གི་བསྟན་བཅོས་རྣམ་པ་རིག་པ་ཙམ་དུ་གྲུབ་པ་ལས།

> བརྡ་སྤྲད་དེ་བཤད་པ་ལས་ཇི་སྐད་དུ། མདོ་དག་[6]ལས་རྣམ་པར་ཤེས་པ་ནི་དྲུག་གོ་ཞེས་གསུངས་པ་དེ་ནི་རྗེས་སུ་འགྱུར་བའི་དོན་གྱི་སྒོ་ཡིན་ནོ། །ཡང་ན་རྟེན་དུ་གྱུར་པའི་དབང་པོ་དྲུག་གི་རྗེས་སུ་རྣམ་[54a]པ་[7] དྲུག་གོ་ཞེས་གསུངས་པ་ཡིན་ཏེ་རྣམ་པར་ཤེས་པའི་རྣམ་[8] པའི་བྱེ་བྲག་ནི་ཡང་དག་པར་ན་རྣམ་པ་བརྒྱད་དོ།།

ཅི་སློབ་དཔོན་ཀླུ་སྒྲུབ་ཀྱིས་རྣམ་པ་དྲུག་ཁོ་ནའོ་ཞེས་མ་བཞག་གམ་ཞེ་ན། སྨྲས་པ། ཡང་དག་པར་ན་སློབ་དཔོན་ཀླུ་སྒྲུབ་ཀྱིས་བདུན་དང་བརྒྱད་པ་ཡང་ཡོད་པར་ཡིད་ཆེས་མོད་ཀྱི་

---

[1] SNṬ omits *'di.* [2] *byed pa→byed pa'i don* SNṬ. [3] SNṬ reads *rigs pa.* [4] D,M, and N add in parenthesis *'di mkhas pa gcig 'dug.* [5] The following, lines, up to ...*lang kar gshegs pa'i mdo* have been omitted from D,M,N,O, and P through haplology. [6] *dag* SNṬ. [7] SNṬ reads simply *rten du gyur pa'i dbang po drug go zhes.* [8] *rna ba'i → rnam pa'i* SNṬ.

ཞེས་སོ།།

དེ་ལྟར་འདོད་པ་གསུམ་བཀོད་ནས་ཝེན་ཚེག་རན་ཉིད་ཀུན་ཙང་གི་རྗེས་སུ་འབྲང་ཞིང་སློབ་དཔོན་ལེགས་ལྡན་འབྱེད་ཀྱི་བཞེད་པ་བཀོད་པ་ནི་ད་ལྟ་བོད་དུ་འགྱུར་བའི་དབུ་མ་སྙིང་པོའི་ནང་ན་ཀུན་གཞི་དེ་ལྟར་བཀག་པ་མི་སྣང་ལ་ལེའུའི་མིང་འདོགས་ཀྱང་དེ་འདྲ་མི་འདུག་གོ།

དེས་ན་སློབ་དཔོན་ཝེན་ཚེག་གི་མིང་ལ་འཕང་ཐང་གི་དཀར་ཆག་ཏུ་རྗོགས་གསལ་ཟེར་བ་འདུག་པས་ན་
[1202]རིག་པའི་རལ་གྲི་དྲི་མ་མེད་པའི་རྣམ་ཤེས་དགུར་འདོད་མཁན་རྗོགས་གསལ་དུ་བཞེད་པ་མི་འཐད་དེ། རྗོགས་གསལ་རྒྱ་ནག་ཡིན་ཞིང་། དགུར་ཡང་དག་བདེན་པ་འདོད་ལ། དེ་རྒྱ་གར་བ་ཡིན་པའི་ཕྱིར་རོ།།

དེ་ལྟར་ཚོགས་དགུར་འདོད་པ་དགག་པ་ནི།།

ཚོགས་བརྒྱད་དག་ལས་ལོགས་པ་ཡི། །གཙོ་བོ་རྣམ་ཤེས་ཡོད་གྱུར་ན། །རྟག་པའི་དངོས་པོར་འགྱུར་བའི་ཕྱིར། །ཚོགས་དགུར་འདོད་ལ་སྒྲུབ་བྱེད་མེད།།

ཚོགས་བརྒྱད་ལས་ལོགས་སུ་གྱུར་པའི་གཙོ་བོ་རྣམ་ཤེས་ཡོད་ན་རྟག་པ་ཡང་ཡིན་ལ་དངོས་པོ་ཡང་ཡིན་པ་ཡོད་པར་འགྱུར་ཏེ། དེ་འདུས་བྱས་མ་ཡིན་ཞིང་ཡུལ་དམིགས་པར་བྱེད་པའི་རྣམ་ཤེས་ཡིན་པའི་ཕྱིར་རོ། །ཅི་སྟེ་ཚོགས་བརྒྱད་དུ་མི་འདུ་ཡང་འདུས་བྱས་སུ་འདོད་དོ་ཞེ་ན། །མི་རུང་སྟེ་གཟུགས་དང་ལྡན་མིན་ཡིན་ན་དམིགས་བྱེད་དུ་འགལ་ཞིང་སེམས་བྱུང་ཡང་མིན་ལ་སེམས་སུ་ཡང་[54b]མི་རུང་སྟེ། ཚོགས་བརྒྱད་དུ་མི་འདུ་བའི་རྣམ་ཤེས་ཡོད་པར་འདོད་པ་ལ་ལུང་རིགས་ཡང་དག་མེད་པའི་ཕྱིར་དང་། རྣམ་ཤེས་བདུན་པ་ལེན་པའི་རྣམ་ཤེས་སུ་དེ་བཞིན་གཤེགས་པའི་མདོ་དང་རྒྱལ་བ་བྱམས་པའི་གཞུང་གི་ཆ་གང་དུ་ཡང་མ་གསུངས་པའི་ཕྱིར་དང་། ཤིང་རྟ་ཆེན་པོ་སྐུ་མཆེད་ཀྱི་བཞེད་པ་མིན་ལ་དེ་དག་གི་གཞུང་ལ་ཚད་མ་གྱུར་པ་བློ་བརྟན་རང་དང་ཡང་མི་མཐུན་པའི་ཕྱིར་རོ།།

ཡིད་དང་ཀུན་གཞིའི་དཀའ་བའི་གནས་རྒྱ་ཆེར་འགྲེལ་པ་ལེགས་པར་བཤད་པའི་རྒྱ་མཚོ་ཞེས་བྱ་བ་ལས་རྣམ་ཤེས་ཚོགས་དགུར་འདོད་པ་དགག་པ་སྟེ་ལེའུ་གསུམ་པའོ།།

བཞི་པ་རྣམ་ཤེས་ཚོགས་གཅིག་ཏུ་འདོད་པ་དགག་པ་ལ། ཕྱོགས་སྔ་མ་བརྗོད་པ་དང་། དེ་དགག་པ་གཉིས་སོ། །དང་པོ་ནི།

ཡིད་ཤེས་གཅིག་ཉིད་དབང་དྲུག་གི །རྟེན་ལ་སོ་སོར་རྒྱུ་བའི་ཚེ། །སོ་སོའི་མིང་དུ་བཏགས་པ་ཙམ། །བྲམ་ཟེའི་ཚོམས་དང་སྐྱེ་མཆེད་ནི། །བཅུ་གཉིས་སྟོན་པའི་མདོ་ལས་ཀྱང་། །གཅིག་པུར་གསུངས་དང་རྣམ་ཤེས་[1203]དྲུག །ཡིད་ཀྱི་སྐྱེ་མཆེད་ཡིན་གསུང་ཕྱིར། །ཤེས་ཀུན་ཡིད་ཤེས་གཅིག་པུ་ལོ།།

འདི་བྱུང་སེམས་གཅིག་པུར་སླ་བའི་འདོད་སྦྲུར་དུ་བཤད་དོ། །དེ་ཡང་བྲམ་ཟེའི་ཚོམས་ལས། རིང་དུ་འགྲོ་བ་གཅིག་པུ་རྒྱུ། །གདུལ་བར་དཀའ་བའི་སེམས་འདུལ་བྱེད། །དེ་ནི་བྲམ་ཟེ་ངས་བཤད་དོ།།

ཞེས་གཅིག་པུ་རྒྱུ་ཞེས་སེམས་དེ་གཅིག་པུར་གསུངས་པ་དང་། མདོ་ལས་ཀྱང་

རྣམ་པར་ཤེས་པའི་ཚོགས་དྲུག་ནི་ཡིད་ཀྱི་སྐྱེ་མཆེད་དོ།།

ཞེས་དང་།

རྣམ་པར་ཤེས་པ་དྲུག་གི་ཡུལ་ནི་ཡིད་ཀྱིས་མྱོང་ཞིང་ཡིད་ནི་འདི་དག་གི་སྟོན་པའོ།།

ཞེས་འབྱུང་བའི་ཕྱིར་ཡིད་ཤེས་གཅིག་ཉིད་རྟེན་དབང་པོ་སོ་[55a]སོ་ལ་བརྟེན་ནས་ཡུལ་སོ་སོ་ལ་རྒྱུ་བ་རྣམ་ཤེས་སོ་སོའི་མིང་ཐོབ་པ་ཡིན་ཏེ་དཔེར་ན་ཁང་པ་བུ་ག་མང་པོ་ཡོད་པ་རུ་མར་མི་གཅིག་བདེག་པ་བཞིན་ནོ། །དེ་ལྟར་ཡང་ཐེག་ཆེན་བསྡུས་པར།

ཁ་ཅིག་ནི་ཡིད་ཀྱི་རྣམ་པར་ཤེས་པ་དེ་ཉིད་རྟེན་དེ་དང་དེ་ནས་འབྱུང་པ་ན[1] དེ་དང་དེའི་མིང་ཐོབ་སྟེ། སེམས་པ་ལ་ལུས་དང་ངག་གི་ལས་ཞེས་བྱ་བ་བཞིན་ནོ་སྙམ་མོ། །རྟེན་ཐམས་ཅད་དུ་འབྱུང་བ་ན་སྣ་ཚོགས་ཀྱི་རྣམ་པས་གཉིས་སུ་སྣང་བ་འབྱུང་སྟེ། དེ་དོན་ཙམ་དུ་སྣང་བ་དང་། རྣམ་པར་རྟོག་པར་སྣང་བའི་ཕྱིར་རོ། །གཟུགས་ཅན་གྱི་ཁམས་ན་ནི་ཡིད་ཀྱི་རྣམ་པར་ཤེས་པ་ལུས་ལ་གནས་པའི་ཕྱིར། དེ་ལས་གཞན་པའི་དབང་པོ་གཟུགས་ཅན་ལུས་ལ་གནས[2] པ་བཞིན་དུ་གནས་ཐམས་ཅད་དུ་ཡང་རེག་བྱ་ལ་འཛིན་པར་སྣང་བའང་འབྱུང་ངོ་། །འདིར་ཚིགས་སུ་བཅད་པ།

གང་ཞིག་ལུས་མེད་ཕུག་གནས་ཤིང་། །རིང་དུ་འགྲོ་ལ་གཅིག་པུ་རྒྱུ། །གདུལ་བར་དཀའ་བའི་སེམས་འདུལ་བྱེད། །དེ་ནི་བྲམ་ཟེ་ངས་བཤད་དོ།།

ཡང་

དབང་པོ་ལྔ་པོ་འདི་དག་གི་སྤྱོད་ཡུལ་གྱི་ཡུལ་ནི་ཡིད་ཀྱིས་མྱོང་སྟེ་ཡིད་ནི་འདི་དག་གི་རྟོན་པའོ།།[3]

ཞེས་ཇི་སྐད་གསུངས་པ་ལྟ་བུའོ། །ཡང་སྐྱེ་མཆེད་བཅུ་གཉིས་བསྟན་པ་ལས།

རྣམ་པར་ཤེས་པའི་ཚོགས་དྲུག་ནི་ཡིད་ཀྱི་སྐྱེ་མཆེད་དོ་

ཞེས་ཇི་སྐད་གསུངས་པ་ལྟ་བུའོ།། [1204]

ཞེས་སོ།།

གཟུགས་ཅན་གྱི་ཞེས་པ་ནས་སྣང་བ་ཡང་འབྱུང་ཞེས་པའི་བར་གྱི་དོན་ནི། ཡིད་ཤེས་དེ་ལས་གཞན་

---

[1] 'jug pa ni D,O,P. [2] *snang→gnas* Nagao. [3] *ston pa* D,M,N,O,P.

པའི་དབང་པོ་གཟུགས་ཅན་ལྔ་པོ་རྣམས་ལུས་ལ་གནས་པ་སྟེ་དབང་པོ་དེ་དག་ལ་ཕན་པ་དང་གནོད་པ་བཞིན་གཟུགས་ཅན་གྱི་ཁམས་ན་ཡིད་ཤེས་[55b]ལུས་ལ་གནས་པས་དེའི་རྟེན་བ་ལུས་ཀྱིའང་ཡིན་ཅིང་ལུས་ཀྱི་གནས་ཐམས་ཅད་དུ་རེག་བྱ་ལྟེ་ཡང་སོགས་ལ་འཛིན་པར་ཡང་སྣང་ཞེས་པའོ། །རྣམ་པ་གཉིས་སུ་སྣང་ཞེས་པ་ཡིད་ཤེས་དེའི་ཆ་གཅིག་ནི་དོན་ཙམ་དུ་སྣང་ཞིང་རིག་ལ་ཞེན་ཅིང་རྟོག་པ་མེད་ལ་ཆ་གཅིག་ནི་དོན་དུ་སྣང་བ་ལ་ཞེན་ཅིང་རྟོག་པས་ན་ཡིད་ཤེས་ཀྱང་ཡིན་པའི་ཕྱིར་རྟོག་མེད་ཁོ་ནར་འགྱུར་བའི་སྐྱོན་མེད་ཅེས་པའི་དོན་ནོ། །ཁུངས་གཉིས་པར་སྟོན་པ་ཞེས་པ་ནི་ཡིད་ཀྱི་དབང་གིས་འགྲུབ་པའི་དོན་ནོ།།

གཉིས་པ་དེ་དགག་པ་ནི།

ལུང་དོན་གཞན་དུ་ནུས་ཕྱིར་དང་། །དབང་ཤེས་ཀྱིས་ཀྱང་ཕྱོགས་གྱུར་དང་། །འདས་དང་མ་
འོངས་འཛིན་འགྱུར་ཕྱིར། །ཚོགས་གཅིག་འདོད་པ་མུན་སྤྲུལ་ལོ།།

རེ་ཞིག་ལུང་ལས་རྣམ་ཤེས་གཅིག་ཏུ་མི་འགྲུབ་སྟེ་འདི་ལྟར་གཅིག་པུ་རྒྱུ་ཞེས་པ་ཡིད་ཤེས་ཁོ་ན་ལ་དགོངས་ཤིང་དབང་པོ་ལྔའི་སྤྱོད་ཡུལ་ལ་ཡིད་རྒྱུ་བ་དང་ཡིད་དབང་ཤེས་ཀྱི་སྔོན་པར་གསུངས་པ་ནི་རིམ་པ་ལྟར་ཡིད་ཀྱི་ཤེས་པས་ཆོས་ཐམས་ཅད་འཛིན་པ་དང་། ཡིད་ཤེས་ཀྱི་མཐུས་དབང་ཤེས་ཡུལ་ལ་འཇུག་པ་ཡོད་པ་དང་། དེ་དག་ཡུལ་ལ་མི་འཕྲོ་བར་ནང་དུ་སྡུད་པ་ཡང་ཡིད་ཤེས་ཀྱི་ནུས་པ་ལ་དགོངས་པ་ཡིན་པའི་ཕྱིར་དང་། ཚོགས་དྲུག་ཡིད་ཀྱི་སྐྱེ་མཆེད་དུ་གསུངས་པ་སྐྱེ་མཆེད་བཅུ་གཉིས་སུ་བྱེད་པ་ལ་སྐྱེ་མཆེད་གཞན་དུ་གཞག་ཏུ་མེད་པས་དེར་བཤད་ཀྱི་,ཡིད་ཤེས་སུ་སྟོན་པ་མ་ཡིན་ཏེ། ཡིད་དང་ཡིད་ཤེས་གཅིག་མ་ཡིན་པའི་ཕྱིར་རོ།།

རིགས་པས་ཀྱང་མི་འགྲུབ་སྟེ། གལ་ཏེ་གཅིག་ན་དབང་ཤེས་ཀྱིས་ཀྱང་ཕྱོགས་གྱུར་རྟགས་ལས་དཔོག་པ་དང་། འདས་མ་འོངས་འཛིན་པ་སྲིད་པར་འགྱུར་ཏེ་ཡིད་ཤེས་ཡིན་པའི་ཕྱིར་རོ། །ཡང་ཡིད་ཤེས་ཀྱང་རྟོག་མེད་ཁོ་ནར་[1205]འགྱུར་ཏེ། དབང་ཤེས་[56a]དང་རྫས་གཅིག་པའི་ཕྱིར་རོ།།

ཅི་སྟེ་དེ་གཅིག་ཀྱང་དོན་ཙམ་དུ་སྣང་བ་དང་ཞེན་ཅིང་རྟོག་པའི་ཆ་གཉིས་ཡོད་ཅེས་མ་བརྗོད་དམ་ཞེ་ན། ཆ་གཉིས་ཀྱང་ཡིན་ལ་རྫས་གཅིག་པུ་ཡང་ཡིན་པ་འདི་ནི་ལྷ་རྣམས་དགའ་བར་བྱེད་ཀྱི་དོན་ཤེས་པ་ནི་མ་ཡིན་ནོ།།

ཚོགས་གཅིག་ཏུ་འདོད་པ་འདི་ཐེག་བསྡུས་སུ་དངོས་སུ་མ་བཀག་ཀྱང་ཚོགས་བརྒྱད་སྒྲུབ་པ་ཉིད་འདི་བཀག་པ་ཡིན་ནོ། །བཤད་སྦྱར་དུ་འདིའི་འགྲེལ་པར་མ་བཀག་མོད་འོན་ཀྱང་གོང་དུ་ཡིད་ཤེས་ཀྱི་རྟེན་གྱི་སྙིང་གི་གཟུགས་སུ་འདོད་པ་བཀག་པ་འདིའི་ཡང་དགག་པའོ།།

རྣམ་ཤེས་བརྒྱད་ལས་གྲངས་མང་བ་དང་ཉུང་བར་སྨྲ་བ་ལ་ལུང་རིགས་ཀྱི་གནོད་པ་ཡོད་པ།

དེ་ཕྱིར་ཡིད་ཆེས་ལུང་རིགས་ཀྱིས། །གྲུབ་པ་རྣམ་ཤེས་བརྒྱད་ཡིན་ཕྱིར། །གསང་བའི་གནས་ལ་མི་ཞུམ་པའི། །མཁས་པས་བརྒྱད་ཉིད་འདོད་པར་བྱ།།

དེ་བཞིན་གཤེགས་པའི་གནས་ཟབ་མོ་ཀུན་གཞི་དང་། རྣམ་པར་རིག་པ་ཙམ་གྱི་ལྟ་བ་ལ་མི་སྐྲག་པའི་མཁས་པ་རྣམས་ཀྱིས་ཚོགས་བརྒྱད་ཉིད་དུ་འདོད་པར་བྱའོ།།

ཡིད་དང་ཀུན་གཞིའི་དཀའ་བའི་གནས་རྒྱ་ཆེར་འགྲེལ་པ་ལེགས་པར་བཤད་པའི་རྒྱ་མཚོ་ཞེས་བྱ་བ་ལས་རྣམ་ཤེས་གཅིག་པུར་འདོད་པ་དགག་པ་སྟེ་ལེའུ་བཞི་པའོ།།

གཞན་གྱི་ངལ་བརྒྱས་འབད་ཀྱང་ཤིན་ཏུ་རྟོགས་དཀའི་གནས། །ཇི་བཞིན་རྟོགས་མ་ནུས་པ་ཡིད་དང་ཀུན་གཞིའི་གནས། །སྐུ་མཆེད་གཞུང་དང་དེ་འགྲེལ་དགོངས་པ་ཇི་ལྟ་བཞིན། །བླ་མའི་དྲིན་གྱིས་ངས་འདིར་མ་འདྲེས་རྫོགས་པར་བཀོད།།

ལན་མང་ཐོས་པས་ཚིག་ཙམ་ཤེས་གྱུར་ཅིང་། །འདོད་པ་རིམ་པས་ཁ་ཏོན་བྱང་བ་ཅན། །ཡི་གེ་ཙམ་གྱིས་ཚིག་པར་འཛིན་པ་ཡི། །མཁས་པའི་ཤ་ཚུགས་[56b]ཅན་རྣམས་མགུ་དཀའ་མོད།།

ཐུབ་པའི་གསུང་དང་ཤིང་རྟ་ཆེ་རྣམས་ཀྱི། །གཞུང་ལུགས་འབྱེད་ལ་གཞན་དྲིང་མི་འཛོག་ཅིང་། །མུན་སྤྲུལ་བརྫ་ཡིས་བློ་གྲོས་མ་དཀྲུགས་པའི། །མཁས་པས་མཁས་པའི་ཡིད་[1206]རབ་འཕྲོག་པར་བྱེད།།

རྒྱ་ཆེན་རྒྱ་མཚོ་ལྟ་བུ་ཡི། །རྣམ་རིག་གཞུང་ལ་སྦྱངས་གྱུར་པ། །དེ་དག་གིས་ནི་རྣམ་ཤེས་འདི། །གཟུ་བློས་རིགས་དང་མི་རིགས་དཔྱད།།

གལ་ཏེ་རིགས་པ་ལྟ་ན་ལྷང་། །ཕྲ་ཞིང་ཕྲ་ལ་བདག་འདྲའི་བློ། །འཁྲུལ་མི་སྲིད་པ་མ་ཡིན་ཕྱིར། །ཅི་སྟེ་མིན་ན་གཞན་དུ་ཕྱིས།།

དེ་ལས་ཐོབ་པའི་རབ་དཀར་[1] དགེ་བ་འདི། །འདི་དང་ཕྱི་མ་ཀུན་ཏུ་མི་ཟད་གཏེར། །གཏེར་ཆེན་བུམ་བཞིན་དཔག་མེད་ཡོན་ཏན་དག །དག་དང་མ་དག་འགྲོ་ལ་སྩོལ་གྱུར་ཅིག། གཞན་ཡང་སྐྱེ་ཞིང་སྐྱེ་བ་ཐམས་ཅད་དུ། །སྡོམ་བརྩོན་དམ་པའི་རྗེས་སུ་འཇུག་པ་དང་། །ཐུབ་པའི་གསུང་གི་བདུད་རྩི་འཐུང་བ་དང་། །ཀུན་ལ་བྲན་བཞིན་ཁེངས་དང་བྲལ་གྱུར་ཅིག།

ཡིད་དང་ཀུན་གཞིའི་དཀའ་བའི་གནས་རྒྱ་ཆེར་འགྲེལ་པ་ལེགས་པར་བཤད་པའི་རྒྱ་མཚོ་ཞེས་བྱ་བ་འདི་ནི་མི་འཕྲོགས་པའི་མཁྱེན་རབ་དང་ཐུགས་རྗེ་དཔག་ཏུ་མེད་པ་མངའ་བས་གདུལ་བྱ་བགྲང་ལས་འདས་པའི་

[1] *dka'* O,P.

ཐར་པའི་ལམ་གསལ་བར་མཛད་པ་དོན་གྱི་སླད་དུ་མཆན་ནས་སློས་ཏེ་ཆོས་ཀྱི་རྗེ་དོན་གྲུབ་རིན་ཆེན་ཞབས་ཀྱི་རྟུལ་ཕྱི་བོས་ལེན་ཅིང་ཆེ་རབས་དུ་མར་ཚོགས་གཉིས་རླབས་པོ་ཆེ་བསྒྲུན་པས་དེ་བཞིན་གཤེགས་པའི་གསུང་རབ་ཕལ་མོ་ཆེ་མཐོང་བ་ཙམ་གྱིས་ཐུགས་སུ་ཆུད་ཅིང་ཐུབ་པའི་གསུང་གི་མཛོད་ཀྱི་གཅེས་པ་རྙེན་ཅིང་འགྲེལ་བར་འགྱུར་བ་ཟབ་མོའི་དོན་ལ་ཤེས་ནས་ཐེ་ཚོམ་བསལ་བ་ཆོས་ཀྱི་སྤྱན་ལྡན་ཆེན་པོ་རིད་མདའ་བ་གཞོན་ནུ་བློ་གྲོས་ཀྱི་ཞབས་ཀྱི་པད་མོ་གུས་པས་[57a]བསྟེན་པས་རྒྱལ་བའི་གསུང་གི་ཕྱོགས་རེའི་དོན་ལ་བློའི་འཇུག་པ་ཙུང་ཞིག་སད་པ། ཤར་མདོ་སྨད་པ་སྡེ་སྣོད་གསུམ་པ་བློ་བཟང་གྲགས་པས་མཁས་ལ་གྲུབ་པ་བརྙེས་པའི་དམ་པ་དུ་མས་བྱིན་གྱིས་བརླབས་ཤིང་གངས་རིའི་ཁྲོད་པ་རྣམས་ཀྱི་རྡོ་རྗེའི་གདན་དཔལ་ལྡན་ས་སྐྱའི་ཆོས་གྲྭ་ཆེན་པོར་སྦྱར་བ་འདིས་བསྟན་པ་དང་སེམས་ཅན་དཔག་ཏུ་མེད་པ་ལ་ཕན་ཐོགས་པར་གྱུར་ཅིག།

BIBLIOGRAPHY

Indian sūtras and śāstras mentioned in the Introduction and text are listed alphabetically (Devanāgarī) by title in the first section; Tibetan commentaries are listed alphabetically (Tibetan) by author in the second section; works by modern writers are listed alphabetically by author in the third section.

I Indian Sūtras and Śāstras

Abhidharma-kośa-kārikā (Vasubandhu). Gokhale (1946).

Abhidharma-samuccaya (Asaṅga). Pradhan (1950). Trans. Rahula (1971).

Abhidharma-samuccaya-bhāṣya (Jinaputra or Sthiramati). Tatia (1976).

Abhisamayālaṁkārālokā Prajñā-pāramitā-vyākhyā (Haribhadra). Wogihara (1932-35).

Abhisamayālaṁkāra-nāma-prajñā-pāramitopadeśa-śāstra-kārikā (Maitreya). Wogihara (1932-35).

Abhisamayālaṁkāra-vṛtti (Ārya Vimuktisena). First *abhisamaya* ed. by Pensa (1967). Skt. title of P5185, *[Ārya-]pañcaviṁśati-sāhasrikā-prajñā-pāramitopadeśa-śāstrābhisamayālaṁkāra-vṛtti.*

Ārya-gambhīra-saṁdhi-nirmocana-sūtra-ṭīkā (Won ch'uk). In Tib. *Dgong 'grel gyi grel chen.* P5517.

Triṁśikā Vijñāpti-mātratā-siddhi (Vasubandhu). Levi (1932).

Dharma-dharmatā-vibhāga[-kārikā] (Maitreya). In Tib. *Chos dang chos dbying rnam byed tshig le'u byas pa.* P5524.

Pratītya-samutpādādi-vibhaṅga-nirdeśa/Pratītya-samutpāda-vyākhyā (Vasubandhu). In Tib. *Rten cing 'grel par 'byung ba dang po dang rnam par dbye ba bshad pa.* P5495.

Pratītya-samutpādādi-vibhaṅga-nirdeśa-ṭīkā (Guṇamati). P5496.

Bodhicaryāvatāra (Śāntideva). Bhattacharya (1960).

Bodhicaryāvatāra-pāñjikā (Prajñākaramati). Vaidya (1960).

Madhyamakāvatāra (Candrakīrti). In Tib. *Dbu ma la 'jug pa.* La Vallée Poussin (1907-12).

Madhyānta-vibhāga (Maitreya). Nagao (1964).

Madhyānta-vibhāga-bhāṣya (Vasubandhu). Nagao (1964).

Mahāyāna-saṁgraha (Asaṅga). In Tib. *Theg pa chen po bsdus pa.* Lamotte (1973).

Mahāyāna-saṁgraha-bhāṣya (Vasubandhu). In Tib. *Theg pa chen po bsdus pa'i 'grel pa.* See Lamotte (1973).

Mahāyāna-saṁgrahopanibandhana (Asvabhāva). In Tib. *Theg pa chen po bsdus pa'i bshad sbyor.* See Lamotte (1973).

Mahāyāna-sūtrālaṁkāra (Maitreya). Levi (1911).

Mūla-madhyamaka-kārikā (Nāgārjuna). See La Vallée Poussin (1903-13).

Yukti-ṣaṣṭikā (Nāgārjuna). Lindtner (1982).

Ratnāvalī (Nāgārjuna). Tucci (1934-36). For Tib. text see Hahn (1982). P5658.

Ratna-gotra-vibhāga-mahāyānottara-tantra-śāstra (Maitreya?). Johnson (1950).

Laṅkāvatāra-sūtra. See Nanjio (1956).

Viṁśatikā Vijñāpti-mātratā-siddhi (Vasubandhu). See Levi (1932).

Vivṛta-guhyārtha-piṇḍa-vyākhyā/Vivṛta-gūḍhārtha-piṇḍa-vyākhyā. Author unknown. In Tib. *Don gsang ba rnam par phye ba bsdus te bshad pa.* P5553.

II Tibetan Commentaries

Kun dga' rgyal mtshan (Sa skya Paṇḍita). *Thub pa'i dgongs pa rab tu gsal ba.* In *Complete Works of the Great Masters of the Sa skya sect of Tibetan Buddhism,* vol. 5:1-50. Tokyo: The Toyo Bunko, 1968.

___. *Tshad ma rigs pa'i gter.* In *Complete Works of the Great Masters of the Sa skya sect of Tibetan Buddhism,* vol. 5:155-167. Tokyo: The Toyo Bunko, 1968.

___. *Sdom pa gsum gyi rab tu dbye ba'i bstan bcos.* In *Complete Works of the Great Masters of the Sa skya sect of Tibetan Buddhism,* vol. 5:297-321. Tokyo: The Toyo Bunko, 1968.

Ke'u tshang blo bzang 'jam dbyangs smon lam. *Rnal 'byor spyod pa pa'i lugs kyi yid dang kun gzhi'i rtsa 'grel gyi dka' gnas gsal byed nyi zla zung 'jug.* In the *Collected Works of Ke'u tshang sprul sku blo bzang 'jam dbyangs smon lam,* vol. 1:181-254. Dharamsala: LTWA, 1984.

Klong chen rab 'byams pa dri med 'od zer. *Sems dang ye she kyi dri lan. Zhal gdams dris lan skor: chos gzhi rin po che'i phreng ba*: 377-393. In *Miscellaneous Writings (Gsung thor bu)* vol. 1:247-393. Delhi: Sanje Dorje, 1973.

Dkon mchog 'jigs med bang po. *Grub pa'i mtha'i rnam par bzhag pa rin po che'i phreng ba.* Mundgod, India: Dre-gomang Buddhist Cultural Association, 1980.

Mkhas grub dpal bzang po. *Rje btsun bla ma tsong kha pa chen po'i ngo mtshar ma du byung ba'i nam par thar pa dam pa'i 'jug ngog. Lhasa gsung 'bum*, vol. Ka:2-144. New Delhi: Ngawang Gelek Demo, 1977.

Gung thang dkon mchog bstan pa'i sgron me. *Yid dang kun gzhi'i dka' gnas rnam par bshad pa mkhas pa'i 'jug ngog.* In *Collected Works of Gun-than dkon-mchog bstan-pa'i sgron-me*, vol. 2:275-402. New Delhi: Ngawang Gelek Demo, 1972.

Go rab 'byams pa bsod nams seng ge. *Sdom pa gsum gyi rab tu dbye ba'i rnam bshad rgyal ba'i gsung rab kyi dgongs pa gsal ba.* In *Complete Works of the Great Masters of the Sa skya sect of Tibetan Buddhism*, vol. 6:119-199. Tokyo: The Toyo Bunko, 1968.

___. *Sdom pa gsum gyi bstan bcos la dri shing rtsod pa'i len sdom gsum 'khrul spong.* In *Complete Works of the Great Masters of the Sa skya sect of Tibetan Buddhism*, vol. 6: 240.4-273.2. Tokyo: The Toyo Bunko, 1968.

Lcang skya rol pa'i rdo rje. *Grub mtha'i rnam par bzhag pa.* Sarnath: Pleasure of Elegant Sayings Press, 1970.

Stag tshang lo tsa ba shes rab rin chen. *Grub mtha' kun shes nas mtha' bral grub pa zhes bya ba'i bstan bcos rnam par bshad pa legs bshad kyi rgya mtsho.* Thim phu: Kun bzang stobs rgyal, 1976.

Thu'u bkvan blo bzang chos kyi nyi ma. *Grub mtha' thams cad kyi khungs dang 'dod tshul ston pa legs bshad shel gyi me long.* Sarnath: Chos je lama, 1963.

Bu ston rin chen grub. *Chos mngon po kun las btus kyi ṭīk rnam bshad nyi ma'i 'od zer. The Collected Works of Buston*, vol. 20:79-748. Ed. by Lokesh Chandra. New Delhi: International Academy of Indian Culture, 1967.

Blo bzang chos dbyings. *Kun gzhi'i thal 'phreng yig cha'i rje su 'jug pa.* Buxa: Shes rig 'dzin skyong slob gnyer khang, 1964.

Blo bzang 'jigs med. *Yid and kun gzhi'i rtsa ba'i mchan 'grel.* In *Rare Texts of the Bla-brang Bkra-sis-'khyil Tradition.* New Delhi: Kalsang Thabkay, 1974.

Blo bzang thugs rje. *Yid dang kun gzhi'i dka' gnas rgya cher' grel gyi gnad don gsal bar byed pa'i mtha' yod padma dkar po'i phreng ba blo gsal mgul rgyan.* No place, no date. Listed in Odani and Kalsang (1986).

Blo bzang dam chos rgya mtsho, Rong tha che tshang sprul sku. *Rnam rig pa'i lugs kyi yid dang kun gzhi'i don cung zad bshad pa ngo mtshar gzugs brgya 'char ba'i me long.* In *Collected Works of Blo bzang dam chos rgya mtsho*, vol. 1. New Delhi:

Ngawang Sopa, 1975.

Dbu pa blo gsal. *Grub pa'i mtha' rnam par bshad pa'i mdzod.* In Mimaki (1983).

'Brug rgyal dbang blo bzang 'phrin las rnam rgyal. *'Jam mgon chos kyi rgyal po Tsong kha pa chen po'i rnam thar.* Ed. Tshe-tan Zhabs-drung. Xining: Quinghai People's Publishing House, 1984.

Tsong kha pa blo bzang grags pa. *Skyes bu gsum gyis nyams su blangs pa'i rim pa thams cad tshang bar ston pa'i byang chub lam gyi rim pa.* Blockprint by Pad Dkar. Dharamsala 1974. Also P6001.

___. *Dge bdun nyi shu bsdus pa, zhugs dang gnas pa'i skyes bu chen po rnams kyi dka' gnas* (alternative name *Dge bdun nyi shu bsdus pa rjes gnang dang zhugs gnas?*). In *Legs bshad gser gyi phreng ba*:1281-1290. Mtsho sngon mi rigs dpe skrun khang, 1986.

___. *Sde bdun la 'jug pa'i sgo don gnyer yid kyi mun gsel.* In *Legs bshad gser gyi phreng ba*:1207-1244. Mtsho sngon mi rigs dpe skrun khang, 1986.

___. *Dpal gsang ba 'dus pa'i bshad pa'i rgyud ye shes rdo rje kun las 'tus pa'i rgya cher bshad pa rgyud bshad thabs kyi man ngag gsal bar bstan pa. Lhasa gsung 'bum*, vol. Ca:450-586. New Delhi: Ngawang Gelek Demo, 1977.

___. *Dbu ma la 'jug pa'i rgya cher bshad pa dgongs pa rab gsal.* Vārāṇasī: Dge ldan sphyi las khang, 1973. Also P6143.

___. *Zhugs pa dang gnas pa'i skyes bu chen po rnams kyi rnam par bzhag pa blo gsal bgrod pa'i them skas.* In *Legs bshad gser gyi phreng ba*:1291-1359. Mtsho sngon mi rigs dpe skrun khang, 1986.

___. *Shes rab kyi pha rol tu phyin pa'i man ngag gi bstan bcos mngon par rtogs pa'i rgyan 'grel pa dang bcas pa'i gya cher bshad pa'i legs bshad gser phreng zhes bya ba.* In *Legs bshad gser gyi phreng ba*:1-1112. Mtsho sngon mi rigs dpe skrun khang, 1986. Also *Lhasa gsung 'bum*, vol. Tsa. New Delhi: Ngawang Gelek Demo, 1977.

___. *Gsung rab kyi drang ba dang nges pa'i don rnam par phye ba gsal bar byed pa legs par bshad pa'i snying po.* Vārāṇasī: Dge ldan sphyi las khang, 1973. Also P6142.

___. *Gsen yig. Lhasa gsung 'bum*, vol. Ka. New Delhi: Ngawang Gelek Demo, 1977.

___. *Bsam gzugs zin bris.* In *Legs bshad gser gyi phreng ba*:1245-1260. Mtsho sngon mi rigs dpe skrun khang, 1986.

Zha dmar bstan 'dzin. *Lhag mthong chen mo'i dka' gnad rnam brjed byang du bkod pa dgongs zab snang ba'i sgron me.* Delhi: Mongolian Lama Guru Deva, 1972.

Rang 'byung rdo rje. *Rnam shes ye shes 'byed pa'i bstan bcos.* In *Dbu ma gzhan stong skor bstan bcos phyogs bsdus deb dang po*:49-62. Gangtok: Karma Shri Nalanda Institute, 1990.

Red mda' ba gzhon nu blo gros. *Dbu ma la 'jug pa'i rnam bshad de kho na nyid gsal ba'i sgron ma.* Sarnath: Sakyapa Student Union, 1982.

Rong ston shes rab kun rig. *Shes rab kyi pha rol tu phyin pa'i man ngag gi bstan bcos mngon par rtogs pa'i rgyan ces bya ba'i rnam bshad tshig don rab tu gsal ba.* Delhi: Ngawang Tobgay, 1972.

Śākya mchog ldan. *Shing rta chen po'i srol gnyis kyi rnam par dbye ba bshad nas nges don gcig tu bsgrub pa'i bstan bcos kyi rgyan. Collected Works*, vol 2:471-619. Thim phu 1978.

Sa bzang Ma ti Paṇ chen. *Dam pa'i chos mngon pa kun las btus pa'i 'grel pa shes bya ba rab gsal snang ba.* Gangtok: Gon po Tseten, 1977.

Bsod nams rgyal mtshan. *Byang chub sems dpa'i spyod pa la 'jug pa rnam par bshad pa dgongs pa nges par gsal ba.* In *A 14th century Sa-skya-pa Commentary on Śāntideva's Bodhi-caryāvatāra by bla ma dam pa Bsod nams rgyal mtshan.* New Delhi: Ngawang Topgay, 1973.

III Works by Modern Writers

Anacker, Stefan. (1984) *Seven Works of Vasubandhu.* Delhi: Motilal Banarsidass.

Batchelor, Stephen. (1979) *A Guide to the Bodhisattva's Way of Life.* Dharmsala: LTWA.

Bhattacharya, V. (1960) Ed. *Bodhi-caryāvatāra.* Bibliotheca Indica 280. Calcutta: Asiatic Society.

Brown, Brian Edward. (1981) "The Buddha Nature: A study of the *tathāgata-garbha* and *ālaya-vijñāna.*" Ph.D. dissertation. Fordham University.

Das (Bahadur), Sarat Chandra. (1985) *Tibetan-English Dictionary.* Calcutta, 1902; reprint ed., New Delhi.

Dasgupta, S.B. (1974) *An Introduction to Tantric Buddhism.* 3d edition. University of Calcutta.

Davidson, Ronald Mark. (1985) "Buddhist Systems of Transformation: Āśraya-parivṛtti/parāvṛtti Among the Yogācāra." Ph.D. dissertation. University of California (Berkeley).

de Jong, J.W. (1977) Ed. *Madhyamaka-kārikā.* Adyar: Theosophical Society.

Demiéville, Paul. (1987) "The Mirror of the Mind." In P.N. Gregory (1987):13-40.

Dhargyey, Ngawang. (1975) *A Short Biography and Letter of Je Tzong-k'a-pa.* Dharamsala: LTWA.

Dreyfus, George. (1991) "Ontology, Philosophy of Language, and Epistemology in Buddhist Tradition." Ph. D. dissertation. University of Virginia.

Dutt, N. (1966) Ed. *Bodhisattva-bhūmi.* Patna: K.P. Jayaswal Institute.

Friedmann, D.L. (1984) Trans. *Sthiramati, Madhyānta-vibhāga-ṭīkā.* Utrecht 1937; reprint ed. Talent (Oregon): Canon Publishers.

Gokhale, V.V. (1946) "The Text of the *Abhidharma-kośa-kārikā* of Vasubandhu." Journal of the Bombay Branch of the Royal Asiatic Society. New Series, vol. 22:72-102.

___. (1947) "Fragments from the *Abhidharma-samuccaya* of Asaṅga." Journal of the Bombay Branch of the Royal Asiatic Society. New Series, vol. 23:13-38.

Gregory, P.N. (1987) Ed. *Sudden and Gradual Approaches to Enlightenment in Chinese Thought.* Studies in East Asian Buddhism no. 5. Honolulu: University of Hawaii.

Griffiths, Paul, J. (1986) *On Being Mindless: Buddhist Meditation and the Mind-Body Problem.* Lasalle, Illinois: Open Court.

Gyatso, Tenzin (Dalai Lama XIV). (1984) *Kindness, Clarity and Insight.* Ed. Jeffrey Hopkins and Elizabeth Napper. Ithaca: Snow Lion.

Hakamaya, Noriaki. (1978) "Araya-shiki sonzai no hachi ronshō ni kansuru shobunken." *Komzawa Daigaku Bukkyōgakabu Kenyū Kiyo* 36:1-26.

Hahn, Michael. (1982) Ed., *Nāgārjuna's Ratnāvalī.* Bonn: Indica et Tibetica.

Hopkins, P.J. (1977) *Tantra in Tibet.* London: Allen and Unwin.

___. (1980) *Compassion in Tibetan Buddhism.* Valois, N.Y.: Snow Lion.

Huntington, C.W., Jr. (1989) *The Emptiness of Emptiness.* Honolulu: University of Hawaii.

Iida, Shotaro. (1980) *Reason and Emptiness: A Study in Logic and Mysticism.*Tokyo: Hokuseido Press.

Jackson, David. (1990) "Sa skya Paṇḍita the 'Polemicist': Ancient Debates and Modern Interpretations." JIABS 13.2 :17-116.

Johnston, E.H. (1950) Ed. *Ratna-gotra-vibhāga-mahāyānottara-tantra-śāstra. Journal of the Orissa and Bihar Research Society,* 26, part I.

Karmay, Samten Gyaltsen. (1988) *The Great Perfection (rDzogs chen). A Philosophical and Meditative Teaching in Tibetan Buddhism.* Leiden: E.J. Brill.

Kaschewsky, R. (1971) *Das Leben des lamaistischen Heiligen Tsongkhapa Blo-bzang grags-pa (1357-1419)*. 2 vols. Wiesbaden: Otto Harrassowitz.

Lai, Whalen and Lancaster, Lewis R. Eds. (1983) *Early Cha'n in China and Tibet.* Berkeley Buddhist Series, no. 5. Berkeley: University of California.

Lamotte, Étienne. (1934-35) "L'Ālaya-vijñāna (Le Réceptacle) dans le *Mahāyāna-saṁgraha* (chap. 2)." MCB:169-255.

___. (1935) Trans. *Saṁdhinirmocana Sūtra: L'Explication des mysteres.* Louvain: Institut Orientaliste.

___. (1970) Trans. *Le Traité de la Grande Vertu de Sagesse de Nāgārjuna* (*Mahāprajñā-pāramitā-śāstra*). Vol. I and II: Bibliothèque du Muséon, 18. Louvain: Institut Orientaliste, 1949; reprinted 1967. Vol III, IV and V: Publications de l'Institut Orientaliste de Louvain, 2, 12, and 24. Louvain: Institut Orientaliste, 1970, 76 and 80.

___. (1973) *La Somme du Grand Véhicule D'Asaṅga (Mahāyānasaṁgraha).* Two vols. Publications de L'Institut Orientaliste de Louvain, 8. Louvain-la-Neuve: Université de Louvain.

La Vallée Poussin, Louis de. (1907-12) Ed. *Dbu ma la 'jug pa* [and] *rang 'grel* (*Madhyamakāvatāra* [and] *bhāṣya*). Bibliotheca Buddhica 9. St. Petersburg.

___. (1903-13) Ed. *Mūla-madhyamaka-kārikās de Nāgārjuna avec la Prasannapadā Commentaire de Candrakīrti.* Bibliotheca Buddhica 4. St. Petersburg; reprint ed. Osnabrück 1970.

___. (1927-28) *Vijñapti-mātratā-siddhi (La Siddhi de Hiuan-tsang).* Paris.

___. (1934-35) "Note sur l'Ālaya-vijñāna." MCB:145-168.

Lopez, D.S. (1987) *A Study of Svātantrika.* Ithaca: Snow Lion.

Levi, Sylvan. (1925) Ed. *Triṁśikā Vijñapti-mātratā-siddhi.* Bibliothèque de L'École des Hautes Études. Paris: Champion. Reproduced Anacker (1984:422-423).

___. (1932) *Matériaux pour l'étude du système Vijñapti-mātra.* Bibliothèque de l'École des Hautes Études, 260. Paris: Champion. Reproduced in Anacker (1984).

Lindtner, C. (1982) *Nagarjuniana: Studies in the Writings and Philosophy of Nāgārjuna.* Indiske Studier 4. Copenhagen: Akademisk Forlag.

McDermott, A. Charlene S. (1973) "Asaṅga's Defense of *Ālaya-vijñāna*: Of Catless Grins and Sundry Related Matters." JIP 1:167-74.

Mimaki, K. (1982) *Blo Gsal Grub Mtha'.* Kyoto: University of Kyoto.

___. (1983). "The *Blo Gsal Grub Mtha'* and the Mādhyamika Classification in Tibetan *grub mtha'* literature." In E. Steinkellner and H. Tauscher, eds., *Contributions on Tibetan Buddhist Religion and Philosophy.* Vienna: Universität Wien:161-67.

Nagao, G. (1964) Ed. *Madhyānta-vibhāga-bhāṣya.* Tokyo: Suzuki Research Foundation.

___. (1982). *Shōdaijōron* (*Mahāyāna-saṃgraha*) vol. 1, Tohoku 4183; Tokyo Reprint no. 5410. Kodansha, Tokyo.

Nanjio, Bunyiu. (1956) Ed. *Laṅkāvatāra-sūtra.* Bibliotheca Otaniensis, vol. 1. Kyoto: Otani University.

Napper, Elizabeth. (1989) *Dependent Arising and Emptiness.* Boston: Wisdom.

Obermiller, E. (1931) "The Sublime Science of Maitreya." Acta Orientalia 9:81-306.

___. (1934-35) "Tsong-kha-pa le Pandit." MCB 3:319-338.

___. (1935) "Bu ston's History of Buddhism and the *Mañjuśrī-mūla-tantra.*" JRAS:303-7.

___. (1980) *History of Buddhism, Being an English Translation of Bu Ston Rin po che's Chos 'byung.* Heidelburg, 1933; reprint ed. Delhi.

Odani, Nobuchiyo. (1985) *Daigōshōgonron no Kenkū* ("*Mahāyāna-sūtrālaṅkāra*"). Buneidō, Kyoto.

Odani, Nobuchiyo and Kalsang (Skal bzang), Tshul khrims. (1986) "A Study of the *Ālaya-vijñāna* and *mano-vijñāna*: *Kun gzhi dka' 'grel* by Tsong kha pa." Kyoto: Buneidō.

Overmyer, Daniel L. (1976) *Folk Buddhist Religion: Dissenting Sects in Late Traditional China.* Cambridge: Harvard University Press.

Pensa, Corrado. (1967) Ed. *L'Abhisamayālaṁkāra-vṛtti di Ārya-Vimuktisena, Primo Abhisamaya.* Serie Orientale Roma, 37. Rome: Is.M.E.O.

Pradhan, Pralhad. (1949) "A Note on the *Abhidharma Samuccaya Bhāṣya* and its Author Sthiramati (?)." Journal of the Orrisa and Bihar Research Institute 35:34-46.

___. (1950) *Abhidharma Samuccaya of Asaṇga.* Santiniketan: Viśva-bharati.

Rahula, W. (1971) *Le compendium de la super-doctrine (philosophie) (Abhidharmasamuccaya) d'Asaṅga.* Publications de l'École Française d'Extrême-Orient 78. Paris: École Française d'Extrême-Orient; reprint ed.

Ruegg, D. Seyfort. (1963) "The Jo nang pas: A School of Buddhist Ontologists According to the *Grub Mtha' Śel gyi me loṅ.*" JAOS 83.1:73-91.

___. (1966) *Life of Bu ston Rin po che.* Serie Orientale Roma, 34. Rome: Is.M.E.O.

___. (1969) *La Théorie du Tathāgata-garbha et du gotra.* Publications de l'École Française d'Extrême-Orient 70. Paris: École Française d'Extrême-Orient.

___. (1989) *Buddha-nature, Mind and the Problem of Gradualism in a Comparative Perspective.* London: School of African and Oriental Studies.

Shastri, S.D. (1981) Ed. *Abhidharma-kośa and Bhāṣya of Ācārya Vasubandhu with Sphūṭārthā Commentary of Yośomitra.* Varanasi: Bauddha Bharati.

Schmithausen, Lambert. (1987) *Ālaya-vijñāna. On the Origin and the Early Development of a Central Concept of Yogācāra Philosophy.* Studia Philologica Buddhica. Monograph Series IVb. Tokyo: The International Institute for Buddhist Studies.

Snellgrove, David. (1987). *Indo-Tibetan Buddhism.* 2 vols. Boston: Shambhala.

Suzuki, D.T. (1968) Trans. *The Lankāvatāra sūtra.* London: Routledge and Kegan-Paul.

Tatia, N. (1976) Ed. *Abhidharma-samuccaya-bhāṣya.* Patna: K.P. Jayaswal Institute.

Tatz, Mark. (1985) *Difficult Beginnings. Chandragomin.* Boston: Shambhala.

___. (1986) *Asaṅga's Chapter on Ethics With the Commentary of Tsong-kha-pa, The Basic Path to Awakening, the Complete Bodhisattva.* Studies in Asian Thought and Religion, vol. 4. Lewiston/Queenston: Edwin Mellen Press.

Thurman, Robert. (1981) Ed. *Life and Teachings of Tsong Khapa.* Dharamsala: LTWA.

___. (1985) "Tsong-kha-pa." *Soundings in Tibetan Civilization:* 372-382. Ed. by B.N. Aziz and M. Kapstein. New Delhi.

___. (1989) *The Speech of Gold. Reason and Enlightenment in Tibetan Buddhism.* Princeton University Press, 1984; reprint ed. Delhi: Motilal Banarsidass.

Tshe-tan Zhabs-drung. (1982) *Bstan rtsis kun las btus pa.* Xining: Quinghai People's Publishing House.

Tucci, G. (1930) "A Fragment from the *Pratītya-samutpāda-vyākhyā* of Vasubandhu." JRAS:611-623.

___. (1934 and 1936) Ed. and trans. "The Ratnāvalī of Nāgārjuna." JRAS 1934:307-25; 1936:237-52, 423-35.

Vaidya, P.L. (1960) Ed. *Bodhi-caryāvatāra with the Commentary Pañjikā.* Buddhist Sanskrit Texts 12. Darbhanga: Mithila Institute.

van der Kuijp, Leonard W.J. (1983) *Contributions to the Development of Tibetan*

Buddhist Epistemology. Wiesbaden: Franz Steiner.

___. (1985) "Apropos of a Recent Contribution to the History of the Central Way Philosophy in Tibet: Tsong-kha-pa's *Speech of Gold*." Berliner Indologische Studien 1:47-74.

Wangyal, Geshe and Cutillo, Brian. (1988) *Illuminations: A Guide to Essential Buddhist Practices.* Novato, California: Lotsawa.

Wayman, Alex. (1979) *Calming the Mind and Discerning the Real.* New York: Columbia, 1978; reprint ed. Delhi: Motilal Banarsidass.

___. (1991) *Ethics of Tibet. Bodhisattva Section of Tsong-Kha-Pa's Lam Rim Chen Mo.* New York: State University of New York Press.

Wilson, Joe Bransford Jr. (1984) "The Meaning of Mind in the Mahāyāna Buddhist Philosophy of Mind Only (*Cittamātra*): A Study of a Presentation by the Tibetan Scholar Gung tang jam bay yang (Gung thang 'jam pa'i dbyangs) of Asaṅga's Theory of Mind-Basis-of-All (*Ālaya-vijñāna*) and Related Topics in Buddhist Theories of Personal Continuity, Epistemology and Hermeneutics." Ph.D. dissertation. University of Virginia.

Wogihara, U. (1973) *Abhisamayālaṁkārālokā Prajñā-pāramitā-vyākhyā. The Work of Haribhadra.* Tokyo: The Toyo Bunko, 1932-35; reprint edition. Tokyo: Sankibo Buddhist Book Store.

Index